Evolutionary Phonology

Evolutionary Phonology is a new theory of sound patterns which synthesizes results in historical linguistics, phonetics, and phonological theory. In this groundbreaking book, Juliette Blevins explores the nature of sound patterns and sound change in human language over the past 7,000–8,000 years, the time depth for which the comparative method is reasonably reliable. This book presents a new approach to the problem of how genetically unrelated languages, as far apart as Native American, Australian Aboriginal, Austronesian, and Indo-European, can often show similar sound patterns, and also tackles the converse problem of why there are notable exceptions to most of the patterns that are often regarded as universal. It argues that in both cases, a formal model of sound change incorporating misperception and variable articulation can account for attested sound systems without reference to markedness or naturalness within the synchronic grammar.

Wide-ranging, clearly structured, and original, this book will be of key interest to all linguists working in phonology, phonetics, historical linguistics, and language change.

JULIETTE BLEVINS was formerly Visiting Professor at the Department of Linguistics, University of California, Berkeley from 2002, and joined the Department of Linguistics at the Max Planck Institute for Evolutionary Anthropology, Leipzig, in Fall 2004. Her research interests span almost every domain of phonology, including syllable structure, tone, feature structure, stress, and metathesis. In addition to numerous articles on phonology, morphology, and sound change, she has also previously published *Nhanda: an aboriginal language of Western Australia*, and is currently working on a grammar and dictionary of Yurok, an endangered language of northwestern California.

Evolutionary Phonology

The emergence of sound patterns

Juliette Blevins

CAMBRIDGE
UNIVERSITY PRESS

PUBLISHED BY THE PRESS SYNDICATE OF THE UNIVERSITY OF CAMBRIDGE
The Pitt Building, Trumpington Street, Cambridge, United Kingdom

CAMBRIDGE UNIVERSITY PRESS
The Edinburgh Building, Cambridge, CB2 2RU, UK
40 West 20th Street, New York, NY 10011–4211, USA
477 Williamstown Road, Port Melbourne, VIC 3207, Australia
Ruiz de Alarcón 13, 28014 Madrid, Spain
Dock House, The Waterfront, Cape Town 8001, South Africa

http://www.cambridge.org

First published 2004
Third printing 2006

Printed in the United Kingdom at the University Press, Cambridge

Typeface Plantin 10/12 pt.   *System* LATEX 2$_\varepsilon$ [TB]

A catalogue record for this book is available from the British Library

Library of Congress Cataloguing in Publication data
Blevins, Juliette.
Evolutionary Phonology: the emergence of sound patterns / Juliette Blevins.
    p.   cm.
Includes bibliographical references and index.
ISBN 0 521 80428 0 (hardback)
1. Grammar, Comparative and general – Phonology.   2. Linguistic change.
I. Title.

P217.3.B585   2004
414 – dc22   2003061549

ISBN 0 521 80428 0 hardback

For Jim,

ardutha,

'nenos,

'ek-hireh wettel

Contents

Contents   ix

Preface

This is a book about phonology or sound patterns of the world's languages. In this book I present a new synthesis of historical and non-historical accounts of sound patterns. Anyone who studies phonology soon comes to realize that many sound patterns occur with more-than-chance frequency. Other sound patterns are quite rare. In this book, I provide evidence that recurrent sound patterns are the transparent result of recurrent sound change, where sound change is a direct consequence of the indirect transmission of language across generations. Other recurrent sound patterns reflect direct inheritance from a mother tongue. Rare sound patterns are either the result of uncommon sound changes, or result from the combined effects of independent sound changes. Certain sound changes are more common than others because they are rooted in the way we hear and speak. By attributing common sound patterns to phonetically based sound change, there is no need to encode the same phonetic explanations in synchronic grammars. Synchronic grammars model speakers' knowledge of language. In the realm of sound patterns, synchronic grammars include seemingly universal categories of features, segments, syllables, and other prosodic categories. At the same time, they encode many language-specific sound patterns. By viewing recurrent sound patterns as instances of parallel or convergent evolution in the domain of speech perception and production, synchronic grammars can be modeled as pure expressions of grammatical knowledge.

This book is about how the mature human language faculty, in all its complexity, has given rise to thousands of languages which, in many cases, though genetically unrelated, show similar sound patterns. Contrary to what the title may imply, this is not a book about the evolution of language in the human species. Though I do draw parallels between the evolution of sound patterns and Darwin's theory of natural selection, these parallels are largely metaphorical. This book does not deal with the biological or neurological foundations of language and should not be read as a neo-Darwinian treatise. The period of study is roughly the past 7,000 years – extremely short by biological standards, but a widely accepted estimate of the approximate time depth for which the comparative method of historical reconstruction is reliable.

The parallels between biological evolution and language change across generations must be metaphorical by definition. While the brain's general capacity for language is genetically transmitted from one generation of humans to the next, the ability to speak *a particular language* is not transmitted in this way. On the contrary, natural first-language learning occurs through complex social interactions. And evidence is mounting that a large amount of the knowledge we have of language is highly language specific, from fine details of pronunciation, to ways in which events are situated in time and space. If so much of language learning involves acquired knowledge, then we cannot make a direct parallel between inherited genetic traits and inherited features of language; direct inheritance in genetics is the norm, while indirect inheritance (via human transmission) is the norm in language transmission. Whenever evolutionary models are mentioned then, I will try to be explicit about where parallels are helpful and enlightening, and where they may be misleading.

This book is written for anyone with a general background in linguistics, whose interests include sound patterns, sound change, and the relationship between phonetics and phonology. It is not meant to be an introduction to phonology, nor is it meant solely as an advanced technical work for specialists in the field. Rather, it is written for enquiring minds who would like to understand why the sound systems and sound patterns of languages are the way they are. Those with serious interests in phonology, phonetics, sound change, typology and universals, markedness theory, explanation and naturalness, and the relationship between synchrony and diachrony will find, in this volume, a link between all these domains of inquiry. Those with interests in biological properties of the human organism and evolutionary theory will find in this volume explanations for structure in one component of human language – the sound system – which essentially demonstrate the emergent character of many structural properties.

This book should also be of interest to scholars in closely related fields (e.g. neurology, psychology, computer science, philosophy, anthropology) who have come to question the view that the grammars of all languages are basically the same due to inherited properties of the human species. A bold claim of this model is that the precise set of sounds, sound sequences, and context-determined sound alternations found in a given language are all *learned aspects of grammar*. These aspects of grammar are language-specific and subject to a great deal of variation across languages. In other words, cross-linguistic tendencies are real things in the same way that natural selection is real. Natural selection may result in brightly colored foul-tasting butterflies alongside well-camouflaged sweet-tasting moths. The cooccurrence of bright colors/bad taste and camouflage/good taste however is not attributed to any intrinsic property of particular butterflies or moths. On the contrary, we know very well that many other combinations of properties can and do exist. The *tendency* for certain combinations to be more common than others in the natural world can, in many cases, be seen as a consequence of natural selection: an association of bright colors and bad taste warns predators of a sickening meal; the absence of such colors will yield higher rates of predation, unless an organism has other means of avoiding capture, e.g. well-developed camouflage. In the field of linguistics, it has become quite common to attribute recurrent properties or combinations of properties to intrinsic properties of the language faculty. In this book, I show that many of these recurrent properties are the result of common pathways of language evolution. If a particular sound change can be shown to be common, then the sound pattern which results from that sound change is predicted to be common. This simple relationship between common sound change and common sound patterns appears to account for the majority of attested recurrent sound patterns in the world's languages.

For courses in phonology, phonetics, or historical linguistics, this book will fill a noticeable gap: while standard textbooks often address phonetic explanations for sound change, or phonetic explanations for synchronic phonological patterns, there are few texts where phonetic explanations, sound change, and synchronic sound patterns are connected in a coherent way. For courses in phonological theory, chapters can be used to stimulate debate in numerous areas, including: explanation in phonology; the role of naturalness and markedness in grammar; the inventory of phonological universals; the nature of phonological conspiracies; methods of assessing phonological productivity; the interpretation of data from language acquisition; and models of phonologization. A student of experimental or descriptive phonetics will find in this book a concrete example of how phonetic science informs linguistic theory. It is only through detailed understanding of speech perception and production that we come to understand the range of phenomena which underlie regular sound change. To the extent that sound change defines synchronic sound patterns, this detailed understanding is invaluable to advances in the field. For historical linguistics, this book provides a general link between neogrammarian discoveries, advances in modern phonetics, and phonological theory. It can be read as an expanded treatise on the nature and role of regular sound change in grammar, as a general reification of the importance of historical explanations in our conceptions of grammar, or as an exemplification of the non-teleological nature of sound change when viewed in the broadest terms.

For readers with interests in evolutionary biology, I suggest that this book be read as a complement to other work in the field of language evolution. Collections such as Briscoe (in press), Hurford et al. (1998), and Knight et al. (2000) provide a wide range of views on the evolution of linguistic form and grammatical structure. This book can be seen as picking up from the point where Lindblom (1998), Kohler (1998), de Boer (2001), and others leave off. Once a system of categories and contrasts has been established, what are the forces which continue to shape sound systems, and which have led to similar sound patterns in so many of the world's languages? How can regular sound change, as one aspect of language evolution, shed light on the synchronic patterns which modern phonology attempts to formalize? What aspects of linguistic phonetics and language structure lead to ambiguity or biases in the acquisition process? Are there default strategies in language acquisition which play a role in regular sound change? And more generally, in comparing language evolution with biological evolution, what parallels are useful and instructive? Is there a role for natural selection in the world of sounds?

The general outlines of Evolutionary Phonology are presented in part I, with empirical support and exemplification in part II. Theoretical implications are discussed in part III. I ask the forbearance of the non-phonologist for the amount of data and technical detail discussed in part II. Given the somewhat controversial nature of the approach, I feel obligated to present its empirical basis in some detail. At the same time, at the risk of alienating those with little phonetic background, I have presented only the barest outlines of cross-linguistic patterns, phonetic explanations, and experimental findings, hoping that those with interest will consult the sources cited in the text. For those with backgrounds in the biological sciences, there is a brief reference to the evolution of toepads in lizards in chapter 2, and to frog calls in chapter 6; otherwise, the comparison with biological systems, as stressed in chapter 2, is strictly metaphorical. For those interested in language acquisition, a close reading of chapter 2, where the general model of sound change is spelled out, can be combined with relevant facts from the acquisition literature summarized in chapter 9. As the empirical basis of this work lies equally in historical linguistics, phonetics, modern phonological theory, and language acquisition, there is no way the range of debate in all of these domains can be properly represented within a single volume. Wherever possible, I have given key references within each subfield which summarize the range of empirical data relevant to points under discussion.

While this book can be read as a modern neogrammarian treatise, its empirical foundations are the sound patterns which characterize synchronic phonological systems. Historical explanations are not only meant to account for language-particular detail, but also for the broad range of cross-linguistic generalizations characteristic of synchronic sound patterns. Phonetic science is a tool which allows us to understand how and why regular sound change occurs. Where regular sound change remains unexplained, it is only a matter of time before phonetic hypotheses can be tested in the laboratory. It is my hope that this book will serve as a catalyst for future phonetic studies whose results will provide explanations for sound patterns which are not yet well understood.

This book is the culmination of nearly twenty years of cross-linguistic research in phonology. This research includes studies of: syllable structure (Levin 1985a, 1987a; Blevins 1995a, 2001b, 2002a, b, 2003a, to appear a); stress (Levin 1988a, 1988b; Blevins 1992; Blevins and Harrison 1999); tone (Blevins 1993b, 1995b); segment structure (Blevins 1994a, 2003a); laryngeal phonology (Blevins 1993a, 2002b, 2003a; Blevins and Marmion 1995); prosodic phonology and morphology (Levin 1983, 1985b; Blevins 1994b, c, 1996, 1999b, 2003b); segment underspecification (Levin 1987b, c; Blevins 1993c); and sound change (Blevins 1997, 1999a, to appear b, c; Blevins and Blust 2003; Blevins and Garrett 1993, 1998; Blevins and Marmion 1994; Garrett and Blevins to appear). Past and current research, as reflected in this book, covers a wide range of languages, including, but not limited to, Austronesian, Native American, Australian Aboriginal, and Indo-European languages. Despite the wide range of topics and languages covered, a theme runs through many of these studies, one which provides the foundation for this work: phonological theory will be greatly enriched by providing precise analyses of largely ignored, misunderstood, problematic, and exceptional facts. In the course of investigating exceptional patterns, it becomes clear that the exceptions cannot be understood without first understanding the basis of the original phonological generalization they appear to violate. It is this search for understanding that has led slowly, but steadily, to the approach presented here.

As I write these words, I am conscious of the fact that another language will die this month, and more this year. Whether you, as a reader, are convinced by the linguistic arguments in this book or not, let me try to convince you here of something different, which I firmly believe. The science of linguistics advances as we come to understand the possible range of variation within and across languages. Much of this understanding is impossible without examining language in its social and cultural context. For this reason, the future advance of the scientific study of language depends, in part, on the survival of endangered languages and cultures. In this book alone, I rely on data from hundreds of languages, most of which are endangered. Many of the central arguments I present could not be made but for the hard work of linguists who have devoted their lives to language description and language maintenance. And I am not alone. The phonological literature is filled with seminal references to endangered and dormant languages, from Yowlumne here in California, to Lardil of Mornington Island. Whether you are a general reader, a professional linguist, a linguist-in-training, or a tropical fish specialist working in the forests of Mexico, look around you, and see if there is any way you can help an endangered language survive. As students of language, language endangerment threatens us all. Let us all try to do something, before it is too late.

Acknowledgments

This book, like most, is not the work of an isolated individual. There are many people who have provided me with guidance, encouragement, data, arguments, counterarguments, and more, who I would like to briefly acknowledge.

I thank my first linguistics professors, Joe Malone of Barnard College, and the late Robert Austerlitz of Columbia University for providing me with a solid introduction to sound patterns of the world's languages, from Irish, Semitic, and Turkish, to Finnic and Gilyak, and for encouraging me to pursue a career in linguistics.

I thank those at MIT who educated me in phonological and syntactic theory, and who were always willing to listen and ready to argue: my generous teachers, Morris Halle, Donca Steriade, Noam Chomsky, and the late Ken Hale, and fellow student Bill Poser, who remains a constant source of remarkable facts and phonological rarities. The arguments continue as does the learning, and the friendships remain strong.

At the University of Texas at Austin I was lucky to have a range of colleagues with their own take on sound patterns and sound change who all helped me define my own views, including Andrew Garrett, Bob Harms, Bob King, John Kingston, Björn Lindblom, Armin Mester, Scott Myers, and Tony Woodbury. I thank my many wonderful students at the University of Texas who allowed me to discover my own teaching style, and to be just as engaged in their own research as in my own.

I thank my former colleagues at the University of Western Australia, Shelly Harrison, John Henderson, and Alan Dench, for supporting my work on Australian Aboriginal languages, and for sharing their descriptive work with me, even in its early stages. I am also thankful to the Australian Research Council and AIATSIS for grant support from 1995 to 1999 for research on Australian sound patterns.

I am grateful to Larry Hyman, former Chair of Linguistics at the University of California, Berkeley, for inviting me to share some of the ideas in this book in the form a two-week lecture series at Berkeley in 1999, and again as a phonology seminar in 2002. I also thank Larry, and current Chair, Leanne Hinton, for extending my visit to the 2002–2003 academic year, and Paula Floro, Belén Flores, and Esther Weiss for their administrative assistance and goodwill. Without this extension, this book would not be finished. Thanks also to Andrew Garrett, Sharon Inkelas, John Ohala, and Ian Maddieson for valuable feedback during my regular visits to Berkeley, and to the students in the Evolutionary Phonology seminar in the spring of 2002 for their contributions and patience as this work took shape in the classroom. Additional thanks to Emmon Bach, Roger Higgins, David Lightfoot, Andy Spencer, and in the world of biology, Molly Morris and Kevin de Queiroz, for stimulating discussion and much encouragement.

My view of sound patterns is informed not only by the many descriptive grammars available in print but also by patient teachers who have allowed me to attempt my own grammatical descriptions. If there is anything that has led to my appreciation of language-specific aspects of grammar and their historical origins, it is this work. Sincere thanks to my Nhanda teacher, Lucy Ryder of Northampton, Western Australia; may she and her language rest in peace. Ongoing thanks to my Yurok teachers, Aileen Figueroa of Westhaven, California, and Jimmie James of Hoopa, California, and to the Language Committee of the Muwekma Ohlone Tribe for allowing me to learn the Chochenyo language in the context of their revitalization movement.

I would like to give special thanks to several linguists who have had a significant influence on my work, knowingly or unknowingly. I thank Andrew Garrett for inspiring me to enter the world of historical linguistics, and for his contributions to earlier collaborations, and careful reading of so much of my own work. Andrew has been, and continues to be, a stimulating colleague, and I hope that this general thanks will make up for whatever is missing in subsequent pages. I also offer special thanks to Bob Blust for careful reading of parts of this manuscript, and for providing detailed replies to my queries over the years. As may be clear from the many references to his work which appear in the following pages, I have been greatly influenced by Bob's oeuvre, much of which has served as a catalyst for my own historical explanations of recurrent sound patterns. In the world of synchronic phonology, two people are owed special thanks. The first is Donca Steriade, whose extreme theoretical positions have always been instructive. While we agree on much, it is our disagreements which have been most constructive in shaping this book. I would also like to thank John McCarthy for his past support and correspondence. I moved to Western Australia in 1992, and was therefore quite far from the epicenter of Optimality Theory which was shaking ground around then. In the relative isolation of Perth, I read and worked, and began to question some of the basic assumptions of modern phonological theory. I am grateful to John for replying to so many of my queries, and for keeping me on his mailing list for so many years. I also thank the same four people for their professional support. My career has taken some odd turns, geographically and otherwise, and having this support has made it easier to do what I felt was right.

I am grateful to Professor Gillian Brown at the Research Centre for English and Applied Linguistics, University of Cambridge, for providing me with an academic home on arrival in England, and to former colleagues at the University of Luton for providing generous research time. For their support and encouragement in the final stages leading up to publication, I thank: Farrell Ackerman, Barry Alpher, Steve Anderson, Bob Blust, Joan Bybee, Terrence Deacon, Paul Kiparsky, David Lightfoot, Teresa McFarland, Bill Poser, Chilin Shih, Richard Sproat, and Andy Wedel.

The deepest thanks go to my family. Thank you to all the Blevins, for staying close, despite the distance. Thank you Dad, Marc, El, Sara, Dan, Nic, Ben, Dani, David, Julia, and Sophia, for all that love, for nourishing my heart and soul, for reminding me to save something for the sequel, and for laughing at words like *incredulity* and *rhinoglottophilia*. To my beloved children – Molly, Lucy, and Rebecca – thank you for being so patient while Mummy finished her book, for showing me the brightness of Nana in the sky, and for being the wonderful children you are. To my husband, Jim, who I can never thank enough, thank you again for everything, and more.

Part I

Preliminaries

The formation of different languages and of distinct species [is] . . .
curiously parallel . . . We find in distinct languages striking homologies
due to community of descent, and analogies due to a similar process of
formation . . .   Darwin (1871: 465–66)

1 What is Evolutionary Phonology?

> In language, as in nature in general, everything moves, everything is alive
> and changing.   Baudouin de Courtenay (1897/1972)

1.1   Relating sound patterns to sound change

The field of modern linguistics is conventionally divided into distinct subfields, defined by the questions they address and analytical methods they
use to answer these questions. Establishing a clear separation between the
components of a synchronic description has proved particularly useful
in investigating the distinctive properties of sound systems (phonology),
words (morphology), and phrases (syntax). Yet the strict segregation of
synchronic and historical description has a rather different character, as
it is very often the case that these subfields overlap in their coverage. The
post-Saussurean tradition has tended to dismiss historical explanations
as entirely irrelevant to the task of synchronic description, on the grounds
that the speaker of a language cannot be expected to know the history
of that language and "a segment does not know where it came from"
(Lass 1984: 178). This essentially ahistorical perspective leads to considerable redundancy, as numerous commentators have observed, since
many patterns with a well-understood historical basis or origin must be
reencoded in synchronic accounts. The fact that such patterns typically
lack system-internal motivation within the synchronic grammar has likewise expanded the inventory of "universals" that must be attributed to a
linguistic system because they cannot in any way be deduced or inferred
from other properties. The predictable effect has been a general extension
of synchronic descriptions and mechanisms to encompass nearly all patterns and generalizations within a linguistic system, irrespective of their
status or origin.

    A central claim of the present work is that this "one size fits all" method-
ology invariably fails to explain – and often fails even to describe accurately – many of the sound patterns that recur in the world's languages.
On the other hand, phonetically motivated accounts of the origin and

3

development of common sound changes provides the basis for a genuine explanation. This type of explanation offers perceptual or articulatory motivations for recurrent sound patterns in place of *a priori* claims that these patterns arise because they are intrinsic to the organization of the synchronic system.

The overlap between the subject matter of phonology and historical linguistics is particularly striking. Phonology is the study of sound patterns, their nature and use. In attempting to model sound patterns, linguists have studied the phonological systems of most of the world's languages and language families. This large corpus of descriptive studies has served as the primary database for work within phonological typology. Typologists have spent centuries cataloguing recurrent and unattested sound patterns across independent languages, language families, language areas, and language types. These sound patterns fall into many different categories. Among these we find studies of segment inventories, segment sequences, syllable types, stress patterns, tone patterns, feature distribution, and studies of common alternation types. Alternations between sounds in related words have been categorized as instances of assimilation, dissimilation, deletion, insertion, metathesis, coalescence, breaking, lenition, fortition, and neutralization, with further subdivisions within each of these.[1]

Historical linguistics is the study of language change and relationships among languages. In attempting to model patterns of change, linguists have studied sound change in many of the world's languages and language families. Sound changes fall into many different categories. It is noteworthy that the majority of commonly attested sound changes in the world's languages are mirrored by synchronic alternations of precisely the same type. Sound changes give rise to changes in segment inventories, segment sequences, syllable types, stress patterns, tone patterns, and feature distribution. Moreover, these sound changes are, precisely like synchronic alternations, categorized as instances of assimilation, dissimilation, deletion, insertion, metathesis, coalescence, breaking, lenition, fortition, and neutralization. At a much finer level of detail, the most common sound changes and the most common types of synchronic alternations are nearly coextensive. The many common sound changes which have direct parallels in synchronic sound patterns include velar palatalization, final obstruent devoicing, vowel nasalization before nasal consonants, and place assimilation of nasals to following oral stops.

---

[1] Phonology has been extended to the study of signed languages used by the Deaf, where visual image patterns replace sound patterns as the object of study. For an overview, of current issues in sign language phonology, see Brentari (1995). A brief discussion of the relevance of sign language phonology to evolutionary approaches can be found in 11.1.

The pervasive parallels between common types of sound change and common synchronic alternations, has suggested to many, notably the neogrammarians, that synchronic sound patterns are a direct reflection of their diachronic origins, and, more specifically, that regular phonetically based sound change is the common source of recurrent sound patterns. Evolutionary Phonology investigates this hypothesis and explores its consequences for phonological theory and models of sound change. However, before elaborating this approach, it is worth clarifying a guiding methodological principle.

All else being equal, simpler grammatical models are usually preferred to more complex ones. More specifically, any model which duplicates explanations, within or across domains, is in some basic sense more complex than one which does not. Hence, if we can demonstrate that principled diachronic explanations exist for particular sound patterns, considerations of simplicity would seem to dictate that explanations for the same phenomena should not be imported into, or otherwise duplicated within, synchronic accounts. In all cases where clear diachronic explanations exist for a particular synchronic pattern, this diachronic explanation makes a synchronic account redundant, since the optimal description should not account for the same pattern twice. To take just one concrete example, if it can be shown that final obstruent devoicing is a common sound change with a principled phonetic explanation, then we can recognize many synchronic prohibitions against voiced obstruents in final position as the direct result of this common sound change (see chapter 4). The resulting patterns of voiced versus voiceless obstruents must be describable within synchronic grammars, but the grammars do not need to explain the absence of voiced obstruents in final position. Any cross-linguistic statements of this sort merely duplicate an explanation which already exists independently in the diachronic domain. A central premise of Evolutionary Phonology, then, is that principled diachronic explanations for sound patterns replace, rather than complement, synchronic explanations, unless independent evidence demonstrates, beyond reasonable doubt, that a separate synchronic account is warranted.

The idea that common sound patterns reflect common sound changes, and that historical explanations have priority over synchronic ones, are views that have been expressed many times in the history of linguistics. In the study of sound change, the neogrammarians were renowned for their belief that the formal and functional status of an element within a synchronic system could be understood only in terms of its diachronic origins (see chapter 3). Though the neogrammarian view is no longer quite so widely assumed as a consequence of Saussure's reorientation of the field, it is nonetheless endorsed by many general grammarians, historical linguists, typologists, phonologists, and phoneticians of the twentieth century. Consider, for example, Jesperson's (1924) position that to truly understand a linguistic system "we must know how it came to be." A similar position is taken by Greenberg in his discussion of phonological typology. He suggests that diachronic processes explain frequently occurring sound patterns, and stresses the complementary nature of diachronic and synchronic considerations in characterizing universals of sound patterns (Greenberg 1966a, 1978). Sampson (1970: 618–19) likewise questions the status of morphophonemic rules in synchronic grammars, and the general overlap of historical and synchronic explanations:

> If morphophonemic rules may indeed be thought of as reconstructions of history, we are then free to ask whether this part of the phonological component, as distinct from the MS [morpheme structure constraints: JB] or phonotactic rules, has any place in a description of linguistic competence . . . the latter could simply be interpreted as universal constraints on the nature of possible sound-changes; and as for the former, if regularity of alternations may be explained as due to a historical sound-change having applied to a situation not exhibiting alternation in the relevant respect, *there is certainly no need to give a second explanation of the same facts in terms of synchronic linguistic competence.* (emphasis added: JB)

In modern phonological theory, the precise locus of explanation has been variable (see chapter 3). Nevertheless, in one of the few careful evaluations of the role of extra-grammatical factors in shaping synchronic sound systems, Anderson (1981: 497) suggests that "we can only determine that some property is to be attributed to the essential nature of language *if it does not seem to have an account in more general terms*" (emphasis added: JB). In studies of the phonetic basis of sound change, it is taken for granted that the majority of recurrent sound patterns can be explained in terms of phonetically natural processes. Consider, for example, the introductory remarks to Hombert et al.'s (1979) detailed phonetic study of tonogenesis: "Sound changes or sound patterns that are attested in diverse, widely-separated languages cry out for an explanation by what is common to all speech communities: the physical apparatus which humans use to produce and perceive speech. One such sound change that reveals many striking common patterns is the development of tone."

Despite the consensus that frequent sound patterns reflect common phonetically motivated sound change, there is no single work which demonstrates this point comprehensively and in detail. This gap in the literature is noted by Ferguson (1990: 59–60), in his essay on one particularly common sound change, that of *s* > *h*:

> One of the most powerful tools in the armamentarium of linguists engaged in the study of diachronic phonology is the often implicit notion that some changes

are phonetically more likely than others. Thus if a linguist finds a systematic correspondence between [g] and [dʒ] in two related language varieties, it will be reasonable to assume that the stop is the older variant and the affricate the younger one until strong counter evidence is found. The linguist makes such an assumption because experience with many languages has shown that the change of [g] to [dʒ] is fairly common and tends to occur under certain well-documented conditions whereas the reverse change is unusual and problematic. This line of argumentation has been employed, either explicitly or implicitly, since the earliest days of modern historical linguistics.

Because of the importance of this methodological tool, one might expect that general treatises and introductory textbooks on historical linguistics would devote considerable space to a presentation of the relative probabilities of various possible sound changes, as well as explanatory factors accounting for them. Also, because of the centrality of alternations and processes to the field of phonological theory, one might expect that general treatises and introductory textbooks in phonology would devote considerable space to this topic. Unfortunately, authors of books on historical linguistics or phonological theory have a great deal of other ground to cover, and this simple but important concern tends to be neglected.

Evolutionary Phonology addresses itself directly to this basic but central concern. This study fills a gap in the literature by providing a sustained argument demonstrating that a broad range of phonological phenomena can be explained in terms of common phonetically motivated sound change. Evolutionary Phonology constitutes a concrete and comprehensive attempt to explain the majority of the world's recurrent sound patterns in terms of well-understood instances of phonetically motivated sound change. As a concrete model, it incorporates current models of articulatory phonetics, speech perception, and language acquisition. As a comprehensive model, it summarizes a great deal of work in experimental phonetics, typology, variation, and theoretical phonology, and relates this to centuries of work modeling sound change and sound patterns. As an explanatory model, it locates the domain of explanation for many recurrent synchronic patterns in the diachronic dimension.

1.2 A formal model of sound change

One important component of Evolutionary Phonology is a model of phonetically based sound change which is broad enough to handle all the various types of attested change, and constrained enough to rule out unattested changes. A precise model of sound change is proposed in chapter 2, and incorporates two observations regarding human language which should be fairly uncontroversial. First, *all spoken language is characterized by a wide range of phonetic variation, some of which is language specific, and some of which is determined by physical properties of the human vocal apparatus.* One dimension of this continuum of variation is that determined by careful versus casual speech, a dimension sometimes quantified in terms of articulatory effort. Another dimension of this continuum is fast versus slow speech, which may involve articulatory compression or expansion along the temporal dimension. Other relevant dimensions of variation in this model include frequencies of particular phonetic variants: frequencies are expected to be highly variable across speakers and across time, since they are determined by a wide range of factors including lexical frequency, frequency of contexts involving careful versus casual forms, and social variables (age, gender, class, etc.) associated with particular phonetic variants. A second observation is that, though language transmission from one generation to the next is constrained by perceptual, articulatory, cognitive, and social factors, *language transmission is, by its very nature, indirect and imperfect.* Within this imperfect system of transmission, sound change may be viewed as the norm, not the exception. Since every individual will have slightly different early childhood experiences, every individual will, by definition, form a grammar based on distinct sets of surface forms.

The range of sound patterns investigated in part II support the general model of sound change in three respects. First, the suggested typology of sound changes with sources in misperception, ambiguous segmentation, and ambiguity due to variation is descriptively adequate. Second, where sound changes appear to defy this typology, they can be shown to have non-phonetic origins. Third, and most strikingly, the general model of sound change makes predictions regarding phonetic preconditions of change which find general support in experimental and typological studies. Implications of this particular model of sound change are explored in part III. One implication of the model is that most aspects of sound patterns constitute learned language-specific information. A corollary of the model is the regularity hypothesis: phonetically based sound change is typically regular because sound change is a subcase of normal acquisition of phonological contrasts and categories.

1.3   Types of explanation: historical, phonetic, formal, and non-teleological

This locus of explanation in Evolutionary Phonology places it at some distance from other phonological models, where explanation is attributed directly to synchronic principles. The working hypothesis supported throughout this volume is that *recurrent synchronic sound patterns have their origins in recurrent phonetically motivated sound change.* As a result, there is no need to directly encode the frequent occurrence of these patterns in synchronic grammars themselves. Common instances of sound change give rise to commonly occurring sound patterns. Certain sound patterns are rare or unattested, because there is no common pathway of change which will result in their evolution.

What are the frequent sound patterns exhibited by the world's languages? What are the recurrent sound patterns which phonological theory attempts to explain? Many generalizations have been discovered in different domains. In (1) I list a sample of these, organized in terms of sound patterns they attempt to characterize. Some of these will be mentioned later in the book. The purpose of this brief discussion is to exemplify significant ways in which explanation within Evolutionary Phonology differs from other approaches to sound change and sound patterns.

(1) Examples of generalizations over sound systems of the world's languages
  i. SEGMENT INVENTORIES
    a. If a language has only three vowels, it will usually have /i, u, a/
    b. All languages have voiced sonorants and voiceless obstruents in their segment inventories.
    c. In the series of voiced stops /b d g/, /g/ is most likely to be missing.
    d. No language contrasts voiceless laryngealized obstruents with their voiceless ejective counterparts.
  ii. STRESS PATTERNS
    e. There are languages in which stress falls consistently on the first syllable of the word, or the last syllable of the word, but there are no languages in which stress falls regularly on the middle syllable of the word (e.g. the second syllable of a three-syllable word, the third syllable of a five-syllable word, and the fourth syllable of a seven-syllable word.)
    f. There are languages in which stressed syllables must be separated by single unstressed syllables, and others where stressed syllables must be separated by two unstressed syllables, but there are no languages where stressed syllables must be separated by three unstressed syllables.
    g. There are languages with long vowels and short vowels where all long vowels must be stressed, but there are no languages with long and short vowels where all short vowels must be stressed.

iii. PHONOTACTICS

    h. In nearly all languages, each consonant in a syllable-internal obstruent cluster must agree in laryngeal features.

    i. In many languages, each consonant in an obstruent cluster must agree in laryngeal features.

    j. In many languages, there is no possible laryngeal contrast for obstruents in pre-obstruent position.

    k. In languages where there is no possible laryngeal contrast for obstruents in pre-obstruent position, laryngeal contrasts are neutralized in this position in derived environments.

One question that has driven research in phonology and phonetics is *why* generalizations like those in (1) exist. How are they best explained? Are they best stated in terms of phonological primitives, as reflections of phonetic properties of speech, or a mix of the two? What are their origins? Are they tied to intrinsic properties of synchronic grammars, or is their appearance a consequence of the historical development of language? Do they serve a clear function in making speech easier to perceive or pronounce? Are certain properties, like those in (1h–k) related? Should some of these properties be viewed as accidental, or are there clear deterministic pathways in the course of language evolution? Of course, for each sound pattern in (1), there could be a different combination of answers to these questions, and a single generalization could also have multiple overlapping explanations.

    The range of explanations offered for recurrent sound patterns can be illustrated with reference to the examples in (1). Consider, for example, the generalization in (1a), which suggests a general preference in three-vowel systems for the vowels /i, u, a/. In the twentieth century, this typological generalization seems to have been first discovered by Trubetzkoy, who wrote, in a letter to Jakobson in 1928:

In the meantime I have started working on something else which fascinates me. I have compiled all vocalic systems I knew by heart (thirty-four in all) and tried to compare them . . . I will continue my work on them until I have collected about one hundred languages. The results are extremely strange. All systems can be reduced to a small number of types and can always be represented by symmetrical diagrams . . . There are some laws about the "formation of systems" which can be seen without difficulty . . . I believe that the empirical laws discovered in this way will be of great importance . . . (Jakobson 1975: 320)[2]

---

[2] Trubetzkoy's impressions are consistent with the findings of Maddieson (1984: 153–54), based on the UPSID database of 317 languages representative of the world's major

Trubetzkoy (1929, 1939) expands on his notion of the "formation of systems." In this work, he proposes one of the first feature systems for vowels which attempts to encode generalization (1a) by combining two phonological features, one of aperture (or sonority), and the other of timbre (place of articulation). His claim was that, with very few exceptions, aperture and timbre features were basic oppositions in all vowel systems. If the vowel system was triangular, it would involve a single vowel specified with the maximal degree of aperture /a/. The contrast between /i/ and /u/ was the addition of the timbre contrast to the close class of vowels. Trubetzkoy's approach classified the generalization in (1a) as an essentially phonological one, arising from constraints on the combinatory properties of phonological features. However, as our understanding of the physical properties of speech has deepened, other explanations for this universal tendency have been proposed. Within the quantal theory of speech (Stevens 1972), where quantal signals are those for which a distinct acoustic signal is achieved through a relatively imprecise gesture, [i], [u], and [a] are more quantal than other vowel sounds, and therefore better phonological categories. Another account of the same facts invokes the principle of vowel dispersion. This principle, first proposed by Liljencrants and Lindblom (1972), and elaborated by Lindblom (1986), suggests that vowels are evenly and widely distributed in the psychoacoustic vowel space. In other words, vowel systems are preferred to the extent that the perceptual space between vowels is maximized (independent of the ease or difficulty of the gesture). Under their account, for a three-vowel system, perceptual distance alone predicts the phonological categories /i, u, a/.[3] The quantal and dispersion approaches can each be viewed in either synchronic or diachronic terms. If vowels require too precise a gesture to generate distinctive categories, or, if they are too close in the perceptual vowel space, a synchronic distinction is impossible. At the same time, given that speech is transmitted by articulators which can lack precision, and that transmission occurs in a generally noisy environment, the accuracy of transmission of utterances from one generation to the next will depend to a great degree on the ease of articulation and ease of discrimination of different sounds. Language evolution will tend to converge on quantal vowels, or on vowel systems which obey the dispersion principle.

Maximal perceptual distance has also been suggested to account for the apparent universal in (1b): all spoken languages make use of sonorants

---

genetic groupings. Lindblom (1986) and De Boer (2001) treat similar generalizations as emergent properties of sound systems.

[3] Though see Maddieson (2003) on problems in extending this account to four-vowel systems.

and obstruents (Lindblom and Maddieson 1988).[4] This generalization can be explained in terms of maximal phonetic contrast at the syntagmatic level. The most dissimilar sounds in terms of their intrinsic sonority are voiced vowels and voiceless obstruents. Voiced vowels are the loudest sounds, while voiceless obstruents involve long durations of silence, and are therefore the quietest sounds. Strings containing these two sound types in alternating sequences will result in maximal sequential contrast, which facilitates the perceptual saliency of each element in turn. The fact that all languages have voiceless obstruents, but not all languages have voiced obstruents, has been claimed to follow from the marked nature of obstruent voicing. For Trubetzkoy (1939) this was a purely phonological property, though it could just as well be seen to follow from physiological facts about speech: obstruents which are produced without any active gesture at the larynx will be voiceless due to the raised intraoral air pressure which, with the vocal folds in their neutral position, inhibits vocal fold vibration.[5]

Within inventories of voiced obstruents, the fact that /g/ is more likely to be missing than /d/ or /b/ (1c) is also attributable to the physics of voicing in stop consonants. This gap has a simple aerodynamic explanation: where voicing of oral stops is concerned, the greater the volume of the supralaryngeal air chamber, the longer voicing can be sustained. In other words, all else being equal, voicing can be sustained longest in [b], less long in [d], and for a shorter time still in [g] (Javkin 1977; Ohala and Riordan 1979; Ohala 1983a, 1995a). Of the three voiced stops, [g] is most likely to undergo devoicing to [k], since it is the least compatible with sustained voicing. In this case, synchronic constraints like *g have also been proposed to account for the same gaps, though they are unable to directly associate this gap in phoneme inventory with the arguably related fact that in contexts of devoicing, /g/ is more likely to devoice than /d/ or /b/.

The lack of a contrast between voiceless laryngealized obstruents and ejectives noted in (1d) can be viewed as the result of the synchronic phonological feature system: the laryngeal features [-voiced, constricted glottis], specify both types of sounds. In this case, the feature system offers no way of distinguishing more than one category of voiceless obstruent

---

[4] In fact, the generalization Lindblom and Maddieson account for is much more specific: in segment inventories, approximately 70 percent of consonants are obstruents, while only 30 percent are sonorants. This near-constant distribution across languages is attributed to the large perceptual space of obstruents, in contrast to the much smaller one for sonorants.

[5] Ladefoged and Maddieson (1996: 53) suggest there may actually be two phonetic types of voiceless stops in the world's languages: one involving active vocal-fold opening, and the type described in the text, where voicelessness is a consequence of modal voicing decay during stop closure.

with glottal constriction. Again, however, a promising phonetic explanation is available. Sounds produced with constriction at the glottis will very often generate creak or glottal pulses in surrounding vowels. If this glottal pulsing is used as a significant cue for both sound types, then they may be unlikely to cooccur in a single language, due to high rates of perceptual confusions. Support for this position is found in languages like Yapese and Yurok, which show variation between these two phonetic realizations of a single phonological category.

Competing phonological and phonetic explanations have also been proposed for the three generalizations in (1e–g) which relate to stress patterns. If stress is seen as serving a delimitative function at the level of the phonological word, then word-medial stress (1e) is ruled out, since this does not serve to delimit the word edge (Martinet 1961: 87). Non-functional phonetic historical explanations have been proposed for other aspects of stress systems. For example, the generalization in (1f) notes that there are no systems where stress falls on every fourth syllable, in contrast to the attested systems where stress falls on every other syllable, or every third syllable. One suggestion in the literature is that these patterns reflect the typical tonal melodies of stressed syllables and patterns of tonal association (Blevins and Harrison 1999). If stressed syllables are typically associated with H, LH, or HL, but not longer melodies, then the longest sequence of stress + unstressed syllables will be three: two syllables to realize the bi-tonal pattern, plus one syllable with no realization of stress. Note that this proposal does not formally rule out a language with a swwwswww . . . stress pattern. It merely points to an association between the rarity of such systems and the rarity of single *HLH melodies associated with stress or accent.

The generalization in (1g) states an implicational universal between vowel length and stress. This universal appears to follow from the phonetic content of stress. Stressed vowels have more acoustic energy than unstressed vowels (Gordon 1999, 2002). Longer vowels have more acoustic energy than shorter vowels. All else being equal then, a long vowel will always be perceived as having more stress than a corresponding short vowel, so that a system with stressed short vowels, but unstressed long vowels is unlikely to evolve. This principle is typically written in to synchronic theories of syllable weight: if a language shows a weight distinction, VV rimes will be heavy and V rimes will be light. But, as with the contrast between ternary and quaternary alternating stress systems, it is reasonable to ask whether we really need to rule out other types of systems, given that perceptual principles make them unlikely to arise.

The generalizations in (1h–k), have again been explained in phonological and in phonetic terms. In early work on phonological markedness,

Trubetzkoy proposed that for phonological systems like East Caucasian, which contrasts voiced/voiceless and ejective/non-ejective sounds, the unmarked obstruents are voiceless and non-ejective.[6] Trubetzkoy further suggested that the unmarked element of an opposition always appears in positions of neutralization. Only later were aspects of language use and phonetic content incorporated, when Trubetzkoy (1939) suggested that unmarked members of an opposition class occur more frequently in continuous speech than marked members, and that this might be related to Zipf's Law (Zipf 1935: 96–97), which holds that the less complicated the phonetic realization of a phoneme, the greater its frequency. Chapter 4 looks in depth at generalizations like those in (1h–k) and concludes that all such patterns follow from regular phonetically based sound change.

This brief summary of the kinds of explanations offered for universals and universal tendencies illustrates some of the major splits in the domain and nature of explanations offered for recurrent properties of synchronic sound patterns in the world's languages. Two basic questions largely define the range of approaches and their basic assumptions. Are explanations for sound patterns located in the diachronic or synchronic dimension? And are explanations for sound patterns goal-directed and teleological, directly invoking notions of articulatory ease, perceptual distance, ease of learnability, or other characteristics of "optimal" sound patterns? These two questions are logically distinct, and define the four-way contrast shown in (2).

(2)   APPROACHES TO EXPLANATION IN PHONOLOGY
    i. Synchronic, not goal-directed (e.g. Saussure 1949; Hockett 1955; Chomsky and Halle 1968)
    ii. Synchronic, goal-directed (e.g. Trubetzkoy 1939; Prince and Smolensky 1993)
    iii. Diachronic, goal-directed (e.g. Grammont 1933; Lindblom 1986)
    iv. Diachronic, not goal-directed (e.g. Andersen 1973; Ohala 1981; Evolutionary Phonology)

In (2i), a range of synchronic non-teleological frameworks are listed. Structuralist principles like those pertaining to rule simplicity and the symmetry of phoneme inventories are seen as unmarked properties of sound systems, but there is no direct reference to teleological principles within the synchronic grammar itself. These approaches differ from

---

[6] Interestingly, the early Sanskrit grammarians, including Pāṇini, writing several hundred years BCE, used the term *gʰoṣavant* 'having tone' for the voiced consonants and the *agʰoṣa* 'toneless' for the voiceless consonants, suggesting that voiced consonants have something which voiceless consonants lack.

Prague school and more recent Optimality approaches, where grammars directly encode the status of unmarked (optimal) versus marked (non-optimal) properties. The many accounts which attribute cross-linguistic generalizations in sound patterns to diachronic explanation also divide into teleological and non-teleological approaches. In the most phonetically sophisticated accounts, sound change is quantified directly in terms of the opposing forces of maximizing contrast and minimizing effort (e.g. Lindblom 1986). A coherent alternative to this approach, and the one argued for here, is that recurrent sound patterns in the world's languages are best explained in terms of phonetically motivated sound change, but sound change itself is non-optimizing. Sound change may result in a less effortful pronunciation, or more extreme perceptual contrast, but these are emergent, non-deterministic, properties of change which reflect common sources of sound change, and nothing more.

Another difference between the approaches outlined in (2) concerns the role of phonetic explanation. While the general approaches in (2i) and (2ii) do not directly incorporate phonetic explanations into synchronic grammars, many of their descendants do. Standard generative approaches gave rise to Natural Phonology (Donegan and Stampe 1979), which directly incorporates phonetic naturalness, and early Optimality work, where reference to phonetic explanation was minimal, has given rise to descendent approaches which make direct reference to fine aspects of phonetic representation (Kirchner 2000; Flemming 2001).

Evolutionary Phonology has much in common with other schools of historical and synchronic analyses of sound systems, but, as sketched in chapter 3, presents a distinctive synthesis of these ideas, which is informed by the descriptive, typological, and theoretical advances in phonetics and phonology over the past century. Evolutionary Phonology shares with the nineteenth-century neogrammarian doctrine the view that synchronic sound patterns are best understood in terms of their diachronic origins. At the same time, it differs significantly from the neogrammarian tradition in its amplified model of sound change, and in the attempt to model synchronic systems in their own terms. The interrelationships established between diachrony and synchrony in Evolutionary Phonology are closest, at least in spirit, to the work of Baudouin de Courtenay (Stankiewicz 1972). However, the use of underlying and surface forms, phonemes specified in terms of distinctive features, and autosegmental and prosodic representations, make Evolutionary Phonology distinctly modern. The historical phonetics which underlie regular synchronic patterns and their propagation across generations are similar to those proposed by Grammont (1933). But where Grammont explains sound change in terms of an interplay of the "la loi du moindre effort" ('the least effort principle') and "le besoin de clarté" ('the need for clarity'), Evolutionary Phonology acknowledges the accidental nature of change.

The claim that phonetically based sound change is non-optimizing is most closely associated with the work of Ohala (e.g. Ohala 1971, 1974b, 1981, 1990, 1993). In much of this work, the primary focus is on the acoustic auditory signal in speech perception. Since the acoustic signal is the only physical manifestation of communication between speaker and listener, the listener must rely on information in the signal to determine the phonological structure of the utterance. Sound change occurs in various circumstances: when the listener is unable to decode the speech signal in precisely the same way that the speaker meant it to be decoded; when listeners misperceive utterances; when phonetic variation gives rise to tokens with distinct phonological interpretations; when a given utterance has multiple phonological interpretations; when redundant properties of speech gradually exceed the limits of redundancy and require independent specification. However, there is no single guiding principle to these events. Sound change is essentially random and non-optimizing. There is no teleology in this model of sound change. Sound change, at the level of the individual, occurs because certain acoustic auditory signals are inherently ambiguous in terms of their phonological structure, while others are easily misperceived. Chapter 2 amplifies Ohala's model to incorporate sound change whose ultimate source is the phonetic variation inherent in the speech stream, and to account for both phonetic and phonological change. Within this amplified model, all regular phonetically based sound change occurs without a specific goal or purpose. Sound change happens because of the way we produce and hear speech. It does not happen in order to improve speech in any way.

In general discussions of linguistic explanation, functional approaches to grammar are sometimes distinguished from formal approaches. These terms are used in very different ways by different linguists. For example, McCarthy (2002: 220) defines functional approaches as those which "look for explanations that go beyond the properties of formal grammar." Under this definition, any approach, like Evolutionary Phonology which places the bulk of explanation for sound patterns in the diachronic dimension, is a functionalist approach. However, there are other definitions of functionalism which draw a slightly different line of division. For example, usage-based models of phonology (e.g. Bybee 2001) associate functionalism with acceptance of the hypothesis that sound patterns are not independent of language use and the communicative function of speech. Under this definition, Evolutionary Phonology is largely non-functionalist. Although language use will determine frequency effects which can play a role in sound change, inherent phonetic variation, ambiguities of the speech signal, and probabilities that a particular signal will be misperceived, follow directly from aspects of the human articulatory and perceptual system, and are, to a great extent, independent of language use and communicative function.

In the same way, the term "formal" is often equated with explanations which are embedded within synchronic grammars. However, there is no principled reason to limit formal properties of grammar to synchronic analyses. Chapter 2 proposes *a formal model of sound change* which specifies the precise conditions under which ambiguity arises for the listener. By making precise the phonetic conditions under which ambiguity can arise, certain types of phonetically based sound change are expected to be common, while others are predicted not to occur. For example, context-free devoicing of [g] to [k] is expected to be more common than similar devoicing of [d] or [b] because air pressure above the glottis will increase faster in [g] than in articulations with greater intraoral air volume. On the other hand, a context-free change of [t] to [m] should not occur: spontaneous nasalization is not associated with voiceless stops, nor is there any evidence suggesting that due to phonetic similarity, listeners will mistake [t] for [m]. Throughout this volume, the predictions of the model of sound change proposed are evaluated in the light of the known cases of regular sound change and found to be strongly supported. To recapitulate, unlike other approaches, Evolutionary Phonology proposes historical explanations for synchronic sound patterns which are both formal and non-teleological.

1.4 The evolutionary metaphor

The field of historical linguistics has long recognized that theories of language limited to the evolutionary concepts of ontogeny and phylogeny are insufficient in characterizing the true nature of language. What is missing in these models is characterization of the imprecise transmission of language from one generation to the next – the source of language change. Evolutionary Phonology is the general study of sound patterns in relation to language change. There is of course a risk that the term "Evolutionary" may be misunderstood in the present context. "Language evolution" is used in two separate senses: to refer to the origins of language in the human species and its biological evolution, or to language change as a form of knowledge exchange across generations without biological change. It is in this second sense that Evolutionary Phonology is evolutionary.[7] At the same time, the allusion to Darwinian thinking is intentional, since comparisons with biological evolution will at times be useful and instructive.

As remarked above, Evolutionary Phonology is the study of synchronic sound patterns as reflections of their natural history. Synchronic sound patterns are those which exist at a given point in time, independent of their history. In many cases, recurrent synchronic sound patterns can be shown to emerge naturally from the imprecise transmission of language across generations. Within Evolutionary Phonology, many cross-linguistic generalizations, like those listed in (1), are argued to be the result of *parallel evolution*. Parallel evolution is the case where identical phonetically motivated sound changes occur independently in different languages, giving rise to similar sound inventories, phonotactics, or patterns of alternation. The analogy here is with biological evolution and natural selection as first proposed by Darwin (1859). As detailed in chapter 2, certain traits, like toepads in lizards, have evolved at least three separate times in lizard history. In each case, toepads appear as a natural adaptation to arboreal habitats, where the ability to cling can be a life or death matter. Similarly, certain sound patterns, like those in (1h–k), have arisen independently in many unrelated languages, and can all arguably be explained by phonetic conditioning factors, as detailed in chapter 4. Whether or not a language allows distinctive voicing in word-final position is not a life or death matter for anything but the voicing contrast itself and any previous meaningful contrasts it once conveyed. Nevertheless, there is still drama within the domain of sounds: contrasts die, new contrasts evolve, and old contrasts mutate. The world of sounds is ever-changing, and understanding mechanisms of change allows us to see synchronic phonology in a new light.

Evolutionary Phonology is of course not a theory of language evolution based on natural selection. Though it is sometimes useful to draw parallels between the evolution of sound patterns and Darwin's theory of natural selection, these parallels are largely metaphorical, and are used to highlight the non-teleological character of sound change. This book does not deal with the biological or neurological foundations of language and should not be read as a neo-Darwinian treatise. It does not deal with the evolutionary beginnings of language as so many other works do (e.g. Aitchison 1996; Hurford et al. 1998; Carstairs-McCarthy 1999; Knight et al. 2000), and it deals uniquely with sound patterns which are

---

[7] Hurford (1990) suggests the term "glossogeny" for the cultural phenomenon of language change which constitutes the primary object of study of historical linguistics. However, in the phonetics and phonology literature, "sound change" is in common usage, and is wholly unambiguous.

directly inherited. The period of study is roughly the past 7,000 years – extremely short by biological standards, but a widely accepted estimate of the approximate time depth for which the comparative method of historical reconstruction is reliable. Documented sound changes in language during this time period are not assumed to have any genetic basis in the human organism, nor to have resulted in linguistic systems which are any more adaptive, in the biological sense, than those which preceded them.

In addition, all sound changes explored in this book are examined at the level of the individual language learner. While this is clearly a simplification of reality, the simplified model makes predictions which are confirmed with striking regularity. Of course, for a sound change to be recognized, it must usually spread to other members of a community. The study of how sound change spreads involves studies of societal interactions and relationships, and forms one of the core areas of sociolinguistics (Weinreich, Labov, and Herzog 1968; Labov 1972, 1994, 2001). This study focuses only on sound change at the level of the individual which *can spread* and give rise to sound change at the level of the speech community. Within the sociolinguistic literature, these phonetic changes are sometimes viewed as the "seeds" or ultimate sources of sound change. Moreover, though contact-induced changes are mentioned briefly, in contrast to sound changes which reflect direct inheritance, this book does not deal at any length with the many interesting sound changes which result from language contact and diffusion, and have no clear biological analogue (Thomason and Kaufman 1988).

1.5   Pure phonology

Though a majority of the recurrent sound patterns in the world's languages appear to be the result of parallel evolution, within Evolutionary Phonology, the explanation for phonological patterns can reside in synchronic grammar, diachronic evolution, or both. The correct locus of such explanations is entirely an empirical question, and part of this book is devoted to empirical studies demonstrating the limits of diachrony in explaining synchronic phonologies. By extracting from synchronic phonologies all patterns whose explanation is found in the diachronic domain, we are able to investigate the essence which remains.

Anderson (1981: 509) presents a clear statement of the problem:

On the one hand, we find that a great many phonological rules are tantalizingly close to some sort of phonetic explanation; but on the other, we find that when we try to pin them down in such terms, they have evidently been transformed into something which is no longer merely "functional phonetics." An adequate account of the nature of phonological structure will have to deal with both of these aspects of the phenomena: it must provide some basis for the apparent connection between phonetic and phonological effects, but must also recognize the essential independence of the latter domain by rigid deterministic control of the former.

There are wide-ranging consequences of an evolutionary perspective for models of synchronic grammar. One important consequence is that there is no clear role for markedness within synchronic phonology. Absolute universals and universal tendencies in sound patterns emerge from general pathways of language change, and have no independent status in the grammar. In fact, as demonstrated in part II, there is a great deal of empirical evidence against the direct incorporation of markedness into synchronic grammars. Few, if any, markedness principles proposed in phonology encode anything more than statistical probability. There are counterexamples to nearly every universal constraint or principle and most proposed universals, as well as counterexamples to them, have straightforward diachronic explanations. Even in cases where markedness constraints are obeyed, incorporation of markedness into synchronic grammars fails to explain why only a subset of alternation types are typically associated with particular markedness constraints.[8]

If recurrent sound patterns are not handled by a theory of markedness or general phonological constraints, then what form do they take in the synchronic phonology? What does pure phonology look like? The position developed here is that most recurrent aspects of sound patterns found in the world's languages are encoded as language-specific synchronic constraints. These constraints are stated in terms of independent phonological primitives which include distinctive features, segments, length, and prosodic categories (mora, syllable, foot, prosodic word, etc.). Most phonological approaches agree that phoneme inventories, representing the phonemic contrasts of a language, are learned aspects of a grammar.[9] Evolutionary Phonology carries this one step further and suggests that everything from fine aspects of phonetic detail, to phonotactics, exceptionless alternations, and morphologically governed alternations, constitute learned knowledge as well. As argued in chapter 9, there is no obvious learnability problem in this domain. Phonological systems are finite and relatively small. In contrast to syntactic systems which have been claimed to present the learner with data of "degenerative quality and narrowly limited extent" (Chomsky 1965), phonological

---

[8] Here I refer to the gaps in factorial typologies within Optimality approaches noted by Wilson (2001) and Myers (2002).

[9] One exception is Optimality Theory (Prince and Smolensky 1993; McCarthy 2002). On language-specific learning in phonology and phonetics, see chapter 9.

systems provide an abundance of stimuli, with productive phonological alternations robustly cued. While this model might appear to put a large burden on the language learner, there is mounting evidence that the human mind is specially equipped to handle precisely this sort of learning task (Jusczyk 1992).

Evolutionary Phonology represents then a serious attempt to deal with the connection between phonetic and phonological patterns, and the essential independence of phonological primitives. By detailing the way in which regular phonetically motivated sound change gives rise to recurrent synchronic sound patterns, the role of phonetic explanation in phonology can be restricted to the diachronic domain. Idealized synchronic phonologies are pure phonology, and make no reference to phonetic explanation, or non-contrastive phonetic features. Only by extracting phonetic explanations and placing them in their proper domain, can we begin to see the aspects of synchronic grammars which demand synchronic explanations.

1.6   Organization of this book

The body of this book is organized as follows. Leading on from this overview of the model, part I continues with two other introductory chapters. Chapter 2 uses biological evolution as a metaphor for linguistic evolution. Sources of change are identified and a formal model of sound change is proposed. Direct inheritance, convergent evolution and parallel evolution are compared in biological and linguistic domains, and the role of natural selection is briefly considered. Providing biological metaphors for linguistic systems highlights the importance of separating diachronic and synchronic explanation, and of distinguishing historical accident from synchronic determinism and *vice versa*. Chapter 3 places the leading ideas in Evolutionary Phonology in a historical context. Since Evolutionary Phonology diverges quite dramatically from many contemporary approaches, it is instructive to investigate the precise points of disagreement, and where these points of disagreement originate in the history of the field.

The bulk of the volume, part II, is devoted to empirical studies of sound patterns and their origins. Chapters 4 and 5 focus on phonotactics, or context-sensitive sound patterns involving the distribution of features and segments. Laryngeal features are the subject of chapter 4, and place features are the subject of chapter 5. A range of common sound patterns are investigated in chapter 6, with the goal of providing historical phonetic explanations within a formal and phonetically informed model of change. Chapter 7 explores the evolution and behavior of geminate consonants. A prediction of the evolutionary approach is that geminate distribution and behavior will reflect historical pathways of evolution. These predictions are borne out, and are incompatible with synchronic accounts which attempt to associate geminates with consistent cross-linguistic properties. Chapter 8 investigates uncommon sound patterns, distinguishing between those for which rarity is likely an accident, and those for which rarity implies some degree of articulatory or perceptual difficulty. Methodological suggestions are made for distinguishing rare from difficult sound patterns, and the role of morphological paradigms and independent phonetic contrasts in supporting tenuous contrasts is explored.

Part III assesses theoretical implications of the evolutionary approach. Chapter 9 highlights the implications for synchronic grammars. Marked-ness and naturalness are shown to be emergent properties of synchronic phonologies. Sound patterns are argued to be learned aspects of language structure, while the feature system, prosodic organization, and their combinatorics are potentially innate. The productivity of alternations is important, but non-productive alternations are also learned, and unnatural rules seem no more difficult to acquire than alternations whose phonetic origins are still transparent. The distinction between productive and non-productive sound patterns is identified as essential to the proper modeling of phonological systems. However, when investigated closely, productivity appears to involve levels of gradation which are also highly suggestive of learned knowledge. Chapter 10 assesses the compatibility of Evolutionary Phonology with standard historical accounts of sound change. The regularity of sound change is shown to be a derivative feature of the model. Slight modifications are made to Labov's resolution of the neogrammarian controversy, and the arguments against the role of teleology in sound change are strengthened. Chapter 11 concludes with a sketch of how the principles of analysis in Evolutionary Phonology can be extended to other areas of grammar.

1.7   Orthographic conventions in this book

Every effort has been made to minimize the use of special symbols and technical notation in this volume, though in some cases, this is unavoidable. Symbols in square brackets, e.g. [i], are those of the International Phonetic Alphabet (IPA) (The International Phonetic Association, 1999), and can be accessed via the International Phonetic Association website: http://www.arts.gla.ac.uk/IPA/ipa.html. Symbols in slash brackets, e.g. /i/, represent phonologically significant contrasts within a given language, and may differ from surface phonetic forms.

Where language data are cited in running text, italics indicate use of the native orthography, e.g. English *bird*, French *oiseau*, etc. Where multiple orthographies are in use, forms cited are most often in the orthography of the primary data source. In some cases, cover symbols are used to represent phonologically significant subclasses of sounds. These include V for vowels; C for consonants (or non-syllabic segments); N for nasals; and R for liquids. Any deviation from these conventions is explicitly noted in the text.

1.8   A concise summary of Evolutionary Phonology

The leading ideas and results of Evolutionary Phonology are summarized in (3)–(5) below and expanded and supported in subsequent chapters.

(3)   CENTRAL PREMISE OF EVOLUTIONARY PHONOLOGY
       Principled diachronic explanations for sound patterns have
       priority over competing synchronic explanations unless
       independent evidence demonstrates, beyond reasonable doubt,
       that a synchronic account is warranted.

(4)   HYPOTHESES SUPPORTED BY EMPIRICAL
       INVESTIGATIONS (part II)
       a. Common sound patterns typically result from common
          phonetically motivated sound change.
       b. Rare sound patterns are not the result of common
          phonetically motivated sound change.
       c. Synchronic properties of particular sound patterns are better
          explained in diachronic terms than in terms of synchronic
          phonological universals.
       d. Sound change is not goal-directed.
       e. Rare sound patterns may be rare as a consequence of sound
          change, or may reflect accidental gaps in sound pattern
          distribution.

(5)   SOME CONSEQUENCES OF THE APPROACH (part III)
       a. New phonetic explanations are proposed for previously
          problematic instances of sound change and sound patterns.
       b. Markedness constraints are excised from synchronic
          grammars.
       c. Distinctive features and prosodic categories may be innate,
          but their combinatory possibilities in synchronic grammars
          and their precise phonetic realizations are learned.
       d. Phonetically based sound change is typically regular at the
          level of the individual.

As noted above, Evolutionary Phonology attempts to explain the striking similarities in sound patterns across unrelated languages in terms of parallel evolution. Recurring independent diachronic developments are circumscribed by the interaction of articulatory and perceptual properties of speech, and ways in which these properties are abstracted into phonological representations. These diachronic developments have sound phonetic bases, but they are non-teleological and frequently non-optimizing. Recurrent sound change is the source of many recurrent sound patterns. However, sound change has no common design or purpose, as reflected in the thousands of ways languages can differ from one another, and in the notable exceptions to proposed phonological universals. To understand how language change can result in recurrent sound patterns and dramatic linguistic diversity, let us now look more closely at evolution in language and elsewhere.

2   Evolution in language and elsewhere

> It is a natural principle that the script and the sounds of language differ according to time and place.   Chén Dì (1541–1617)

Darwin's (1859) theory of the evolution of life forms has been used as a metaphor for historical developments in other fields almost since its conception. Darwin himself made use of the language-equals-species comparison, and this has continued in the modern field of linguistics, being most apparent in the field of historical linguistics. Mother languages develop, split into daughter languages, which in turn develop and split, much like the speciation of biological organisms. As biological organisms become extinct, languages also die, never to be heard again. The gradual change of languages in isolation in contrast to abrupt shifts which may occur through social contact have been likened to the punctuated equilibrium characteristic of biological evolution (Thurston 1987).[1] Environmental conditions leading to linguistic diversity, including richness of natural resources and geographic isolation, are similar to those associated with extreme localism and higher rates of speciation in life forms.[2] And, reflecting the similarities between models of genetic inheritance and those of language change, the trees used to represent linguistic relationships have a similar form and interpretation to those used in modern cladistics. A mother node (e.g. Proto-Indo-European) defines a genetic family of languages, with daughter nodes (Indo-Iranian, Balto-Slavic, Germanic, etc.) defined by shared linguistic innovations.

However, it has long been recognized that language change differs in significant ways from biological evolution, and that comparisons between

---

[1] Thurston's model of linguistic gradualism and punctuated equilibrium as applied to the languages of North-Western New Britain differs from that popularized by Dixon (1997).

[2] The split of a mother language into distinct dialects, and, eventually, distinct languages, correlates most closely with geographic and social isolation. This is evident in much of Amazonia, New Guinea, and equatorial Africa which have more languages per square mile than most other parts of the world, or did, until times of contact. Contact-induced language death has had a significant effect on linguistic diversity in these geographic areas, as elsewhere.

the two systems must remain metaphorical.[3] Historical linguistics, the study of language change, is limited to approximately the past 5,000–7,000 years. Ancient writing systems go back no farther than 5,000 years, and the rate of language change makes historical reconstruction difficult for time depths greater than about 7,000 years. At the same time, human fossil remains reveal brain and vocal tract structures suggesting that the modern human language faculty is at least 50,000–100,000 years old.[4] The linguistic study of language change then, is not the study of the evolution of language in the human species, or the study of the biological evolution of the language organ. The study of language change over the past 5,000–7,000 years assumes a mature human language faculty, and must attribute changes in the sound and shape of languages to cultural evolution. Language is passed along, like other knowledge, from one generation to the next; where an individual is isolated from the culture, it is not passed along, and where whole cultures die, languages die as well. Throughout this book language evolution refers to documented and hypothesized changes in linguistic systems which constitute one focus of historical linguistics. Evolutionary Phonology is the study of sound systems as a function of language evolution in this historic sense.

In Evolutionary Phonology, the metaphor of biological evolution is borrowed to model a very specific aspect of language change: regular phonetically based sound change and regular phonetically based sound inheritance at the level of the individual.[5] At the most general level, it can be observed that sound patterns and living organisms change over time. More narrowly, a comparison is made between errors in DNA replication and errors in sound replication. In both cases, changes resulting from errors in replication are random and non-optimizing. At the same time, the primary source of shared characteristics in biological organisms and language is direct inheritance. To my knowledge, no one has made use of the evolutionary metaphor at the level of speech production and perception to model sound patterns in precisely this way.[6] What Evolutionary Phonology offers is a way of viewing sound change in terms

---

[3] See Dalby (2002, chapter 1) for a succinct summary of differences between biological evolution and language change, with special reference to language contact.

[4] Fitch (2000) reviews evidence suggesting that Neanderthals may have had greater capacities for speech than attributed to them by Lieberman (1984).

[5] Whether or not these sound changes spread throughout the speech community depends on a range of social factors which will not concern us here. See Labov (2001) for a comprehensive survey of the issues involved.

[6] A non-metaphorical evolutionary model of the emergence of sound patterns can be found in Steels (1998) and De Boer (2001). Jakobson (1929) and Kiparsky (1995) propose similar models, but with the selectional mechanism of language transmission heavily determined by phonological markedness principles which are not assumed within Evolutionary Phonology.

of well-understood biological concepts including parallel evolution, convergent evolution, direct inheritance, adaptation, and disaptation. Many recurrent sound patterns are argued to be the result of recurrent sound changes, and do not merit inclusion in the class of properties attributed directly to the human genetic language faculty. The biological metaphor is particularly useful here, since human languages are arguably already highly adapted to human learning capacities (Locke 1983; Lindblom 1986; Deacon 1997).[7]

While the evolutionary metaphor informs this study, it is worth stressing that no direct reference is made to evolutionary principles in the formal model of sound change presented in this chapter, in the sound patterns reflecting common sound change discussed in part II, or in the leading ideas and results of the model summarized in 1.7. Where some linguists find it useful to compare synchronic rule systems to the rules of chess, or to imagine the human language faculty as a parallel distributed processor, in the domain of sound change, analogies with biological descent are revealing. Sound patterns are viewed as emergent properties of synchronic grammars in the sense of Lindblom et al. (1984). There is no need to encode the primary content of phonological representations and constraint systems in the human mind, since these properties can be shown to emerge from natural processes of language change inherent to the transmission of language from one generation to the next.

2.1   Language evolution

Evolution is ongoing in all forms of life, as it is in all languages. Life forms change over time and are able to pass these changes on to future generations. Evidence for continuous change in living creatures is everywhere: in the varieties of domesticated plants and animals, in the varieties and distributions of wild creatures, and, most dramatically, in the fossil record (Darwin 1859). Like living organisms, languages change over time and these changes may be passed on to future generations. Evidence for continuous change in languages also surrounds us.

Ancient writing systems serve as the fossil record, preserving on stone or paper what was once a living spoken language. Long before Lamarck and Darwin were documenting biological evolution in all its forms, the Chinese scholar Chén Dì (1541–1617) used ancient Chinese texts to identify sound correspondences between Old and Middle Chinese. Chén Dì was lucky, since the *Shījīng* (c. 500 BCE) included Chinese poems

---

[7] See also Briscoe (2000) on the coevolution of language and the language-acquisition device.

organized by tone and rhyme, which could be compared directly to the *Qièyùn*, a rhyming dictionary of the eighth century. Prior to Chén Dì's discoveries, the differences in rhyming schemes between the two texts were viewed as liberties or laziness on the part of *Shījīng* poets, or as evidence for changes in the poetic rhyming rules over the centuries, from imperfect to perfect rhymes. Chén Dì, perhaps the first true historical linguist of the modern era, laid the foundation for all subsequent work on the history of Chinese by showing that differences between *Shījīng* and *Qièyùn* rhymes followed from the simple fact that languages change over time.[8]

If written texts are the fossil records of language, how does the metaphor proceed? What circumstances approximate "Variation Under Domestication," the first chapter of *The Origin of Species*? In this chapter, Darwin highlights the extreme degree of intra-species variation found in domesticated plants and animals, suggesting that it is the unusual circumstance of domestication which allows otherwise useless, cumbersome or even monstrous features to be passed along. In his case study of pigeon varieties, Darwin (1859: 84–85) concludes that these breeds:

. . . though agreeing generally in constitution, habits, voice, coloring, and in most parts of their structure, with the wild rock-pigeon, yet are certainly highly abnormal in other parts of their structure: we may look in vain throughout the whole great family of Columbidae for a beak like that of the English carrier, or that of the short-faced tumbler, or barb; for reversed feathers like those of the jacobin; for a crop like that of the pouter; for tail-feathers like those of the fantail.

What explains the seemingly greater diversity and abnormalities of cultivated animals and plants when compared to their counterparts in the natural world? Darwin's hypothesis, now substantiated by modern genetics, was that "this greater variability is simply due to our domestic productions having been raised under conditions of life not so uniform as, and somewhat different from, those to which the parent-species have been exposed under nature" (1859: 71). Domestic plants and animals do not compete for nourishment as they do in the wild, as this is supplied. They are taken out of their natural habitats, rendering some of their adaptive features no longer useful. At the same time, features which might lead to quick demise in a natural world full of predators are freely passed along to future generations when those predators are absent.

Potential linguistic analogues to the abnormalities of domesticated pigeons can be seen in the unnatural situation where language acquisition is directly influenced by prescriptive laws or by spelling pronunciations,

---

[8] See chapter 2 of Norman (1988) for a concise history of Chinese historical phonology. The quote at the beginning of this chapter is taken from Norman (1988: 42).

where spelling conventions influence pronunciation. In the naturalistic home or community setting, children go about acquiring language with very little help. Where they are corrected, corrections are typically ignored, and a word or phrase which receives too much attention, even in the form of praise, may go unused for some time. The primary ingredients of healthy language acquisition in children are healthy social interactions, including language input, and healthy individuals. Provided these basic conditions are met, the bulk of language acquisition, including natural processes of sound change, takes place within the first three to five years of life, well before most literacy skills are acquired.[9] However, unnatural conditions may impinge on the naturalistic setting. Prescriptive grammarians may decide to impose their views of the way language should be spoken on others. Or, literacy skills may give rise to pronunciations which are altered in line with orthographic representations. As a result of these influences, a natural sound change may be arrested or reversed, giving rise to the sound-based equivalent of the pouter's crop or the fantail's bulky display.

Consider one small but striking case in the history of English in the context of cross-linguistic sound patterns. All languages have voiced sonorant consonants, where sonorants include glides, liquids, and nasals, but very few of the world's languages have a contrast between voiced and voiceless sonorants. Limiting our attention to labio-velar glides, it appears to be the case that no language in the world contains /ʍ/, a voiceless labio-velar glide, without also having /w/, a voiced labio-velar glide, and very few languages tolerate a contrast between these two sounds.[10] In the context of sound patterns at large then, the contrast between /w/ and /ʍ/ could be seen as *comparatively* useless or cumbersome, as opposed to the contrast between, e.g. /w/ and /j/, which is widespread in the world's languages.

British English at one time had a phonemic contrast between /w/, a voiced labio-velar glide and /ʍ/, a voiceless labio-velar glide. These two sounds were able to distinguish sound–meaning pairs like *weather* and *whether*, and still do in dialects of Scots English (Ladefoged and Maddieson 1996: 326), where the original contrast is maintained, and in many varieties of American English (Labov 1994: 314). In the English fossil record, there is much evidence for this contrast: words spelled with *wh* generally reflect old *ʍ while *w* reflects *w. Compare *whit* versus *wit*, *which* versus *witch*, *where* versus *wear*, *whine* versus *wine*, etc. However,

---

[9] This is not to say that grammars change little after the age of five. Vocabularies continue to increase over a lifetime, and significant grammatical changes can take place as well, but are typically associated with sociolinguistic variables.

[10] Ladefoged and Maddieson (1996: 326) list only three other languages with an underlying /w/ versus /ʍ/ contrast: Klamath, Yao, and Aleut.

in most dialects of English, there is no longer a /ʍ/ phoneme; the previously voiceless glide has become voiced [w] (e.g. *awhile*), or voiceless [h] (e.g. *who*), and there is only a single voiced labio-velar glide /w/.[11] The merger of *ʍ and *w in Modern English is not unexpected. Just as the fantail's surplus of tailfeathers might hinder flight and lead to decreased survival rates in the wild, there is evidence that the rarity of /w/ versus /ʍ/ contrasts in the world's sound systems is a function of phonetically determined low survival rates. Voiceless sonorants like [ʍ] have very little acoustic energy, are hard to hear, and may be lost over time, or reinterpreted as contextual variants of their voiced counterparts. In English and many other languages, voiced sonorants like /w/ are commonly devoiced due to coarticulatory laryngeal gestures. Additional factors which may play a role in this merger are the low functional load of the *w*/ʍ contrast, and the fact that other voiced/voiceless sonorant pairs in English are non-contrastive.[12]

However, the merger of /w/ and /ʍ/ was seen as a minor catastrophe in the eyes of prescriptive grammarians who saw loss of a phoneme as a sure sign of language decay. In this case, exercises were devised to reintroduce the contrast to American schoolchildren who had lost it ("repeat '[ʍ]ich [w]itch is [ʍ]ich?', and 'I [w]onder [ʍ]ether the [w]eather [w]ill change?' 100 times please"), with spelling conventions making the task somewhat easier. For some speakers, the prescriptive enterprise was successful, and a contrast between /w/ and /ʍ/ was maintained, or reestablished (though never in all the places it occurred historically), buttressed by the archaic English spelling system. Though the contrast between /ʍɪtʃ/ and /wɪtʃ/ may not conjure up images of bizarre domestic pigeon breeds alongside their svelte wild cousins, an instructive parallel exists. Just as the English carrier pigeon's beak can be viewed as a strange deformity, the isolated low-functioning voiced/voiceless contrast between /w/ and /ʍ/ in American English can be classified as a phonological abnormality. In English, the natural demise of this contrast has been artificially delayed or reversed through unnatural means: enforced practise and repetition, combined with spelling pronunciation.

As with living creatures, however, the varieties and distribution of wild or natural languages provide us with the most abundant evidence for constantly evolving linguistic structures. Every historical study of language is able to identify differences in speech across time. And every living language that has been studied involves variation within and across

---

[11] For documentation of this sound change in progress in American English, and a similar analysis, see Locke (1983: 206–8).

[12] See Labov (1994: 328–29) for multiple variables which may play a role in mergers. In Scots English, the maintenance of the contrast may be related to the feature of pre-aspiration which is absent in dialects where merger occurred.

speakers. This variation may be random or predictable; it may be related to rate of speech or not; and it may be related to any number of social variables, including age, gender, socioeconomic status, adolescent peer groups, or a multitude of other quantifiable factors (Labov 1994, 2001). Differences in sound patterns may be very small across generations, but they exist and provide evidence for the constant evolution of language. In the natural history of language, sounds change over time. Let us now look closely at how and why sound change occurs.

2.2   Sources of natural sound change

Evolution is a fact about life and language. But how does evolution take place? How do things change? Living creatures pass on their genetic blueprint through DNA. Errors occur when DNA is replicated, and these errors result in subsequent changes in the life form. Languages have a much less precise inheritance mechanism than DNA. There is no miracle molecule at work. A child is born and learns natural language through exposure to that language as it is spoken in the surrounding speech community. Granted, there are neurological mechanisms involved which appear to make language learning very different from other learning tasks, but there is no direct replication of language in anything resembling a genetic blueprint. Languages are learned over the course of years, with a learning process of trial and error which is highly individualistic. No two children will experience the exact same linguistic input in their early years of life, and no two children, including identical twins, acquire language in precisely the same way. The world is a very noisy place, and it is in the context of this noise that language is transmitted. Given all of these factors, language change appears to be the rule, not the exception.

In this context, let us focus on language evolution in a very particular sense. First, we will confine our investigation to sound patterns and sound change. Second, we will look at language as it is transmitted from one individual to another, without considering additional social factors which also clearly play a role in language change (Labov 1994, 2001). With this narrow focus, we can return to the original observation – that languages differ from living organisms in their fairly imprecise method of transmission. This process of transmission involves a speaker providing input to a listener, with the listener attempting to internalize the speaker's grammar in order to understand speech. The process of transmission takes place in a sea of noise and starts from a point where the human infant listener has no knowledge of any sound–meaning associations in the speaker's language. We will assume throughout that the speaker's performance directly reflects his or her language competence, ruling out speech errors on the part of the speaker. Under these conditions, where can error creep in?

What is responsible for the exact or inexact transmission of sounds across generations? What general models can be used to explain recurrent types of sound change in the world's languages?

The great majority of regular sound changes in evidence in the world's languages appear to be phonetically motivated.[13] Evolutionary Phonology associates errors in transmission of sound patterns with the general typology of phonetically conditioned sound change in (1). This typology highlights three distinct natural phonetic sources of sound change which I refer to as CHANGE, CHANCE, and CHOICE throughout this volume.[14] One factor is the probability of an acoustic signal being misheard by the listener/learner in the course of language acquisition. If some signal A can be misheard as B, then a change of A > B is phonetically motivated on the basis of perceptual similarity. If a sound change has perceptual similarity as its primary basis, it is classified as an instance of CHANGE (1i). A distinct source of sound change involves the localization of non-local percepts. All speech involves some degree of coarticulation between adjacent segments (Hardcastle and Hewlett 1999). If, in the course of language acquisition, a segmental representation is acquired, long-domain acoustic properties will give rise to ambiguities involving segmentation. If a sound change has ambiguous segmentation as its primary basis, it is classified as an instance of CHANCE (1ii).

(1)   GENERAL TYPOLOGY OF SOUND CHANGE IN
       EVOLUTIONARY PHONOLOGY (S = speaker, L = listener)
       i. CHANGE: The phonetic signal is *misheard* by the listener
           due to perceptual similarities of the actual utterance with
           the perceived utterance.
           Example: S says [anpa]
                    L hears [ampa]
       ii. CHANCE: The phonetic signal is accurately perceived by
           the listener but is intrinsically phonologically ambiguous,
           and the listener associates a phonological form with the
           utterance which differs from the phonological form in the
           speaker's grammar.
           Example: S says [ʔa̰ʔ] for /aʔ/
                    L hears [ʔa̰ʔ] and assumes /ʔa/

---

[13] For discussion of some potential cases of regular sound change without identifiable phonetic explanations, see Blust (2003).

[14] Small capitals are used to distinguish these technical terms from their common usages. When referring to the formal model of phonetically based sound change in (1), I will use the term "CCC-model" where CCC abbreviates CHANGE, CHANCE, and CHOICE. Also, from this point on, I will use "sound change" to refer to phonetically motivated sound change, referring specifically to other types of change (e.g. lexical diffusion, analogy, contact-induced change) where necessary.

iii. CHOICE: Multiple phonetic signals representing variants
of a single phonological form are accurately perceived by the
listener, and due to this variation, the listener (a) acquires a
prototype or best exemplar of a phonetic category which
differs from that of the speaker; and/or (b) associates a
phonological form with the set of variants which differs
from the phonological form in the speaker's grammar.

Example: S says [kakáta], [kãkáta], [kkáta] for /kakata/
L hears [kkáta], [kãkáta], [kakáta] and
assumes /kkata/

A third source of sound change is the intrinsic variability of speech along
the hyper-to-hypoarticulated continuum (Lindblom 1990a). In all languages, speech varies according to rate. If, from the pool of variants, a
listener chooses, as basic, a form which was non-basic for the speaker,
sound change can occur. If a sound change has phonetic variation as its
primary basis, it is classified as an instance of CHOICE (1iii).

Misperception or confusion of one phonetic percept with another
under CHANGE is common and well documented. Laboratory experiments documenting perceptual biases range from the propensity to perceive [ki] as [tʃi] (Guion 1996, 1998), and [θ] as [f] (Eilers 1977), to the
interpretation of a nasalized vowel [Ṽ] as [ṼN] (Kawasaki 1986; Lahiri
and Jongman 1990). In the example illustrated in (1i), a speaker says
[anpa], but the listener hears [ampa]. This is one instance of a much
more general pattern where an intervocalic heterorganic sequence of nasal
stop followed by oral obstruent is misperceived as an intervocalic homorganic nasal-obstruent sequence. What phonetic principles underlie this
misperception? The sounds [n] and [m] are produced at distinct points
of articulation, alveolar and labial respectively; these two sounds differ
acoustically, both in terms of the formant transitions from the preceding
vowel into the nasal, and in terms of the values of their nasal antiresonances. Some languages do contrast [n] and [m] in the same context
(e.g. Ngiyambaa bunbil 'pillow, for beating time to singing and danc-
ing' versus bumbil 'instrument for mimicking emu calls as a lure'), so it
is clearly possible for humans to distinguish these sounds in this context. Nevertheless, misperceptions of this type occur with greater than
chance frequency, and are argued by Ohala (1981, 1985, 1990, 1993)
to result from the intrinsic weakness of place cues for the nasal in contrast to those of the following pre-vocalic stop.[15] Notice that all instances
of CHANGE, by definition, will involve changes in *pronunciation* between
the speaker and listener. Whether these changes in pronunciation lead to

---

[15] This imbalance leads to asymmetries in misperception: [anpa] is frequently misheard as
[ampa], but not as [anta]. See chapter 5 for further discussion of related asymmetries.

phonological reanalysis on the part of the listener is not determined by the source of change itself. In a language where [n] and [m] contrast in other contexts, e.g. word-initially before vowels, or intervocalically, the sound change shown in (1i) will typically lead to phonological reanalysis of /anpa/ to /ampa/. If however, there are limited environments where [n] and [m] contrast, the listener may assume /n/, and incorporate place assimilation into the grammar. In the first case, CHANGE gives rise to a change in both pronunciation and phonological representation; in the second case, it is instantiated by a change in pronunciation and a new phonological alternation. One phonetic source of sound change, then, is misperception on the part of the listener. Certain misperceptions, or perceptual confusions, are more likely to occur than others, and give rise to instances of CHANGE. While all cases of CHANGE involve a change in pronunciation, associated changes in phonological representation may, but need not, occur.

A final comment on CHANGE regards the difficulty of finding empirical evidence for it in children's speech. As detailed in 9.1, there is good evidence that during the first three to four years of speech, the majority of a child's mispronunciations reflect maturational constraints on production, not reflections of language competence. Fully mature segmental organization is generally not complete until the early school years. During the early stages of acquisition, children's pronunciations can be quite far from adult norms. In the earliest stage (nine to eighteen months), whole syllables are left unpronounced, CV syllables predominate, and only a small number of basic consonants are used. However, even by three to four years when closed syllables, consonant clusters, and fricatives appear, many reductive strategies are still found in children's speech, including unstressed syllable reduction ([æmz] for *animals*), final consonant loss ([fɔ] for *thought*), cluster reduction ([saimi] for *slimy*), consonant harmony ([lɛloʊ] for *yellow*), and a variety of segment substitution processes ([taʊ] for *cow*, [mu:b] for *move*, [siŋ] for *thing*, etc).[16] If children mishear the speech around them, and as a consequence attempt to pronounce misheard words, there may be no evidence of this change in the child's speech for the simple reason that the child is far from being able to coordinate the articulatory gestures involved in accurate production of adult targets. At the point at which a child finally does produce a string like [ampa] instead of adult [anpa], an attentive adult who actually perceives a consistent difference between these two forms is more likely to be delighted at hearing [ampa] as opposed to [pa], [aapa],

---

[16] These examples from different children are taken from appendix 9.1 of Vihman (1996: 238–239).

or some other more distant variant, than engage the child in a mini-session of articulatory phonetics. Given this, during the point at which sounds are being misheard, the adult has no real clues as to a child's grammatical restructuring. There is good reason to believe then, that at the level of the individual, sound changes with sources in CHANGE can slip into a child's grammar almost unnoticed, providing the seeds for one source of phonetically based sound change within the wider speech community.

Intrinsic phonological ambiguity under CHANCE is also well documented.[17] The term CHANCE refers to the fact that, unlike CHANGE, there is no language-independent phonetic bias involved in this type of sound change; the signal is inherently ambiguous, though independent structural features of the language may give rise to higher probabilities for one phonological analysis than another. Some reanalyses of this sort are regular metatheses and regular dissimilations (Ohala 1993; Blevins and Garrett 1998, to appear; Ritchie 1999). Sound changes of this sort most commonly involve phonetic features with multisegmental domains, like the example of laryngealization in (1ii).[18] The example in (1ii) shows the speaker producing [ʔa̰ʔ], a short laryngealized vowel, preceded and followed by glottal closure. Vowel laryngealization is a phonetic feature associated with glottal stops, and glottal stops are often redundant properties of laryngealized vowels. If the listener assumes any phonetic redundancy within the string, then there are at least four potential phonological analyses of [ʔa̰ʔ]: /ʔa/, /aʔ/, /ʔaʔ/ or /a̰/. If /ʔa/, /ʔaʔ/ or /a̰/ is chosen, a sound change has occurred.

There are three important ways in which CHANCE differs from CHANGE. First, CHANCE does not involve misperception on the part of the listener. Second, CHANCE does not involve any immediate change in pronunciation on the part of the listener. A gradual shift in pronunciation can evolve as a consequence of the new phonological analysis, but it need not. A third difference between the two sources of sound change involves inherent biases versus priming effects. In CHANGE the probability of a sound change occurring is generally related to biases in the human perceptual system; in CHANCE, pre-existing sound patterns

[17] Any phonetic string in isolation is ambiguous with respect to multiple phonological representations. However, context-dependent regularities in phonetic realization of phonological categories within and across words and phrases typically allow the language learner to zero in on a phonological analysis which matches that of the speaker. We are still at an early stage in understanding precisely how such generalizations are extracted from the speech stream. Relevant studies of speech perception are cited throughout this volume, and a range of perspectives is presented in Ferguson et al. (1992).

[18] Difficulties in feature localization may also arise as a result of auditory decoupling which may occur in the perception of sibilant and click noise (Blevins and Garrett, to appear).

within the ambient language being acquired may produce priming effects which increase the probability of sound change.[19]

This last difference highlights an intriguing property of the general model of sound change in (1): sound changes are modeled as probabilistic, with higher probabilities of occurrence relatable to other phonetic features of the language in question, or to general strategies involved in extracting sound patterns from the acoustic signal. For example, if a language has a high token frequency of CV syllables, then a listener hearing [ʔa̰ʔ] may be more likely to interpret this as an instance of /ʔa/ than /aʔ/. The listener makes a simple frequency-based inference: most syllables are CV, therefore [ʔa̰ʔ] is most likely CV, therefore, posit /ʔa/. In chapter 6, the common structure-preserving nature of several different types of sound change is attributed to language-specific factors of this sort. Chapter 6 also suggests a general preference rule involved in phonological acquisition: all else being equal, a single segmental source is assumed for a particular phonetic/phonological feature. This principle will rule out /ʔaʔ/ as a potential underlying form in (1ii), since laryngealization is associated with two segments, giving preference to /ʔa/, /aʔ/, or /a̰/.

Both CHANGE and CHANCE involve idealizations of the phonetic world, since both take as input single invariant tokens of a particular speech form. However, all spoken languages involve a great deal of intraspeaker variability in the phonetic realization of phonological forms. Intraspeaker variability is arguably a manifestation of accordian-like transforms of the speech stream, from the forceful, maximally segmentable stretched-out profile of clear speech, to the lax, coarticulated, and highly compressed mumble of casual speech. In CHOICE, intraspeaker phonetic variability is the source of sound change. The term CHOICE refers to intrinsic choices offered to the language learner in observing phonetic variation: these include choices for the center or prototypical exemplar of a particular category, as well as choices as to which variant should be chosen when different variants suggest different phonological forms. Following Lindblom (1990a, 1998), intraspeaker variation is viewed as a direct manifestation of the continuum from hyperarticulated listener-oriented "clear" speech (Moon and Lindblom 1994) to reduced, hypoarticulated "casual" speech (Lindblom et al. 1992; Willerman 1994).[20] In clear speech, the speaker articulates more forcefully: segments are generally longer and ambiguities due to

---

[19] See 6.4 and 9.2 where these priming effects are attributed to Structural Analogy.

[20] This is part of the H&H theory of Lindblom (1990a). Evolutionary Phonology adopts the H&H *description* of intraspeaker variation as a function of the hyper-to-hypoarticulated

coarticulation are reduced. In casual speech, the opposite holds: segments are generally shorter, and coarticulation is extreme. Consider the pronunciations of /ka-kata/ 'to laugh' in Bellonese, a Polynesian Outlier language of the Solomon Islands. In hyperarticulated speech, there is a full vowel in each syllable: [ka.ka.ta]. However, in fast speech, the vowel flanked by adjacent consonants is not pronounced and we find [kkata]. Intermediate forms present the listener with a short vowel between the identical consonants: [kăkata]. In this example, two related choices present themselves. First, which *phonetic variant* of the word 'to laugh' is the prototypical one? Second, should this word, and others with the same patterns of vowel reduction, be represented phonologically with or without a vowel between the two identical consonant sounds? A naive view might be that speakers will choose /kakata/ due to the fact that two of the three basic variants contain a vowel. However, there is growing evidence that token frequency plays an important role in the acquisition of sound patterns (Skousen 1989; Bybee 2001; Pierrehumbert 2001). If [kakata] has the lowest token frequency, occurring only in careful speech, ritual speech, or song, listeners may base their hypotheses on other, more common, everyday variants. Another complicating factor in this example, which I return to in 6.2.2, is that the variable vowel always has the same quality as the vowel of the following syllable, and hence is *predictable*. If the vowel in [kăkata] is short enough, and of predictable quality, it may be interpreted not as a phonological vowel, but as a transition associated with phonetic release of the /k/ sound.[21] In this example, where the historical form is /kakata/, choice of /kkata/ by the listener is an instance of sound change. Many examples of CHOICE are illustrated in chapters 6 and 7, and sound changes which combine CHOICE with CHANGE or CHANCE are also discussed. The most important defining characteristic of CHOICE is its source in intrinsic phonetic variation. As a consequence of its source in variation, changes in token frequencies of particular phonetic variants are catalysts in CHOICE. To clarify this last point, it will be useful to lay out the model of sound change in somewhat more detail.

In (2), the model of sound change proposed in (1) is amplified by showing cases where no sound change occurs (2i), by integrating phonetic variation into all types of change, and by identifying universal aspects of

---

speech continuum. However, unlike H&H theory, it does not view sound change as "improving" speech along this continuum. Rather, a stochastic model is adopted in which changes in frequency of particular phonetic variants result in shifts along the hyper-hypoarticulation axis.

[21] The non-contrastive status of release in the world's languages is discussed in 2.5 in the context of non-aptive features of speech.

the phonetics-to-phonology mapping. In (2), three independent phonetically governed sound changes are illustrated: fronting of the back vowel [u] adjacent to a dental/alveolar consonant under coarticulation, *ut > yt (Ohala 1981); *θ > f due to perceptual similarity of lamino-dental and labio-dental fricatives [θ] and [f] (see 6.1.1) and *t' > $\textit{ʔ}$, the change of a voiceless glottalized (unreleased) stop to a glottal stop, which results from anticipation of glottal closure combined with absence of release (see chapter 5).

As is well known, the mappings between acoustic features and units of perception are of a non-trivial nature:

> The basic elements of language, its consonants and vowels, are not objective, physical units, but rather psychologically defined entities that can be reliably identified only by a human listener. Speech is not a simple left-to-right sequence of discrete and invariant alphabetic segments such as we see on a printed page. The reason for this is that we do not speak phoneme by phoneme, or even syllable by syllable. Typical rates of speech – 10 to 15 phonemes/second – are possible because we coproduce, or coarticulate, the units. At each instant, our articulators are executing overlapping patterns of movement that may correspond to several neighbouring phonemes, including phonemes in neighbouring syllables. The result of this shingled pattern of movement, is, of course, a shingled pattern of sound, in which the acoustic structure of a given consonant or vowel varies from one context to another. Thus, the units of the acoustic signal do not correspond, one for one, with the units of perception. (Studdert-Kennedy 1998: 169–70)

Nevertheless, assuming that speech, at some level, is represented in terms of segments and features, universal aspects of the mapping, listed in (3) can be defined. The numbered arrows in (2) refer to the steps listed in (3); double-shafted arrows in (2) indicate predicted directions of change given phonological restructuring.

(2)   A formal model of sound change with examples

    i. No sound change

Speaker	Listener
/ut/	/ut/
↓1	↑3
[ut,ʉt,yt . . .]$_{Vi}$ 2→	[ut,ʉt,yt . . .]$_{Vi}$

    ii. CHANGE: sound change via misperception

Speaker	Listener
/θa/	/fa/
↓	↑3
[θa . . .]$_{Vi}$ 2→	[fa . . .]$_{Vj}$

iii.   CHANCE: sound change via "mis-application" of
phonetic-phonology mapping

Speaker	Listener
/yt/	/ut/
↓1	↑3

[yt . . .]$_{Vi}$ 2→   [yt . . .]$_{Vj}$ ⇒ [ʉt,yt, . . .]$_{Vj}$

iva.   CHOICE: sound change from phonetic variation (change in
variant frequency)

Speaker	Listener
/ut/	/yt/
↓1	↑3

[yt,ʉt, . . .]$_{Vi}$ 2→   [yt,ʉt . . .]$_{Vi}$
4↑
[ʉt,yt, . . .]$_{Vj}$

ivb.   CHOICE: sound change from phonetic variation (change in
variant set)

Speaker	Listener
/ut/	/yʔ/
↓1	↑3

[yʔ . . . yt']$_{Vi}$ 2→   [yʔ, . . .]$_{Vj}$
4↑
[yt',yʔ . . .]$_{Vi}$

(3)   Universal decomposition of sound change
Step 1: Universal and language-specific phonetics give rise to a
range of surface forms in natural speech production,
abbreviated here by [ ]$_V$ (= [ ] and its phonetic
variants), where subscripts indicate identity, or lack
thereof, and are listed in order of decreasing
frequency.[22]

---

[22] Within some models of phonologization, a distinction is made between universal phonetic properties, and language-specific ones. For example, Hyman (1977) identifies a
state where a language has automatic lowering of F_0 following a voiced consonant due
to universal phonetics, and a subsequent state where lowering of F_0 is too great to be
attributed to universal phonetics. Hajek (1997: 21) also distinguishes language-specific
phonetic rules from universal phonetic rules. In the model proposed in (2), there is no
formal difference between variants determined by universal phonetics and those determined by language-specific properties; in both cases, a set of variants is defined from
which the listener *qua* learner must acquire language-specific phonetics, and at the same
time, extract from acoustic data significant sound patterns and contrasts. Within this
model, the enhancement of F_0 lowering following a voiced consonant is no different in

Step 2: Utterance (set) is perceived "correctly" (i, iii, iv), or "incorrectly" (ii).

Step 3: Utterance is associated with a phonological form on the basis of

    a. Universal knowledge (features, prosodic categories)

    b. General segmentation and pattern matching algorithms

    c. Default mapping principle: one-to-one association between features and segments

    d. Other ambient sound patterns of the language being acquired

    e. Relative frequency of variants

Step 4: Shift in variant frequencies from speaker as child to speaker as adult

In (2i), there is no sound change, and both the range of phonetic surface forms and their relative frequencies, and the phonological interpretation of the sequence are directly inherited.[23] The context-free *θ > f in (2ii) is an example of CHANGE with variation playing no role. In (2iii), CHANCE is illustrated by the dissimilatory change *yt > ut. In this example, the listener attributes the frontness of [y] to the effect of the following [t], and on this basis, posits an underlying form which lacks the shared assimilatory feature. Because the speaker's [yt] was an instance of /yt/, the listener's /ut/ constitutes a sound change. Notice again that in (2iii), there is no immediate change in pronunciation. The double-shafted arrow in (2iii) shows the predicted direction of change for this particular sequence. Because the vowel has been analyzed as /u/, it will most likely move towards other phonetic tokens of /u/ in the language if they exist.

In (2iv), two cases of CHOICE are diagrammed. (2iva) involves a simple vowel change *ut > yt, where the high frequency of fronted variants of /u/ gives rise to a category shift. In (2ivb) a more complex example of CHOICE is illustrated by *ut > $y\mathfrak{r}$. Here, there is an overt change in pronunciation. Whereas the speaker has tokens [yt'] and [y$\mathfrak{r}$], due to the high frequency of [y$\mathfrak{r}$], the listener adopts this as the basic form from which the phonological representation is extracted. The interest of this type of example relates to loss of the phonetic conditioning factor for vowel fronting: due to a sound change of *t > t' > $\mathfrak{r}$ (cf. a similar change

---

nature from the enhancement of a pre-existing language-specific feature, like the extreme vowel lengthening found in English preceding voiced consonants. The model in (2) is meant to capture subphonemic sound change as well as phonologization.

[23] For evidence supporting the learned status of detailed phonetic knowledge, including patterns of variation, see Pierrehumbert (1994, 2000, 2001), Bybee (2001), and Warner et al. (2002).

in many dialects of English), the *t which conditioned vowel fronting is lost. Variation plays a direct role in the changes in (2iva) and (2ivb), but not elsewhere.

A few remarks are in order regarding step 3 of (3), where a listener extracts generalizations from the raw acoustic signal based on, at least, the factors listed. Universal aspects of phonetic and phonological knowledge include audible phonetic features, distinctive phonological features, segments, and prosodic structures, which can be all be identified by human infants, as summarized in Werker and Pegg (1992), and reviewed in 9.1. General segmentation or pattern-matching algorithms are, to a large extent, unexplored. For the purposes of this volume, all that is important is that frequency of particular variants can play a role in the learner's development of phonetic and phonological categories. The approaches consistent with this model of sound change include: Skousen's (1989, 1992) analogical model; the WRAPSA (Word Recognition and Phonetic Structure Acquisition) model of Jusczyk (1992); Stemberger's (1992) connectionist view; Pierrehumbert's (2001) exemplar dynamics; Wedel's (2003) analogical modeling of sound patterns invoking self-organizing principles; and analogical learning confirmed by the experimental results in Ernestus and Baayen (2003). In all of these approaches, token frequency may play an important role in sound patterns, and may initiate instances of sound change with sources in variation. Given that the set of utterances which any child hears in the course of language acquisition will be different from that of the next child, with different frequencies of, e.g. word variants, the model in (2)–(3) implies that every individual's grammar will be different at the level of phonetic implementation. This recognition of minute differences in individual grammars sets Evolutionary Phonology apart from other approaches where speakers of the same language are assumed to have the same grammar.

The importance of frequency in instances of CHOICE within this model is worth highlighting. In traditional neogrammarian treatments, gradual articulatory drift was attributed to "mechanical" factors, which in step 1 of (3) are the transforms of speech which occur at different rates, and which distinguish clear speech from casual speech. However, what remained unexplained within the neogrammarian account was *why* these mechanical shifts took place. Within the model of sound change proposed in (1)–(3), there is an uninteresting, but testable answer given. Mechanical shifts in pronunciation take place at the level of the individual when the input the learner is exposed to gives rise to different relative frequencies of variants from that which gave rise to the speaker's grammar. That frequency effects play a role in shaping sound patterns is well demonstrated (Bybee 2001; Bybee and Hopper 2001). By allowing frequency effects to guide a language learner's phonological generalizations, shifts in articulation can be modeled as shifts in the perceptual-acoustic space defined by token frequencies.[24] CHOICE, as modeled in (1)–(3), incorporates change at the subphonemic level (changes in pronunciation) as well as changes which are often referred to as "phonologizations," where there is a change in some aspect of the phonological system.

A final aspect of CHOICE which I return to in 8.3 is that it is the sole locus of what is sometimes termed "teleology" in sound change. When a range of variants exists for a particular word, a speaker may choose one variant over another to maximize contrast with an otherwise homophonous word. I suggest in 8.3 that this type of choice on the part of the speaker is typically limited to paradigm-internal contrasts, and can account for certain cross-linguistically rare feature contrasts.

There are several important differences between the model in (1)–(3) and other treatments of phonologization (e.g. Hyman 1977; Ohala 1981; Hajek 1997). First, step 1 of (3) assumes no fundamental distinction between universal phonetic rules and language-specific phonetic implementation rules. This is based on empirical findings questioning the universal/language-specific phonetics dichotomy. Kingston and Diehl (1994) suggest that much of phonetic interpretation is controlled or language-specific, and that far more articulations are directly controlled by speakers than was previously thought. Of particular interest is their finding that the lowering of F_0 on vowels after voiced consonants in English occurs even in contexts where the phonologically [+voiced] segment *is not phonetically voiced*, or in any obvious way phonetically distinct from allophones of the [−voiced] category in other contexts. If this lowering occurs in the absence of the phonetic feature which is universally associated with it, then clearly, it is no longer the result of automatic phonetic processes. At the same time, studies of coarticulation suggest general trends related to other language-specific factors (Manuel 1999). Inter-speaker variation shows that some speakers have little coarticulation

---

[24] Kiparsky (1988: 373), citing Jespersen (1886/1993) and Nyman (1978) attributes the causal link between frequency and sound change to redundancy: "frequent items are more easily guessed by the hearer, so the speaker can afford more reduced pronunciations of them, which then may be lexicalized." In other words, reduced variants of high-frequency words will be more common than reduced variants of lower-frequency words, but reduced variants of lower-frequency words may still occur. In order to account for the "lexicalization" referred to by Kiparsky, frequency effects are incorporated in the model of sound change.

Many factors can give rise to changes in the frequencies of phonetic variants from one generation to the next, from changes in use of lexical items to increased use of particular genres which occupy one extreme of the hyper-to-hypoarticulation continuum. These frequency changes give rise to the seemingly non-deterministic pathways of change (e.g. lenition versus fortition) observed through this volume.

compared with others "who show relatively extensive temporal and spatial coarticulatory effects" (Manuel 1999: 189). It is unclear how such intra-speaker variation can be accounted for without some blurring of the universal/language-specific boundary. As suggested by Manuel (1999: 189), the role of contrast may "set a maximum limit on coarticulation, but has little to say about how it is further limited."

Another difference between the CCC-model and more circumscribed accounts of phonologization is that it incorporates context-free splits and mergers. This is not true of Hyman's (1977) model. Hyman's assumption is that the evolution of a new contrast implies or leads to the loss of a former contrast – that there is an inevitable trading relationship between contrasts: "*the development of a phonological rule carries the seeds of its own destruction*" (Hyman 1977: 412). However, there are context-free sound changes (e.g. $*\theta > f$) which involve changes in phonological representation but no trading relationship. And there are also processes like the phonologization of vowel harmony, where the trigger of the assimilatory change is not lost, though a shift from variable coarticulation to harmony needs to be modeled. Even if Hyman's model is restricted to the evolution of new phonological contrasts or phonological alternations, the descriptive generalization does not hold. In many languages, [s] is palatalized to [ʃ] adjacent to [i], but this does not typically result in a shift from /i/ to /ɨ/, when a contrast between /s/ and /ʃ/ evolves. A final difference between the CCC-model of sound change and those of Hyman (1977), Ohala (1981), and Hajek (1997), is the prominent role given to phonetic variation in instances of CHOICE, and the integration of frequency effects in determining the output of sound change under CHOICE.[25]

The central role of phonetic variation in defining the choice space for sound change has been suggested by Sievers (1881), Passy (1890), Ohala (1974a, 1989), Kiparsky (1988, 1995) and many others. However, there are few accounts in which frequency effects are modeled in sound change. One notable exception is Watson (1999), who highlights the role of frequency with reference to sound changes like the one diagrammed in (2iva):

Ohala is inexplicit as to why listeners of one generation should have a different response to such variability from their forebears, suddenly failing to do the appropriate filtering out of contingent features. A cause of this may be a statistical change in the pattern of variability . . . (Watson 1999: 160)

Watson provides an analysis for how a /VN/ sequence with a small amount of contextual nasalization, (a) below, shifts phonetically to [ṼN] with a

---

[25] Hajek (1997: 21) acknowledges variation in production as a constant which "may result in gradual, subtle but ultimately cumulative shifts in articulatory and acoustic targets" but does not build this directly into his model or typology of sound change.

greater amount of contextual nasalization, (b) below, which is phonologically reinterpreted as a nasalized vowel:

Time 1: [VN] with small amount of contextual nasalization   (a) V [−nasal]
Time 2: [ṼN] greater amount of contextual nasalization   (b) V [+nasal]

His analysis makes direct reference to changes in the statistical frequency of variation:

> The essential factor in bringing about this abduction is the individual variability already discussed in coarticulation . . . At time point 1, a majority of speakers in a language community produce vowel nasalization only to extents consistent with . . . that is with no phonological specification of vowel nasality, only [VN] coarticulation. Even at this stage, a minority of speakers might show significantly more nasalization . . . this need not effect the community's norms. However, this may be changed by a small sociolinguistic shift. If a higher proportion of speakers (or speakers from a higher status group) shift to a larger degree of coarticulation (which they can do without any necessary change in their own phonological representations), new generations of speakers will be led to infer phonological structure (b) rather than (a). (Watson 1999: 166)

Other recent models incorporating frequency effects include Bybee (2001) and Pierrehumbert (2001).

Though the CCC-model isolates distinct phonetic sources of ambiguity, it will often be the case that a single sound change has multiple sources. For example, nasal place assimilation in VNTV is characterized as a cannonical instance of CHANGE, though many languages allow for coarticulation of N and T in non-careful speech, suggesting that CHOICE may also be involved (see chapter 5). Coarticulation is a natural feature of speech at normal rates, and can give rise to inexact transmission of speech, as in the case of CHANCE illustrated in (1ii) and (2iii) above. At the same time, the speaker's ability to control a phonetic continuum from casual to clear speech can be understood as a potential check on the segmentation problem. But this intraspeaker flexibility results in variation, feeding CHOICE, which can also result in sound change. To summarize, CHANGE, CHANCE, and CHOICE are intrinsic features of the inexact language inheritance mechanism and constitute primary sources of sound change at the level of the individual.

2.3   Non-optimal sound change

Though Darwin was unaware of DNA as the conduit for genetic inheritance, one of the most important aspects of his theory of evolution is the assumption that changes which occur in the course of evolution are random. The study of genetic mutations is in its infancy, yet, as far as we can tell, these mutations are non-optimizing in the sense that they do not necessarily result in a better organism (Gould and Lewontin 1979). Like genetic mutations, the three phonetic sources of sound change defined in 2.2 are in no way goal-directed. Sound change happens, but it does not occur in order to make speech easier to articulate, easier to perceive or easier to transmit; it does not necessarily result in a more symmetrical, more stable or generally improved phonological system; for every case where it happens, there is a parallel case where it does not happen.

The non-optimizing nature of sound change finds empirical support in cross-linguistic studies of metathesis (Blevins and Garrett 1998, to appear). Many cases of CHANCE like *aʔ* > *ʔa* in (2ii) can be paired with mirror-image changes in other languages. For example, in Slavic *VR* > *RV*, where *R* is a liquid, but in Le Havre, a Romance language, *RV* > *VR*. Any claim for Slavic that *RV* is generally better (phonetically or phonologically) than *VR* will have to contend with the fact that *RV* sequences are eliminated in favor of *VR* sequences in Le Havre.[26] And, there are many languages in which *VR* and *RV* sequences have endured: in Standard French, most native words beginning in *prV* . . . reflect Latin *prV*, while in many Pama-Nyungan languages, Proto-Pama-Nyungan **VR* is reflected as *VR*. In both cases, direct inheritance reflects the stability of these sequences over hundreds or thousands of years.

A different argument against optimizing sound change is that a single sound change may simplify articulation at the cost of perceptual saliency or vice versa. In Bellonese where /kakata/ has at least three perceptually distinct surface forms, [ka.ka.ta], [kākata], and [kkata], the listener must choose between at least two phonological representations /kakata/ and /kkata/. The casual speech variant, [kkata], is, one might argue, easier to articulate, since it involves less articulatory effort, with one less vowel gesture than the careful-speech variant. Ease of articulation, then, might favor /kkata/. At the same time, positing /kkata/ means that the language has a new phonological contrast between /kkata/ and /kata/. As noted in chapter 7, pure durational contrasts like [kk] versus [k] are difficult to perceive in word-initial position, and often lead to neutralization of the length contrast in this position. One problem, then, is that where ease of articulation favors /kkata/, maintenance of perceptual contrast favors /kakata/. While it is conceivable that tradeoffs of this sort may be

---

[26] The proponent of optimizing sound change can always revert to the position that *RV* is better in Slavic, while *VR* is better in Le Havre. The problem, discussed further in 10.3, is that from the same proto-language, different languages evolve, while from the same language, different dialects emerge. If *VR* is better in Le Havre, why isn't it also better in French? See 6.3 and 9.2.2 for a non-teleological account of structure preservation in sound change.

calculated for any pair of phonetic forms, a serious problem is the fact that phonological representations like /kakata/ have *multiple phonetic variants*.[27] Intraspeaker variability itself makes the calculation of phonetic optimality of phonological forms intractable. In order to calculate ease of articulation or perceptibility values for /kakata/ versus /kkata/ we must know precisely how each will be phonetically implemented by the articulators. But, as already demonstrated, intraspeaker variation provides a range of alternatives which differ precisely in these values. In fact, as a case of CHOICE, at the point in time where /kakata/ is reanalyzed as /kkata/, there is no difference in the articulatory space associated with each of the two forms.

Finally, we turn to the most interesting challenge for a model of non-optimizing sound change, the case of CHANGE. Recall the observation that [anpa] may be misheard as [ampa], but [anpa] is not misheard as [anta]. The unidirectionality of this misperception smacks of optimization. Ohala's (1990b) general explanation for this sound change is the weakness of perceptual cues to place of articulation in the post-vocalic pre-obstruent environment, and their strength in pre-vocalic position. In functional terms, /n/ versus /m/ before /p/ is hard to hear, so the contrast is eliminated.[28] However, Ohala's experimental evidence indicates that speakers simply *do not hear* [np] as [np] a good part of the time. No principle of optimization is necessary, since the sound change follows from the way our auditory system processes speech. In other cases of CHANGE, an optimization approach is disconfirmed by the same sort of bidirectionality exhibited by metathesis sound changes. An instructive case is the perceptual affinity between nasality and aspiration, known as rhinoglottophilia (Matisoff 1975: 265).[29] Breathiness and nasalization have similar acoustic effects on the vowel spectrum (Ohala 1975: 303), and these spectral similarities can result in misperception of breathiness as nasalization (Ohala 1980, 1987; Klatt and Klatt 1990). In the natural world of sound change, nasalization appears as a reflex of aspiration in Bzhedukh and Shapsegh, two Caucasian languages, while the Owerri

---

[27] Lindblom (1986, 1998) suggests an equation for optimal systems of phonetic contrasts, balancing articulatory ease with perceptual ease. However, in his equation the size of the inventory is predetermined. In natural language learning, we cannot assume that the listener arrives at inventory size before segmental contrasts are discovered.

[28] An articulatory argument might also be made, since [np] requires two articulatory gestures, while [mp] has only one. However, as pointed out by Ohala, this account cannot explain why sound changes like *np > mp involving regressive assimilation are extremely common, while shifts of *np > nt, involving similar articulatory simplification but progressive assimilation, are rare.

[29] It is instructive in the phonological domain, because both nasality and aspiration are usually viewed as marked properties of vowels. And it is instructive in the phonetic domain because both aspiration and nasality shrink the perceptual vowel space.

dialect of Igbo shows aspiration as a reflex of nasalization (Blevins and Garrett, 1993). The inevitable conclusion is that sound patterns, like organic forms, are "not an array of optimal adaptations to their immediate surroundings, but complex products of history, not always free to change in any direction that might 'improve' them" (Gould 1990: 67).

If the three basic types of sound change in 2.2 are non-optimizing, then what factors are responsible for the sound patterns which repeat themselves in one language family after another? Why do so many unrelated languages have word-final devoicing, with word-final voicing a rarity? Why does word-final place neutralization of /p, t, k/ occur with greater-than-chance frequency, while similar word-initial neutralizations are unattested? Why do consonantal length contrasts tend to exist in the middle of words and not at word edges? And why is it possible to come up with near-exceptionless phonological generalizations? If changes which give rise to these patterns cannot always be seen as improvements on the sound shape of language, what does give rise to these striking similarities in form?

2.4   Sources of similarity

When a biological character in one organism resembles that of another, there are four logical sources for the observed similarity. The first and most usual explanation is that similar characters reflect *direct genetic inheritance*. In this case, the species are genetically related and the feature in question has been acquired by descent from a shared ancestor which also had this feature. The importance of inheritance as an explanation for shared biological features is stressed by Gould (1983: 80), replying to Dobshansky's (1951) application of adaptive landscape to the question of discontinuous distribution of species:

... surely the cluster of cats exists primarily as a result of homology and historical constraint. All felines are alike because they arose from a common ancestor shared with no other clade. That ancestor was well adapted, and all its descendants may be. But the cluster and the gap reflect history, not the current organization of ecological topography. All feline species have inherited the unique cat *Bauplan*, and cannot deviate far from it as they adapt, each in its own particular (yet superficial) way. Genealogy, not current adaptation, is the primary source of clumped distribution in morphological space.[30]

---

[30] Physical environment appears to play a very minor role in shaping language. Multiple languages (so far as one can tell, any possible subset of natural languages) can be acquired by a single child in any part of the world. This context-free gift for multilingualism signals the essential independence of language structure and transmission from broad aspects of the physical environment and the human genetic code. Nevertheless, there

The acceptance of direct genetic inheritance as a prime component of linguistic structure was fundamental to the neogrammarian tradition of the nineteenth century, but generally abandoned by the Chomskian generative tradition.[31] Though the generative view is perhaps not as farfetched as Dobshanksky's model of species distribution they share a methodological fallacy: a mechanism (like adaptive landscape or innate properties of universal grammar) which can explain *some* aspects of regular distribution is taken to explain *all* aspects of regular distribution, despite the existence of alternative explanations, including direct inheritance.[32] Within Evolutionary Phonology, the source of similarities across languages is the subject of empirical investigation. Where a common ancestor possesses a sound pattern found in one of its descendants, and where it can be shown that there is a direct path of inheritance between these languages and sound patterns, the sound pattern of the descendant language is explained through descent, and synchronic principles proposed to derive it are likely to be superfluous. Most Indo-European languages have closed syllables of the form CVC. Should this be surprising, given that Proto-Indo-European also had closed syllables, and that many of these were directly inherited by daughter languages? In language, as in life, the primary source of shared characteristics is direct genetic inheritance.

A second account of similar characteristics in different organisms highlights the fact that the characteristics are not as similar as they look. If the characteristics are only superficially similar, having arisen through different developmental pathways from different ancestral conditions, the development is referred to as *convergent evolution*. A well-studied biological example involves the eyes of vertebrates and those of cephalopods (cuttle-fish, nautilus, octopus, etc.). These eyes have superficial similarities, but are very different in design and function, and have evolved independently. So, in language, superficially similar sound patterns may have arisen in different ways from different kinds of sound change.

---

are interesting speech modes which appear to have evolved relative to aspects of the physical environment. One example is whistled speech, where words are whistled instead of spoken. In Pirahã, an Amazonian language, whistle speech is used during rainforest hunts (Everett 1986). The rainforest is arguably one of the noisiest natural environments encountered, and so it is not surprising that a speech mode with better overall acoustics than the spoken word has arisen in its depths.

[31] See chapter 3 for a brief general history of explanation in phonology.

[32] Within generative models, direct genetic inheritance has relevance only to the periphery of the grammar, and no relation to its core, which includes most, if not all, commonly recurrent grammatical properties. Regularity in form is not the result of inheritance. Only peculiarities of grammar are viewed as "historical residue." As Lightfoot (1999: 13) puts it: "We shall look to history . . . to understand the quirks of the modern language."

Convergent evolution in language is visible at many different levels. Words can be very short, consisting of two or three sounds, and sound inventories can be quite small (20–30 phonemes), so the probability of two words with a similar sound–meaning relationship occurring among the 4,000 or so languages, all with vocabularies of tens of thousands of words, is very high.[33] An example of convergence at the lexical level is the word for 'dog' in English and in Mbabaram, an Australian Aboriginal language of the Cape York Peninsula. In both languages, one sound sequence associated with this general meaning is [dɔg]. Though the Mbabaram word and the English word have similar sounds and meanings, we know that the general relationship between sound and meaning in language is an arbitrary one.[34] In this case, then, the resemblance between the English and Mbabaram words for 'dog' is either the result of convergent evolution (e.g. an accident), or a result of borrowing. Comparative work on the languages of Cape York allows us to identify this as a case of convergent evolution: Mbabaram /dɔg/ derives from Proto-Paman *gudaga 'dog,' by four regular sound changes: *gudaga > gudɔga > udɔga > dɔga > dɔg (Hale 1964, 1976a, b). The superficial relationship between the English and Mbabaram words is a spurious one, and unlikely to illuminate fundamental aspects of sound patterns or sound change.

More relevant to this study are cases of convergent evolution at the level of sound patterns and sound inventories, independent of meaning. In one relevant case, an inherited feature of one language is non-inherited in another.[35] Convergent characteristics are found in Japanese and Gilbertese, a Micronesian language. In both languages, the only possible word-final consonants are nasals.[36] Though these look like superficially similar constraints, they have arisen in different ways. In Pre-Gilbertese, all inherited forms with final nasals were once vowel-final. Loss of word-final voiceless vowels has left the nasal exposed in final position (Blevins 1997). In Old Japanese, all words also ended in vowels. However, the development which led to final nasals was not one of sound change, but of language contact (Shibatani 1990: 121–22). Borrowings from Chinese languages containing nasal-final words are the source of nasal-final words in Middle Japanese. Again, a superficial relationship,

---

[33] See Ringe (1999) where the problem of random cognate sets for CVC roots is detailed.

[34] Exceptional lexical classes with non-arbitrary sound–meaning correspondences include sound symbolism, baby-talk, and onomatopeia.

[35] Of course, there is no direct analog to borrowed features in the biological world, though hybridism and new technologies in inter-species organ transplants come close.

[36] In Japanese, the only nasal found word-finally is a nasal glide. In Gilbertese /m, n, ŋ/ are all licit word-finally.

in this case, between Japanese and Gilbertese, cannot be explained by a single phonetic or phonological principle.[37]

Another case of convergent evolution is the emergence of similar sound patterns or contrastive oppositions which arise by very different types of sound change. For example, consonantal length contrasts may evolve through vowel loss between identical consonants, as in the *kakata > kkata change in Bellonese, or through post-tonic lengthening of an earlier short consonant, as in Buginese takke 'stick' from Proto-Austronesian *təkən. Chapter 7 details seven distinct general pathways leading to the evolution of consonantal length contrasts. The importance of convergent evolution in this case study is that distinct evolutionary pathways give rise to distinct cases of geminate behavior within synchronic phonologies.

A final case of convergent evolution is the existence of identical sound changes with distinct evolutionary sources. Consider a sound change involving vowel loss: $V > \emptyset$. Vowel loss can arise from CHANGE, in the case where, for example, a short final voiceless vowel is not perceived due to its weak intensity. But vowel loss can also result from CHOICE, as in the Bellonese *kakata > kkata example. Whether misperception or CHOICE is the source of sound change has implications for the form of synchronic grammars, as demonstrated in chapter 7. Another example of a multi-source sound change are common assimilations like *np > mp. As already discussed, this sound change can result from CHANGE, as described in 2.2, where [anpa] is misheard as [ampa]. But the same sound change can also arise from CHOICE: in many languages, including English, /np/ sequences are produced as [np] in clear speech, but can be pronounced as [mp] in casual speech (e.g. [ɪnpʊt], [ɪmpʊt] for 'input'). The sound change *np > mp may be an instance of CHANGE, CHOICE, or a combination of the two. Where two common sound changes converge on a single sound pattern, such sound patterns are expected to be more common cross-linguistically than cases where convergence is not a factor.

Convergent evolution contrasts with a third logical possibility for the evolution of like characters: *parallel evolution*. In biological systems, parallel evolution describes similar developmental modifications which evolve independently. Under parallel evolution a feature with more than one evolutionary origin comes into existence by similar developmental processes from similar ancestral conditions.[38] For example, within the family of

---

[37] Though the argument is made that instances of convergent evolution reflect a general cross-linguistic preference for nasal codas. See, for example, Herbert (1986, section 6.1.4), and the discussion in 6.6.

[38] In the field of evolutionary biology, parallel evolution contrasts with convergent evolution. In convergent evolution two independently evolved features which are superficially

lizards, toepads have evolved independently in three lineages: *Iguanidae*, *Scincidae*, and *Gekkonidae* (Larson and Losos 1996). If we view toepads in functional terms, then in all three cases, a similar feature has evolved which enhances the clinging ability of lizards in their arboreal habitat.[39] Parallel evolution is also apparent in the world of sounds. For example, word-final devoicing of obstruents has evolved independently in at least three different subgroups of Indo-European: Romance (Catalan, Friulian), Germanic, and Slavic. Or, to take another example, consider the sound change *np > mp which was used in 2.2 to illustrate CHANGE as a source of sound change. Many of the world's languages show homorganicity constraints on intervocalic nasal–stop sequences. In chapter 5 I show how these constraints result from the independent occurrence of CHANGE in unrelated language families. Since CHANGE has solid phonetic foundations, and can be simulated under laboratory conditions, attempts to attribute this homorganicity constraint to features of the synchronic grammar alone seem misguided. In sum, a central finding of Evolutionary Phonology is that the changes which give rise to truly similar sound patterns in genetically unrelated languages are most often the result of parallel evolution.

A final source of similarity across features are physical constraints on the form and function of the organism. Within biology, these are usually associated with aspects of an organism's growth and development, and may include anything from laws of physics relevant to embryonic development, to biochemical processes regulating common patterns of spots and stripes on felines and shellfish (Stewart 1998). Properties which derive from *synchronic constraint systems* are the primary object of study in most modern schools of phonology where elaborate theories of rules and representations are constructed to account for these properties.[40] Languages which prohibit heterorganic nasal–stop clusters are accounted for by featural licensing constraints on place of articulation. The absence of epenthesis into geminates is attributed to the structural representation of geminates as linked structures. Synchronic metathesis is expressed in terms of competing phonotactic constraints in distinct morphological environments. Though all of these analyses are claimed to reflect innate

---

similar arise by different developmental pathways from different ancestral conditions. As mentioned earlier, eyes of vertebrates and eyes of cephalopods (octopus, squid, etc.) are a case in point. See Larson and Losos (1996) for precise phylogenetic definitions. I make a similar distinction between convergent and parallel evolution in language.

[39] At the structural level, the toepads are only superficially similar, and constitute a case of convergent evolution (Larson and Losos 1996: 192).

[40] The terms "constraint" and "rule" are used interchangeably in reference to phonological theories, unless the precise issue of constraint systems versus rules systems is the focus of discussion.

properties of synchronic grammars, as general accounts they are both too weak, and too strong. In part II I offer alternative historical explanations for these same sound patterns based on the CCC model of sound change.

The purpose of this book is to demonstrate that many of the similarities in sound shape across languages are best explained in terms of parallel evolution or direct genetic inheritance. Examples of parallel developments abound in the world of sounds, as they do in the natural world. Where regular sound change is involved, it is shown to have one of the three sources detailed in 2.2. With this foundation, synchronic grammars are liberated from the burden of explaining most cross-linguistic similarities in sound patterns, and can be modeled to best describe attested patterns and alternations. Synchronic constraint systems are minimal in form. They specify phonological categories – featural, segmental, and prosodic – and they specify possible relationships between these categories. Synchronic constraint systems do not express the occurrence of similar sound patterns across languages, when these sound patterns can be shown to have their source in direct inheritance, convergent evolution, or parallel evolution. In sum, the phonological landscape is much like that in evolutionary biology: genealogy, not synchronic constraint, is the primary source of non-random distribution. Within the realm of inherited features, parallel and convergent evolution play a significant role in shaping sound patterns. Convergent evolution may give rise to similar sound patterns with distinct phonological behavior, while parallel evolution is the primary source of phonotactic regularities in feature distribution.

2.5   Natural selection in a world of sounds

No discussion of Darwinian evolution would be complete without mentioning natural selection. Darwin's theory of *natural selection* is built on the premise that life forms which survive to pass along their genes to future generations are those which are well adapted to the environment in which they live. An *adaptation*, in the technical sense, is a character resulting from natural selection to serve a particular biological role. As emphasized by Gould (1991: 12):

The essence of Darwin's theory lies in his contention that natural selection is the creative force of evolution – not just the executioner of the unfit. Natural selection must construct the fit as well; it must build adaptation in stages, by preserving, generation after generation, the favorable part of a random spectrum of variation . . . variation must be random, or at least not preferentially inclined toward adaptation. For, if variation comes prepackaged in the right direction, then selection plays no creative role, but merely eliminates the unlucky individuals who do not vary in the appropriate way.

We have already established that, like genetic variation, sound change at the level of the individual is non-optimizing, or, in Gould's terms "not preferentially inclined toward adaptation." If this is so, is there an analogue to natural selection in the world of sounds? Are sound patterns which are passed down from one generation to the next well adapted to their environment? What would adaptation look like in the world of sounds?

Before answering these questions, let us look at a clear case of adaptation in the reptilian world. A prime example of adaptation through natural selection is the case of lizard toepads mentioned earlier (Larson and Losos 1996). The ancestors of all lizards were terrestrial and had claws, not toepads. Accurate genetic grouping of lizards and their lineages allows us to determine that toepads evolved at least three separate times in the lizard family: in *Iguanidae*, *Scincidae*, and *Gekkonidae*. All lizards with toepads appear to have enhanced clinging ability, suggesting that this may be an adaptation to life in the trees (Irschick et al. 1997). Support for this view comes from the fact that in each of the three cases studied, toepad evolution is simultaneous with evolution of use of arboreal habitats. The chance probability of each instance of toepad morphology and enhanced clinging ability occurring on an arboreal lineage is $P = 0.028$, allowing Larson and Losos (1996: 206) to conclude that "expanded toepads in lizards have evolved as an adaptation to increase the clinging ability in arboreal situations."

Now let us return to the linguistic questions posed above. Are sound patterns which are passed down from one generation to the next well adapted to their environment? What would adaptation look like in the world of sounds?[41] One analogue to natural selection at the phonetic level are neutralizing cases of CHANGE, like the $*np > mp$ discussed in 2.2. In this case, a contrast in place of articulation for nasals is neutralized in pre-obstruent position.[42] In this instance, misperception is a function of the higher probabilities of misperception of certain sounds and sound

---

[41] Recall that I am limiting myself to study of language evolution over the past 7,000 years or so. For discussion of language as an adaptive feature at the level of the human species, and nineteenth-century views on its evolution, see the collection of essays in Harris (1996). For a wide range of modern perspectives on language evolution and the emergence of phonology and syntax see Hurford et al. (1998).

[42] Observe that not all cases of CHANGE are neutralizing. For example, with rhinoglottophilia, misperception of breathiness as nasalization or nasalization as breathiness does not alter the number of phonological contrasts in the language. In simply shifting from one phonetic feature analysis to another, there is no principle of natural selection at work. Breathiness and nasalization are both well adapted to the phonetic environments in question, as indicated by the retention of these features as a set. They are simply so perceptually similar that, without further phonetic enhancement, they are easily confused.

sequences than others which result from aspects of the human auditory system. If a contrast between two sounds is just barely perceptible in a particular phonetic environment, its chances of survival in a noisy world are slight. Notice that we are talking about contrastive categories, not individual sounds. Furthermore, contrasts must be considered within their phonetic environment. In reconsidering the case of CHANGE where [anpa] is heard as [ampa] it makes very little sense to compare the sounds [n] and [m] outside the specific environment in which they occur. In the same sense that the usefulness of claws and toepads cannot be assessed outside particular physical environments in which they occur, there is no sense in which /n/ is a better or more useful nasal consonant than /m/ or *vice versa*.[43] Adaptation occurs with respect to a specific phonetic context. In attempting to account for recurrent phonotactic patterns, then, a linguistic counterpart of natural selection may play a role precisely where misperception results from the weakness of a particular perceptual contrast in a specified phonetic environment.

The same mechanism of natural selection responsible for syntagmatic sound patterns could govern paradigmatic phonological contrasts and their phonetic instantiations. Categorical perception is the phenomenon whereby, given a range of acoustic tokens along a gradient scale, a listener identifies those at the periphery of the scale with different categories, while those in the middle have no more than chance probability of being classified into one category or the other. To take a concrete example, in many languages, what distinguishes a [p] sound from a [b] sound in the syllables [pa] versus [ba] is voice-onset time – the time between the release of the lips for the bilabial stop and the onset of voicing for the following vowel. By presenting listeners with a range of voice-onset times, two categories and a rough category boundary are established. Categorical perception for a wide range of phonological features (laryngeal, place, manner, tone) has been established for infants only a few days old, and has also been demonstrated for chinchillas and quail (see 9.1).[44] Humans are born with a pre-set mechanism for discriminating speech sounds, and the consonant and vowel categories of natural language can be viewed as adaptations to these settings. Phonetic instantiations of phonological categories are a subset of those distinguishable at birth, and a range of studies demonstrates that language-specific overrides of universal categorical contrasts, not their acquisition, are the hallmark of early phonological

---

[43] The claim has been made that coronal consonants are phonologically unmarked, and that /n/ is better than /m/ in some absolute way. In 5.5 I argue against this position.

[44] Categorical perception looks biologically ancient. So does left hemisphere specialization for vocal communication, which has now been demonstrated in monkeys, mice, hamsters, birds, and frogs (Studdert-Kennedy 1998: 173).

learning (Jusczyk 1992; Werker and Pegg 1992). An explanation, then, for recurrent phonetic instantiations of phonological categories is that these instantiations are an adaptation to the phonetic space defined by categorial perception. Category boundaries, where misperception is the norm, are avoided. Though I will continue to assume, based on evidence from infant perception studies, that phonological features and categories constitute part of universal grammar, arguments along these lines lead one to explore the possibility that these aspects of linguistic structure are also emergent.

At an altogether different level, the listener's acceptance of intraspeaker variation (the source of sound change in CHOICE) can be viewed as an adaptation to the limits of human vocal tract anatomy and muscular control. Coordination of distinct articulatory gestures is highly inexact in speech. Implementing a phonological sequence like /ns/ requires transition from a physical state where the velum is lowered, and there is complete oral closure produced by the tongue tip touching the alveolar ridge, to a following state where the velum is raised, and the tongue tip is slightly lowered to create turbulent noise as the air passes between the tongue and the alveolar ridge. Exact coordination of velic movement and tongue-tip movement would give rise to [ns], where the velum is raised precisely at the same time as the tongue-tip is lowered. This sort of precise coordination of articulators, however, is not found in natural speech. Instead, tongue-tip lowering may slightly anticipate velic raising, producing [nˢs], or velic raising may slightly precede tongue-tip lowering, producing [nᵗs]. An example of this second kind is found in English. Consider the often indistinguishable pronunciations of the words *prince* and *prints* as [prɪnᵗs]. If listeners were unwilling to accept [nᵗs] as a phonetic variant of /nt/, the communicative function of language would be greatly impaired. It follows that the general facility listeners have in associating careful and casual speech forms can be viewed as an adaptation to physical constraints on speech production.

Finally, it is possible that sound patterns are adaptive in terms of the mechanisms of language acquisition.[45] If certain phonological systems

---

[45] The obvious fact that all natural languages are learnable (by children before the critical age) could also be attributed to adaptation, in the form of coevolution, though it could just as well be accidental. There is no evidence that the process of language acquisition has changed significantly over the past 7,000 years, nor is there any obvious external source capable of introducing unlearnable systems into the domain of natural language. So, for recent history, there is no plausible way of testing this hypothesis. However, calculations like those of Lindblom (1986) and Lindblom and Maddieson (1988) are highly suggestive of this type of coevolution as a constant force shaping vowel and consonant systems respectively.

See Bever and Langendoen (1972) on language change as an interplay of ease of learning and ease of perception.

or generalizations are learned faster than others, and if a first workable hypothesis allows the learner to dispense with other possibilities, then phonological systems which are learned first will have the best "fitness." In the example of CHANCE discussed in section 2.2, a phonetic string [ʔa̰ʔ] occurs as a speaker's phonetic realization of the phonological sequence /aʔ/. However, given that the creakiness of the vowel may be a redundant feature of an adjacent glottal stop, and that creaky voiced vowels can give rise to redundant preceding and following glottal stops, the listener has a choice of phonological analyses. Did the speaker mean to say: /ʔa/, /aʔ/, /ʔaʔ/ or /a̰/? If certain phonological generalizations are acquired more quickly than others, the choice space may be reduced. For example, imagine that a learner has already posited a phonological constraint, based on other sound patterns, which forbids closed syllables (syllables in which a non-vocalic element follows the vowel). A grammar incorporating this constraint eliminates the closed syllables /aʔ/ and /ʔaʔ/ from the choice space due to a pre-existing hypothesis about the form of the grammar (even if this hypothesis is ultimately not the right one.) In this case /ʔa/ and /a̰/ have better fitness with respect to the evolving grammatical system in the mind of the speaker.

Some specific features of sound patterns may be adaptive in more than one dimension. An interesting feature of all documented natural spoken languages is that there is never a phonological contrast between a released stop (e.g. [k°]) and an unreleased stop (e.g. [k̚]) in word-final position. A released stop is one where oral closure is released while air is still flowing, and before intraoral air pressure has subsided. An unreleased stop involves release of oral closure after intraoral air pressure has decayed. Though this feature cannot partake in phonological contrasts, it can be controlled and specified at the phonetic level. In some languages, like Marshallese, word-final consonants are typically released. In other languages, like Cantonese, they are not. If release versus non-release can distinguish the surface phonetics of word-final stops in different languages, why is this contrast not coopted into phonological systems? I suggest that phonological specification of release is a highly non-aptive feature. First, consider the fact that words are most commonly produced in contexts where they are followed by other words. In a string of sounds, where a word-final stop is followed by a word-initial vowel, the smoothest articulatory trajectory involves releasing the stop into the following vowel. On the other hand, where a word-final stop is followed by another stop, the smoothest articulatory trajectory involves an unreleased stop followed by a released stop. Second, intraspeaker variation can be viewed as a continuum from hyperarticulated clear speech to hypoarticulated casual speech as already discussed. If clear speech serves the purpose of eliminating potential ambiguities created by the coarticulatory properties of casual speech, then clear speech is a domain where release can serve a very useful function. Since unreleased stops lack phonetic release features which may instantiate phonologically contrastive features of aspiration, glottalization, and major place of articulation, among others (see chapters 4 and 5), limiting the release/non-release opposition to the phonetic domain allows for recovery of potentially contrastive phonological features in hyperarticulated speech. In actual usage, this is the norm: "His name is [mæt°] not [mæk˺]!," where [mæt°] is produced with an audible release of the /t/. The absence of phonological contrasts between released and non-released stops can be viewed as an adaptive feature of sound systems in at least two respects then. First, it is adaptive in articulatory terms, since the smoothest transitions between stops and following vowels involve release, while those between stops and following stops do not. If release is specified independent of the sound which follows, ease of articulation will be hampered. The second way in which purely phonetic release is adaptive is in terms of its discriminating function in hyperarticulated speech. All spoken languages contrast stops at major points of articulation, and many make laryngeal contrasts as well. Though phonetic cues for these features may be lost in contexts where ease of articulation leads to absence of release, they can be recovered in careful speech where release is introduced.

Just as certain sound patterns look highly adaptive, so others smack of *non-aptation* or *disaptation*. In evolutionary biology, if a character cannot be distinguished from its genetic antecedents with respect to conferring an advantage to the organism possessing it, it is called a non-aptation. Disaptation refers to the case where the genetic antecedent has greater utility to the organism than its evolved counterpart (Baum and Larson 1991; Arnold 1994).[46] Both of these categories suggest characters whose evolution is inconsistent with natural selection, and there are few if any convincing examples of this in the biological literature. In speech, we can look for such cases at the limits of perceptibility, where non-aptive features may arise fleetingly and, just as quickly, disappear. One recently verified case is the contrast between two degrees of nasalization in Palantla Chinantec, an Otomanguean language. In this language, a contrast exists between oral vowels, lightly nasalized vowels, and heavily nasalized vowels. Palantla Chinantec is the only reported language in the world in which degree

---

[46] In biological models, it is important to distinguish primary and secondary non-aptation and disaptation. Primary non-aptation and disaptation are cases where a character replaced one of equal or superior utility at its origin; secondary cases occur by evolutionary changes in selective regime (Baum and Larson 1991; Arnold 1994).

of nasality (lightly versus heavily) is phonologically contrastive. Interest-ingly, speakers have difficulty perceiving differences between lightly and heavily nasalized vowels, and this contrast might also stretch the limits of velic control. Nevertheless, the contrast exists. It was first reported by Merrifield (1963: 5): "certain idiolects of Palantla Chinantec exhibit two degrees of nasalization which occur in identical environments, thus defin-ing lexical contrasts." Subsequent confirmation comes from Ladefoged (1971) and Merrifield and Edmondson (1999) who demonstrate a con-trast between oral syllables, heavily nasalized syllables, and lightly nasal-ized syllables. The contrast between heavily and lightly nasalized syllables involves two quantifiable parameters: in heavily nasalized syllables, nasal airflow begins shortly after the syllable-initial consonant, and continues at a relatively steady level through the syllable, while in lightly nasalized syllables, low-volume nasal airflow begins roughly halfway through the nuclear vowel and gradually increases through to the end of the syllable. While Palantla Chinantec is the only language known to contrast degree of nasality, not all speakers of the language exhibit two degrees of nasaliza-tion in their speech. For some speakers, oral and lightly nasalized vowels fall together as oral, while for others, lightly and heavily nasalized vowels merge into a single nasalized category. The contrast is dying, confirm-ing the suspicion that it is disaptive, or at least non-aptive. But, if natural selection does play a role in language evolution, how did this contrast arise in the first place? Two grammatical relationships may have played a role. First, heavy nasalization is associated with animacy in some lexical pairs. Second, light nasalization evolved in some verbs from the inflectional person–number suffix /n/, via the sound change *VN > lightly nasalized vowel. In this case the phonetic feature of light nasalization may have been temporarily bolstered by its association with a specific morphosyntactic feature.[47] As these grammatical distinctions erode, so does the phono-logical contrast: for many speakers of Palantla Chinantec today, there is only a binary contrast between oral vowels and nasalized vowels, as in so many other languages.

In this section I have suggested some ways in which natural selection may play a role in the evolution of sound patterns. The clearest cases with biological parallels are neutralizing cases of CHANGE and recurrent phonological partitioning of the phonetic perceptual space. Intraspeaker variation defined in terms of hyper- and hypoarticulated speech can also be seen as an adaptation to the imprecise muscular control involved in

---

[47] Relations between phonological contrast and the functions of these contrasts within the grammar as a whole are one focus of the Firthian school of prosodic phonology (e.g. Firth 1948; Henderson 1949). In 8.3 the potential role of paradigms in contrast maintenance is explored.

articulation of speech sounds. I have also pointed to the possibility that sound patterns could be adaptive with respect to grammatical generalizations arising in the course of language acquisition. A feature which might be viewed as adaptive in its ease-of-articulation function and maximize-contrast function at the phonetic level is the apparent universally non-contrastive status of stop-release. In this case, importation of release from the phonetic to the phonological domain would arguably result in a non-aptive feature. As far as we know, this has never occurred. However, non-aptation may be visible in linguistic systems. The Palantla Chinantec distinction between three degrees of nasalization is arguably non-aptive compared with the simple nasal/oral contrast from which it descends. In this case, associations between these phonological categories and semantic or morphosyntactic features may have given rise to strengthening of the weak feature. However, subsequent decay of these associations has left the degree of nasalization contrast on the verge of extinction.

As Rose and Lauder (1996: 9) point out in the introduction to their volume on modern views of adaptation:

Adaptation is no longer something that can be safely assumed by evolutionary or other biologists. Indeed, the more one examines the concept, the more it comes to resemble a newly landed fish: slippery, slimy, obstreperous, but glittering with potential. There it is, flapping about, full of energy, but the significance of all the commotion is not clear.

In the same way, adaptation cannot be assumed within Evolutionary Phonology. It may further our understanding of CHANGE, but be irrelevant to sound change arising from CHANCE or CHOICE. The question is an empirical one, and throughout this volume, we will consider its glittering potential and, at the same time, question its significance.

Throughout this chapter concepts in evolutionary biology have been used as metaphors for language change. I do not claim that language evolution is structurally identical to biological evolution, nor that Darwinian principles of natural selection can be applied to living organisms and languages in precisely the same way. One purpose of this comparison is to make a clear distinction between the mechanisms of change spelled out in 2.2, their non-optimizing character outlined in 2.3, and possible instances of natural selection discussed above. Another important role of this comparison is to emphasize the four logical sources of resemblance between sound patterns laid out in 2.4. Similarities in sound patterns are often the result of direct genetic inheritance. In other cases, recurrent sound patterns may reflect convergent or parallel evolution. Finally, there is the possibility that regularities in sound patterns are a direct result of synchronic constraint systems.

From this point on, the biological metaphor will, for the most part, be left behind. While it is useful in understanding why certain patterns are common across languages, its usefulness breaks down when key mechanisms of change are compared. There are no direct counterparts to genetic mutation, biological inheritance, or natural selection in the sound changes which characterize language evolution for the last 7,000–8,000 years. Instead, it is more instructive to study the phonetic basis of sound change, the transmission of a learned code across generations of individuals, and the aspects of listener bias and learning algorithms which might limit the phonological choice space. Sound patterns have their own natural history, and it is this history which is documented in part II.

3 Explanation in phonology: a brief history of ideas

> The mechanism of a language (its structure and composition) at any given time is the result of all its preceding history and development, and each synchronic state determines in turn its further development.
>
> Baudouin de Courtenay (1871/1972: 63)

> On enseigne partout qu'elles sont encore inconnues et mystérieuses. C'est inexact. Mais il n'y a pas une cause, il y en a un grand nombre, et l'erreur . . . a été . . . lorsqu'ils ont reconnu une cause de changements phonétiques, de croire qu'elle était la seule cause et de vouloir tout y ramener.
>
> Grammont (1933: 174)

The study of sound patterns goes back thousands of years. Pāṇini and his Indic contemporaries formulated phonetic laws and phonological rules over 2,000 years ago. Under the influence of Hindu and Chinese grammarians, King Seijong (1417–50) and his court advisors devised a writing system for Korean, *hankul*, which demonstrates a clear understanding of the phonemic principle and a sophisticated use of distinctive phonological features. Building on Chén Dì's (1541–1617) principle of historical change, early Qing dynasty scholars like Gù Yánwǔ (1613–82) and Duàn Yùcái (1735–1815) made significant steps in the reconstruction of Old Chinese sound patterns. On the other side of the world, Sir William Jones (1746–94) observed in 1786 that Sanskrit, Greek, and Latin showed similarities of form suggestive of a family relationship. This observation inspired the European scholars Franz Bopp (1791–1867) and Jacob Grimm (1785–1863), forefathers of the neogrammarian movement. During the late nineteenth century, correspondences between Indo-European languages were established, regular sound changes were proposed, and the reconstruction of Proto-Indo-European was well underway. All of this work placed a primary emphasis on the description of sound patterns. Phonetic laws and phonological rules were documented and formalized; phonetic and phonological features were identified and systematized; and sound correspondences between languages were used to formulate laws of sound change.

A search for deeper explanations characterizes the last century of research. Phonologists are now trained to ask why sound patterns are the way they are. What explains Pāṇini's sandhi rules where $a + i \rightarrow e$ and $a + u \rightarrow o$? Why do all languages make use of the same basic set of phonological features? Why were syllable-initial consonant clusters lost between Old Chinese and Middle Chinese? What explains the Germanic sound change known as Grimm's Law where $*p > f$, $*t > \theta$, and $*k > \chi$, and why are similar changes found in many unrelated languages?

This chapter presents a brief history of ideas surrounding three types of explanation in phonology: historical, teleological, and phonetic. Historical explanations account for synchronic properties of grammar in terms of their diachronic origins. Teleological explanations of sound patterns see them as improving speech in some concrete way. And phonetic explanations detail how articulatory, acoustic, and perceptual properties of speech underlie aspects of phonological form. One goal of this chapter is to illustrate how Evolutionary Phonology builds on earlier explanations of similar phenomena, presenting a useful synthesis of results from the neogrammarian tradition, the Kazan school, generative phonology, and modern work in phonetics. This chapter also illustrates where Evolutionary Phonology diverges from earlier approaches, and underscores the ways in which it represents a plausible alternative to structuralist and modern generative explanations of sound patterns.[1]

3.1   Historical explanation

Sound patterns can be studied across time and at a single point in time. In the first case, sound change is the primary object of study. In the second, phoneme inventories, phonotactics, alternations, phonological representations, and constraint or rule systems are the focus of investigation. Diachronic and synchronic studies both attempt to capture broad typological generalizations which appear to recur with greater than chance frequency in the world's languages. These distinct domains for explanation suggest the possibility that certain aspects of sound patterns are best explained in terms of their history, while others are best explained in terms of synchronic aspects of sound systems.

Historical explanation was a fundamental component of neogrammarian thought, as expressed in the work of Hermann Paul, Karl Brugmann,

---

[1] See Robins (1997) for a concise history of linguistics from the classical period onwards, and Morpurgo-Davies (1998) for an in-depth history of nineteenth-century linguistics. On the history of modern phonology, see Fischer-Jørgensen (1975) and Anderson (1985). See Kiparsky (1988) on the relationship between sound change and phonological change in the nineteenth and twentieth centuries.

August Leskien, Hermann Osthoff, and others. Paul (1886/1920) boldly states that the only valid scientific study of language is historical. Features of modern languages were subject to seemingly arbitrary variation, and could only be truly understood in terms of their history. A parent language was reconstructed on the basis of related daughter languages, with sound laws established to relate stages of development.[2] System-internal relationships (vowels versus consonants; voiced versus voiceless; initial versus final, etc.) were fundamental to reconstruction. But these synchronic features were seen as useful descriptive devices, not as explanations in and of themselves.

The central role of history in shaping sound patterns was shared by Baudouin de Courtenay (1845–1929), founder of the Kazan school. As summarized in the opening quote of this chapter, Baudouin de Courtenay stressed the general understanding of language development in linguistic science and the role of history in the development of rule systems. He was perhaps the first to treat exceptional sound patterns as "historical residue," and to recognize in lexical diffusion the seeds of innovation: "seeming grammatical exceptions can be explained by the history of the language, and are either remnants of past 'rules' or harbingers of future ones" (1871/1972: 52). While Baudouin was insistent on the characterization of synchronic grammars, he criticized others for failing to view grammars from a historical perspective:

The greatest heights were attained by the Indic grammarians . . . But the Indic grammarians lacked a feeling for history and were unable to grasp the significance of gradual development, historical sequence, or chronology in general. As a result, their findings lay, so to speak, on a single temporal plane; everything happened simultaneously, as though there were neither a past nor present nor future. Thence also the purely mechanical character of their grammatical rules; they give excellent prescriptions for the formation of all kinds of grammatical forms, but we would look in vain for a scientific explanation of the ways and means by which these forms originated. (Baudouin 1895/1972: 147–48)

Here Baudouin praises the Indic scholars for their comprehensive descriptions, but is acutely aware of their failure to explain why synchronic rules systems have the properties they do. In Baudouin's view, synchronic systems could only be fully understood by explaining how they came into existence.

---

[2] Lehmann (1992: 27) notes the general influence of the Romantic movement on historical linguistics of the same period. The Romantics put great emphasis on understanding contemporary systems of law, social customs, folktales and language in terms of their historical development. Lightfoot (1999, section 2.4) focuses on the theme of historical determinism which can be seen to unify nineteenth-century intellectual thought in biological evolution, political science and linguistics.

A clear discontinuity exists between the purely historical explanations of the neogrammarians, the mix of historical and synchronic explanation of the Kazan school, and the primary synchronic explanations suggested by Saussure. Saussure's method of the early twentieth century isolated synchronic systems, and was widely adopted by generative grammarians from the 1950s to the present.[3] Saussure (1949: 19) acknowledged the substantial contributions of the neogrammarians, but at the same time, dismissed their work in the context of the fundamental problems of language structure:

si grands que soient les services rendus par cette école, on ne peut pas dire qu'elle ait fait la lumière sur l'ensemble de la question, et aujourd'hui encore les problèmes fondamentaux de la linguistique générale attendent une solution.

Saussure believed that the nature of language could only be revealed by synchronic study of grammar, where synchronic systems are idealized unchanging language states, and grammar is an internalized rule system in the mind of the speaker. The synchronic study of language was diametrically opposed to diachronic study, where focus was not on grammar, as Saussure defined it:

La linguistique statique ou description d'un état de langue ne peut être appelée *grammaire*, dans le sens très précis, et d'ailleurs usuel, qu'on trouve dans les expressions "grammaire du jeu d'échec", "grammaire de la Bourse", etc., où il s'agit d'un objet complexe et systématique, mettant en jeu des valeurs coexistantes.

La grammaire étudie la langue en tant que système de moyens d'expression; qui dit grammatical dit synchronique et significatif, et comme aucun système n'est à cheval sur plusieurs époques à la fois, il n'y a pas pour nous de "grammaire historique"; ce qu'on appelle ainsi n'est en réalité que la linguistique diachronique. (1949: 185)

Saussure's analogy between language and the game of chess is instructive. Saussure is interested in the game of chess as defined by its rule system. One can ultimately discover the rules of chess by observing many games. History is irrelevant to this discovery. Likewise, the rules of a synchronic grammar constitute a system which exists independent of its historical development. Saussure's enormous posthumous influence on the field

---

[3] The descriptivist tradition in the US, including the work of Sapir, Bloomfield, and Hockett, appears to place great value in historical explanation, though this value is rarely mentioned explicitly. For example, Sapir (1921), chapter 8, is entitled "Language as a historical product: phonetic law." In this chapter, Sapir follows neogrammarian tradition. However, apart from the chapter title, there is no general reference to primary historical explanations for synchronic patterns. In other parts of the world, there are small pockets where attempts have been made to integrate diachronic and synchronic approaches to language, for example, the work of Hagège and Haudricourt (1978) and Hagège (1993).

gave rise to a clear split within the field of linguistics proper. Historical linguistics contracted to become just the study of language change,
centered on reconstruction and genetic relationships, while general linguistics developed an exclusively synchronic focus. By the middle of the
twentieth century, the chasm between the two areas of study was so deep
that Hjelmslev (1953) described historical and general linguistics as two
separate disciplines.

This schism between diachronic and synchronic linguistics continues
to the present. Chomsky's Saussurian conception of generative grammar
as a synchronic rule system disembodied from its history has been influential in maintaining this divide. The generative model was extended
to phonology in Chomsky and Halle (1968), where sound patterns are
described and formalized, but "scientific explanation of the ways and
means by which these forms originated," so important to Baudouin, is
entirely absent. An inspection of introductory linguistics texts makes the
divergence between synchronic and diachronic fields clear. Sound change
is a topic for texts in historical linguistics. To the extent that it is covered
in phonology texts, it is used to illustrate properties of synchronic systems, such as the ubiquity of natural classes, rule ordering as a function
of historical age, abstractness, or naturalness.

Kenstowicz's (1994) text, *Phonology in Generative Grammar*, highlights
the continued separation of the two subdisciplines in the study of sound
patterns. On the first page of this book, the major goal of generative
linguistics is defined: to solve "Plato's problem" (Chomsky 1986) – the
observation that "any speaker knows many surprising things about the
structure of his or her language, things whose internalization is difficult to
understand if based solely on evidence from the linguistic environment."
Chomsky's approach is to ascribe this knowledge to aspects of Universal
Grammar (UG), and this is precisely the path followed by Generative
Phonology:

There are many recurrent aspects of phonological structure of a highly specific
and rich character whose acquisition cannot be explained on the basis of analogy
or stimulus generalization in any useful sense of these terms. These properties
are also most naturally explained as reflections of UG. (Kenstowicz 1994: 2)[4]

In Kenstowicz's volume of over 500 pages, only ten are devoted to discussion of historical phonology (pp. 115–25). There is no suggestion

---

[4] See chapter 9 for general arguments against the "poverty of stimulus" in phonology,
and for evidence that many aspects of phonological structure are acquired on the basis
of analogy or stimulus generalization. To my knowledge, there is no argument in the
literature that phoneme inventories, stress patterns, tone patterns, phonotactics, and regular phonological alternations cannot be acquired on the basis of generalizations gleaned
directly from auditory input.

that recurrent sound change might explain the general aspects of phonological structure Kenstowicz refers to. On the contrary, Kenstowicz uses historical evidence to further support aspects of synchronic analyses. For example, in summarizing Bloomfield's reconstruction of Proto-Algonquian and Sapir's work on Proto-Athabaskan, Kenstowicz's primary focus is reference to natural classes and general features of phonological representations:

These data provide an impressive demonstration of the regularity of sound change . . . They also demonstrate that sound change operates over natural classes of sounds . . . Both properties follow from the basic premise of generative phonology that a language's vocabulary is stored in the memory of individual speakers as phonological representations composed of strings of feature matrices that can be modified in very precise ways by the ordered application of context-sensitive phonological rules. (1994: 124)

Kenstowicz' apparent lack of interest in historical explanations for recurrent sound patterns is typical of the field of generative phonology as a whole, and characterizes subsequent developments in Optimality Theory as well. Synchronic universals or tendencies are assumed to follow from cross-linguistic synchronic constraints on the form and content of grammars. Historical explanations are only proposed for peripheral, quirky, or otherwise anomalous properties of synchronic systems. Despite the pervasiveness of this view, there have nevertheless been individual attempts to integrate historical linguistics and phonological theory.

Kiparsky's work, as represented in the 1982 collection, *Explanation in Phonology*, has been influential in this area. Kiparsky's most general contributions involve attempts to explain historical developments in terms of phonological principles (see Kiparsky 1982a, 1988, 1995, 2002). Kiparsky (1965) made concrete the abstract psychological notions which played a role in Baudouin and Saussure's models of sound change by distinguishing *innovation* from *restructuring*. Innovation is a change in the way phonological representations are executed by a speaker, while restructuring is the resulting revision in the phonological representation. In this way, Kiparsky introduced the synchronic division of competence and performance into the realm of sound change. Kiparsky's (1965) formalization of innovations represents another application of synchronic principles to aspects of language change. Following Halle (1962) and Klima (1964), innovations were encoded as newborn phonological rules within synchronic rule systems, with restructuring dependent on other aspects of grammar:

the more highly structured form of language postulated by the theory of generative grammar, together with the goal of giving in a grammar an explicit account of the regularities of a language, often leads to a synchronically motivated retention of earlier underlying representation and incorporation of innovations as phonological rules, often in a synchronic order that matches their relative chronology . . . it depends on the structure of the language whether an innovation leads to restructuring. (1965/1982a: 5)

Kiparsky's introduction of surface and underlying forms in sound change, and his formulation of innovations as phonological rules, both illustrate his general strategy of importing synchronic explanation into the diachronic domain. In Kiparsky's (1970/1982a: 55) view, developments in generative grammar were exerting a powerful and largely beneficial influence on historical linguistics.

At approximately the same time that Kiparsky was using generative rules and representations to model sound change, a number of linguists, including Bach and Harms (1972), Vennemann (1972b), Skousen (1972), and Hyman (1975, 1977), were giving serious reconsideration to the role of diachronic explanation in synchronic grammars. Cases of seemingly unnatural synchronic alternations were studied. These alternations, sometimes referred to "crazy" rules (Bach and Harms 1972), lacked phonetic motivation, and could not be assigned any systematic synchronic explanation.

In (1) four general sources of unnatural sound patterns are distinguished.

(1)   Four potential sources of phonetically unnatural sound patterns

	Original sound change	Subsequent development
a. analogy	$*XaY > XbY$	a or b extended to new environments on the basis of non-phonetic factors
b. rule inversion	$*XaY > XbY$	$b \rightarrow a/{\sim}X{\sim}Y$
c. rule telescoping	$*XaY > *XbY > XcY$	$a \rightarrow c/ X\_Y$
d. accidental convergence	various	surface pattern is generalized

Analogical change (1a) is conditioned by non-phonetic factors, and typically affects the structure of morphological paradigms. The neogrammarians drew an important distinction between sound change, which was claimed to be regular, and analogical change, which could result in non-systematic or irregular sound correspondences. A well-studied example of analogical change is found in Ancient Greek, where coronal

stops /t, tʰ, d/ surface as *s* before /m/. Nasal-induced coronal spirantization does not correspond to any attested regular sound change and
has no plausible articulatory or perceptual basis. Unsurprisingly, parallel
synchronic alternations are not described for unrelated languages. Nevertheless, the origins of these unnatural alternations in Ancient Greek
are not mysterious. Brugmann (1878: 81 n.1) and Schmidt (1885) note
that the pattern is rooted in the finite paradigm of perfect middle verbs,
with further analogical developments detailed by Garrett and Blevins (to
appear). The most important of these was the extension of stem-final /s/,
which occurred in the perfect middle of verbs ending in coronal stops,
to first-person forms. Originally, the stem-final *s* alternant occurred only
before suffixes beginning with coronal stops. Leveling of the paradigm
by extending the *s*-final stems to first-person forms resulted in a surface
alternation between coronal stops and *s* before /m/-initial suffixes. This
pattern was then generalized to other derived environments.

Another general source of unnatural sound patterns is rule inversion (1b) (Venneman 1972b). Rule inversion originates with a context-
sensitive sound change, X*a*Y > X*b*Y. As a result of this change, the synchronic grammar may have instances of *a* alternating with *b*. If *a* and
b are both in phonological contexts which are easily defined in terms
of natural classes and prosodic constituency, then it is possible for language learners to take /b/ as underlying and *a* as derived, inverting the
historical relationship. A well-known case of rule inversion involves the
English rhotic glide [ɹ], which was lost post-vocalically in syllable rhymes
in certain Southern British dialects (Vennemann 1972a; McCarthy 1991;
Blevins 1997). In many dialects of British English, a non-historical [ɹ]
occurs between a lax word-final vowel and a following word-initial vowel:
I like Rosa, but *Rosa[ɹ] is leaving now*; *I saw Bill*, but *I saw[ɹ] Allison*, etc.
Historically, it is clear that [ɹ] was lost from post-vocalic position within
the syllable rhyme: *bird* > b[ɜː]d, *bar* > b[aː], etc. However, surface [ɹ]/Ø
alternations resulting from this sound change could be interpreted as
instances of deletion or insertion by language learners, since, in both
cases, the phonological environments were transparent, and could be
stated in terms of natural classes of sounds. Like the Ancient Greek rule
of pre-/m/ spirantization, English [ɹ]-insertion does not correspond to
any attested regular sound change: spontaneous [ɹ]-epenthesis between
vowels has no plausible articulatory or perceptual basis (Blevins 1997).
Although, *a priori*, as a rule of consonant-epenthesis, it does not appear
as "crazy" as the Ancient Greek alternations mentioned above, cross-
linguistically, the only languages which show synchronic rules of rhotic-
insertion are precisely those which have undergone historical rhotic-loss
(Blevins 1997, to appear b).

Another source of unnatural sound patterns is rule telescoping (1c), which collapses a historical sequence of phonetically motivated sound changes $a > b > c$, etc. Though each step in the sequence is phonetically motivated, there is no evidence for intermediate stages in the synchronic grammar, which simply attests a alternating with c, where this alternation has no plausible phonetic motivation. A case discussed by Hyman (1975: 174–75) is $p \rightarrow s/\_i$ in some Bantu languages, which stems from sound changes occurring before the Proto-Bantu super-high vowel $^*i̱$. The realization of /p/ as [s] before [i̱] is unattested as a regular sound change. High vowels like [i̱] often induce palatalization and/or affrication, due to coarticulation and aerodynamic factors, respectively, but there is no plausible phonetic explanation for the change in place and manner of articulation from p, a bilabial stop, to s, an alveolar fricative. Examples of intermediate developments of Proto-Bantu $^*pi̱$ in other languages reveal the diachronic evolution of $^*pi̱$ to $si̱$. In this case, there is a sequence of changes: $^*pi̱ > {}^*p^j i̱ > {}^*t^s i̱ > si̱$. In this chain, every link involves a phonetically plausible sound change which is attested elsewhere. A shift of plain to palatalized consonant like $^*pi̱ > p^j i̱$ in the environment of a high vowel is unremarkable; coarticulation of this sort is commonplace in the world's languages (Ladefoged and Maddieson 1996). The subsequent shift of $^*p^j i̱ > t^s i̱$, perhaps the most unusual link in the chain, has a solid perceptual explanation, first noted by Ohala (1978a: 373):

F2 transition for the palatalized labial is more similar to that for the dental than it is to that for the plain labial . . . If a listener were to miss the noise burst cue . . . the consonant would very likely be taken for a dental. Moreover, the impression that such stops were dentals or palatals would be reinforced by any fricative noise generated from the rush of air through the narrow palatal constriction.

Outside Bantu, similar palatalized labial to coronal shifts are described for Teták dialects of Czech (Andersen 1973), and similar changes may have occurred in the history of Proto-Algonquian, Proto-Salish, the Romance languages, and languages of the Balkans (Thomason 1986). The subsequent development of a fricative from an earlier affricate, $^*t^s i̱ > si̱$, is unremarkable: similar changes are found in many unrelated languages, with deaffrication related to the weakness of the stop percept and strength of fricative noise in this environment. In Bantu languages in which $p \rightarrow s/\_i$, p is retained in non-palatalizing environments, while [s] is a surface alternant precisely where the phonetic chain of palatalizing events has occurred.

A final general source of unnatural sound patterns, rarely discussed, is accidental convergence (1d). Independent sound changes of various sorts may result in exceptionless surface patterns which are generalized by language learners, despite their non-homogeneous origins. An example which will be discussed further in chapter 9 is the surface phonotactics of certain Paman languages of Australia. In some of these languages, like Oykangand (Sommer 1969, 1970), the two regular sound changes in (2) have given rise to cross-linguistically unusual phonotactics where all words begin with vowels and end in consonants, as in the sentence *og arŋg aŋguɲang eŋkoɟiy uwal ay iɲun* 'I gave (some) water to the young child in the shade.'

(2)   Two Northern Paman sound changes (following Hale 1964, 1976a, b)
    a. Initial C-loss: $^*C > \emptyset$ / $_{Word}[\_$
    b. Final V-loss: $^*V > \emptyset$ /$\_]$ $_{Word}$

The convergence of (2a) and (2b) on this particular sound pattern is accidental. Initial C-loss is found in many other Paman languages without final V-loss (Hale 1976a). And final unstressed V-loss is found in many of the world's languages where initial C-loss in unknown. That this sound pattern plays an active role in the phonology of Oykangand is evident in all processes which access syllabification: . . . VC_1V . . . strings are syllabified as . . . $VC_1.V$ . . . , reflecting word-based generalizations whose significance I return to in 9.1.5.

The fact that unnatural sound patterns can result from the natural developments outlined in (1) suggests that all phonologies should be a mix of natural and unnatural rule types. This is essentially the conclusion reached by Bach and Harms (1972) and Anderson (1981). Bach and Harms attribute natural rules to the phonologization of regular phonetically motivated sound change, and see no reason to build naturalness into synchronic accounts:

the fact that languages have plausible rules is . . . the result of strong naturalness constraints on the initiation of phonetic rules. These constraints are essentially diachronic and should not be incorporated into the simplicity metric. (Bach and Harms 1972: 18)

Anderson (1981: 536) is in agreement: "although phonological rules are by no means limited to 'natural processes,' they typically originate in the phonologization of such processes, and their subsequent restructured forms often relate to such a basis." Many languages have alternations which appear to be phonetically motivated because these alternations directly reflect sound changes which are phonetically natural. However, other unnatural alternations are attested, suggesting that naturalness plays no role in constraining synchronic systems.

Though the majority of work in phonological theory from the mid-1980s forward makes no principled distinction between natural and unnatural rule types, this contrast is central to Evolutionary Phonology. Natural sound patterns are precisely those with well-documented phonetic origins, and are transparent reflections of the phonologization of regular phonetically based sound change. Unnatural sound patterns may be the result of direct inheritance, or have one of the sources in (1). Synchronic constraints incorporating naturalness or markedness are misguided, since whether a sound pattern is natural, crazy, or somewhere in between, is wholly a function of its history. Sound change is phonetically natural, but phonological constraints need not be. Phonetically motivated sound changes with high frequency will result in common synchronic sound patterns in cases where these sound patterns are not obscured by other changes like those shown in (1).

Evolutionary Phonology accepts direct inheritance, parallel evolution, and the components of the formal model of sound change in 2.2 as the basic mechanisms giving rise to recurrent synchronic sound patterns. Historical explanations are primary in accounting for recurrent features of sound patterns across unrelated languages. At the same time, synchronic phonology defines contrastive features, segments, and prosodic categories which constrain the output of sound change in the course of acquisition. By combining historical phonetic accounts of sound change with synchronically defined constraints on pathways of phonologization, Evolutionary Phonology provides a synthesis of neogrammarian and generative approaches to sound patterns: historical explanation is combined with precise description of the form and content of synchronic grammars.

3.2   Teleological explanation

Section 1.3 surveys the different types of explanation in phonology. Teleological or goal-directed explanations are those which view sound patterns as moving towards optimal targets.[5] The most common teleological explanations in phonetics and phonology invoke notions of articulatory ease and perceptual distance. A particular sound change or sound pattern

---

[5] Recall from 1.3 that teleological explanations are distinguished from general functional explanations. For many linguists, functional explanations are those which directly invoke the communicative function of language. For other linguists, functional explanations are those which make reference to properties which are not part of formal grammar. The merger of teleological and functional explanation occurs in models where constraints like "minimize effort" and "maximize contrast" are part of the formal grammar itself (e.g. Kirchner 2000; Flemming 2001).

occurs in order to minimize articulatory effort while another occurs in order to maximize perceptual contrast. A related teleological explanation is that sound patterns arise in order to make languages easier to learn. Ease of learnability is usually assumed as a subcase of the first two goals: if a particular sound pattern occurs in order to facilitate speech production or speech perception, then it will presumably be easier to learn. In the majority of models in which teleological explanations are suggested, it is the perpetual conflict between effort minimization and contrast maximization which leads to variety and complexity in the world of sounds.

Many historical linguists in the mid-to-late nineteenth century viewed sound change as constantly improving articulatory or perceptual ease. This perspective was partly due to Darwin's influence, and partly due to the influence of Friedrich Max Müller and Baudouin.[6] Arguably Müller's greatest claim to fame in this area is his direct influence on Darwin. Citing Müller, Darwin (1871: 88) suggests that ease of articulation leads to sound change: "the better, the shorter, the easier forms are constantly gaining the upper hand, and they owe their success to their inherent virtue." Where Müller's approach is primarily an attempt to apply Darwinian principles of natural selection to language evolution, Baudouin's approach is more considered. With detailed principles of phonological analysis in mind, Baudouin highlights the optimizing nature of sound change in terms of phonetic form and more abstract psychological form. In his "statement of Linguistic Principles" Baudouin proclaims:

The cause, the impulse for all linguistic change, is a tendency toward convenience, toward a minimum of effort in three areas of linguistic activity: in pronunciation (phonation), in hearing and perception (audition), and in linguistic thought (cerebration). (1897/1972: 213)

Perhaps the best-known proponent of teleological explanations for sound change is Grammont (1933). In part II of *Traité de phonétique*, Grammont presents one of the most comprehensive inventories of sound change to date, focusing on the phonetic sources of sound change. Grammont (1933: 175–79) suggests multiple influences on sound change including: race, climate, political structure, social factors, and analogy. He localizes sound change in the imperfect process of child language acquisition, but his primary explanation for most of the phonetically based cases of sound changes discussed in this part of the volume is the balance between "la loi du moindre effort" ('the law of least effort') and "le besoin de clarté" ('the need for clarity'):

---

[6] Though Friedrich Max Müller and Baudouin were influential in importing teleological explanations into the field of historical linguistics, these views never came to be associated with the general neogrammarian program, as discussed below.

La loi du moindre effort. Il est certain que cette loi joue un grand rôle dans l'évolution des langues, et qu'en particulier tous les phénomènes d'assimilations, à quelque degré et sous quelle forme que ce soit, lui sont dus. Mais, si elle était seule à régir l'évolution phonétique des langues, tous les mots arriveraient assez vite à se réduire à une seule syllabe, voire à un seul phonème. Elle a contre elle la loi du plus grand effort, ou plutôt du besoin de clarté, qui commande toutes les différenciations et tous les renforcements. (Grammont 1933: 176)[7]

Grammont's position is similar to the modern H&H theory of sound change (Lindblom 1986, 1990a; Lindblom et al. 1995). Within this model articulatory reduction and elaboration on the part of the speaker result from articulatory economy and intensional auditory contrast respectively. Communicative effectiveness demands that each of these forces be maximized wherever possible. Though the H&H proposal attempts to explain 'on-line' variability in speech in terms of "the continual tug-of-war between production and perception demands," Lindblom (1998: 245) also suggests that sound change might involve evaluation of these changes: "if the change facilitates articulation and perception . . . its probability of acceptance goes up. If the change violates the criteria, it is likely to be rejected."

The neogrammarians soundly rejected teleological explanations for sound change. Their view was that sound change was the end result of gradual, minute, and essentially random changes in articulation.[8] The non-teleological view is maintained by most modern Indo-European scholars and by the majority of historical linguists. Lehmann (1992: 207) in his *Historical Linguistics* text, for example, summarizes his position as follows: "We conclude that assumption of change towards ease of articulation in accordance with the principle of least effort is based on an inadequate view of language." Lass (1980, 1997) argues against general functional explanations, not only in phonology, but for other domains as well. And Ohala's (e.g. 1983a, 1990b) position that sound change is non-optimizing has already been mentioned in relation to his experimental evidence and explanations for the phonetic bases of sound change. In his influential paper on the role of perception in consonantal place-assimilation, Ohala (1990b: 266) presents what might be viewed as the

---

[7] "The law of least effort. It is clear that this law plays an important role in the evolution of languages, and that, specifically, all assimilatory phenomena to whatever extent and in whatever form, are due to it. But, if only this law governed the phonetic evolution of languages, every word would quickly be reduced to a single syllable, even a single phoneme. Working against this law is the law of most effort, or rather, the need for clarity which gives rise to all contrasts and all fortitions" (trans. JB).

[8] One exception was the neogrammarian account of metathesis which did not lend itself to treatment in terms of gradual shifts in articulation.

most modern and phonetically informed restatement of the neogrammarian position that sound change is not goal directed:

these results reinforce a non-teleological view of sound change, that is, that neither
speaker nor hearer chooses – consciously or not – to change pronunciation . . .
Rather, variation occurs due to "innocent" misapprehensions about the interpretation of the speech signal or . . . to listeners' inexperience. In this respect
sound change is not unlike the transmission of scribal errors in the copying of
manuscripts. It does not occur to "optimize" speech in any way: it does not make
it easier to pronounce, easier to detect, or easier to learn.[9]

While the neogrammarian movement and many of its modern descendants reject teleological explanations for sound change, the split between twentieth-century historical linguistics and synchronic linguistics
remarked on above has led to a similar bifurcation in terms of ultimate
explanations for sound patterns. Within synchronic studies, explanations
for phonological contrasts and alternations have been viewed in terms of
theories of markedness or naturalness. Marked patterns are rare, unnatural, and non-optimal, while unmarked patterns are thought to be frequent, natural, and optimal. The earliest formulations of markedness
were purely structural. In describing the notion of distinctive phonological oppositions, for example, Trubetzkoy (1931: 97) says:

the one member has the particular property or has it in its positive form, the other
does not have it or has it in its negative form. We designate the former as marked
and the latter as unmarked.

However, this notion of markedness was soon coupled with teleological notions of articulatory complexity. Unmarked members of an opposition were simpler and more natural than marked members (Jakobson
1937; Trubetzkoy 1939). The neutral position was that of normal breathing, with markedness assessed in relation to this baseline, as defined by
Trubetzkoy (1939: 146): "In any correlation . . . a 'natural absence
of marking' is attributed to that opposition member whose production
requires the least deviation from normal breathing." A further innovation was the association of markedness values with neutralization and
frequency. In positions of neutralization where the composition of the
variant is not environmentally conditioned, only the unmarked member of an opposition class occurs (Trubetzkoy 1935, 1939). This allowed

[9] The analogy between speech errors and transcription errors is also made by Baudouin
(1876–77/1972: 92) in his discussion of sound change: "The beginnings of dynamic
sound change (alterations) conditioned by their physical (physiological) properties . . .
Different categories of sound changes: assimilation, dissimilation, metathesis and others.
Comparison with similar phenomena in writing (slips of the pen) and in everyday events."
To my knowledge, Baudouin is the first linguist to suggest the listener as the source of
sound change, in the specific sense in which it occurs in Ohala's research program.

Trubetzkoy (1939: 262) to claim that the unmarked member of a privative opposition is more frequent in the phonological surface representations of a particular language than the marked member.

The history of markedness and naturalness in the twentieth century is a somewhat odd one. In *The Sound Pattern of English* (*SPE*; 1968), which served as a catalyst for much subsequent work in generative phonology, Chomsky and Halle fail to incorporate an explicit theory of markedness into their analyses. In chapter 9 of *SPE* the authors discuss this weakness, and suggest a system of linking rules which give weighted values to fully specified phonological representations. By incorporating substantively motivated feature-marking conventions, an attempt was made to make natural rules simpler under the proposed evaluation metric. However, with the exception of Kean (1975), this aspect of generative phonology was not explored seriously. Throughout the 1970s, markedness in generative phonology continued to be an informal aspect of analyses, with the naturalness of rules evaluated primarily with respect to the given body of knowledge surrounding phonetically natural sound patterns, or typologically common sound patterns like those documented in Greenberg (1978). Textbook presentations of generative phonology maintained the view that a synchronic account of naturalness or markedness should exist, though no specific proposals were put forth. The brief discussion of Kenstowicz and Kisseberth (1979) is typical:

Any adequate theory of phonology must contain postulates that will define natural sound changes.[10] Although many of these can be expressed by appeal to the notion of assimilation defined over the features of a feature system, it is clear that not all natural sound changes fit into this mold. For example, many languages have a rule converting consonants to ? or *h* in preconsonantal and final position. Such a process is clearly not assimilatory in nature. Nevertheless phonological theory must have some apparatus for expressing the fact that neutralization to a glottal stop in these positions is a natural rule as opposed to, say, neutralization to *l*. (Kenstowicz and Kisseberth 1979: 251)

One notable exception to this informal reference to markedness was the theory of Natural Phonology, as developed by Stampe (1973) and Donegan and Stampe (1979).[11] The imperative to build natural phonological processes into phonological theory was directly expressed in this

---

[10] It is clear from the context of this discussion that "natural sound changes" refers to natural synchronic alternations. The particular example being discussed is rounding of /i/ to *u* in Igbo reduplication, when the stem-initial segment is labial. This alternation might be expressed as $i \rightarrow u/ \underline{P} + P$, where P is labial, and $+$ marks the reduplicative prefix boundary.

[11] See also the approaches of Venneman (1972a) and Hooper (1976), where phonology and markedness were equated.

approach. All humans were claimed to be born with innate natural phonological processes, like final obstruent devoicing. These innate phonological processes were, in turn, claimed to have natural phonetic explanations relating, for the most part, to articulatory ease. These universal natural processes could be inhibited by exposure to conflicting data in order to maximize existing contrasts in the language being acquired. In other words, common sound patterns, like final devoicing, were explained in terms of teleological principles which were direct components of the synchronic grammar. The process of final devoicing makes speech easier to pronounce, therefore, it is a natural phonological process, and will occur in the course of language acquisition unless the learner is exposed to surface forms which conflict with its output. Where standard generative accounts of the 1960s and 1970s failed to incorporate formal models of explanation, Natural Phonology allowed explanation to limit its descriptive domain, having little to say about unnatural sound patterns of the sort mentioned in 3.1.

As the focus in phonology moved from phonological rules to representations in the 1980s, Prague school conceptions of markedness were revived. Kiparsky (1982b), Archangeli (1984), and Pulleyblank (1986), among others, suggested that markedness and naturalness could be directly related to feature specification or presence versus absence of structure. Unmarked feature values were taken to be absent in underlying representations while marked feature values were present. Though attempts were made to equate feature-filling rules with unmarked processes, and feature-changing rules with more marked processes, this line of investigation met with serious empirical difficulties (Steriade 1995).[12]

The end of the twentieth century has seen a revival of interest in incorporating markedness and goal-directed explanations into formal approaches to synchronic phonology. Within Grounded Phonology (Archangeli and Pulleyblank 1994: 177), path conditions which define paradigmatic linkings of phonological features "must be phonetically motivated." The phonetic motivations in Grounded Phonology involve both articulatory ease and increased perceptual contrast. For example, relationships between feature values for [high] and [ATR] are grounded in the tendency for interdependence between tongue root and tongue body movements (Archangeli and Pulleyblank 1994: 174–75), ultimately related to articulatory ease.

A more extreme integration of teleological principles into synchronic grammars is found in Optimality Theory (Prince and Smolensky 1993;

---

[12] The problems were so serious that Mohanan (1991) and Myers (1991) proposed full feature specifications, with modern versions of *SPE* linking rules to capture synchronic notions of naturalness and markedness.

Kager 1999; McCarthy 2002), as its name suggests. Within Optimality approaches, the synchronic grammar is itself a combination of ranked markedness and faithfulness constraints. Faithfulness constraints require identity between input and output candidates under evaluation, while markedness constraints evaluate output candidates, favoring certain sound patterns over others. Markedness constraints evaluate only output structures in Optimality Theory and have a system-internal function which distinguishes them from Prague school conceptions of markedness. Cross-linguistic tendencies, absolute universals, and implicational relations are not direct evidence for markedness constraints within Optimality Theory. Rather, the only primary evidence for markedness constraints in this theory is the correctness of the typologies they predict under permuted ranking of all possible constraints within the universal constraint set. Constraint-ranking within Optimality Theory defines a surface form as the most harmonic candidate for a given input when evaluated against the language-particular constraint rankings. Given a constraint ranking, the grammar is formulated to provide an optimal candidate for any given input. Synchronic sound patterns are explained within Optimality Theory as being the most harmonic members of their candidate sets. All phonology is goal-directed in the sense that all synchronic phonology is expressed as constraint satisfaction at some level. Like the earlier developments of markedness in the Prague school, the earliest formulations of markedness within Optimality Theory were purely structural. However, markedness constraints have been equated by many researchers with notions of articulatory complexity and perceptual contrast (Steriade 1999a, 2001; Kirchner 2000; Flemming 2001), in line with Kager's (1999: 11) suggestion that "phonological markedness constraints should be phonetically grounded in some property of articulation and perception."

Within Evolutionary Phonology there is no notion of improvement that guides the development of sound patterns within the diachronic or synchronic dimension. The precise mechanisms of sound change proposed in 2.2 are stochastic, and the spread of any sound change at the level of the individual within a speech community involves yet further chance occurrences. Nevertheless, this model of sound change can account for common recurrent sound patterns in the world's languages and at the same time model the fact that a particular sound change may occur in one daughter language but not in another. Although perception and production play a significant role in all types of regular sound change modeled in 2.2, the only place where minimal effort and maximal contrast have any role is in defining the hypo-to-hyperarticulated speech continuum which can seed instances of sound change, and in apparent instances of CHOICE (see 8.3) where maintenance of paradigmatic contrast may be involved. Empirical support for this non-teleological view of sound change and synchronic sound patterns is presented throughout the remainder of this volume. On this view, there is no need to use markedness to incorporate notions of phonetic complexity directly into synchronic phonological description. Articulatory ease and perceptual contrast may play an indirect role in the typology of sound change, but the end results of these sound changes are phonological systems which are independent of their phonetic origins, and may ultimately obscure them. Synchronic sound patterns which appear natural are those which have not strayed far from their phonetic origins. Unnatural sound patterns, on the other hand, are those where a single sound change has been inverted, layered over with others, or diluted with the effects of analogical change. Currently, as emphasized in chapter 9, there are no criteria by which natural and unnatural sound patterns can be distinguished in synchronic grammars, provided both types are regular. Given this, a formal distinction between the two seems unwarranted and indeed misguided.

3.3   Phonetic explanation

A basic question is: why do sound systems pattern the way they do, and not otherwise? One of the most widely accepted explanations for regularities in synchronic phonological systems is that they are the grammaticization or formalization of earlier phonetic patterns. The recognition that certain sound patterns, like palatalization before high vowels, bear a striking resemblance to phonetic coarticulatory aspects of speech has led many researchers to propose that synchronic alternations can be explained in phonetic terms. Significantly, this type of phonetic explanation can be invoked without reference to teleology or goal-oriented change. To take just one example, synchronic metathesis rules very often have their origins in cases of CHANCE: a phonetic feature of long duration gives rise to temporal ambiguity, and is reinterpreted in its non-historical position (Blevins and Garrett 1998, to appear). However, in such cases, resulting metathesized forms are not claimed to be easier to articulate, easier to perceive, or easier to learn. Phonetic explanation then, is not intrinsically teleological, though, as discussed in 3.2, most teleological explanations proposed for sound patterns have a phonetic basis.

Paul (1886) presents two categories of sound change: *Lautwandel* ('phonological change') where articulation of a speaker changes gradually giving rise to inherited articulatory changes in the listener, and *abweichende Neuerzeugung* ('imperfect learning') where a listener's phonological analysis differs from that of the speaker.[13] Phonological change is clearly related to phonetic variation, however, unlike the H&H model, where articulatory changes are goal-directed, or the present model, where articulatory changes are the result of changes in input frequencies, no neogrammarian account is given for gradual articulatory shifts in one particular direction versus another. Paul's imperfect learning, on the other hand, views ambiguity of analysis as the source of change. A speaker assigns a distinct phonological representation to the phonetic string, and this ultimately has consequences for articulation. While Baudouin makes specific reference to the possibility of misperception as the source of sound change, perception-based explanations are not found in the mainstream neogrammarian literature.

The idea that synchronic phonological alternations are the grammaticization or formalization of earlier phonetic patterns is attributable to Baudouin de Courtenay, "the first linguist to propose explicitly that all systematic phonological variation originates in the phonologization of phonetic detail" (Anderson 1985: 76). Baudouin's views of the relationship between sound change and synchronic alternations were radical for his time, and revealed a great sensitivity to the intricacies of phonetic detail, and a firm commitment to the psychological nature of phonological representations. Within Baudouin's collected works, every potential source of regular sound change is alluded to. Consider, for example, the case where a particular phonetic string is commonly misheard due to intrinsic strengths and weaknesses of particular perceptual cues. Baudouin (1876–77/1972: 93) appears to refer to just this case when he writes of "the discrepancy between the physical nature of sounds and their significance in the mechanism of language and in the people's linguistic feeling," where "linguistic feeling" was Baudouin's term for psychological construct or mental representation. This notion is made more precise in later work. In his assessment of phonetic laws of sound change, Baudouin (1910/1972: 267) emphasizes:

the importance of errors in hearing (*lapsus auris*) . . . as a factor of change at any given moment of linguistic intercourse . . . Experimental methods can help to define the types and directions of these errors which depend on physical conditions, on the sense of hearing of individuals, and on the degree of morphologization and semasiologization of the mobilized articulatory and auditory representations.

Baudouin (1910/1972: 261–62) also saw the inherent ambiguity of the phonological analysis of a phonetic string as a source of sound change:

---

[13] Translations of Paul's terms are those first used by Kiparsky (1965).

"The acoustic impressions activate *sensory nerves* which transmit these impressions to the cerebral center. The *apperception* of the received impressions takes place in this system. Thanks to apperception, each representation is potentially and actively *associated* with and enriched by other existing representations." Here Baudouin seems to make reference not only to the ambiguous nature of certain phonetic symbols, but also to the role of other sound patterns within a language in guiding the listener to a particular mental representation of speech. Variation as the source of change is also noted. In considering the origins of the variation between [t] and zero word-finally in Rezian, Baudouin points out that: "there are differences of tempo and style of speech. On the one hand, though more rarely, there is a greater or lesser degree of solemnity and carefulness; on the other hand, in everyday life there is a greater or lesser degree of carelessness" (Baudouin 1929(2)/1972: 292–93). From these sources of sound change, traditional phonological alternations were classified into two categories: those which transparently reflected their phonetic origins ("those that developed directly from divergents or neophonetic alternations that have lost their live anthropophonic cause"), and those which did not transparently reflect their phonetic origins ("those that have gone through several stages") (1895/1972: 184–95). Again, this typology anticipates the recognition of natural and unnatural rule types discussed earlier.

It is difficult to trace direct descendants of Baudouin's ideas concerning phonetic sources of sound change, listener-oriented sound change, and historical phonetic sources of phonological alternations. Similar ideas have been developed, apparently independently, in a number of contemporary approaches, though, of the work cited in this chapter, only Anderson (1985) makes direct reference to Baudouin.[14] A related view of phonologization is elaborated in Hyman (1972, 1973, 1977), though, as noted in 2.2, this model is restricted to one stage of one particular subcase of sound change. Ohala's phonetic explanations for sound patterns (1974a, b, 1975, 1981, 1983a, 1985, 1990b) also bear a striking resemblance to the leading ideas of Baudouin. If anyone has carried out the experimental work suggested by Baudouin on the direction of "errors in hearing" in the quote above, it is Ohala and his colleagues. And Baudouin's reference to variation as the source of change is developed most directly in the H&H model, though again, there is no evidence of direct intellectual lineage.

The attempt to encode phonetic explanation in terms of markedness was discussed in the previous subsection. Yet it is the near absence of

---

[14] Locke (1983: 209) makes reference to Baudouin's modern conception of phonologization.

phonetic explanation that is more characteristic of much work in generative phonology, with the exception of work in Natural Phonology noted above. In Natural Phonology (Stampe 1973; Donegan and Stampe 1979), the object of study was limited to phonetically natural regular sound patterns. While this approach facilitates the understanding of phonological alternations as natural phenomena with clear phonetic origins almost by definition, it does so by arbitrarily limiting the scope of phonological description. As detailed in Bach and Harms (1972), Hyman (1972, 1973, 1977), and part II of this book, there are phonetically natural historical pathways to phonologically unnatural sound patterns. And phonological rules appear to have the same formal status regardless of their naturalness quotient. As noted in 3.2, phonetic explanations for markedness constraints have been introduced in Grounded Phonology (Archangeli and Pulleyblank 1994) and in some Optimality accounts (Steriade 1997; Kirchner 2000; Flemming 2001). Recent collections on this topic include Hume and Johnson (2001) and Hayes et al. (to appear). McCarthy (2002: 222–27) points to several problems with phonetically motivated constraints of this sort. First, like the external naturalness postulates of the *SPE* tradition, they may be "inert but admired"; the theory is essentially the same, whether constraints have phonetic motivation or not. A second problem involves the introduction of gradience into constraint evaluation: phonological targets involve categorical distinctions which may not surface once the gradient nature of individual utterances is modeled.

3.4   Explanation in Evolutionary Phonology

Evolutionary Phonology proposes historical, non-teleological, phonetic explanations for synchronic sound patterns. Cross-linguistic similarities which occur with greater than chance frequency are viewed as the result of direct inheritance or parallel evolution. Unnatural sound patterns can also be viewed as the result of regular historical changes like those sketched in (1). In either case, the primary explanation for a synchronic sound pattern is historical. The formal model of sound change proposed in 2.2 points to the intrinsic ambiguity of certain phonetic strings as the source of potential reanalysis. By limiting phonetic explanation to the diachronic component, the integrity of synchronic phonological systems remains uncompromised.

We have seen in this chapter that many of the fundamental concepts incorporated into Evolutionary Phonology have a long and distinguished history. In many ways, Evolutionary Phonology may be seen as instantiating the research program suggested by Anderson (1985: 346) with origins in the Kazan school:

a fundamentally modular theory with a serious claim to genuine explanatory capacity already exists *in posse* in the views of Baudouin and Kruszewski . . . On that picture, the phonetic capacities of speakers function to determine the "raw material" for sound change . . . which serve as the source of synchronic regularities in natural language systems. The impact of such "natural processes" on phonological systems, however, is a result both of their substantive content and of the interaction of this with the processes of phonologization and historical change – for they are no longer phonetically determined in their essence, once incorporated into the grammar of a language. Many (if not most) of the details of such a theory remain to be developed, but at least in outline it appears to present the possibility of achieving an understanding of the scope of "phonetic explanation" in phonology, without abandoning the requirements of comprehensive and accurate description.

Evolutionary Phonology integrates the neogrammarian view of sound change originating in random articulatory drift, with two schools of phonetic research: Lindblom's modeling of the hyper-to-hypoarticulated speech continuum, and Ohala's listener-oriented approach to sound change. It is closest in spirit and execution to the research program defined by Baudouin, and recognizes explicitly that natural sound patterns are those which arise from regular phonetically motivated sound change. There are three identifiable types of phonetically governed sound change, and each has a slightly different explanatory profile. Recall from 2.2 that language-internal origins of sound change at the level of the individual speaker include CHANGE, CHANCE, and CHOICE. CHANGE and CHANCE are categories derivative of Ohala's work, while CHOICE can occur only where there is synchronic variation along the hyper-to-hypoarticulation continuum. In this last case, the minute changes of articulation assumed by the neogrammarians are actual features of synchronic systems with their notion of "random imperceptible articulatory drift" associated with changes in token frequencies of particular phonetic variants.

Goal-directed sound change is nearly absent within Evolutionary Phonology. Features of a particular language (e.g. high frequency of open syllables) may result in priming effects in the course of learning which yield higher probabilities for reanalysis of one particular percept than another, but they need not. As discussed in chapter 2, a phonetic percept [ʔV̰ʔ], with a long-domain feature of laryngealization is ambiguous between /ʔV/ and /Vʔ/ among other segmentations. In a language where the majority of syllables have the form CV, a learner may be more likely to analyze [ʔV̰ʔ] as /ʔV/ rather than /Vʔ/ due to the high frequency of CV syllables. However, there is no reference in the model to /ʔV/ being better in any definable way: it is not necessarily easier to pronounce, easier to distinguish from other percepts, or easier to learn than /Vʔ/. The model is intentionally agnostic regarding optimal sound patterns, and probabilistic regarding sound change. It attempts to accurately model the fact that highly marked sound patterns do occur, and that, from a given language source, sound change may or may not occur. The only place where teleological sound change is recognized is in limited instances of CHOICE (see 8.3) where antihomophony constraints may act as catalysts or inhibitors of sound change. The general non-teleological nature of Evolutionary Phonology distinguishes it from the H&H model of sound change, and from many modern Optimality approaches. Sound change and sound patterns are not goal directed. If they appear to be, it is only because in comparing any two sound patterns, XaY and XbY, one can *always* define XaY as better along some dimension, and XbY as better along another.

Another feature absent from Evolutionary Phonology is direct reference to naturalness or markedness, distinguishing it from the Prague school and its descendants. Some synchronic sound patterns are natural and others are not, but no synchronic system appears to differentiate sound patterns on this basis. Frequently occurring sound patterns can be understood in terms of frequencies of sound changes which give rise to them. Most of these will be natural, since all regular sound changes with phonetic sources are, by definition, natural, but some, like alternations stemming from rule inversion, will not be. Building naturalness or markedness into synchronic accounts seems unwarranted, and leads to a range of problems, in part II of this volume, where unnatural sound patterns are involved. Without direct reference to markedness within synchronic systems, are there heuristics for identifying marked versus unmarked features of sound systems? Some possibilities are suggested in chapter 8.

Evolutionary Phonology satisfies at least two of the desiderata set out in Anderson (1985: 346), by offering explanations for natural phonological systems, and by insisting on the modularity of phonological and phonetic levels of representation:

There is clearly something general and natural about phonological systems which is not represented in a system of the SPE type; and it is plausible to seek explanations of that fact in the organic basis of human phonetic capacities. Where natural phonology and the theory of markedness in SPE go astray . . . is in trying to incorporate this explanation directly into the descriptive framework for phonology. We should instead recognize the modularity of language: the fact that it represents the intersection of a number of distinguishable domains, each subject to its own principles.

Substantive universals define synchronic phonological systems, and include distinctive features, segments, syllables, and other levels of the prosodic hierarchy. However, the combinatorial possibilities of these building blocks are not obviously constrained by synchronic principles, but rather by their particular histories.

The remainder of this book is organized as follows. Part II presents empirical support for Evolutionary Phonology and part III examines theoretical implications of the approach. The synthesis that emerges adopts historical explanations from the neogrammarian and Kazan traditions, and appeals to phonetic explanations to account for the majority of the world's recurrent sound patterns. Evolutionary Phonology also develops a contemporary variant of Baudouin's view of systematic phonological variation as the phonologization of phonetic processes, informed by our current understanding of phonetics and cross-linguistic typology. Evolutionary Phonology is an attempt to document the scope of historical explanation in phonology, without abandoning the requirements of comprehensive and accurate synchronic description. The model of synchrony which emerges is not a homogeneous one: some alternations are natural and others are not; some generalized phonotactics are accidental and others are not; some constraints are violable and others are not.[15] While this model may not have great esthetic appeal, it is the only one consistent with the range of facts presented in this volume.

Evolutionary Phonology develops Baudouin's claim that phonetic explanation is limited to the diachronic dimension. Phonetics and phonology are separate levels of linguistic representation. The phonetic sources of sound change are those formalized in 2.2, and reflect the basic mechanisms of change suggested in Baudouin's work. The typology of sound change is based on the type of phonetic explanation offered, and in this way differs from traditional typologies of sound change where one finds lists of assimilation, dissimilation, deletion, insertion, etc. A regular assimilatory sound change like $^*np > mp$ has at least two potential origins. It may arise as a simple case of CHANGE, where [np] is misheard as [mp], or it could be an instance of CHOICE, where phonetic realizations of $^*np$ include [np] and [mp], with high token frequency of [mp] providing the basis of phonological (re)analysis on the part of the listener. At the same time, other sorts of non-local assimilations, like the umlaut of $^*u > y \ / \ \_Ci$, are not, as far as is known, the results of CHANGE. By classifying regular sound changes in terms of their phonetic origins, we can pose, for any given sound change $^*XaY > XbY$, the questions in (3).

---

[15] Jackendoff (2002, chapter 6) argues for a similarly non-homogeneous view of grammar. For example, in his view, the lexicon is not merely a collection of minimal syntactic units, but also includes words and phrases, and may include whole sentences and entire discourses.

(3)   Phonetic sources of sound change: three questions
    i. Can XaY be misheard as XbY?
      If yes, CHANGE is possible source.
    ii. Are there multiple analyzes of XaY which include XbY,
      aXY, XYa, etc.?
      If yes, CHANCE is possible source.
    iii. Is XaY a slow- or fast-speech variant of XbY, Xab Y, XY,
      etc.?
      If yes, CHOICE is possible source.

The rest of this book is an attempt to demonstrate that answers to the
questions in (3) bring us closer to a real understanding of the origins of
sound patterns. By modeling sound change as a mapping between one
synchronic grammar and the next, synchronic phonology remains a pure
non-teleological system of abstract features and categories, with phonetic
explanation limited to the diachronic dimension.

Part II

Sound patterns

Evolution is the epitome of inscrutability, indirectness, and opportunism – seldom following an obvious or elegant path.

Deacon (1997: 46)

4   Laryngeal features

Les changements phonétiques sont les manifestations et les réalisations
de tendances, que la langue a contractée au cours de sa vie antérieure.
Ces changements sont désignés par le nom de *lois phonétiques*.

Grammont (1933: 166)

4.1   Phonological features and laryngeal features

If there is one point of agreement within phonetic and phonological
theory, it is that the segments which compose speech are not indivisible
primitive units of speech. Instead, the general view is that segments are
the simultaneous realization of smaller units, known as *features*. Features
play a significant role in defining sound change and sound patterns. At the
phonetic level, there are potentially gradient and potentially imperceptible *phonetic features*; at the phonological level, there are *distinctive features*
which are typically privative (single-valued) or binary-valued, and which
define contrasts which are typically perceptible to all human newborns
(Werker and Pegg 1992). These distinctive features are the basis of all
attested phonological contrasts. Two primary arguments exist for distinctive features. One argument is that they correspond quite closely to
innate perceptual categories demonstrated in newborns and young children (9.1). Another argument is that they allow the statement of what
appear to be significant generalizations across sound patterns.

In this chapter, characteristic patterns of laryngeal feature distribution
are investigated.[1] Laryngeal features are those which characterize the state

---

[1] Languages on which generalizations are based include: Lithuanian, German, Frisian,
Sanskrit, Russian, French, Catalan, English, Attic Greek, Polish, Maithili, Lamani (Indo-
European); Kiowa (Kiowa-Tanoan); Yokuts, Kashaya, Miwok, Klamath, Tsimshian,
Nez Perce; Afar (Cushitic); Dinka (Nilotic); Ngizim (Chadic); Korean; Hungarian
(Finno-Ugric); Kolami (Dravidian); Yateé Zapotec (Otomanguean); Tamazight
Berber (Afro-Asiatic/Berber); Arabic, Syrian, Eastern, Moroccan, Iraqi Arabic (Afro-
Asiatic/Semitic); Totontepec Mixe (Mixe-Zoque); Nhanda (Pama-Nyungan); Lac
Simon (Algonquian); Wantoat, Kalam (Papuan); Sre, Pacoh (Mon-Khmer); Chepang,

of the larynx or vocal folds, and the acoustic and perceptual features associated with these states. Though it is necessary to distinguish dozens of phonetic categories which contrast gradient voice onset times, degrees of laryngealization, and pulmonic versus laryngeal airstream mechanisms (Gordon and Ladefoged 2001), for the purposes of describing contrasts in phonological segment inventories, only three phonological features appear necessary. These features are often labeled as [voiced], [spread glottis], and [constricted glottis].[2] While labeling and precise definitions of these features may be disputed, there are two aspects of the feature system which are non-negotiable. First, phonological features are distinct from gradient phonetic properties, and typically reflect categories which have multiple distinct phonetic instantiations or cues. Second, no reference is made in phonological systems to non-contrastive features (e.g. the release of stops, 2 ms of voice-onset time, laminal interdental versus laminal dental, etc.) Each of these properties is integral to the explanations provided for typical cases of regular sound change. Because phonological features are distinct from gradient phonetic properties, and there is typically no one-to-one relationship between a phonological feature or category and a single phonetic characteristic, reinterpretations of the phonetic signal in the form of slight shifts of whole categories within the psycho-acoustic space are expected.

Within a single language, identical phonological feature specifications can be associated with highly distinct phonetic features depending on phonological context, or on other segment-internal feature specifications. Consider the phonetic contrast between pre- and post-aspirated segments. Though these two sounds clearly constitute different acoustic and auditory categories, in Icelandic (Thráinsson 1978), regular alternations condition pre- and post-aspirates, which are in complementary distribution. In other languages, like Twampa (Thelwall 1983; 334) post-aspirates have optional pre-aspirated variants in certain contexts. The same sort of phonetic variation characterizes segments defined as [constricted glottis]. In Klamath (Barker 1964; Blevins 1993a), sonorants with this feature are pre-glottalized, while obstruents are realized as ejectives. For more examples of this kind, see Kingston (1990). The

---

Mikir, Sherpa (Tibeto-Burman); Lushootseed, Twana, Bella Coola, Montana Salish, Shuswap (Salishan); Palauan, Marshallese (Austronesian); Nootka, Kwakiutl (Wakashan); Haida (isolate); Mbe (Niger-Congo/Bantu), as well as others mentioned in the text. This set includes 52 languages from 22 different language families.

[2] Here I do not include laryngeal "tone" features. For an overview of the relationship between laryngeal features and tone, see Yip (1995: 484–88). On the evolution of tonal systems from F_0 perturbations associated with consonantal laryngeal features, see Hombert et al. (1979). And for phonological systems where tone features interact with other laryngeal features, see Hyman (1973).

phonological identity of pre- and post-aspiration, and of pre-glottalization and post-glottalization (or ejection), is strongly supported by the fact that no languages are reported to contrast segments with respect to these dimensions alone. Our starting point for the investigation which follows, then, is that a limited number of phonological categories or segment types are defined by a limited set of phonological features.

4.2   The phonetic basis of sound patterns

Since the introduction of distinctive features into phonological theory, the majority of phonotactic constraints have been stated in terms of natural classes defined by distinctive features. One fundamental observation which emerges from the cross-linguistic study of the distribution of laryngeal features is that segments with identical phonological feature representations may have dramatically different patterns of distribution. For example, there is a strong cross-linguistic preference for post-aspiration of consonants to occur pre-vocalically, while pre-aspiration of consonants is generally found post-vocalically. Accounting for this general type of distributional pattern is problematic for most phonological approaches, since pre-aspirates and post-aspirates are non-contrastive, and therefore are assumed to have identical phonological representations. One might think of this as an isolated problem, relating only to the characterization of aspiration, but the same problem occurs again and again: recurrent phonotactic patterns seem directly related to *non-distinctive* properties of sound patterns, and yet, phonological characterization of these patterns must be stated without reference to non-distinctive properties, missing important generalizations.

How can this problem be overcome? Two logical alternatives present themselves. One possibility is to abandon a pure phonological feature system by introducing phonetic detail into phonological representations. This is the position taken, for example, by Steriade (1993, 1999a), Kirchner (2000), and Flemming (2001). In these accounts, sound patterns are defined with direct reference to phonetic features as well as phonological ones. This alternative eliminates any principled distinction between phonological and phonetic representations, or phonological and phonetic features, and attempts to build phonetic explanations into phonological representations and constraints themselves. A second alternative, and the one defended throughout this book, is to maintain a pure categorical phonology, free of phonetic detail. This view of phonology, similar to that conceived of by the Prague school, represents all and only the features, segments, and prosodic categories which are *contrastive* in the world's languages. Within Evolutionary Phonology, the phonotactic regularities exhibited by synchronic phonologies appear to be sensitive to phonetic detail because they are arguably, in many cases, the transparent result of phonetically motivated sound change. Since phonetically motivated sound change is well evidenced in the historical record, and can be simulated in the laboratory, relying on such factors to explain recurrent relationships between feature distribution and non-distinctive properties of speech appears to be the null hypothesis.

A primary argument for Evolutionary Phonology over alternative approaches is that phonetically motivated sound change is already accepted as one explanation for properties of synchronic sound systems. Any model which incorporates phonetic detail into phonological systems in order to explain synchronic regularities is essentially duplicating an explanation which already exists in the diachronic dimension. Under this account, there is no pre-determined set of phonological constraints in the mind of the speaker which gives rise to recurrent sound patterns. Rather, the phonotactic regularities examined in this and following chapters are *emergent universals* in the sense of Deacon (1997: 115–16):

Grammatical universals exist, but . . . their existence does not imply that they are prefigured in the brain like frozen evolutionary accidents. In fact, . . . the universal rules or implicit axioms of grammar aren't really stored or located anywhere, and in an important sense, they are not *determined* at all. Instead . . . they have emerged spontaneously and independently in each evolving language, in response to universal biases in the selection processes affecting language transmission. They are convergent features of language evolution in the same way that the dorsal fins of sharks, ichthyosaurs, and dolphins are independent convergent adaptations of aquatic species. Like their biological counterparts, these structural commonalities present in all languages have each arisen in response to the constraints imposed by a common adaptive context. Some of the sources of universal selection on the evolution of language structures include immature learning biases, human mnemonic and perceptual biases, the constraints of human vocal articulation and hearing . . . to name a few. Because of these incessant influences, languages independently come to resemble one another, not in detail, but in terms of certain general structural properties . . .

In the following section I summarize ways in which languages independently come to resemble one another in terms of the distribution of laryngeal features.

4.3   Recurrent patterns of laryngeal feature distribution

The distribution of distinctive laryngeal features on consonants is severely limited in many languages. Obstruent voicing, aspiration, and ejection are often limited to certain positions, while distinct distributional constraints are found for sonorant voicelessness and sonorant laryngealization. As documented by Lombardi (1991), Steriade (1999a), Fallon (2002), and Blevins (2003a) among others, there is general similarity across languages with respect to: (i) the neutralizing feature or features; (ii) the positions in which neutralization occurs; (iii) the direction of neutralization; and (iv) distinct neutralization patterns for laryngeal features of obstruents and sonorants.

In (1)–(3) I summarize some of these recurrent patterns with respect to their phonetic status as release features, realized at consonant release, or closure features, realized at the onset of consonant closure.

(1) Release feature pattern: obstruent voicing, obstruent post-aspiration, obstruent ejection
   (i) PHONETIC FEATURES: post-aspiration, post-glottalization, ejective release, release cues for voicing (burst strength, VOT, F_0 values, F_1 values)
   (ii) PHONOLOGICAL FEATURES: [voiced], [spread glottis], [constricted glottis]
   (iii) COMMON POSITIONS OF CONTRAST: before sonorants
   (iv) COMMON POSITIONS OF NEUTRALIZATION: before obstruents, word-finally
   (v) COMMON DIRECTION OF NEUTRALIZATION: neutralization is either
     a. to the voiceless unaspirated member of the series, or
     b. in obstruent clusters, the result of regressive assimilation

(2) Closure feature pattern: sonorant pre-glottalization
   (i) PHONETIC FEATURE: pre-glottalization
   (ii) PHONOLOGICAL FEATURES: [−syllabic, +sonorant, constricted glottis]
   (iii) COMMON POSITIONS OF CONTRAST: after vowels
   (iv) COMMON POSITIONS OF NEUTRALIZATION: after consonants, word-initially
   (v) COMMON DIRECTION OF NEUTRALIZATION: to the plain voiced member of the series

(3) Closure feature pattern: obstruent pre-aspiration
   (i) PHONETIC FEATURE: pre-aspiration
   (ii) PHONOLOGICAL FEATURES: [−sonorant, −continuant, spread glottis]
   (iii) COMMON POSITIONS OF CONTRAST: after vowels, sometimes after sonorant consonants

>   (iv) COMMON POSITIONS OF NEUTRALIZATION: after
>   obstruents
>   (v) COMMON DIRECTION OF NEUTRALIZATION:
>   neutralization is either
>   a. to the voiceless unaspirated member of the series, or
>   b. in obstruent clusters, the result of progressive
>   assimilation

No phonological system is known to contrast post-aspirated stops with their pre-aspirated counterparts. Nevertheless, this phonetic difference appears to determine the general sound patterns of aspirated stops both within and across languages. Compare the common patterns involving post-aspiration, a release feature, in (1), with those of pre-aspiration, a closure feature, in (3). The patterns are near mirror images of each other. Post-aspirates contrast most widely in pre-vocalic position, while pre-aspirates are most likely to contrast in post-vocalic position. The cross-linguistic regularities in this distribution are problematic for phonological theory since all aspirated oral stops will have the same basic feature representation.

The patterns in (1) and (2) are also near mirror images. Compare ejective obstruents and their distribution with pre-glottalized sonorants. Though both segment types are characterized by the same distinctive feature, [constricted glottis], neutralization of ejection is common before obstruents and word-finally, while neutralization of glottalized sonorants is typical word-initially and after consonants. As far as I am aware, there are no reported cases of ejectives neutralizing to plain stops word-initially or post-consonantally, highlighting the distinctive patterns of contrast for closure and release features documented by Steriade (1999a).[3]

Perhaps the most well-known and well-studied examples of laryngeal neutralization involve obstruent devoicing. Given a language where voiced and voiceless obstruents contrast in some environments, there are typically other environments in which voicing is non-contrastive. In unrelated languages across the world we find that the voicing contrast is neutralized for obstruents, that this neutralization tends to occur word-finally and/or in pre-obstruent position, and that neutralization in word-final position is to the voiceless phone, while neutralization in pre-obstruent position is typically either to the voiceless phone, or subject to regressive voice assimilation. This pattern is included in (1).

The emergent sound patterns summarized in (1)–(3) do not appear to be the result of chance occurrences. Word-final neutralization of laryngeal release features is common, while word-initial neutralization of the same

---

[3] Context-free shifts from ejective to plain stops are reported in Fallon (2002, chapter 3).

release features is unattested. At the same time, word-initial neutralization of sonorant pre-glottalization is common, while word-final neutralization of pre-glottalization is rare. The significance of these distinct patterns of contrast and neutralization cannot be overstated. Phonological features show distinct patterns of distribution which appear to be dependent, at least in part, on their phonetic realization. In 4.4, historical phonetic explanations are proposed for these common and recurrent sound patterns. However, before turning to these, it will be useful to briefly review how and why such patterns are best characterized in terms of parallel evolution.

General accounts of similarity were reviewed in 2.4. Recurrent sound patterns may be the result of shared inheritance, convergent evolution, parallel evolution, or diffusion through language contact. For the majority of languages included in the surveys cited above, diffusion can be ruled out as the source of similarity. Many of these languages are spoken on different continents or islands, with no evidence of contact between them. For example, there is no evidence of linguistic contact between Korean speakers, Dinka speakers of Saharan Africa, Wantoat speakers of New Guinea or Klamath speakers of south-central Oregon, and yet all of these languages have sound patterns of the type summarized in (1). Diffusion of laryngeal sound patterns from neighboring languages can often be ruled out as well. For example, although Yurok is spoken close to other languages with glottalized sonorants, the same languages show no evidence for the Yurok pattern of neutralization conforming to (2). As a consequence, the sound patterns on which the generalizations in (1)–(3) are based are ones which appear to have evolved spontaneously many times in the natural course of language change.

Ruling out diffusion as an explanation for these common sound patterns still leaves open the possibility that they are nothing more than chance resemblances. As Blust (1990: 24) notes:

Ideally, in evaluating the role of chance as an explanation we should have access to a statistical model which states how many times a given sound change might be expected to occur in relation to the null hypothesis. Unfortunately, no such model is available, and we are consequently forced to fall back upon an impressionistic statement.

This is still the case over a decade later, and we are forced to rely on linguistic intuitions as to what constitutes "more than chance frequency" for a given pattern. However, if chance were entirely responsible for the patterns of laryngeal feature distribution just summarized, then we would expect similar frequencies for other "chance" events. If there is no principled difference between word-final devoicing and word-final voicing, both being the possible result of chance events, then how are we to explain the high frequency of the first pattern in contrast to the low frequency of the second? Likewise, if the association between release versus closure features and positions of contrast is the result of chance, what could possibly explain the common neutralization of post-aspiration in word-final position, in contrast to the rarity of rules neutralizing pre-aspiration in precisely the same environment? If common sound patterns are the result of phonetically motivated sound change, then a starting point for a statistical model is the observation that sound patterns which can result directly from phonetically motivated sound change will be more common than ones which cannot, and those which have multiple sources in sound change will be more common than those with single sources. This starting point will allow us to account for the very high frequency of word-final devoicing in contrast to the high frequency of word-final de-aspiration, and the apparent absence of regular word-final voicing.

With diffusion and chance incapable of explaining the recurrent nature and high frequency of the sound patterns in (1)–(3), we are left to conclude that these patterns of laryngeal feature distribution are instances of shared inheritance or parallel evolution. A great many of the genetic relationships among the world's languages have been established by use of the comparative method. Widely agreed-upon genealogies exist for many language families, including Algonquian, Austronesian, Indo-European, Mayan, Niger-Congo, Semitic, and Sino-Tibetan, to name just a few. Given well-understood genetic relationships among languages, it is often possible to determine whether or not a particular sound pattern is the result of direct inheritance, or not. While many similar patterns of laryngeal feature distribution *are* the simple result of shared inheritance, a great many are not. Historical records of Sanskrit allow us to reconstruct ancient patterns of laryngeal feature distribution, and to see the extent to which these have been directly inherited by modern Indic languages like Gujarati and Punjabi. But for each case of direct inheritance, there are near-identical patterns of laryngeal feature distribution in an unrelated language or language family. Klamath, Korean, Dinka, and Wantoat were mentioned earlier. Genetic affiliations of Klamath and Korean are debated, but each language certainly qualifies as independent stock from any of the other languages with similar sound patterns. Dinka is a Nilotic (Nilo-Saharan) language of the Sudan, and Wantoat, a language of Morobe Province, Papua New Guinea, has been assigned to the Trans-New Guinea phylum. Similarities between Proto-Indo-European, Gujarati, and Punjabi might be the result of direct inheritance, but those between Indic, Klamath, Korean, Dinka, and Wantoat are not.

The strongest evidence for parallel evolution, however, are cases where it can be demonstrated that a particular sound pattern was not a feature of the mother tongue, and that it is the result of an innovation. The reconstruction of languages and language families has uncovered thousands of sound changes, which, when studied closely, provide the empirical base for parallel evolution as the source of common sound patterns. To take just one example, consider the common distribution of contrastive voicing summarized in (1). Lithuanian, an Indo-European language, allows voicing contrasts in obstruents before vowels and sonorants, but neutralizes these contrasts elsewhere. The same sound pattern has evolved independently within the Slavic, Germanic, and Italic subgroups of Indo-European. Within Italic, this pattern has evolved in Catalan, but not in French. Within West Germanic, the pattern has evolved in German, but not in English.[4] In sum, findings in historical linguistics present a wealth of evidence for parallel evolution in the world of sounds. Similar instances of phonetically based sound change occur in language after language. These sound changes are both the locus of phonetic explanation and the source of synchronic regularities in Evolutionary Phonology. It is to these sound changes that we now turn.

4.4 Explanations for patterns of laryngeal feature distribution

The general hypothesis of Evolutionary Phonology, and the one argued for throughout this book, is that parallel evolution is associated with phonetically based sound changes which recur with more than chance frequency due to inherent features of the human perceptual and articulatory system. The formal model of sound change proposed in 2.2 predicts that any sound change with sources in CHANGE, CHANCE, or CHOICE will give rise to sound patterns that are more frequent than those which do not have their sources in natural sound change. Common sound patterns will typically reflect common instances of sound change. In this section, the common patterns of laryngeal feature distribution in (1)–(3) are associated with common instances of sound change. The overarching generalization is that positions of contrast for a particular feature are those in which neutralizing sound change is unattested, while positions of neutralization are precisely those where phonetically motivated sound change is common.

4.4.1 Release features

Let us focus on the most significant generalizations which have emerged from the cross-linguistic study of laryngeal feature distribution, many of

---

[4] In fact, English dialects with word-final devoicing are reported. One case in Appalachian American English is discussed in 10.2.

them originally due to Steriade (1999a). One important generalization is that phonetic features timed with release have distributional patterns which are distinct from those timed with the onset of constriction or closure. A related generalization is that release features tend to be neutralized before obstruents and word-finally, while closure features tend to be neutralized after consonants and word-initially. In addition, there appears to be a significant tendency to devoice obstruents in word-final position, even in languages where voicing is primarily cued by segment-internal voicing or duration, as opposed to differences in voice onset time.

Why are release features like post-aspiration and ejection neutralized before obstruents and word-finally? Recall the discussion of variability in articulation in 2.2. There it was observed that stop–release is not distinctive in any attested spoken language. In some languages, like English, the release of word-final stops is optional. In other languages, like Marshallese, there is a strong tendency for final stops to be unreleased. In still other languages, like German, there is a strong tendency for final stops to be released. While a given language, dialect, or speech style may show a particular tendency for release or non-release of word-final stops, this phonetic feature is never contrastive. In fact, when careful speech is elicited, one often finds that non-released stops are released. In general, hyperarticulated speech may transform unreleased stops into released stops. In 2.5 I suggest that release as a distinctive phonological feature would be particularly nonaptive given the frequency of pre-vocalic contexts. Whatever the explanation, however, the fact remains that release is a variable feature of pronunciation for some sounds in nearly all well-described languages.

Now, consider how variability in release might give rise to the observed patterns of neutralization. There are many languages like Klamath, where distinct laryngeal series of stops are distinguished primarily in terms of release features. In Klamath, with plain voiceless, voiceless aspirated, and voiceless ejectives, voice onset time and burst quality appear to be the primary phonetic cues for the laryngeal contrast: plain stops differ from aspirated stops in VOT values, while ejectives differ from the other two series in possessing a glottal release which follows the oral release. Ejectives also carry longer VOTs than plain stops, and ejectives will typically differ from the aspirated stops in showing no formant structure following the moment of oral release. What happens to the three-way laryngeal contrast for oral stops when a word-final or pre-obstruent stop is unreleased? Without audible release, the primary phonetic cues for the three-way contrast are no longer perceptible, resulting in high probabilities of neutralizing sound change.

In this case, the phonetic source of sound change is two-fold involving CHOICE and CHANGE. First, there is the fact that, for all languages, the continuum of careful to casual speech allows for variation in the (audible) release versus non-release of consonants involving oral closure. If the frequency of unreleased variants is higher than that of released variants, these forms can become new norms of pronunciation – a simple and common case of CHOICE. For many segment types, like [m], release versus non-release may not result in any general increased instances of misperception. However, where laryngeal contrasts like those described for Klamath are involved, the absence of release will result in reduction of primary phonetic cues for laryngeal contrasts, with a greater likelihood of the unreleased stops being perceived by language learners as stops lacking aspiration or ejection. Note that the speaker may still be carrying out the same laryngeal timing sequence for the production of unreleased aspirates and ejectives; however, the absence of release will make these articulatory movements less perceptually salient, or even inaudible.

By expressing the relationship between non-release and neutralization in terms of sound change, a restricted phonetic typology is defined.[5] First, there will be languages which maintain a surface contrast between, e.g., plain obstruents and obstruents contrasting in laryngeal release features in final and pre-obstruent position. In these languages, by definition, stops will be audibly released. Languages of this type include Lushootseed (Urbanczyk 1995, 1996) and Bella Coola (Nater 1984), where ejectives and plain obstruents are contrastive in all positions, and there is audible release. Second, there will be languages in which neutralization of laryngeal release features occurs precisely in positions where obstruents are not released. A language of this type is the dialect of Bengali described by Kenstowicz (1994: 193), where aspiration and breathy voiced release are neutralized word-finally, and in pre-obstruent position, but obstruent voicing is maintained. A third type of language will reflect a *superficial* development from the Bengali stage to a subsequent one: neutralization patterns will reflect earlier non-release, but obstruents will be phonetically released. Klamath, as described by Barker (1963, 1964) reflects this language type. In this last case, the intrinsic variability of consonant release plays a role in rendering a once transparent relationship between phonological patterns and phonetic source translucent.[6]

---

[5] This typology may have practical applications. For example, in efforts to reconstruct the phonetics of Coahuilteco for the purposes of language revitalization, this typology has been useful. Ejectives clearly contrast with plain stops, but should they be produced as ejectives in pre-consonantal and final position or not? Troike (1996: 651) has discovered at least one example where an expected sequence of ejectives *p't'* is written as *pt'*, suggesting that Coahuilteco obstruents are not released in pre-consonantal position.

[6] This sort of translucency is problematic for Steriade's (1999a) account in which parallel phonetic and phonological phenomena are accounted for by the same constraints.

But what of the many other cases where neutralization in VC_1C_2V is to the laryngeal features of C_2? What phonetic fact explains the common pattern of regressive voice assimilation in obstruent clusters? As demonstrated by Raphael (1981) and Slis (1986) for voicing, there is a general perceptual preference for the cues present in stop bursts and C–V transitions to take precedence over those in the V–C transition, all else being equal. Viewed in this light, regressive voice assimilation involves a classic case of CHANGE: a sequence like [apda] is misperceived as [abda], resulting in regressive voice asssimilation. The same explanation can be given for assimilation in longer obstruent clusters, like the pattern found in Russian, where all obstruents take on the voicing feature of the last obstruent in the cluster.[7]

Finally, notice that this released-based account, originally due to Steriade (1999a), makes two predictions concerning voicing contrasts in stops versus fricatives, assuming that fricative voicing is typically cued by segment-internal noise (or duration) as opposed to release features. First, there are predicted to be languages in which stops undergo laryngeal neutralization due to non-release, but fricatives do not. This pattern is found in Turkish, where the voicing contrast for stops and affricates is neutralized word-finally and in pre-consonantal position, but the voicing contrast for fricatives is maintained in the same contexts. Second, across-the-board laryngeal neutralization of stops and fricatives under non-release is unexpected, unless laryngeal features of fricatives are specifically associated with release, an apparent cross-linguistic rarity.[8] This second prediction appears to be in conflict with the many languages which show consistent word-final devoicing of both stops and fricatives. In 4.4.4 I suggest an alternative pathway to final devoicing which predicts final devoicing of both stops and fricatives.

4.4.2   Closure features

If the absence of release can explain the most general features of laryngeal release feature distribution in (1), is there a mirror-image explanation for

---

[7] Work with chinchillas and quails shows evidence of categorical perception for voicing contrasts in oral stops (Kuhl and Miller 1978; Kluender, Diehl, and Killeen 1987). If their categories are based on similar perceptual features, chinchillas and quails should show the same tendencies in misperception, mistaking [apda] for [abda], and mistaking [abta] for [apta]. As far as I know, this prediction has not been tested.

[8] The segment types involved would be post-aspirated, ejective, or post-glottalized fricatives. Burmese has post-aspirated fricatives; ejective fricatives are found in Hausa and Tlingit; and post-glottalized fricatives are reported for Amharic and Yapese (Ladefoged and Maddieson 1996: 178–79; Demolin 2000; Maddieson 1998). In Tlingit, where consonants are typically audibly released in all positions, ejective fricatives occur in pre-consonantal and final position (Story and Naish 1973; Maddieson et al. 2001).

the distributional patterns of the closure features of pre-glottalization and pre-aspiration summarized in (2) and (3)? Before answering this question, it is important to recognize that these two cases have significant differences which cannot be ignored. First, though there are many languages where a contrast between plain and pre-aspirated obstruents is absent in word-initial position, there are few languages in which phonological alternations provide evidence of neutralization in precisely this position. Since, within Evolutionary Phonology, regular phonological alternations are often the fossilized reflexes of regular sound change, this gap is puzzling, and suggests that the absence of pre-aspirates in word-initial position may be partly independent of neutralizing sound change. On the other hand, similar alternations in unrelated Yurok and Yokuts suggest that the restriction of pre-glottalized sonorants to post-vocalic position may, at least in some languages, be the direct result of neutralizing sound change. Given these differences, this subsection will limit itself to potential sound changes resulting in common distributional patterns of pre-glottalization in (2). In 4.4.3 an additional factor is suggested in the cross-linguistic distribution of pre-aspirates, one which is independent of laryngeal neutralization.

If the primary cue for sonorant laryngealization in some languages is creak on a preceding vowel, or a glottal stop preceding sonorant modal voicing, then it is not surprising that in contexts where a preceding vowel is absent, neutralization occurs. Unlike the account of release features, there is no reference to variation in this account. In a language like Yurok (Robins 1958: 9), with a contrast between /w/ and /w'/, where /w'/ is phonetically realized as a glide with preceding creak or glottal closure, utterance initial [ʔw] can be easily misheard by the listener as [w]. In this context, primary phonetic cues of creakiness on a preceding vowel or the post-vocalic silent interval of the glottal stop are absent. Over time, we expect that word-initial glottalized sonorants in languages with consistent sonorant pre-glottalization will tend to neutralize to plain sonorants, based on the perception of these segments in phrase-initial and postconsonantal positions.[9]

Timing of laryngeal articulations relative to oral constriction is often reversed for obstruents and sonorants (Sapir 1938, Kingston 1985), with laryngeal events typically timed to peak at release for obstruents, but at onset of oral closure in sonorants. Along with these differences in timing,

---

[9] It would be of great value to study the frequency of single-word utterances or single-word phrases in child-directed speech. If more content words occur either phrase-initially or phrase-finally in child-directed speech than in non-child-directed speech, a child may be more likely to generalize from phrase-final to word-final context, or from phrase-initial to word-initial context on the basis of raw phonetic token frequency effects.

we find significant differences in distributional patterns. Neutralization of obstruent release features is determined by the phonetic context immediately following the obstruent, while neutralization of sonorant onset features is determined by the phonetic context immediately preceding the sonorant. In the case of obstruent release features, the overarching generalizations can be explained by the presence versus absence of consonant release. For pre-glottalized sonorants, seemingly significant cross-linguistic generalizations can be explained in terms of the presence versus absence of a preceding phonetic context facilitating the perception of creak or a silent glottal closure. In both cases, common sound changes are suggested which lead to common sound patterns: in the first case, the absence of release leads to neutralizing sound change for non-released stops; in the second case, regular sound change takes pre-glottalized sonorants to plain sonorants in phrase- or word-initial position.

4.4.3   The origins of obstruent pre-aspiration

Though pre-glottalization of sonorants and pre-aspiration of obstruents may both be classified as phonetic closure features, significant differences set them apart. Despite distributional constraints, there is little evidence from phonological alternations or the historical record suggesting neutralization of obstruent pre-aspiration in word-initial or post-consonantal position. In fact, a contrast between post-aspirated and unaspirated stops is found initially, in languages like Icelandic, Gaelic, Nukuoro, and West Futuna, suggesting that initial position is not a position of neutralization for the phonological contrast, but one where the contrast has a *distinct phonetic realization*. In all of these languages, pre-aspirates are realized as post-aspirates word-initially.

Another significant difference between pre-aspirates and post-aspirates involves duration. While languages with allophonic pre- and post-glottalized sonorants provide little evidence of consistent durational difference between these two segment types, pre-aspiration differs significantly from post-aspiration in terms of duration. Thráinsson (1978) notes for Icelandic that "pre-aspiration typically has a normal segment length in Icelandic, whereas postaspiration is much shorter . . . This suggests that pre-aspiration is not simply the inverse of postaspiration, as its name and some phonetic descriptions might lead us to believe."[10]

Both the distribution of pre-aspirates and their bisegmental durations in some languages suggest potential historical origins in geminates or

---

[10] The length associated with pre-aspiration in Icelandic is also found in Skye Gaelic, but not in Lewis Gaelic where pre-aspirates are as short as other stops (Ladefoged and Maddieson 1996: 72).

consonant clusters. Geminates and consonant clusters in many languages are absent word-initially, and word-finally, but present intervocalically (see chapters 5 and 7). Consonant clusters and geminates typically have longer durations than single segments, in the same way that pre-aspirated segments in languages like Icelandic are longer than their post-aspirated counterparts. It is possible, then, that some of the synchronic distributional constraints on pre-aspirates may reflect earlier distributional constraints on geminates or consonant clusters. An investigation of the history of obstruent pre-aspiration in a variety of genetically unrelated languages yields some support for this hypothesis (Blevins and Garrett 1993): in all cases where evidence is available, and where language contact is not involved, pre-aspirates seem to derive from earlier geminates or clusters. For example, in Lule Sami, pre-aspirates reflect medial geminates in other dialects, while in Cree, where pre-aspirates are found only after vowels, they are the result of a *CC > hC sound change (Bloomfield 1946: 88–90).[11]

4.4.4   Final devoicing

Some laryngeal features are cued by phonetic features internal to a segment. One case of this kind is the obstruent voicing contrast: in some languages, the primary cue for voiced (versus voiceless) stops is closure voicing and/or closure duration. While most languages combine segment-internal voicing and duration cues with differences in VOT, preceding vowel length, F_0 and F_1 values on adjacent vowels, and burst duration and amplitude, there are some languages like French, Catalan, and Thai where primary phonetic cues for the voicing contrast are closure voicing and closure duration. Since, in at least some languages, the cues for voicing are internal to the segment, and not aligned with stop release, presence versus absence of release should not result in neutralization of the voicing contrast. Nevertheless, we find that in languages like Catalan and Thai there is no voicing contrast for obstruents in word-final position. Assuming that the phonetic realization of voicing in these languages has been constant for some time, final devoicing cannot be attributed to the absence of release.

This finding should not be surprising since a purely release-based approach to final neutralization of voicing contrasts also makes the wrong predictions with respect to stops and fricatives. Under a purely

---

[11] In Ojibwe, clusters whose first member continues Proto-Algonquian *h, *x, *ʔ, or *θ are realized in some dialects as "fortis" or long stops *pp, kk, cc, tt* and in others as pre-aspirated stops.

release-based approach, word-final fricative devoicing is unexpected, since fricative voicing is cued by presence versus absence of noise during the fricative noise portion of the segment. And yet, many languages, including German and Russian, show devoicing of stops and fricatives word-finally. If release cues are not involved, what other phonetic factors might play a role in the evolution of word-final obstruent devoicing?

In Smith's (1997) detailed phonetic study of the devoicing of /z/ in American English, devoicing is found to be most common in two different contexts: first, where the fricative is followed by another voiceless consonant; and second, at the ends of words and phrases, and in unstressed syllables. Smith (1997) identifies two distinct causes of devoicing. In the first case there is glottal abduction, and transglottal airflow is insufficient for vocal-fold vibration. Glottal abduction occurs in anticipation of a glottal opening in a following voiceless sound, and also prepausally. A reduced glottal abduction gesture may also occur in contexts of reduction. These findings are consistent with the common devoicing of final unstressed vowels in many languages (see 8.2.1), as well as the offglides to voicelessness which, for example, are possible after all Klamath word-final segments (Blevins 1993a). A second cause of devoicing identified by Smith is when the transglottal pressure differential is too small to allow voicing. This study suggests then that there are quantifiable articulatory and aerodynamic factors which may lead to obstruent devoicing preceding other voiceless obstruents, and obstruent devoicing phrase-finally. In the current model of sound change, these articulatory and aerodynamic factors, in particular those which result in word- and phrase-final devoicing, shape the set of phonetic variants from which learners must choose to model their own sound system. Smith's (1997) study, then, suggests a phonetic source of devoiced final obstruents (and sonorants) for sound change with sources in CHOICE which is independent of release features.

An additional potential phonetic source for cross-linguistic word-final obstruent devoicing is also independent of closure and release cues and non-assimilatory in nature.[12] In many languages, a phrase-final syllable is longer in duration than a segmentally identical phrase-medial syllable (Klatt 1975; Wightman et al. 1992; Fougeron and Keating 1997). Phrase-final or pre-pausal lengthening can often result in segments which are two to three times longer than their non-lengthened counterparts. In some languages, like Modern Hebrew (Berkovits 1993), final lengthening has the greatest effect on final plosives and fricatives. In addition, as noted first by Catford (1977), there is a near universal association between

---

[12] I thank John Ohala for his comments on early versions of this hypothesis.

consonant duration and voicing: in obstruents, voiced obstruents are shorter than their voiceless counterparts. Together, these two observations suggest that phrase-final lengthening is one phonetic source of word-final obstruent devoicing, and that perceptual and articulatory factors may both be involved.

If phrase-final lengthening results in lengthening of closure duration, obstruent voicing can be inhibited.[13] The standard explanation for the association between length and voicelessness is aerodynamic: when the vocal folds are in the position for modal voicing, soon after obstruent closure, voicing ceases due to the supralaryngeal pressure resulting from the oral closure if no other strategies (e.g. relaxation of oral soft tissue, tongue root advancement, jaw lowering, etc.) are made use of to sustain vocal-fold vibration. In addition, longer stop duration can contribute to a percept of voicelessness, since voiceless stops are typically longer than their voiced counterparts, or have lower V-to-C durational ratios than their voiced counterparts (e.g Kohler 1979). A working hypothesis then is that due to common phrase-final lengthening, phrase-final consonants may be lengthened. As a result of this lengthening, two things may happen: voicing may be inhibited as a result of prolonged closure duration; or final lengthened voiced obstruents may come to have durations not unlike voiceless obstruents in non-final position, and be misperceived as voiceless. Either factor could result in a listener categorizing a word-final voiced obstruent as voiceless.

The proposed analysis has neither of the weaknesses of the purely release-based approach outlined above. In languages like French, Catalan, and Thai where primary phonetic cues for the voicing contrast are closure voicing and closure duration, final devoicing can evolve through phrase-final lengthening. In addition, such devoicing should affect both stops and fricatives, since there is no association between devoicing and absence of release. Another welcome result of separate phonetic accounts of general final devoicing and neutralization of release features is that it allows for loss of features like breathy voice under non-release, without neutralization of final voicing. This is precisely the pattern observed in some dialects of Bengali (Kenstowicz 1994: 193), where the word-final contrast between T^h, T, $D^ɦ$, D is neutralized to T versus D, with loss of release features, but no loss of the voicing contrast. Another prediction of a model in which final devoicing is an aerodynamic consequence of final lengthening is that phonetic devoicing will be most common in velar consonants, less common in coronal consonants, and less

---

[13] This is related to the findings of Klingenheben (1927), Jaeger (1978), and Ohala (1983b, 1994a) that geminates tend to be voiceless.

common still in labial consonants (Ohala 1983a). Where final devoicing has been captured in its earliest stages, there is evidence for this pattern. In Tonkawa, word-final *g* is devoiced to [k], but *b, d* are not (Hoijer 1933: 4). In Frisian, where final devoicing of *b, d, g* is of recent origin, Tiersma (1985: 30) reports early studies of the language of Grou by Eijkman (1907) where *b* and *d*, in contrast to *g*, are still voiced. Another implication of the final-lengthening account, also illustrated by Frisian, regards vowel-length effects. If phrase-final lengthening results in generally longer syllables, and if a language already has a long versus short vowel contrast in final syllables preceding voiced stops, then phrase-final lengthening may, in some languages, have a greater effect on consonants following long vowels than short vowels, due to upper limits on the length of sonorant portions of the syllable rime. In Sipma's (1913) grammar of Frisian, there are signs that devoicing has started to take place. Though his transcriptions are not entirely consistent, they suggest that devoicing took place first after long vowels, falling diphthongs, and liquids, and only later after short vowels or rising diphthongs (Tiersma 1985: 30).

At the same time, the suggestion that phrase-final lengthening may play a role in final devoicing is not meant to rule out other phonetically based sound changes which may result in convergent sound patterns. If final lengthening and final non-release both play a role in neutralization of voicing contrasts, this neutralization is expected to be more common than final neutralization of aspiration or ejection, which occurs only under non-release. This explanation is also not meant to rule out other potential factors, such as those noted by Smith (1997). Vocal-cord abduction in pre-pausal position is not uncommon. However, in languages where this occurs and appears to be phonologized (e.g. Klamath), both obstruents and sonorants are followed by audible voicelessness word-finally.[14]

4.4.5   Common cases of sound change

In (4) sound changes giving rise to some of the common patterns of laryngeal feature distribution in (1)–(3) are classified and summarized.

---

[14] Baudouin (1895/1972: 209–10) was perhaps the first linguist to explicitly note that sound changes like final devoicing not only occur in mature linguistic systems, but that they also independently arise in the course of language acquisition. Stampe (1969) refers to similar sound patterns in child-language development as "phonological processes," and suggests that they are part of universal strategies used in the course of language acquisition. However, see 9.1.4, where most aspects of sound patterns during early stages of language acquisition are argued to be due to maturational constraints on production. In child-language phonology, neutralization of voicing contrasts is found word-initially as well as word-finally, supporting this general view.

(4)   Some sound changes resulting in recurrent patterns of
       laryngeal feature distribution

Sound change	Type	Phonetic basis
i. $T^h > T^{\urcorner}$, $T' > T^{\urcorner}, D > T^{\urcorner}$	CHOICE + CHANGE	i. variation provides released and unreleased tokens of stops, with unreleased tokens most common in certain positions (finally, pre-consonantally); ii. If a stop is unreleased, laryngeal features typically associated with release can be absent, or misperceived as being absent.
ii. $'R > R/ X\_$ (X not a vowel)	CHANGE	Sonorant pre-glottalization is cued by vowel shift from modal voicing to creak or glottal stop. When vowel is absent, pre-glottalization is commonly misperceived as being absent.
iii. $[-son] >$ $[-voiced] / \_ //$	CHOICE + CHANGE	i. General phrase-final lengthening results in lengthened final consonants; if these variants are taken as basic, sound change can result. ii. Lengthening may inhibit obstruent voicing directly, or lengthened tokens may be may interpreted as voiceless, since voiceless consonants are typically longer than voiced ones.
iv. $T_i T_i > {}^h T$, $T_i T_i > C^h$	CHOICE	Variation in timing of oral and laryngeal gestures can give rise to voiceless geminates produced as pre- or post-aspirated stops. Distribution of resulting aspirates will be identical to original distribution of geminates.

The sound changes proposed in (4i) involve a shift from released to unreleased consonants, and associated neutralizations of release features. The typical contexts for these changes are phrase-final position, word-final position, and pre-obstruent position; less commonly release is lost before other consonants. The changes in (4i) are unattested in pre-vocalic position within the word, since in this context consonants are released. Sound changes like those in (4i) are common because presence versus absence of release can be highly variable across time, speakers, and utterances. Final release may be common in hyperarticulated speech, but may be absent elsewhere.

In (4ii), pre-glottalized sonorants are misheard as plain voiced sonorants when a preceding vowel is absent. This sound change has been phonologized in languages like Yurok, giving rise to alternations, but the same sound change may also account for the limited distribution of glottalized sonorants in languages like Yokuts and Shuswap.

The final devoicing sound change in (4iii) is well documented cross-linguistically, and appears to have multiple sources. By relating this sound change to final lengthening, it is entirely independent of stop release. This is a welcome result since obstruent devoicing in many languages applies to both stops and fricatives, and occurs in languages where voicing is cued by segment-internal features like closure duration and closure voicing. In addition, the possibility of final-stop devoicing via non-release and final lengthening suggests that final-stop devoicing will be more widespread than other types of laryngeal neutralizations, since it has multiple sources. This appears to be the case.

In (4iv), the distribution of pre-aspirates is accounted for, in part, by the reanalysis of geminate obstruents as pre-aspirates. Under this account, distributional constraints on pre-aspiration may be directly inherited, and reflect earlier constraints on the distribution of geminates.

4.5   Exceptional patterns of laryngeal feature distribution

4.5.1   Final voicing

The phonetic-historical explanations proposed above for common patterns of laryngeal feature distribution are also meant to explain the absence or uncommon occurrence of other patterns. Certain patterns of laryngeal feature distribution will be unattested, or extremely rare, since common sound changes will not give rise to them, and other common sound changes will eliminate them. Above, final-obstruent devoicing is suggested as the convergence of at least three independently attested types of sound change: CHANGE based on the common misperception of unreleased consonants as plain voiceless consonants; CHANGE/CHOICE based on phrase-final laryngeal spreading gestures; and CHANGE/ CHOICE based on final lengthening of obstruents which can result in voicelessness or percepts of voicelessness. Together, these three factors are claimed to account for the high frequency of word-final obstruent devoicing cross-linguistically. But these same factors will render other patterns, like final voicing, rare or infrequent.

Natural sound changes giving rise to obstruent voicing are of two basic types: assimilation to a neighboring voiced consonant; or gestural reduction in lenition contexts, with spontaneous voicing or a percept of voicing, as a potential consequence.[15] Since word-final VC# contexts do not provide a natural context for voice assimilation to a neighboring consonant, the only natural source of final voicing for VC# is lenition. However, cross-linguistic surveys of lenition show that voicing is common only in intervocalic contexts (LaVoie 2001: 31–32). In short, there is no single natural sound change which will give rise to sound patterns involving word-final voicing. At the same time, if such a pattern were to arise, either through rule telescoping, analogy, or by chance, the same factors which account for the widespread occurrence of final devoicing would play a role in speeding the decay of the final-voicing pattern. Unsurprisingly, then, there are very few cases of word-final voicing reported in the literature.

Three cases within Austronesian are reported by the same author, and are therefore somewhat suspect. Kähler (1946/1949, 1960), as reported by Robert Blust (personal communication, 2001), transcribes only final voiced stops in two dialects of Malay, though elsewhere (e.g. word-initially and medially) he records a voicing contrast. However, the consistency of Kähler's transcriptions across these three languages, and his mention that final stops are unreleased, suggest that his voiced stop symbols have been used to transcribe precisely the same neutralized segments found in Standard Malay, or languages more distantly related to Simalur. All of these languages have undergone neutralization of final *-b, *-d, *-g to voiceless (unreleased) -p, -t, -k.

Breton (Ternes 1970) has essentially the same distribution of voicing as Lithuanian, with one complication. As in Lithuanian, voicing is contrastive before sonorants, but elsewhere contrasts are neutralized. The difference between Breton and Lithuanian is that in Lithuanian word-final obstruents are voiceless, while in Breton they are voiceless, except

---

[15] In this second case, voicing is often associated with other phonetic features of lenited segments, including shortening of closure duration, reduction of intraoral air pressure, or a shift from stop to continuant. See LaVoie (2001) for many examples.

when a vowel-initial word follows within the phrase, in which case they are voiced. Since, in Breton, word-final obstruents are always devoiced in phrase-final position, or when followed by a consonant, it would seem inappropriate to treat this as an instance of general word-final voicing. Rather, voicing of the word-final segment is an instance of intervocalic lenition at the phrasal level.[16]

Lezgian, a Nakh-Daghestanian language, has a limited set of alternations which suggest final-obstruent voicing through telescoping and rule inversion (Yu 2001). Lezgian has a four-way laryngeal contrast between ejectives, voiceless aspirated stops, voiced stops, and voiceless unaspirated stops. In certain monosyllabic nouns, a plain voiceless stop in pre-vocalic position alternates with a voiced stop in word-final position: *pab/pap-a* 'wife,' *pad/pat-ar* 'side,' *mez/mets-i* 'tongue,' etc. This alternation is not found in polysyllabic unsuffixed nouns, or in other lexical categories. Yu (2001) suggests that these synchronic alternations reflect a historical sequence of intervocalic pre-tonic gemination, where geminates were voiceless, followed by degemination, and rule inversion. Synchronic final voicing in Lezgian, then, appears to reflect historical medial devoicing.

What Breton, its hypothetical descendants, and Lezgian are meant to illustrate is that word-final voicing is not ruled out within Evolutionary Phonology. It is not ruled out as a general sound pattern, and it is not ruled out as the output of a limited set of phonological alternations. Rather, the common sound changes which make word-final devoicing common will make sound patterns limiting final obstruents to voiced ones uncommon. Since exceptionless patterns of word-final voicing will never be the direct transparent result of a phonetically motivated sound change, they are predicted to be less common than patterns of final devoicing. Their rarity follows not from any intrinsic property of synchronic grammars, but from contingent facts about the world.

4.5.2   Initial devoicing

Another rare and unexpected laryngeal feature pattern is word-initial obstruent devoicing. Word-final obstruent devoicing is attributed both to the absence of release and to phrase-final lengthening. Since word-initial pre-vocalic position is a context where obstruents are consistently released, devoicing with the same phonetic source is unexpected. However, phrase-initial strengthening is well documented (Fougeron and Keating 1997; Fougeron 1999). While the effects of phrase-final

---

[16] The French of Quimper has borrowed the word-final devoicing rule from Breton, but not the phrasal rule of intervocalic voicing.

lengthening on consonant length seem more extreme, it is possible that the few reported cases of word-initial devoicing have their origins in phrase-initial lengthening. These include Somali (Armstrong 1934), with devoicing of all voiced stops, and Pennsylvania German, with initial devoicing of /b/ to [p]. In these cases, initial lengthening may inhibit obstruent voicing, or simply give rise to the percept of voicelessness.

In Chamic (Thurgood 1999: 72–73), reflexes of Proto-Chamic word-initial breathy voiced stops have undergone neutralization to voiceless stops when the following syllable begins with a voiceless stop. Where the following syllable begins with a sonorant, breathy voiced stops are maintained initially. And where the following syllable begins with a voiced obstruent, there is maintenance of breathy voicing in Northern Roglai, loss of voicing in Chru and Phan Rang Cham, and variable maintenance of breathy voice in Jarai, and Western Cham. In reflexes of Proto-Chamic monosyllables, voicing is maintained word-initially. Within Chamic, the disyllabic domain is divided into a pre-syllable and main syllable. The pre-syllable is short and unstressed, while the main syllable is longer and stressed. Initial devoicing is limited to pre-syllables, and is conditioned by the laryngeal features of the onset of the main syllable. This then, is not a case of general word-initial devoicing, but a case of obstruent voice assimilation across a short unstressed vowel.

Another pattern which might be erroneously classified as word-initial devoicing is typical of those Pama-Nyungan languages which have only a single laryngeal series of obstruents, and prohibit word-final obstruents. In these languages, obstruents occur either word-initially or between sonorants (intervocalically, or after a sonorant consonant and before a vowel). Nearly all languages with these phonotactics have the same pattern of obstruent voicing: oral stops are voiceless word-initially, but tend to be voiced medially. This is the pattern found, for example, in Panyjima (Dench 1991: 130). This distribution of stop allophones is a consequence of simple intersonorant lenition.

4.6 Summary

In this chapter the most common patterns of laryngeal feature distribution in the world's languages have been attributed to common types of sound change. Certain patterns of laryngeal feature distribution reflect the fact that laryngeal features of obstruents are more perceptually salient in certain contexts than in others. In contexts in which these features are less salient, neutralizing sound changes may occur, and it is these sound changes which are reflected in the most common distributional patterns of laryngeal features. The same phonetic contexts of perceptual saliency define triggers in rules of laryngeal feature assimilation. Phrase-final lengthening as well as the association between phonation types and prosodic boundaries may also play a role in the common process of word-final devoicing.

At the same time, uncommon patterns of laryngeal feature distribution can also be explained in terms of sound change. Final voicing is rare not only because sound changes giving rise to final devoicing are common, but also because there is no single phonetically motivated sound change whose immediate output will give rise to this pattern. Rule inversion and rule telescoping may give rise to patterns of final obstruent voicing, suggesting that the rarity of such patterns does not follow from universal markedness constraints.

Within Evolutionary Phonology, the relationship demonstrated by Steriade (1999a) between positions of laryngeal feature neutralization and phonetic cues for laryngeal features are accounted for by positing phonetically based sound changes with sources in CHANGE, CHANCE, and CHOICE. These sound changes give rise to synchronic sound patterns with similar characteristics, but allow synchronic phonological systems to remain free of reference to phonetic features, and to diverge dramatically from phonetically natural sound patterns when rule inversion, rule telescoping, analogy, or language contact are involved.

5   Place features

Certain typical mechanical tendencies there are (e.g. nb > mb or –az >
-as or tya > tša), but a complete theory of sound change has to take
constant account of the orientation of sounds in our sense.

Sapir (1925)

5.1   Phonological place features

In this chapter, characteristic patterns of consonantal place feature distribution are investigated.[1] Place features of consonants are those which
typically characterize the active articulators involved in consonantal constriction, and the acoustic and perceptual features associated with movements of these articulators. The classification of sounds in terms of place
of articulation is as old as the field of linguistics itself. References to labial
versus lingual articulations are found in the work of the Indic grammarians dating back to 500 BC, and the Korean writing system *hankul* devised
by King Sejong has a distinct symbol for each major point of articulation.
The International Phonetic Alphabet is organized with columns indicating place of articulation and every phonological feature system has some
way of distinguishing sounds produced by the lips from those produced
by the tongue blade or the tongue body.

Major or primary place features are those which distinguish the major
points of articulation, distinguishing labial, coronal and dorsal sounds.
For the purposes of describing place contrasts in phonological segment

---

[1] In addition to those mentioned explicitly in the text below, languages on which generalizations are based include those already mentioned in chapter 4 (see footnote 1), and
the following 47 languages from 10 distinct families: Japanese; Italian, Gujarati (Indo-
Aryan/I-E); Koya (Dravidian); Finnish (Finno-Ugric); Eskimo; Ubykh (Caucasian);
Proto-Pama-Nyungan, Nhanda, Wajarri, Pintupi/Luritja, Arrernte, Alyawarre, Kaytetye,
Mbabaram, Djinang (Pama-Nyungan); Selayar, Konjo, Makasar, Bugis, Uma, Minangk-
abau, Sa'ban, Kelabit, Totoli, Talaud, Ratahan, Duri, Wolio, Acehnese, Toba Batak, Leti,
Woleaian, Saipan Carolinian, Ponapean, Manam, Tuvaluan, Kapingamarangi, Mussau,
Dobel (Austronesian); Middle Chinese, Ningde, Fuzhou, Old Mandarin, Peking, Ling-
bao (Chinese); Diola Fogny (West Atlantic/Niger-Congo).

inventories, at least three phonological features appear necessary to distinguish the major points of articulation. These are often labelled as [labial], [coronal], and [dorsal], referring to the lips, front of the tongue and back of the tongue respectively.[2] Within each major articulator class, secondary or minor articulations are distinguished. Within the class of labial sounds, bilabials can be distinguished from labio-dentals; within the class of coronals, contrasts exist between retroflex and non-retroflex sounds, and between apicals and laminals; and for dorsals, contrasts between velars and uvulars are not uncommon. For all major places, secondary features of labialization, palatalization, velarization, and pharyngealization can be superimposed on primary articulations. A class feature [PLACE] is used to refer to all place features, when necessary.

Most of the analyses proposed in this and subsequent chapters can be translated into other categorical feature systems, and depend only on some way of representing contrastive place, distinguishing primary place features from secondary ones, and having some way of referring to the class of place features as a whole. As noted in chapter 4, phonological features are distinct from gradient phonetic properties, and can reflect categories which have multiple distinct phonetic instantiations or cues. No reference is made to non-contrastive features (e.g. the release of stops, the precise degree of linguo-palatal contact, etc.) in phonological analyses, though these phonetic features play an important role in the CCC-model of sound change.

5.2   Recurrent patterns of place feature distribution

The distribution of distinctive place features on consonants is severely limited in many languages. Major place contrasts for stops are often limited to certain positions, while distinct distributional constraints are found for nasal stops, and for retroflex/non-retroflex contrasts. As documented by Jun (1995a, b), Steriade (1998), and Blevins (2003a), there is general similarity across languages with respect to: (i) the neutralizing feature or features; (ii) the positions in which neutralization occurs; (iii) the direction of neutralization; and (iv) distinct neutralization patterns for major place features and secondary release features, in contrast to, for example, retroflexion (Steriade 1998).

In (1)–(4) I summarize some of these recurrent patterns with respect to their phonetic status as release features, realized at consonant release, or closure features, realized at the onset of consonant closure.

---

[2] Here I do not discuss pharyngeals, which rarely occur as stop consonants, or glottal stop, which lacks specification for the supraglottal place features discussed in this chapter.

(1)   Release feature pattern: major place contrasts for oral stops
       (i) PHONETIC FEATURES: various, but salient in CV
           transition
       (ii) PHONOLOGICAL FEATURES: [labial], [coronal], [dorsal]
            (for [−continuants])
       (iii) COMMON POSITIONS OF CONTRAST: before sonorants
       (iv) COMMON POSITIONS OF NEUTRALIZATION: before
            stops, word-finally
        (v) COMMON DIRECTION OF NEUTRALIZATION:
            a. Word-finally: to ʔ
            b. In stop clusters: the result of regressive assimilation

(2)   Release feature pattern: major place contrasts for nasal stops
       (i) PHONETIC FEATURES: various, but salient in CV
           transition
       (ii) PHONOLOGICAL FEATURES: [labial], [coronal], [dorsal]
       (iii) COMMON POSITIONS OF CONTRAST: before sonorants
       (iv) COMMON POSITIONS OF NEUTRALIZATION: before
            stops, word-finally
        (v) COMMON DIRECTION OF NEUTRALIZATION:
            a. Word-finally: to N, a nasal glide, or ŋ
            b. in stop clusters: the result of regressive assimilation

(3)   Release feature pattern: secondary place contrasts for stops
       (i) PHONETIC FEATURES: various, but salient in CV
           transition
       (ii) PHONOLOGICAL FEATURES: [round], [high], [back], etc.
       (iii) COMMON POSITIONS OF CONTRAST: before sonorants
       (iv) COMMON POSITIONS OF NEUTRALIZATION: before
            stops, word-finally
        (v) COMMON DIRECTION OF NEUTRALIZATION: to plain
            stop

(4)   Closure feature pattern: coronal retroflexion
       (i) PHONETIC FEATURES: various, but salient in VC
           transition
       (ii) PHONOLOGICAL FEATURES: [±anterior] for [coronal,
            apical]
       (iii) COMMON POSITIONS OF CONTRAST: after vowels
       (iv) COMMON POSITIONS OF NEUTRALIZATION: after
            consonants, word-initially
        (v) COMMON DIRECTION OF NEUTRALIZATION:
            neutralization is
            a. initially, to a segment phonologically unspecified for
               [anterior]
            b. in stop clusters, the result of progressive assimilation

The general patterns of neutralization summarized in (1)–(4) are supported by the study of phonetic variation, phonological alternations, and sound change. For example, the neutralization of major place features before stops and associated regressive place assimilation is a common feature of coarticulatory patterns, phonological analyses, and diachronic developments. An English speaker says *hatpin*, with verifiable closure between the tongue-tip and the alveolar ridge for the [t], but there is no sign of this closure (or subsequent release) in the acoustic record, where the labial closure for [p] precedes and hides the [t] gesture (Browman and Goldstein 1990; Byrd 1996). Synchronic rules of regressive place assimilation are extremely common, and occur in almost every major language family which has stop clusters. In Manam (Lichtenberk 1983), where, nasal place features are contrastive only before vowels, alternations involving the first-person-singular irrealis prefix /m-/ suggest a synchronic rule of regressive place assimilation (2vb): compare *m-eno* 'I will sleep,' *m-panana* 'I will run,' and *m-mua* 'I will go first,' with *n-doʔi* 'I will take them,' *ŋ-gelea* 'I will shave,' *N-qozomi* 'I will husk it,' *n-nanari* 'I will tell a story,' and *ŋ-ŋara* 'I will swim.' In the historical record parallel sound changes are common. An attested case of historical place neutralization (1vb) is the regressive assimilation in the development from Latin to Italian: *octo* > *otto* 'eight,' *noctem* > *notte* 'night,' *factum* > *fatto* 'done,' *septem* > *sette* 'seven,' etc.

Where secondary features of palatalization, labialization, or velarization are timed with consonant release (3), word-final and pre-obstruent neutralization to the unpalatalized, unlabialized, or unvelarized member of the series may occur. Ladefoged and Maddieson (1996: 357) note that "labialization is typically concentrated on the release phase of the primary articulation that it accompanies . . . and in many languages with labialized consonants the set of syllable-final consonants, if any, does not include labialized ones." In Mbabaram, with contrasting m, $ṇ$, $ɲ$, n, n^w, $ŋ$, all nasals are found word-initially before a vowel, and all except n^w are found word-finally. Another unrelated language with a similar pattern is Gilbertese. In Gilbertese with contrastive nasals m, n, $ŋ$, m^y, nasals are the only possible syllable codas. Word-finally and pre-consonantally, the contrast between m and m^y is neutralized to [m].

In contrast, the most common restriction on contrastive retroflexion is its limitation to post-vocalic position (4). This is documented by Dixon (1980), Hamilton (1995), and Steriade (1998) for the majority of Australian languages, and by Steriade (1998) for many Dravidian and Indic languages as well. To take just one example, in Pintupi, apical contrasts are found intervocalically: *kana* 'alive' versus *kaṇa* 'spear type'; *mina* 'grass sponge' versus *miṇa* 'arm, branch'; *mutu* 'hitting stick' versus *muṯu* 'short'; *ŋunti* 'unreal, make-believe' versus *ŋunṯi* 'nape of neck.' However, word-initially Pintupi has no contrast between the two apical series of stops.

The emergent patterns of place feature distribution summarized in (1)–(4) do not appear to be the result of chance occurrences. Word-final neutralization of major place features is common, while word-initial neutralization of the same features is unattested. At the same time, word-initial neutralization of the retroflex contrast is attested, while (post-vocalic) word-final neutralization of coronal retroflexion is not. As with the patterns of laryngeal feature distribution examined in chapter 4, the significance of these distinct patterns of contrast and neutralization cannot be over-stated. Phonological features show distinct patterns of distribution which appear to be dependent, at least in part, on their phonetic content and realization.

Synchronic patterns appear to reflect phonetic properties of speech, and yet, direct reference to these phonetic properties is illicit within properly constrained phonological systems. Both progressive and regressive assimilation are attested in the world's languages, and phonological systems must be able to express both rule types. A question for phonological theory is why regressive assimilation is so common for major place features, while progressive assimilation is the norm for apical place contrasts. By documenting how these assimilatory patterns can arise through phonetically based sound change, the answer to this question is circumscribed to the diachronic domain. The "typical mechanical tendencies" noted by Sapir at the beginning of this chapter are just that. There is no need to build the consequences of such tendencies into synchronic grammars, since they naturally emerge via regular sound change as language is passed from one generation to the next.

5.3   Explanations for patterns of place feature distribution

5.3.1   Release features

The phonetic explanation of the convergent distribution of major place features for oral and nasal stops is similar to that proposed for the distribution of laryngeal release features. Major place features [labial], [coronal], and [dorsal], define contrasts between labial, coronal, and velar stops. These contrasts are most perceptually salient in environments where the stop is released, and in particular, where it is released into a following vowel. In an early perception study, final unreleased stops were commonly misidentified by English speakers (Householder 1956). Other early results demonstrate the importance of C–V transitions in identifying major place contrasts by showing release cues are normally powerful enough to override other place cues in the V–C transition phase of a stop (Malécot 1958; Wang 1959). More recent findings demonstrate that in a VCV string, perceptual cues present in the C–V transition far outweigh VC cues in identification of major place features (Repp 1977, 1978; Fujimura et al. 1978; Ohala 1990b). As Ohala (1990b) observes, in VC_1C_2V sequences where the C_2V and VC_1 transitions provide conflicting information for place of articulation, it is the C_2V transitions that play the primary role in the identification of place. The implication is that burst properties (amplitude, spectral shape, multiple bursts), VOT and formant onsets and transitions at stop release are the most important phonetic cues for major place of articulation in oral stops, while formant onset and transitions values are primary in the perception of nasal place features. In sum, an essential factor in the correct perception of place of articulation is the presence of C–V transitions which provide salient phonetic cues to stop place. Where an oral stop is unreleased, or where a stop is not followed by a vowel, place features are less perceptually salient, and more likely to be misperceived.

Given this background, we are in a position to understand certain aspects of the patterns summarized in (1)–(3). Major place of articulation shows the pattern of distribution in (3) because place cues are strongest in pre-vocalic position, and successively weaker as pre-vocalic (or pre-sonorant) contexts are lost. In final position, where stops may be unreleased, place is more likely to be misidentified than in pre-vocalic contexts. And in VC_1C_2V contexts, the greater strength of place cues for C_2 may lead to a percept of homorganicity (Ohala 1990b). Sound change involving regressive place assimilation in intervocalic clusters is a proto-typical instance of CHANGE: a speaker says [anpa], but the listener hears [ampa]; a speaker says [apka] but the listener hears [akka] (Ohala 1981, 1985, 1990b, 1993). The same explanation can be extended straight-forwardly to secondary place feature patterns summarized in (3), when features like labialization, palatalization, and velarization are aligned with consonant release.

However, there appear to be significant differences between patterns of final neutralization for oral stops and nasals, as summarized in (1) and (2). Final oral stops are most commonly neutralized not to a single point of articulation, but to laryngeal glides. On the other hand, final nasal stops are often neutralized to the velar nasal or a velar glide. Explanations for these differences are suggested in 5.3.3.

Before turning to patterns involving coronal retroflexion, note that an alternative phonetic explanation for assimilation in CC clusters is not perceptual, but articulatory. Common gestural overlap between adjacent consonants in casual speech may result in a percept of assimilation, even when both articulatory gestures are present (Browman and Goldstein 1990, 1992). Gestures may be hidden when their starting and ending points overlap with pre-existing independent gestures by different articulators. For example, in the phrase *hundred pounds*, perceived as *hundre*[bp]*ounds*, the coronal gesture for /d/ may be hidden by a longer labial gesture, whose closure precedes the coronal closure, and whose release follows the coronal release. Hidden gestures of this sort are recoverable from X-ray data and palatography, though they may be altogether absent in the acoustic record.

While gestural overlap may *contribute* to the general cross-lingusitic pattern of regressive major place assimilation, it is unlikely to be the primary phonetic source of this sound change. In languages where gestural overlap occurs, there are recurrent asymmetries. For example, alveolar stops assimilate to labials and velars more often than the reverse (Gimson 1962; Brown 1977; Blust 1979). Compare casual English *foo*[pp]*rint* (*footprint*) or *sui*[kk]*ase* (*suitcase*) with unattested *ri[tt]*ide* (*riptide*) or *co[tt]*ail* (*cocktail*) (Blust 1979: 103). However, many of the well-documented sound changes involving total regressive place assimilation, like the Italic and Manam examples mentioned earlier, are not sensitive to articulatory differences of the consonants involved.

5.3.2   Closure features

A mirror-image explanation is possible for the patterns of place distribution for contrastive retroflexion summarized in (4) (Steriade 1998). Examination of formant transitions into and out of the apical stops in languages with retroflex versus non-retroflex contrasts shows that this contrast is strongly cued by the formant values of V–C transitions. For example, in Gujarati (Dave 1977) and a number of Australian Aboriginal languages (Butcher, in progress) vowel formants preceding retroflex stops show significant lowering of F3 and F4, whereas non-retroflex sounds do not show this lowering. In these same studies, formant values at stop release are not significantly different for the retroflex and non-retroflex series. Anderson (1997) excised V–C transitions from speech segments in Western Arrernte, an Australian language with an apical contrast, and measured perceptual confusion rates among different points of articulation. She found that listeners correctly identified apicals less than 35 percent of the time, while all other points of articulation (labial, velar, lamino-dental, lamino-palatal) were identified correctly over 85 percent of the time.

Contrastive retroflexion shows the pattern of distribution in (4) then because cues for retroflexion are strongest in post-vocalic position, and successively weaker as pre-vocalic (or pre-sonorant) contexts are lost. In non-post-vocalic positions, cues present in the V–C transition are absent. Confusion rates between apicals are higher, and neutralizing instances of CHANGE are more likely. In initial position, where there is no preceding vowel, retroflexes are more likely to be misidentified as non-retroflexes, and *vice versa*, than in post-vocalic contexts. In VC_1C_2V contexts where both Cs are coronal apicals, the greater strength of place cues for C_1 leads to a percept of homorganicity for the entire cluster. In this context the VC_1 transition will dominate the percept, providing place cues for the entire apical cluster. This is the mirror-image of major place assimilation, where C–V transition cues dominate in the perception of contrasts. Sound change involving progressive place assimilation of this type is another prototypical instance of CHANGE: a speaker says [aṇta], but the listener hears [aṇṭa]. Synchronic alternations reflecting this sound change are described for many languages (Steriade 1998), and include retroflexion of the locative suffix /-ta/ in Kalkatungu, when preceded by a retroflex consonant (Blake 1979).

5.3.3   Final place neutralization

There are significant differences between patterns of final neutralization for oral stops and nasals. Where place neutralization occurs for oral stops *p, t, k*, it often involves neutralization to a laryngeal glide, ʔ, which lacks place features. In contrast, where final *m, n, ŋ* are involved, final place neutralization is commonly to the velar nasal. The different patterns are visible in table 5.1, where reflections of Middle Chinese final consonants are shown for five different daughter languages. Where oral place contrasts are neutralized to glottal stop in Fuzhou, nasal contrasts are neutralized to the velar nasal.

Since V–C transitions for *p, t, k* differ from those for ʔ, the origins for this type of neutralization are more likely to be found in aspects of articulation than perception.[3] I suggest that, as natural sound changes, these be viewed as instances of debuccalization: a stop with laryngeal constriction is either produced without oral stricture, due to lenition of the oral gesture, or, the same stop is produced with anticipation of the laryngeal gesture giving rise to a glottal stop percept. In the first case, CHOICE

---

[3] Significant silent closure interval is a shared percept of *p, t, k* and ʔ. However, if this percept is taken to be the primary source of neutralization, then it is difficult to explain a preference for ʔ over *p, t,* or *k*, in such changes.

Table 5.1 *Reflections of Middle Chinese final consonants (Norman, 1988:*
49, 194, 238)

	Ningde	Fuzhou	Old Mandarin	Peking	Lingbao
*p	p	ʔ	ø	ø	ø
*t	t	ʔ	ø	ø	ø
*k	k	ʔ, k	ø	ø	ø
*m	m	ŋ	m	n	~
*n	n	ŋ	n	n	~
*ŋ	ŋ	ŋ	ŋ	ŋ	ŋ

gives rise to sound change; in the second case, CHOICE and CHANGE
play a role in the reinterpretation of a glottalized stop as a glottal stop. The
general proposal then, for languages like Fuzhou, is final glottalization,
followed by debuccalization: *p' > ʔ, t' > ʔ, k' > ʔ. The fact that closure
durations may differ for stops at different points of articulation means that
debuccalization itself may occur first with the stops of shortest duration,
and only later with those whose closure durations are longer. Coronal
closure durations can be shorter than those for labial and velar stops,
and tongue-tip movements show higher velocities than tongue-dorsum
or lip movements (Kuehn and Moll 1976). A slight anticipation in the
laryngeal gesture for glottalization will drift to the beginning of a coronal
stop closure sooner than it will for labials and velars if their stop closure
durations are longer, or if this drift is associated with faster articulatory
movements. One prediction of this model, then, is that debuccalizations
involving gestural overlap may occur first with coronals, and only later
with stops at other points of articulation. This may lie at the source of the
now well-diffused sound change of final *t* > ʔ in many dialects of English,
in contrast to other points of articulation, where variation is still found
between final *p'*, ʔ and *k'*, ʔ.[4]

In contrast to this recurrent pattern for oral stops, nasal stops do not
generally neutralize to glottal stop. When place contrasts are neutralized
word-finally, the resulting segment is typically a velar nasal. The limited
cues of final unreleased stops have already been noted. Confusion rates for
place of articulation in nasals are very high when the voiced steady-state
portion of the nasal is isolated from preceding and following vocalic transitions (Malécot 1956; Nord 1976). Further, as noted by Ohala (1975),
velar nasals are often produced as nasal glides, without complete oral
closure, and as such, have more in common acoustically with nasalized

---

[4] See Fallon (2002), chapter 4, for more examples of place neutralization under debuccalization.

vowels than with [n] and [m]. I suggest that the common neutralization of *m*, *n*, ŋ > ŋ word-finally is the result of final nasal weakening. Under lenition, *m*, *n*, ŋ are produced sometimes as nasal glides, with incomplete oral closure. Since there is a stronger tendency for the listener to perceive these nasal glides as velar nasals than as nasals at other points of articulation, the perception-based sound change *m*, *n*, ŋ > *N* > ŋ occurs (*N* a nasal glide). In the typology of sound change presented in 2.2, variable lenition is a case of CHOICE, while misperception of the nasal glide as velar nasal is an instance of CHANGE.

Some support for this case of CHANGE can be found in loanword phonology. When words with final nasalized vowels are borrowed into languages which lack a contrast between oral and nasalized vowels, nasalized vowels are typically realized as velar nasals, not as [n] or [m]. For example, French borrowings into German with final nasalized vowels often show two variant pronunciations: one with a final nasalized vowel, and the other with a final velar nasal. German examples include: *Ballon*, *Balkon*, *Bouillon*, *Champignon*, *Saison*, and *Salon*. Since nasalized vowels are generally non-phonemic in German, we can assume that pronunciations with nasalized vowels reflect learned pronunciation, while velar nasal pronunciations reflect the perceptual similarity of nasal glides and velar nasals. Similar facts characterize French loans into Swedish: *arrangemang*, *ballong*, *balkong*, *betong*, *buljong*, *kartong*, *kupong*, *mannekäng*, *restaurang*, *salong*, where *ng* writes a final velar nasal.

In general, place contrasts in nasals are neutralized word-finally when the oral closure gesture is weakened. If there is no lenition of the oral closure gesture, place neutralization is unexpected, since V–C transitions and nasal antiresonances during closure provide cues for nasal place. If lenition occurs, place neutralization to the velar nasal can arise as a consequence of common perceptual confusions between velar nasals and nasal glides.[5] Though, superficially, patterns of final neutralization for voiceless oral stops and nasals might resemble each other, under the proposed analysis, the only common feature is potential lenition of the oral closure gesture under gestural reduction.

5.4   A context-free change of place

Within the CCC-model of sound change, context-free shifts in major place of articulation are predicted only where the sounds in question share perceptual similarities. For example, the shift of θ > f, which has occurred in

---

[5] Cases of final neutralization of /m/ to [n] are discussed in 9.2.2 in the context of language-specific priming effects.

the history of English and Rotuman, is explained in terms of the perceptual similarities of the dental and labio-dental fricatives (see 6.1.1). Similarly, the sound change $k^w > p$, which is documented for British Celtic and Proto-Mixe-Zoquean, is not problematic, since labio-velars and labials also share significant perceptual features. However, a context-free shift of $t > k$ is remarkable and presents problems for the association between phonetically abrupt changes and misperceptions assumed here. In this subsection I speculate on the phonetic basis of $*t > k$ sound changes documented by Blust (1990) for a range of Austronesian languages.

Blust (1990) illustrates a context-free shift of $t > k$ in at least four different groups of Austronesian languages, and presents evidence for these as independent historical developments. In the Polynesian languages, the $t > k$ change is found in Hawaiian, Luangiua, and in Samoan.[6] An unconditioned $t > k$ change is also found in several New Caledonian languages, in Dehu and Iaai of the Loyalty Islands, and in Doura, Kuni, and Lala in south-eastern New Guinea. Other Austronesian languages outside of the Oceanic group with an unconditioned $*t > k$ change are Numfor/Biak, Kisar, Manipa, and Enggano (Blust 1990: 19).[7] Outside the Austronesian family, an unconditioned $*t > k$ change has also been reported for Chama (Eseexa), a Tacanan language of northern Bolivia (Key 1968), and the same $*t > k$ sound change is documented in Orokolo, a Papuan language of the Gulf Province (Brown 1986: xv–xvii).

An intriguing feature of the $*t > k$ change in the Austronesian languages described by Blust is that, with the exception of a few northern New Caledonian languages, the change in question is non-neutralizing. This is because, in all cases, earlier $*k$ has shifted to glottal stop, or, in Gomen, to c. Blust (1990) characterizes the general pattern as a drag chain; the loss of Proto-Oceanic $*k$ leaves a position within the phoneme inventory which is filled by the $*t > k$ change.

I suggest that consonants allow a degree of phonetic variation which is inversely related to the degree of crowding in the acoustic/perceptual space. While this claim is often made for vowels, it is less commonly made for consonants where place contrasts tend to be categorical and non-gradient.[8] This suggestion is based on the degree of variation present in very small consonant inventories. For example, in Rotokas, with only

---

[6] In Samoan the formal style of speech maintains historical $*t$, while in colloquial speech, all ts of the formal style are pronounced as k.

[7] The same $*t > k$ change is limited to final-position in some languages of western Manus. I do not include these languages in the following discussion, since final neutralization of $t > k$ may be related to absence of release, as discussed in 5.3.2.

[8] See Ladefoged and Maddieson (1996: 286–7) demonstrating the extent to which the variation may be contextually conditioned in small vowel systems.

the six consonants *p t k b d g*, the voiced stops are in free variation with voiced continuants and nasals (Firchow and Firchow 1969). Allophones of /b/, /d/, and /g/ include [b, β, m], [d, r, l, n], and [g, ɤ, ŋ] respectively. This free variation between voiced stops and nasal stops is remarkable: in most of the world's languages, contrastive nasal stops are found (though see 8.5) and such variation is absent. Phonetic variation between oral and nasal stops in Rotokas appears to be related to the absence of contrastive nasal stops in the same language.

With this sort of variation in mind, let us consider consonant systems like the Pre-Samoan one. Before the shift of **t > k*, the language had *p t s f m n ŋ l ʔ*, and, due to inherited aspects of syllable structure, all of these consonants occurred only before vowels in CV or CVV syllables. The Pre-Samoan consonant system has only a single place contrast for oral stops, – that between /t/ and /p/. Within this limited oral stop system, language learners hear only [t] and [p] in intervocalic and pre-vocalic positions. As a consequence, it is possible that the same learners attend more to voice-onset time (VOT) and burst properties, than to formant values in V–C and C–V transitions. More specifically, I suggest that, in the course of language acquisition, the [t] versus [p] contrast is initially associated by learners with the categorical distinctions shown in (5). The /t/ category is the stop which is followed by a relatively long voice-onset time, in contrast to /p/ which has a shorter VOT. And, the /t/ category has a high amplitude burst, while the /p/ category is associated with low amplitude bursts.

(5)   Phonetic cues associated with isolated pre-vocalic [p] versus [t] contrasts

		VOT	Burst properties
Category 1	/t/	long	high amplitude
Category 2	/p/	short	low amplitude

Given these initial associations, there is no reason for the language learner to produce a [t] as opposed to a [k] in instantiating the long VOT/high-amplitude burst category. Like [t], [k] has high amplitude bursts in most CV contexts. And VOT for [k] is the longest of the three stops, maximizing the categorial contrast along the VOT axis. Though language learners will not hear [k]s, they will produce them spontaneously in the course of babbling (Locke 1983), and these velars will sound, to the child, like good tokens of Category 1 stops.

While this hypothesis is highly speculative, Plauché (2001) presents experimental evidence supporting VOT as a significant cue for major place of articulation, as well as evidence for *t/k* confusions which support [k] as a possible realization of Category 1 in (5). Nearly all spoken languages have a contrast between coronal and velar stops, and therefore it is difficult to conceive of [t] and [k] as members of a single non-contrastive phonological category. However, there is also evidence for this view from an early observer. Davies (1851: 236) in his *Tahitian and English Dictionary* comments, on *t*, that the Tahitians cannot "perceive the difference between it and *k*." Evidence from loan vocabulary is also consistent with this view: loans with /k, g/ are consistently produced as /t/ in Tahitian.[9] Examples of English loans showing this pattern include Tahitian *tavana* 'governor,' *titeta* 'tea kettle,' *tuava* 'guava,' and *tupere* 'cape gooseberry.'

In sum, the context-free shift of $t > k$ may be viewed as quite common in languages which lack /k/ in their inventories. The fact that /k/ is missing as a contrastive category allows one to view [t] and [k] as members of a single perceptual category defined at the outset of acquisition by the isolated pre-vocalic [t] versus [p] contrast. If a child is exposed only to a place contrast between [t] and [p] in pre-vocalic position, many phonetic features can be viewed as defining contrastive categories. If, as hypothesized above, VOT and burst amplitude are chosen, [k] may serve as, essentially, an allophone of the /t/ category, and may even be regarded by speakers as a better exemplar of this category by virtue of its longer VOT. Since the phonetic cues in (5) defining distinct categories are prominent in C–V transitions, the simple phonotactics of the languages showing $*t > k$ could play a facilitative role in the evolution of this remarkable sound change.

5.5   Coronal: just another place

Many phonologists assume that coronal is the default or unmarked place of articulation for consonants. For example, Kean (1975), based on the frequent occurrence of coronals in segment inventories and their early acquisition, argues that coronal is the neutral or unmarked place feature for stops. Blust (1979) makes a similar claim based on asymmetries in cluster phonotactics: coronal + non-coronal consonant clusters undergo regular assimilation and metathesis, while clusters beginning in non-coronals do not. More recent studies in Parodis and Prunet (1991) suggest that coronals have a special status in phonological systems. They attribute this special status, in part, to the underspecification of coronal place at the point at which certain phonological rules or constraints are active. Underspecified segments are more prone to assimilation and deletion, and may be transparent to the spread of place features. However, as pointed out by McCarthy and Taub (1992), other papers in the same

---

[9] The same is true of loans in formal Samoan.

volume require specification of coronal underlyingly to account for their special behavior: coronal harmony is triggered by coronal-dependent nodes within the feature geometry, while lexical constraints against clusters like *tl also require reference to [coronal] in underlying representations. In fact, none of the arguments for coronals as phonologically unmarked segment types is without internal weaknesses or alternative explanations.

Consider, for example, the high frequency of coronals in segment inventories. One simple explanation for this is that, not taking into account secondary features of palatalization, labialization, velarization, and pharyngealization, there are simply more basic types of coronals (dentals, alveolars, alveo-palatals, retroflexes) than there are of labials or dorsals. An additional factor is the high frequency of sibilants in contrast to other types of fricatives (Maddieson 1984, chapter 3). The high frequency of s-like sounds in the world's languages in contrast to fricatives at other points of articulation could play a role in boosting the overall frequency of coronal segments. Note that the high frequency of s, however, is not just a function of coronal place: θ is also coronal, but it has much lower frequency cross-linguistically than labio-dental f or velar x.

Evidence from language acquisition does not clearly support the view of coronals as easier to produce than labials or velars. Stemberger and Stoel-Gammon (1991: 188) summarize the relative order of acquisition for major place features of stops, pointing out that "Of the three main places of articulation, velars are acquired last by most children. However, studies have found no differences between alveolars and labials, in any position in the syllable." Similar findings are summarized in Vihman (1996), though of the 27 children whose first words are listed in appendix B, 12 produce velars in some context, while only 1 child replaces an initial velar or intervocalic velar with another sound (glottal stop). Given the large number of children who do appear to produce velars in their first words, and the near simultaneous appearance of coronal and labial stops, it is difficult to argue that p, t, and k differ significantly in degree of difficulty independent of phonetic context.[10]

Blust's (1979) observations regarding asymmetries in assimilation and metathesis are real, and demand an explanation. However, the similarity between these patterns and those found in fast speech suggest that they are phonologizations of fast-speech phenomena, explained better in terms of aspects of articulatory timing than segmental markedness, as suggested above. Regressive assimilation in *footprint* in contrast to lack

---

[10] It is only in the context of coordinated gestures that processes like child consonant harmony give the semblance of preference for /t/ over /k/.

of assimilation in *riptide* suggests the patterns of gestural hiding reported in Browman and Goldstein (1990: 214ff). Labial closure may precede coronal closure, hiding the coronal gesture and resulting in a labial-only percept. In fact, there is growing acoustic and articulatory evidence that gestural overlap in coronal–noncoronal stop clusters is greater than that in noncoronal–coronal clusters (e.g. Byrd 1996).

A somewhat surprising aspect of the literature on the unmarked status of coronals is how few references there are to the Jakobsonian notion that neutralization involves a shift to the unmarked member of an opposition.[11] This contrasts with the literature on final devoicing, deaspiration, and deglottalization, which typically refer to neutralization to the unmarked feature value, and which, in feature-geometric terms, represent neutralization as the delinking of a specified feature. The dearth of arguments from place neutralization for coronals as the unmarked place may be related to the rarity of processes showing neutralization of *P, T, K* to *T* or *m, n, ŋ* to *n*.[12] As noted earlier, where complete place neutralization occurs, there are two common patterns outside of assimilatory contexts, both illustrated by the Chinese developments in table 5.1: either the coronal/labial/dorsal contrast is neutralized to a laryngeal segment *ʔ* which lacks place altogether; or, the three-way contrast for nasals is neutralized to *ŋ*. In general then, where neutralizing sound change occurs, there is no association between the direction of neutralization and purported coronal unmarkedness.

A final example of coronals failing to function as the default place of articulation is illustrated, within the diachronic domain, by the recurrent **t > k* sound changes discussed above. In the Polynesian languages,

---

[11] One exception to this is Houlihan and Iverson (1979: 56–57), who mention neutralization of /m/ and /n/ to [n] word-finally in Finnish. Under their account *n* is less marked than *m*, based on Ferguson's (1966) implicational universal stating that the presence of a bilabial nasal implies the presence of a dental or alveolar nasal, but not *vice versa*. An exception to Ferguson's proposed universal is Toaripi (Brown 1968, 1973), an Eleman language of the Gulf Province of New Guinea, which has only a single nasal, *m*.

The Finnish alternation in question appears to be morphophonemic, applying only to a small number of suffixes and does not appear to be productive. For example, the instrumental noun-forming suffix surfaces as *-in* word-finally, but as *-ime-* in other contexts. Though consonant-final loans are rare, some are found with final *m*: *protium* 'protium', *deuterium* 'deuterium', *tritium* 'tritium', *Mannerheimlitto* 'The Mannerheim Union' (Austerlitz 1966).

Another exception is Kiparsky (1995: 669), who claims that "Place neutralization yields coronals." He mentions Finnish as well as Greek, Italian, Croatian dialects, and Fante. See 9.2.2 where the output of nasal place assimilation is attributed to priming effects in language learning.

[12] This is not to say that such sound changes do not exist. For example, Campbell (1998: 173–74) reports a context-free **ŋ > n* change in many Mayan languages, including Yucatec, Cholan-Tzeltalan, and some of the Greater Q'anjobalan languages.

the *t > k change is found in Hawaiian, Luangiua, and in Samoan. In Samoan the formal style of speech maintains historical *t, while in colloquial speech, all /t/s of the formal style are pronounced as k. An intriguing feature of the *t > k changes illustrated is their non-neutralizing status. Within markedness accounts, where unmarked segments are preferred or less costly in segment inventories than marked ones, the attested *t > k changes support the view of dorsal, not coronal, as the unmarked place of articulation for oral stops. Other similar lines of reasoning lead to the same conclusion. If an unmarked segment type is lost, it should be replaced in kind; but if a marked segment type is lost, no such replacement is expected, since the sound system has been simplified. Since in this case, loss of *k gives rise to *t > k, the implication is that the dorsal stop is unmarked. While sociolinguistic variables always appear to be able to trump markedness constraints, it is worth noting in this context that where Samoan formal speech maintains historical *t, colloquial speech shows the *t > k change. Since colloquial speech is usually thought to better reflect the full range of phonetic variation than formal speech, markedness constraints invoking effort minimization are expected to play a greater role in casual speech than in formal speech. Nevertheless, it is in casual speech that k occurs to the exclusion of t, in conflict with the view of coronals as unmarked segment types.

Coronal segments may indeed be special, as suggested by Paradis and Prunet (1991), but there is little evidence that their special phonological status reflects anything more than repeated phonologization of the uniqueness of the articulatory and perceptual properties of sounds produced with the front part of the tongue. Coronal segments may have unique properties, but so do labials and dorsals. Labial segments show up with greater than chance frequency in language games and language disguise (Bagemiehl 1995), while dorsal place, as suggested above, is arguably the most common output of place neutralization for word-final nasals.

Within Evolutionary Phonology there is no encoding of segmental markedness in the grammar. Coronal stops are no more or less marked than stops at other points of articulation. They have a particular phonological representation, which includes the specification [coronal], and they have phonetic realizations, which will include some activation of the tongue blade, and associated acoustic features; and coronals will have some language-specific distribution which may, overtly or covertly, reflect some of their general phonetic characteristics. The simplest explanation of recurrent phonological properties associated exclusively with coronals is that they follow from unique phonetic properties of the same segments. The tendency for coronals to assimilate to following labials in English is one example of a transparent reflection of coronal masking under coarticulation, while the replacement of syllable-final /t/ by glottal stop in many dialects of English can be viewed as a more opaque expression of the same coarticulatory phenomena, where a shorter closure gesture for [t] is the first to show masking due to anticipation of the laryngeal gesture.

Markedness and naturalness are emergent properties of grammar, and are highly context dependent. In word-final position after [i], neutralization of *m, n, ŋ > n* is not unexpected due to coarticulatory effects. Likewise, word-initially, after [u], neutralization of *n > m* may occur. Rather than clutter the synchronic phonology with hundreds, or thousands, of context-sensitive markedness statements, which duplicate phonetically motivated sound change, the null hypothesis is to attribute recurrent sound patterns directly to these sound changes themselves. Within Evolutionary Phonology, theories of phonological markedness and naturalness are replaced with theories of factors which constrain the choice space in which language change and language acquisition take place, and allow for probabilistic modeling of sound change and associated sound patterns.

5.6   Place neutralization and cluster simplification

The analysis of place contrasts and place neutralization presented above has implications for studies of consonant loss and cluster simplification. Wilson (2001) looks at cluster simplification in Diola-Fogny, West Greenlandic, Carib, and Tunica. In all of these languages, in some contexts, a consonant alternates with zero when followed by another consonant. For example, in Diola-Fogny an underlying form /let-ku-jaw/ surfaces as *lekujaw* 'they won't go,' with loss of /t/ before /k/. Wilson takes the loss of C_1 in VC_1C_2V strings to constitute a typological generalization, and proceeds to propose a general phonetic explanation for this pattern. He suggests that common loss of C_1 is the result of poor consonantal cues in this environment. Unless it is released into a vowel, a consonant is defined as 'weak'; and weak consonants are those which are most likely to be lost. Though Wilson's study is confined to cluster simplification, his definition of 'weak consonant' predicts that similar patterns of simplification are expected pre-consonantally and word-finally. In other words, where pre-consonantal consonants are lost, final consonants should be lost as well. This is clearly not the case in Diola-Fogny and West Greenlandic, where final obstruents are common, and word-final place neutralization is unattested.

However, these are not the only facts which might lead one to question Wilson's proposed explanation for the observed patterns of cluster simplification. Recall that, in general, word-final position and word-medial pre-consonantal position may show different patterns of neutralization for place and laryngeal features. Word-final neutralizations of place, which may ultimately give rise to historical final consonant loss, show intermediate stages where place is neutralized, but some consonantal gesture remains. For example, the Chinese data in table 5.1 shows a progression from oral stops to glottal stop to zero. Assuming an initial stage of final glottalized stops, each step in this sequence is a natural phonetically motivated sound change: $*p'$, t', $k' > ? > ø$. In contrast, in word-medial contexts, place assimilation as suggested in (1vb), (2vb) and (4vb) appears to be the most common resolution of a cluster involving a 'weak' consonant in Wilson's sense.

If, as Wilson (2001) suggests, only perception, and not articulation, is involved in determining the patterns of consonant loss in languages like Diola-Fogny and West Greenlandic, it is difficult to understand why, in both of these languages, a heterorganic cluster undergoes *deletion*, rather than surfacing as a geminate. Both languages have geminate obstruents in intervocalic position, and simple misperception of VC_1C_2V, without gestural reduction of C_1, should give rise to a percept of C_2 gemination, not an intervocalic short segment. In fact, within Evolutionary Phonology, the only situation where a direct phonetically motivated sound change $VC_1C_2V > VC_2V$ is predicted is in sound change with sources in both CHOICE and CHANGE, where consonant length is not contrastive. A development of precisely this type is evident in Misantla Totonac (MacKay 1994), where regressive assimilation gives rise to geminates, which, like sequences of adjacent identical segments, undergo degemination, resulting in surface alternations between VC_1C_2V and VC_2V.

The general sound changes investigated in this chapter suggest that there are at least two potential telescoped sources for C_1 weakening and loss in VC_1C_2V where C_1 and C_2 are both oral stops. One scenario involves regressive assimilation, followed by degemination: $VC_1C_2V > VC_2C_2V > VC_2V$. A second pathway is articulatory lenition of the coda followed by further lenition leading to loss: $VC_1C_2V > V\{h,?\}C_2V > VC_2V$. Since neither of these pathways of historical development involves a direct $VC_1C_2V > VC_2V$ sound change, an important question is whether phonetically based sound change of this type exists. Are the alternations in Diola-Fogny and West Greenlandic, which Wilson (2001) takes to be phonetically motivated alternations, truly natural? Or are they the folded transforms of rule telescoping, with intermediate stages of gemination or weakening lost in time?

5.7   Place features and syllable structure

The recognition of cross-linguistic generalizations on the distribution of place features has given rise to phonological analyses where these constraints are expressed as syllable-based statements (e.g. Itô 1986; Goldsmith 1990; Kager 1999). Within these treatments, place features may be licensed by positive or negative constraints on possible syllable codas. Onset position is claimed to license all place features, and homorganicity constraints on coda-onset clusters are accounted for by appeals to coda constraints, combined with onset licensing. Goldsmith's general view of coda consonants follows:

> What is consistently unusual about the coda, in language after language, is that there are far fewer contrasts available in the coda, but, whatever contrasts are available there are a subset of the contrasts available in the first half of the syllable. Thus, the coda is, as we have said, a secondary licenser: it has only a subset of the possibilities of contrast of the first part of the syllable. (Goldsmith 1990: 125)

There is at least one well-described language which violates Goldsmith's claim above. Kashaya, as analyzed by Buckley (1994), has more contrasts in coda position than onset position. Kashaya consonants are $p\ t\ t\ k\ q\ ?$ $p^h\ t^h\ t^h\ c^h\ k^h\ q^h\ p'\ t'\ t'\ c'\ k'\ q'\ s\ \int\ h\ s'\ m\ n\ m^h\ n^h\ m'\ n'\ w\ l\ y\ w^h\ l^h\ y^h$ $w'\ l'\ y'$. In onset position, all segments occur, with the exception of m^h, $n^h,\ w^h,\ l^h,\ y^h,\ w',\ l',\ y'$.[13] In coda position, all segments occur with the exception of the plain voiceless stops $p\ t\ t\ c\ k\ q$ which are neutralized to the aspirated stop series. In sum, of the 38 consonantal phonemes posited, 28, including /m'/ and /n'/, occur in onset position, while only 32 occur in coda position. But there are more serious problems with the general licensing proposals involving the treatment of place features.

In languages like Japanese, where the only consonant clusters are homorganic, and words end in vowels or a nasal glide, licensing approaches claim that the syllable coda cannot license place features (Itô 1986; Kager 1999: 131). However, a logical alternative to this approach is to state Japanese phonotactics in positive terms, allowing place features only before vowels (Blevins 2003a). Support for the second approach is found in the historical development of languages like Saipan Carolinian, which once had the Japanese pattern, but then underwent final vowel loss. Consonants /p, t, k/ which were once medial and pre-vocalic, are now exposed to the word edge. However, nothing else about the general phonotactics of the language has changed. The descriptive problem posed by languages like Saipan Carolinian for coda licensing constraints is that these

---

[13] When /m'/ and /n'/ occur in the onset, they surface as voiced stops.

coda constraints must be qualified so as *not* to apply to word-final codas. Whether the device used is extrametricality, positional faithfulness, or a division into sub-types of codas, one is led to the fundamental conclusion that different phonological behavior may be exhibited by word-final and word-medial codas. Given that these contexts can be distinguished in concrete non-syllable-based terms, the basic question which arises is whether reference to syllables needs to be made at all.[14]

Another descriptive problem with the same approaches is that they cannot be extended from Japanese-like-languages to other languages with similar patterns. While all medial geminate obstruents and homorganic NC sequences in Japanese are heterosyllabic, Woleaian, shows exactly the same distribution of place features as Japanese, but allows tautosyllabic word-initial geminates, while Manam shows the same distribution of place features, but allows tautosyllabic word-initial NC clusters. Since initial homorganic sequences in Woleaian and Manam are arguably not coda-onset sequences, the coda-constraint cannot be extended to them. However, within any model where language-specific constraints may be stated independent of syllable structure, the phonotactics of place in Japanese, Woleaian, and Manam can be accurately captured by a simple constraint which licenses place features in pre-vocalic position only. This is precisely the sort of constraint which is expected, if, as suggested above, recurrent properties of place feature distribution reflect phonetically natural processes.

In sum, the description of synchronic systems of place feature distribution must be data-driven. The most plausible explanations for recurrent aspects of distribution appear to lie, not in the domain of synchronic phonologies, but in the phonetically based sound changes which give rise to them.

---

[14] In the case of Saipan Carolinian with word-final geminates (*takk* 'finished', *xacc* 'good', etc.), even extrametricality is not strong enough a device. Words *tak<k>*, *xac<c>* with extrametrical final consonants, still constitute violations of the constraint against specified place features in the syllable coda.

6   Other common sound patterns

These results add to the growing body of evidence pointing to the crucial role of the listener in initiating certain sound changes . . . This is not to deny that much of the synchronic variation in speech – from which diachronic variation arises – can be traced to the speaker or the physical principles which map articulation to sound . . .   Ohala (1990b: 266)

In this chapter, I investigate potential explanations for common sound patterns not detailed in earlier chapters. For the purposes of this discussion, common sound patterns are those for which there is good evidence of multigenesis. Unlike the uncommon sound patterns detailed in chapter 8, these sound patterns are not limited to a few languages, a few language families, or a small number of geographic regions.

This chapter is organized in terms of the general phonetic source of sound change for the sound patterns in question. Where possible, I begin by demonstrating a particular sound pattern in the synchronic grammar of one or more spoken languages. I then give an example of the same pattern attested as a sound change, and go on to present a phonetic explanation for the sound change in question. After illustrating sound patterns with sources in misperception, feature localization, vowel length, and articulation, I turn to sound patterns with multiple, mythical, and mysterious sources.

6.1   Perception as the primary source of sound change

In chapters 4 and 5, perception-based accounts were proposed for certain recurrent cross-linguistic patterns in the distribution of laryngeal features and place features. C–V transition cues play a primary role in identification of laryngeal release features, major place features, and secondary place release features. When these cues are absent, confusion rates rise, and listeners are more likely to reinterpret the sound in question as belonging to a different category. V–C transition cues play an important role in the identification of pre-aspiration, pre-glottalization, and retroflexion. When these cues are absent, confusion rates rise, and listener-based sound change is again more likely to take place.

There is now a growing phonetic literature on sound patterns whose origins are primarily perceptual (Beddor and Evans-Romaine, in press; van Bergem 1995; Blevins and Garrett 1998, to appear; Foulkes 1997; Guion 1998; Hume and Johnson 2001; Janson 1983; Majors 1988; Ohala 1974b, 1979a, b, 1981, 1985, 1990b, 1995b; Ohala and Amador 1981; Ohala and Busà 1995; Ohala and Lorentz 1977; Plauché et al. 1996, Plauché 2001; Repp and Lin 1989; Ritchie 1999, 2000). In terms of the CCC-model presented in 2.2, these sound patterns have CHANGE or CHANCE as their primary source.

In chapters 4 and 5, I suggest that CHANGE is a primary source of regressive assimilation of laryngeal release features, regressive primary and secondary place assimilation, and progressive assimilation in apical clusters. In this section, other examples of sound patterns are shown to be directly related to percepts which have a greater than chance likelihood of being misidentified or reinterpreted by the listener. This discussion is not meant to be exhaustive, and the interested reader is referred to the literature cited above and below for further examples of perceptually based sound change and for more technical aspects of the phonetic explanations proposed. Here I intend only to highlight the extent to which common sound patterns can originate from acoustic signals which, to the human ear, are perceptually similar.

6.1.1   Context-free changes

Context-free sound changes are generally of two types. They either involve gradual shifts along some articulatory continuum, as in the case of movements of vowels within the vowel space, or they involve shifts between sounds which cannot be accounted for in terms of general articulatory variability. It is this second class of cases and the sound patterns resulting from them that are exemplified here.

A context-free example of this sort is the shift of $\theta > f$ in many dialects of English. The same change appears to be incipient in Veneto dialects of Italian, where [f] and [θ] are in free variation word-initially (MacKay 1995: xvii) and on the remote Pacific island of Rotuma, there is evidence of a similar sound change in the history of Rotuman, where $*t > \theta > f$.

The $\theta > f$ sound change in English is neutralizing, since the contrast between earlier English phonemes /θ/ and /f/ is lost. A merger has occurred – an unremarkable event in the common history of sound systems. But there is something remarkable about this particular change, and that is its phonological and phonetic content. An interdental fricative – a sound made with the tongue blade approaching the upper teeth – has transformed itself into a labio-dental fricative – a sound made by touching the upper teeth to the lower lip. In terms of phonological features, a consonant specified as coronal, non-apical, and non-strident has been transformed into a labial strident sound.

Shifts between interdental and labio-dental fricatives may seem odd from an articulatory perspective, but such sound changes are natural when viewed from the point of view of speech perception. As demonstrated by Miller and Nicely (1955), when noise is used to mask stimuli, the highest confusion rates for English consonants are found between [θ] and [f] and between [ð] and [v]. Subsequent study suggests that it is not the fricative noise which cues differences in these two fricative types, but slight differences in preceding and following formant transitions. In the course of acquisition of English and Rotuman, language learners attending to the fricative noise portion of [θ] and [f] may find no significant differences and categorize them as instances of the same phoneme. Additional evidence for misperception comes from studies of infant perception: unlike nearly all other segmental contrasts tested on infants, the contrast between [θ] and [f] is one which infants have difficulty discriminating (Vihman 1996: 60).

Another example of context-free sound change with perceptual origins is the shift from aspiration to nasalization, or from nasalization to aspiration. Matisoff (1975), who first noticed a relationship between these two phonetic features referred to the phenomenon as "rhinoglottophilia." This particular sound change occurs at the featural level: audible aspiration shifts to audible nasalization and *vice versa*. Again, since context-free sound change is not evidenced by regular synchronic alternations, the closest one can get to documenting such changes as synchronic entities is to capture a sound change in progress. One case of this sort is found in the North-West Caucasian languages Bzhedukh and Shapsegh (Colarusso 1988: 42–43; Blevins and Garrett 1993: 222). In both of these languages, unaspirated spirants contrast with aspirated spirants, and vowels following aspirated spirants are nasalized. In the Israeli dialect of Shapsegh, the sound change is complete. The contrast between aspirated and unaspirated spirants is gone. Instead, formerly aspirated spirants are followed by nasalized vowels (Colarusso 1988: 44–45). Inverse shifts of nasalization giving rise to aspiration are also reported. For example, in the Owerri dialect of Igbo the contrast between aspirated and unaspirated sonorants, fricatives, and palatalized and labialized stops involves both aspiration and nasalization of a following vowel. The segment which has given rise to simultaneous aspiration and nasalization, historically, however, is a nasal (Hyman 1972; Williamson 1973; Ladefoged et al. 1976).

The association of aspiration and nasalization is extremely odd from an articulatory perspective. In general, movements of the velum, which controls nasal airflow, are independent of vocal fold activity. Not surprisingly however, a perceptual link between the two features has been demonstrated. Ohala (1975: 303) describes some of their acoustic similarities:

[h] may produce an effect on vowels that "mocks" that of nasalization. Because of the open glottis during phonation accompanying an [h] (or breathy-voice), the spectrum of the vowel will be changed in the following ways: there will be upward shifting of the formants, especially F1 . . . , increased bandwith of the formants, presence of anti-resonances in the spectrum and an overall lowering of the amplitude of the vowel . . . This is identical to the effect of nasalization on vowels.

Subsequent experiments have shown that spectral similarities between aspirated and nasalized segments can result in misperception of breathiness as nasalization (Ohala 1980, 1987; Klatt and Klatt 1990).

Other more common context-free sound changes with perceptual bases have received a good deal of coverage in the phonetics and phonology literature. One of these is the shift between labialized, velarized, pharyngealized, and retroflex sounds. Similarities between these classes of sounds were noted early in the distinctive feature literature, and captured by the acoustic feature [+flat]. The [+flat] sounds, which included labialized, velarized, pharyngealized, and retroflex sounds were defined by a downward shift of a set of formants, or all formants, or a weakening of some of their upper frequency components (Jakobson, Fant, and Halle 1952: 31; Jakobson and Halle 1956: 26, 28, 31). See Ohala (1985) for further evidence for this acoustic feature.[1]

The perceptual similarities of some of these categories are apparent in sound inventories, variation, loanword phonology, and sound change. For example, until the discovery of a contrast between plain, pharyngealized, and labialized uvular fricatives in the Byzb dialect of Abkhaz (Catford 1977: 193), and similar contrasts for uvular stops and fricatives in Ubykh (Colarusso 1988: 120), pharyngealization and labialization were assumed to be non-contrastive in the world's languages.[2] Even with these discoveries, such contrasts are extremely rare. It is this rarity of contrast which is accounted for in terms of common perceptual confusions between flat sounds. And it still appears to be the case that no language contrasts secondary velarization with secondary pharyngealization.[3]

---

[1] See however Trubetzkoy (1939: 24) and Colarusso (1985, 1988: 221–22) on percepts of palatalization in pharyngealized sounds, possibly related to strong concentrations of energy around around 500 and 1,100 Hz.

[2] A contrast between plain alveolars, pharyngealized alveolars, and rounded pharyngealized alveolars is reported for the Israeli dialect of Shapsegh (Colarusso 1988: 22–23).

[3] Colarusso (1988: 186–88, 290) points to phonetic contrasts of this type in the Bzyb dialect of Abkhaz, and in the second consonant of Georgian harmonic clusters. In the first

Further evidence for a close relationship between velarization and pharyngealization is found in Arabic, where the pharyngealized series of consonants is sometimes produced with pharyngealization, and other times with uvularization, or velarization. In the area of loanword phonology, the substitution of labialization for pharyngealization suggests perceptual similarities between these two categories, as noted by Jakobson, Fant, and Halle (1952: 31): "The fact that peoples who have no pharyngealized consonants in their mother tongue, as for instance, the Bantus and Uzbeks, substitute labialized articulations for the corresponding pharyngealized consonants of Arabic words, illustrates the perceptual similarity of pharyngealization and lip-rounding."

In the area of sound change, we find correspondences between velarization, labialization, and labio-velarization in Micronesian. The reflexes of Proto-Oceanic $*p^w$, $*b^w$, $*m^w$ (Ross 1998) are velarized labial segments in Marshallese (Bender 1968; Choi 1992) and some dialects of Gilbertese (Laver 1994: 326), but labio-velarized labials in Ponapean (Ladefoged and Maddieson 1996: 357–58). Compare Ponapean $naam^w$ 'lagoon,' Marshallese $nam^ɣ$ 'secondary lagoon,' Ponapean $taam^w$, Marshallese $dam^ɣ$ 'forehead'; and Ponapean p^wuus 'navel,' Marshallese $p^ɣicen$ 'navel-3sg.' While we cannot be sure of the phonetic values of $*p^w$, $*b^w$, $*m^w$, they were most likely either velarized labials or labio-velarized labials. In either case, the shifts involved suggest that labialization or labio-velarization can be interpreted as pure velarization or *vice versa*. And a shift from retroflex to velarized appears to have occurred in North-West Caucasian. The majority of languages contrast laminal and apical coronal spirants, the laminals being palatalized and the apicals retroflex. However, in Abkhaz, the series corresponding to retroflexes in other North-West Caucasian languages is realized as velarized (Colarusso 1988: 186–88). In general then, it is rare for labialization, velarization, pharyngealization, and retroflexion to contrast in one and the same language.

However, as with other common sound patterns discussed in earlier chapters, there are exceptions to these tendencies. Colarusso (1988: 262) summarizes the situation:

the complex of features subsumed under the Jakobsonian name [flat] may yet have a place in linguistic theory, perhaps in the area of markedness and phonetic plausibility, where [flat] may offer an explanation for the extreme rarity or nonexistence of contrasts between retroflexed and velarized or uvularized segments, and perhaps between retroflexed and pharyngealized segments as well . . .

case, the underlying contrast is between a laminal palato-alveolar, and a velarized palato-alveolar corresponding to the retroflex series in other North-West Caucasian languages. In the case of Georgian, the velar/uvular contrast is underlyingly primary, not secondary.

In Evolutionary Phonology, where markedness is an emergent property of grammar, the rarity of contrasts between flat sounds is attributed directly to their perceptual similarities. As with sound changes conditioned by release, the role of flat in sound change is purely phonetic, and there is no clear impetus for introducting flat into the phonological feature inventory. Unlike the presence versus absence of stop release, or pre- and post-aspiration which would over-generate distinct phonological categories, [flat] underdetermines contrasts like that between the plain, pharyngealized, and labialized-pharyngealized uvulars in Ubykh. However, like other perceptually salient features of speech, the downward shift of formants present in the realization of all of these contrasts may play a significant role in sound change, increasing probabilities for misperception among like percepts.

6.1.2   Context-sensitive changes

Context-sensitive sound changes are generally, by their very nature never immune to coarticulatory influences. In this brief discussion, I highlight one well-studied case of sound change, which, like the regressive assimilations seen in chapters 4 and 5, appears to have a primary perceptual basis, though coarticulation also plays a role.

While CV coarticulation is the source of many local assimilations, perceptual factors have also been shown to play an important role in sound changes sometimes viewed as assimilatory. A case in point is velar palatalization (Guion 1996, 1998). Many languages show sound changes or synchronic alternations involving velar palatalization before palatal segments. The most common change of this kind is $*k > t\int / \_\{i, j\}$. Palatalizations of voiced velar stops are less frequent than voiceless ones, and velar palatalization is more common before front high vowels/glides than non-high front vowels.

Within the Indo-European family, Old English palatalization of *k, g* before front vowels and Slavic palatalization of *k, g* when followed by front non-low vowels are well documented. Other similar cases are found in the history of Indo-Iranian, Bantu, Chinese, Cowlitz Salish, and Mam (Guion 1998: 20, and references therein). What is remarkable about these velar palatalizations is not only their frequency in the world's languages, but also the fact that the output of the rule is not velar, but a coronal. As summarized by Guion (1996, 1998) coarticulation is able to account for fronting of the tongue body, producing $[k^j]$ a palatalized velar, or [c], a pure palatal, but articulatory factors are unable to explain the shift from velar to alveo-palatal, which involves a change of articulator – from the tongue body for [k], to the tongue blade for $[t\int]$.

A number of experiments carried out by Guion demonstrate that velar stops before front high vowels are acoustically similar to palato-alveolar affricates and that velar stops in the same contexts are easily confused by listeners with palato-alveolar affricates. An additional finding is that the acoustic and perceptual similarity of voiceless velar stops is greater than voiced velar stops. In sum, by making reference to perceptual properties of palatalized velars, Guion (1998) is able to explain the high frequency of velar palatalization in the world's languages, the higher frequency of this change with [k] than [g], the higher frequency of this change with high front vowels than with other vowels, and the shift of articulator from the tongue dorsum to the tongue blade. All of these features characterize historical shifts as well as synchronic alternations. Guion's account also explains the context-free shifts from pure palatals to palato-alveolar affricates that occur in some languages, e.g. in the history of Athabaskan (Krauss 1982).

Velar palatalization serves to highlight the importance of both articulatory and acoustic/perceptual factors in a single sound change: coarticulation is the ultimate source of velar palatalization, but resulting palatalized velars may give rise to coronal percepts. Though few other sound patterns of this type have been examined as carefully, the numerous studies cited at the beginning of this chapter provide preliminary evidence for the role of perception in numerous sound patterns, from apparent debuccalization in *fu/ hu* alternations (Foulkes 1997), to labial-to-coronal shifts under similar coarticulatory palatalization (Plauché et al. 1996; Plauché 2001).

6.1.3   A note on frog calls

The cases of listener-oriented sound change suggested above, and in earlier chapters, highlight the important role of perception in language change. In Evolutionary Phonology common sound patterns are expected to reflect biases of the human perceptual system which emerge in the course of language transmission. This view of sound change follows a long tradition, from the pre-acoustic work of von Raumer, Kruszewski, and Meillet, to the phonetically more sophisticated studies of Jonasson and Ohala. While evolutionary biology serves primarily as a useful metaphor for Evolutionary Phonology, there is good evidence that listener-oriented sound change plays a central role in the evolution of non-human sound systems as well.

An instructive case involves the evolution of frog calls. The general situation is that most male frogs produce mating calls which attract females. These mating calls evolve, with closely related species showing significant differences in call frequency components. A question that can be asked is whether the evolution of male frog calls leads to adaptive changes in the frequency preferences of females, or whether pre-existing features of the female perceptual system can result in adaptive changes in the male call.

Within frogs, the hearing organ important for high-frequency call detection is the basilar papilla. For two closely related species, *Physalaemus coloradorum* and *P. pustulosus*, female frogs show the greatest excitatory frequencies for the basilar papilla at 2200 Hz (Ryan et al. 1990). Of interest is the fact that the males in these two species have different calls. *P. pustulosus* have calls with components at 2200 Hz, while *P. coloradorum* lack a call component at this frequency. Since, in this case, *P. coloradorum* express the primitive state for this character, a working hypothesis is that the *P. pustulosus* males evolved to exploit the perceptual preference in females (Ryan et al. 1990). Because females respond preferentially to calls with components at 2200 Hz, the evolution of this feature in male calls could be viewed as adaptive. Experimental support for this hypothesis was provided by Ryan and Rand (1993). In this experiment, the *P. coloradorum* females were given a chance to show their perceptual preferences. Synthesized calls were produced with and without the 2200 Hz components. These female frogs showed significant preferences for the calls containing a 2200 Hz component, suggesting that the perceptual preference for this frequency is pre-existing, and will be adaptive if the preferred call component arises.

In the frog world, sound change can be a matter of mating and passing genes on to the next generation, or not, while in the human realm, the emergence or elimination of a phonological contrast has few consequences outside of the linguistic system itself. Nevertheless, the parallels between the two cases are instructive. Changes in sound systems may be listener-based and independent of constraints on production and articulation. Whether the listener is a frog or a human, intrinsic features and biases of the perceptual system are likely to show themselves in the course of evolution.

6.2   Articulation as the primary source of sound change

Ohala's quote opening this chapter emphasizes the important role of perception and articulation in sound change. Synchronic variation resulting from the articulatory transforms of speech across various rates and styles plays a fundamental role in shaping sound patterns with sources in CHOICE. Three primary transforms of speech can be distinguished: timings or retimings of articulatory gestures which may result in coarticulation (gestural overlap) or non-overlap; lenitions, where gestures are reduced in length or magnitude; and fortition, where articulatory gestures are strengthened. As reviewed in chapter 3, gradual shifts in articulation have been viewed as fundamental ingredients in sound change at least since the time of the neogrammarians.[4] Entire monographs are devoted to sound change with roots in coarticulation (e.g. Hajek 1997 on vowel nasalization), and a recent volume on coarticulation confirms that "coarticulation is a universal characteristic of human speech production" (Hardcastle and Hewlett 1999: 3). Since few phoneticians or phonologists have disputed this position, I will focus in this section on relationships between synchronic sound patterns and sound change with sources in articulatory variation, and give particular attention to cases where the precise role of articulation has been either disputed, ignored, or misunderstood.

In the typology proposed in 2.2, sound changes with their source in natural articulatory variation are classified as cases of CHOICE. In instances of CHOICE, multiple phonetic variants of a single phonological form are accurately perceived by the listener, but the variation requires the listener to choose a prototype or best exemplar of a phonetic or phonological category; in some cases, involving phonologization, the choice will determine one of two possible phonological representations. The example used to illustrate CHOICE was a case of pre-tonic vowel reduction. A speaker says [kakáta], [kǎkáta], and [kkáta] for /kakáta/. The listener must decide which of these phonetic forms to base a phonological analysis on. If the listener chooses [kakáta] as the best exemplar of this word form, no sound change will have occurred. But if, due to the low frequency of [kakáta] in the input, [kkáta] is chosen instead, a sound change will have occurred. This schematic example, involving vowel reduction and loss, is a classic case of gestural reduction or lenition, and is discussed further in 6.2.2.

Other cases of CHOICE illustrated in chapter 4 include variability in consonant release leading to neutralization of laryngeal release features, variability in the degree of phrase-final lengthening, which can give rise to final devoicing, and variation in the timing of oral and laryngeal gestures in voiceless geminates which can give rise to pre- and post-aspirated segments. In chapter 5, sound changes with sources in CHOICE were shown to include: variability in consonant release leading to neutralization of laryngeal release features, debuccalization of unreleased p', t', k' to glottal stop as a consequence of anticipated glottal closure which may hide the oral gesture; and gestural weakening of oral stop closure in word-final nasals, resulting in nasal glides with [ŋ]-like percepts. In regressive and

---

[4] See Kühnert and Nolan (1999) for a history of coarticulation as a scientific construct in the study of human speech.

progressive place assimilation, the general association between direction of assimilation and the nature of the perceptual features involved makes it appear that CHANGE, not CHOICE, is the dominant phonetic factor. However, place assimilations which are restricted to certain combinations of place-features, like the English coronal-non-coronal sequences studied by Blust (1979), suggest that coarticulation can also play a significant role.

6.2.1   From coarticulation to assimilation and more

The idea that articulation plays a role in defining common sound patterns is rarely debated. Some of the most common sound patterns involve assimilations between adjacent vowels and consonants which can be viewed as phonologized instances of coarticulation. Consider the common palatalization of [s] to [ʃ] adjacent to [i]or [j] which has occurred independently in many of the world's languages, from American English pronunciations of *miss you* as [mɪʃjə], to Yurok [wi ʃoninepek'] for *wi soninepek'* 'I think so.' In English, /s/ can be pronounced as [ʃ] when followed by [j]; in Yurok /s/ is always pronounced as [ʃ] when preceded by [i] within the word. The sound change *s > ʃ/__i in the history of Nahuatl has led to a /s/ versus /ʃ/ contrast. For each of these cases, and many more, there is good evidence that the shift of [s] to [ʃ] is a consequence of coarticulation between [s] and the adjacent palatal vowel or glide.[5] In the English case, where phonetic coarticulation is still the source of [s]/[ʃ] variation, hyperarticulated speech may provide tokens of [s] before [j], but casual speech will often show [ʃ] in the same context. This variation on the part of the speaker defines CHOICE for the listener. The language learner can maintain the system of variation which is in evidence, or, decide that, because of its high frequency, [ʃ] is the appropriate phone for this particular context. In this particular case, a *s > ʃ sound change is unlikely to effect the /s/ of *miss*, *kiss*, etc. since the contexts in which these fricatives are variably palatalized (e.g. before unstressed *you*) are not as common as the contexts in which they are not.

Note that since coarticulation can be both anticipatory or perseverative, there is no *a priori* reason to expect directional asymmetries within the speech stream. Bidirectionality is in fact one characteristic which often distinguishes assimilations with articulatory origins from those with perceptual origins. Compare for instance the Yurok and Pre-Nahuatl patterns of shibilantization above: in Yurok, coarticulation is perseverative, while in Nahuatl, it is anticipatory. This bidirectionality is distinct from

---

[5] Perception may also play a significant role in the phonologization of [sʲ] as [ʃ].

the unidirectional patterns of laryngeal feature assimilation and place assimilation surveyed in chapters 4 and 5.[6]

C–V and V-to-V coarticulation exist in all languages for which articulatory patterns have been studied (Hardcastle and Hewlett 1999). As a consequence, sound changes with sources in coarticulation are predicted to be very common. Phonologized cases of C–V or V–C coarticulation, like the cases of sibilant palatalization just discussed, typically take the form of local assimilation rules where a consonant is specified for secondary features of the adjacent vowel. As phonological rules, these may be referred to as palatalizations, labializations, velarizations, uvularizations, nasalizations, or some combination of these. Though the features of pharyngealization, laryngealization, breathy voice, and rhoticity are also contrastive for vowels in some languages, they are not common, and I know of no well-documented cases of these features giving rise to new contrasts on adjacent consonants via V–C or C–V coarticulation.

Coarticulation between sequential vowels across an intervening consonant appears to be the norm in spoken languages. V-to-V coarticulation refers to the case where, in a VCV sequence, transitions from vowel to consonant and from consonant to vowel are significantly influenced by the quality of the transconsonantal vowel. V-to-V coarticulation is reported by Öhman (1966) for Swedish and English, and has been documented for Spanish and Catalan (Recasens 1987), Arabic (Hussein 1990), Dutch (Van Bergem 1994), and many other languages. Phonologizations of V-to-V coarticulation may take the form of local vowel-to-vowel assimilations (umlaut) or may characterize longer domains (vowel harmony). Rounding, fronting, and backing umlaut or harmonies are well documented in the phonological literature, and occur in many of the world's major language families, including: Altaic, Austronesian (Loniu), Indo-European (Germanic umlaut); Oto-Manguean (Mazahua); Pama-Nyungan (Nyangumarda, Warlpiri, Warumungu); Penutian (Yokuts) and Uralic (Finnish, Hungarian). Foot-based pharyngeal harmony is found in Coeur d'Alene, a Salish language, and a case of stem-level retroflex harmony has been documented for Yurok (Robins 1958: 12–13).[7] Some implications of vowel harmony as an instance of phonologized coarticulation are discussed in Ohala (1994a, b), while Majors (1998) presents

---

[6] See Beckman (1999) for some discussion of the prevalence of C–V over V–C coarticulation. Perseverative shibilantization occurs not only in Yurok, but also in neighboring Karuk (Bright 1957, 1978).

[7] Yurok retroflex harmony appears to be the long-distance effect of a formerly local V–C coarticulatory effect where a retroflex affricate gave rise to retroflexion on preceding non-high vowels. This coarticulatory effect is reported in Wiyot, a related Algic language (Reichard 1925: 8).

phonetic evidence bearing on the evolution of stress-based vowel harmony systems.

Some coarticulatory phenomena give rise to non-assimilatory sound patterns. We have already seen how retiming of oral and laryngeal gestures in, e.g., non-released *t'*, may give rise to a percept of [ʔ], phonologized as debuccalization. Another sound pattern with sources in coarticulation is that involving excrescent oral stops in nasal-fricative clusters. For example, in *prin[t]ce, warm[p]th, young[k]ster*, etc., consonant insertion can be analyzed as a consequence of consonant coarticulation, with anticipation of the velic closing gesture (Ohala 1971, 1974a, 1981, to appear). Finally, coarticulation between adjacent consonants in the form of gestural overlap can give rise to assimilation, or to percepts of consonant loss when one gesture hides another (Browman and Goldstein 1990).

In (1) I summarize the range of sound patterns in the world's languages with evident sources in coarticulation or gestural retiming. This list is not meant to be exhaustive. Rather, it is meant to be suggestive of the extent to which observed synchronic patterns in the form of common alternations or surface true generalizations mirror common instances of sound change with sources in phonetic variation.

(1)   SOUND PATTERNS WITH SOURCES IN COARTICULATION
    i. Assimilatory
       a. local CV, VC, CC, and VV assimilations
       b. vowel harmony
       c. consonant harmony
       d. tone assimilation
    ii. Non-assimilatory segment-internal shifts in featural timing
       f. debuccalization (via laryngeal/oral retiming)
       g. pre-aspiration (via laryngeal/oral retiming)
       h. secondary feature shifts (e.g. post-velarization to pre-velarization)
    iii. Non-assimilatory, other
       i. excrescent C, e.g. *ns* > *nts* (via nasal/oral retiming)
       j. deleted C, e.g. *ktm* > *km* (via gestural hiding of [t])

6.2.2   *Lenition and fortition*

While assimilations, be they local or non-local, are the cases which immediately come to mind when one considers sound patterns with articulatory origins, phonological lenition and fortition processes also appear to have articulatory origins. Support for consonant lenition and fortition as phonologized instances of gestural reduction and gestural strengthening can be found in the growing literature on articulatory phononlogy (e.g. Browman and Goldstein 1990, 1992) H&H theory (e.g. Moon and Lindblom 1994), and in case studies of phonetic correlates of consonant strength (LaVoie 2001; Fougeron and Keating 1997; Fougeron 1999). Whereas lenition occurs in weak prosodic positions, and is typical of casual speech, in clear or careful speech, "talkers shape phonetic patterns for perceptual processing by articulating more forcefully which makes phonetic segments longer and more audible and reduces ambiguities due to coarticulation" (Lindblom 1998: 242).

LaVoie (1996, 2001) presents a cross-linguistic survey of consonant strengthening and weakening in over eighty languages. Consonant strengthening or fortition processes include: gemination, occlusivization/hardening, aspiration, and fricativization of glides. Consonant weakening or lenitions may involve shortening (degemination), voicing, approximantization, debuccalization, and loss. For vowels, strengthening typically involves vowel lengthening and diphthongization (breaking), while vowel weakening is associated with shortening or reduction (with associated quality shifts), devoicing, and loss.[8] In (2) I summarize the range of sound patterns in the world's languages with evident sources in lenition or fortition. Like (1), this list is not meant to be exhaustive. Rather, it is meant to be suggestive of the extent to which observed synchronic patterns in the form of common alternations or surface true generalizations mirror common instances of sound change with sources in gestural reduction and gestural strengthening.[9] Since the articulatory bases of most of these common sound patterns are documented in the literature referred to above, I will say little more about them.

(2)   SOUND PATTERNS WITH SOURCES IN GESTURAL
       REDUCTION AND GESTURAL STRENGTHENING
         i. gestural reduction of consonants
            a. degemination
            b. voicing, approximantization
            c. debuccalization
            d. loss

---

[8] See Barnes (2002) for a comprehensive survey of positional neutralization in vowels.
[9] Prosodic conditions for fortition and lenition require much further study. Ferguson (1990) highlights the distinct pattern of $s > h$ in Ancient Greek and Spanish. In the first case, the sound change occurred intervocalically and word-initially, while in the second, it is confined to syllable coda position, post-vocalically pre-consonantally or word-finally. This example serves to highlight convergence, despite superficial similarity of the two changes. Both, undoubtedly, have articulatory components, but the source of lenition in the two cases may differ in terms of the type of gestural reduction involved, e.g. debuccalization in the Spanish case, but simple temporal reduction in the Greek case leading to an [h]-like percept.

    ii. gestural reduction of vowels
      e. shortening/reduction
      f. loss
   iii. gestural strengthening of consonants
      g. gemination
      h. glide hardening
   iv. gestural strengthening of vowels
      i. lengthening
      j. diphthongization, breaking
    v. gestural strengthening release
      k. release > vowel

One process, however, which is not often discussed is that listed in (2k): the case where a consonant release is strengthened, and as a result, is interpreted by the listener as a vowel. This sound change is often referred to as paragoge or final-vowel epenthesis, and has occurred independently in the history of many Austronesian languages, including Leti, Dobel, and Kambera (Blevins and Garrett 1998: 542). In Dobel, for example, an excrescent [u] occurs after word-final stops. A similar development has occurred in some Sulawesi languages (Mills 1975a, 1975b), as illustrated in table 6.1.

Table 6.1 *Final consonants in Sulawesi languages (from Sneddon, 1993)*

	Totoli	Talaud	Ratahan	Duri	Makasar	Wolio
*p	p	p:a	p	ʔ	ʔ	ø
*t	t	t:a	ʔ	ʔ	ʔ	ø
*k	k	k:a	k	k	ʔ	ø
*m	m	m:a	m	n	ŋ	ø
*n	n	n:a	n	n	ŋ	ø
*ŋ	ŋ	ŋ :a	ŋ	ŋ	ŋ	ø

In Ratahan, Duri, Makasar, and Wolio, loss of final release combined with glottalization, appears to have given rise to place neutralization. However, in Talaud, a different pattern is in evidence, with a paragogic vowel appearing in the context of a lengthened final consonant. Instances like this are attributed to fortition of final consonant release, and are important in highlighting the two extremes of the articulatory continuum which can lead to sound change. Elimination of release, as an instance of gestural reduction, will have many consequences, as discussed in chapters 4 and 5. Strengthening of release, on the other hand, can lead to vowel insertion processes, like that documented for Talaud.

One overlooked aspect of leniting sound change is also worthy of mention. Though the patterns in (2i, ii) have ultimate sources in gestural reduction, the percepts which result from gestural reduction can give rise to phonologized patterns which do not actually directly reflect the lenited articulations. Two cases of this sort are identified by LaVoie (2001): intervocalic voicing of voiceless stops, and intervocalic spirantization of stops. LaVoie's studies of both English and Spanish show that the main acoustic correlate of lenition is decreased duration, and that the phonetic parallels to phonological voicing and fricativization are short duration and incomplete stop closures. Decreased closure duration of intervocalic stops gives rise to a voiced percept in the absence of vocal-fold vibration, while stops with incomplete closure can be perceived as fricatives. These findings highlight the sometimes translucent relationships between phonetics and phonology which Evolutionary Phonology seeks to explain. Speakers do not produce [k] as [g] intervocalically as a result of gestural reduction. In prosodically weak positions, the closure of [k] may be shortened, and linguo-palatal contact may be reduced, resulting in things that *sound* like [g] and [ɣ] to the human ear. When these sounds are reinterpreted and reproduced as [g]s and [ɣ]s, a leniting sound change has occurred.[10]

Gestural reduction of vowels (2ii) is the norm when vowels are unstressed, or in prosodically weak positions. Investigations of fast speech in languages as distant as English and Fijian show that phonological vowels are often absent in the acoustic record. The variation between vowelful and vowelless articulations of the same tokens gives rise to instances of CHOICE, from which historical processes of vowel loss can arise. These include pre-tonic and post-tonic syncopes, where adjacent stressed syllables may result in further reduction of the unstressed vowel. See Barnes (2002, chapter 2) for general patterns of unstressed vowel reduction, and Blevins (to appear a) and Blevins and Blust (2003) for discussion of additional conditions on syncope.

---

[10] The role of perception in leniting sound change creates problems for restrictive phonological accounts. Lenition cannot be modeled as phonological feature loss or delinking (Harris 1997), with subsequent spreading of marked features (Kiparsky 1988), since intervocalic voicing and intervocalic spirantization involve insertion of specified feature values, [+voiced] and [+continuant], which, within constrained theories of underspecification, should be unspecified for vowels. Nor can phonological lenition always be characterized as a decrease in effort (Kirchner 2000), since voicing a stop arguably requires more effort than not. See LaVoie (2001, chapter 6) for similar assessments.

6.3 Feature localization as the primary source of sound change

Certain features are typically local and realized over relatively short time durations, whereas others are typically non-local and realized over relatively long durations. For example, stop bursts are short local events while contrastive pharyngealization of a consonant is typically realized over minimal VC or CV domains, and in some languages, over much longer segmental strings. Other features with typically long domains include: rounding, palatalization, velarization, laryngealization, aspiration/breathiness, retroflexion, and nasalization. Where a particular acoustic property is associated with more than one segment, a problem of feature localization arises. In this section a variety of sound patterns are attributed to shifts of feature localization which occur in the course of sound change, and which are classified as instances of CHANCE.

The general nature of the problem faced by the language learner can be illustrated with a hypothetical instance of pharyngealization. Given a string $C^ʕV^ʕC^ʕ$ where the entire syllable is pharyngealized, what processes play a role in determining localization of the feature in question? If features are associated at some level with unique segments, there are seven logical possibilities for the phonological representation of the pharyngealized $C^ʕV^ʕC^ʕ$ sequence: any of the three segments could carry a secondary pharyngealization feature ($C^ʕVC$, $CV^ʕC$, $CVC^ʕ$); or a pharyngeal glide could be the source of ambient pharyngealization (ʕCVC, CʕVC, CVʕC, CVCʕ). If the historical source of pharyngealization is a pharyngeal glide and the listener posits a pharyngeal glide in a non-historical position, metathesis occurs. If the historical source of pharyngealization is not unique, e.g. the string is historically /$C^ʕVC^ʕ$/, and the listener assumes a unique source of pharyngealization, e.g. /$C^ʕVC$/ or /$CVC^ʕ$/, dissimilation occurs. Another possibility is the case where the historical source of pharyngealization is unique, but the listener attributes it to multiple segments. In this case, a pattern of harmony evolves. In (3) the sound changes are shown schematically for some long-domain feature, F.

(3)   CHANCE as source in metathesis, dissimilation, and harmony

	i. /CVC^F/	ii. /C^FVC^F/	iii. /CVC^F/
Speaker means	i. /CVC^F/	ii. /C^FVC^F/	iii. /CVC^F/
Speaker says	[$C^FV^FC^F$]	[$C^FV^FC^F$]	[$C^FV^FC^F$]
Listener hears	[$C^FV^FC^F$]	[$C^FV^FC^F$]	[$C^FV^FC^F$]
Listener interprets	/C^FVC/	/C^FVC/	/C^FVC^F/, /$C^FV^FC^F$/
Result	metathesis	dissimilation	harmony

6.3.1   Dissimilation

The general model of perceptually based dissimilation in (3ii) is proposed in Ohala (1981), and supported further by Ohala (1986, 1993) and MacEachern (1997) for laryngeal features. Ohala's original idea is that dissimilation is a form of hypercorrection. In attempting to disentangle non-essential automatic phonetic features from essential ones, a phonetic feature covering a sequence of segments may be interpreted as having its source in a single segment, with the sequential spread interpreted as an automatic phonetic effect. In other words, dissimilation occurs when a listener assumes a phonetic source for surface sound patterns which are, in other cases, truly assimilatory effects of coarticulation; the assimilation is "undone" by the listener in mapping the phonetic string to a phonological representation, and dissimilation results.

Grassman's Law in Indo-European involves a regular sound change where $C^hVC^h > CVC^h$, where the dissimilating feature is aspiration. A similar dissimilatory constraint on laryngealization is found in some Mayan languages, where only a single glottalized consonant is possible in a CVC root. Between Old Javanese and modern Javanese, *rVr* shifted to *lVr* (Dempwolff 1934: 36, 96, as cited in Blust 1996a), and a similar dissimilation is found in the history of the Romance languages (Boyd-Bowman 1980). A case of labial dissimilation in Eastern Polynesian (with the exception of Rapanui) involves the change of *faf* > *wah*, where the combined features of noise and labiality occurring in [f] are dissociated. Under sound change, noise is associated with post-vocalic position, while labiality is assigned to pre-vocalic position (cf. Blust 1996a: 98–99). The common changes of $^*C^wu > Cu$ and $^*C^wo > Co$ can be viewed in similar terms. The long-domain feature of labialization is attributed by language learners to a single segmental source. This change is found in Yurok, where in some dialects, the contrast between /k, k'/ and /kw, kw'/ is neutralized to the non-labialized series before round vowels. In all of these cases of dissimilation, a feature which is characterized by a multisegmental domain phonetically and phonologically is located by the listener on a single segment. The result of this monosegmental localization is dissimilation.

6.3.2   Metathesis

This general model is extended to the analysis of perceptual metatheses in Blevins and Garrett (1998, to appear).[11] Under perceptual metathesis

---

[11] In CC-metathesis where both Cs are stops, coarticulation, not perception, is primary. See Blevins and Garrett (to appear) for further discussion.

as schematized in (3i), a long-domain feature is associated with a non-historical position. A common example of perceptual metathesis as sound change are historical inversions of laryngeals *h* and *?* adjacent to vowels. In many languages, *Vh* or *hV* sequences are produced with ambient aspiration or breathiness, while *V?* and *?V* sequences can show ambient laryngealization or creak. The problem of feature localization arises in the course of language acquisition. If a learner attributes the long-domain feature to a laryngeal segment in a non-historical position, laryngeal metathesis has taken place. Laryngeal metathesis has occurred in a wide range of genetically unrelated languages including Arbore (Cushitic), Cayuga (Iroquoian), Bisayan (Austronesian), and Thompson River Salish (Salishan). Indirect support for this perceptual account of metathesis comes from the limited range of features which recur in metathesizing sound changes, including laryngealization, breathiness/aspiration, pharyngealization, palatalization, labialization, and retroflexion (Blevins and Garrett 1998).

6.3.3   Harmony

Phonologization of long-domain features in the form of local CVC harmony is usually treated as a subcase of other instances of coarticulation in the phonetics literature. One potential output of this process is local consonant harmony across an intervening vowel, again as the result of partial hypercorrection. Cases of phonological harmony with phonetic origins in long-domain features are not uncommon. In Cairene Arabic, pharyngealization spreads from a pharyngealized consonant to other tautosyllabic segments (Broselow 1979). In Coeur d'Alene, regressive pharyngeal harmony spreads pharyngealization from a consonant to a preceding vowel, while a rule of progressive harmony spreads pharyngealization from a vowel to a following stressed vowel (Doak 1992). In Caddo, glottalization takes the syllable as its domain when a glottalized sonorant appears in an RVR syllable (Wallace Chafe, personal communication, 2002). In Mayali retroflexion takes the syllable as its domain (Evans 1995a: 739–40). In Ponapean, all labials must be either plain or labialized within a morpheme, reflecting historical local labialization harmony (Rehg and Sohl 1981: 44–46). In all of these cases, what was once a phonologically localized feature with an elongated phonetic domain has been reanalyzed as a long-domain or harmonizing feature within the phonology by the schematic listener-based sound change shown in (3iii).

6.3.4   Compensatory lengthening

Compensatory lengthening is a common sound pattern in the world's languages where loss of one segment is compensated for by lengthening of another. One common sound change of this type involves shifts of $C_1VC_2 \to C_1V$:, where loss of a coda consonant appears to give rise to lengthening of a preceding vowel (de Chene and Anderson 1979). Another common compensatory sound change is $C_1V_1C_2V_2 \to C_1V_1C_2$, where loss of a final vowel in a disyllabic sequence yields apparent non-local lengthening of the vowel in the preceding syllable (Rehg 1984). In Kavitskaya's (2002) comprehensive survey, compensatory lengthening from CVC sequences is found in 57 languages belonging to 18 different language families, while non-local CVCV lengthening is attested in at least 21 languages representing 5 different language families.

Kavitskaya (2002) presents phonetic historical analyses of both CVC and CVCV compensatory lengthening. She argues that both changes are the result of phonologization of pre-existing vowel-length differences. The general hypothesis is that compensatory lengthening results in cases where length, which was once attributable to phonetic factors, is no longer interpreted this way by the listener. Phonetic factors leading to vowel lengthening include longer V–C transitions for particular consonants, longer vowels before particular consonants, and open-syllable lengthening. Under this account, compensatory lengthening is a unique case of CHANCE. Unlike dissimilation, metathesis, and harmony, a long-domain feature, in this case vowel duration, is attributed directly to the vowel, though historically, it is determined by phonetic context.

6.4 Constraints on sound change with sources in CHOICE

In the above discussion, I summarize work suggesting that recurrent sound changes involving dissimilation, metathesis, harmony and compensatory lengthening have a common feature. In these types of sound change, the acoustic record of speech presents the listener with phonetic features whose segmental source is ambiguous. A choice must be made as to where to localize the phonetic feature, and if the listener's choice differs from the speaker's intention, sound change occurs at the level of the individual. In this section, I suggest two universal constraints on sound change with sources in CHOICE.

6.4.1 The Feature-to-segment Mapping Principle

Given the inevitable ambiguities which arise in segmentation of the phonetic signal, it is not surprising that sound changes like those schematized in (3) exist. In fact, it would be quite surprising if they did not. Notice that both metathesis and dissimilation have an interesting property in common: although the feature F characterizes every segment in the phonetic string, the listener interprets F has having a single segmental source, with specification of F occurring only once in the phonological representation. I suggest that this interpretive strategy is a general aspect of the default mapping from phonetic form to phonological representations which takes place in the course of language acquisition. The mapping principle is stated in (4).

(4)   Feature-to-segment Mapping Principle (FMP)
       In the learning algorithm which allows listeners to interpret the phonetic string as a sequence of segments, a phonetic feature, F_p, whose domain overlaps with other segment-defining phonetic features is assumed to have a unique featural source $/S_F/$ in the phonological representation (where F may be a feature or feature-complex).

As stated, (4) will account for the schematic metathesis and dissimilation sound changes shown in (3). This principle can also be seen to play an important role in the phonological interpretation of local C–V coarticulation by requiring that the coarticulated feature have a single segmental source. For example, in a language where coronals are palatalized only before high vowels, the FMP requires that the phonetic sequence [tʲi] be interpreted with a single instance of the phonological palatalization feature. At the phonological level, this feature could be associated with /t/, with /i/, or with both segments. What is ruled out by the FMP are adjacent identical feature specifications as output of the phonetics–phonology mapping.

Note that the phonological forms /C^FVC^F/, /$C^FV^FC^F$/ which are posited by the listener in the case of harmony in (3iii) appear to violate this principle. However, as with the instances of coarticulation just mentioned, these phonological representations can be slightly altered so that the FMP is not violated. Instead of assuming two specified instances of the feature [F] in /C^FVC^F/ or three in /$C^FV^FC^F$/, many-to-one mappings are allowed between features and the segments defined by them. In other words, one instance of the feature F can be associated with multiple segments within the /CVC/ (or longer) domain, in conformity with the Feature-to-segment Mapping Principle.[12] What is ruled out by the FMP are adjacent identical feature specifications as output of the

---

[12] The independent representation of features from the phonological segments they define was a central focus of prosodic phonology, as conceived of by J. R. Firth, and subsequently played a role in the long components of Harris (1951), before becoming the primary concern of autosegmental phonology, as conceived of by Goldsmith (1976), McCarthy (1979), and much subsequent work.

phonetics–phonology mapping. An association between one feature, F, and /CVC/ will not violate this principle.

Reference to adjacent identical specifications brings to mind a principle of phonology which has been claimed to constitute part of Universal Grammar: the Obligatory Contour Principle (OCP). In order to account for the fact that morpheme-internal tone melodies in many languages prohibit sequences of identical tones, Leben (1973) proposed the Obligatory Contour Principle which, in its earliest formulation stated that "Adjacent identical tones are banned from the lexical representation of a morpheme." Subsequently, the OCP was extended from tone to other non-tonal features (McCarthy 1981), prohibiting adjacent identical features or feature complexes in underlying representations. It was also claimed to play an active role in synchronic phonologies by inhibiting vowel loss between adjacent identical consonants (McCarthy 1986).

The Feature-to-segment Mapping Principle in (4) and the Obligatory Contour Principle are similar in their prohibition of phonological representations involving adjacent identical features. However the FMP, as a constraint on phonological acquisition, is not claimed to have any active role in the synchronic phonology of a language. In contrast, the Obligatory Contour Principle is argued to define possible synchronic underlying representations, and to inhibit rule application as well. This view of the OCP has met with serious counterexamples in the phonological literature (e.g. Odden 1988, ch. 7). Once the OCP is demoted to a violable synchronic constraint, as in current Optimality approaches, there is no longer an explanation for the strong cross-linguistic tendencies which it is meant to account for.

However, a stronger argument for the FMP in (4) over the synchronic OCP is the wider empirical coverage of this principle. Recall that the Feature-to-segment Mapping Principle as an interpretive constraint on phonetics–phonology mappings provides a unified analysis of dissimilation, perceptual metathesis, dissimilation, and harmony. The consequence of such a constraint will be visible OCP-like effects in the lexicon, but these are viewed as by-products of acquisition, not as hard-wired constraints on phonological representations. In sum, where the OCP is at once too strong and too weak, the Feature-to-segment Mapping Principle may account for a similar range of sound patterns and relate a range of synchronic sound patterns to their historic phonetic origins.

6.4.2   Structural Analogy

In de Chene and Anderson's (1979: 517) study of compensatory lengthening, they suggested that compensatory lengthening is a structure-preserving sound change, in the sense that a length contrast must already exist in a language for compensatory lengthening to evolve. Subsequent studies have shown this to be incorrect. Compensatory lengthening in at least eight languages has occurred giving rise to new vowel-length contrasts, including Piro (Matteson 1965), Ngajan (Dixon 1990), and Andalusian Spanish (Hock 1986). However, this set of languages is small in comparison to the over eighty languages with well-documented compensatory lengthening where vowel length is pre-existing (Kavitskaya 2002).

I suggest that the greater likelihood of compensatory lengthening to develop in a language with pre-existing length contrasts than in a language without such contrasts reflects potential priming effects on the learner in the course of language acquisition. In languages with pre-existing vowel-length contrasts, the listener is presented with unambiguous tokens of long and short vowels, and categorizes these accordingly. Where phonetically lengthened vowels occur, as in the typical phonetic lengthening contexts described by Kavitskaya (2002), the learner is more likely to categorize these as long vowels for the simple fact that a category of long vowels may already be established. Priming effects may also take the form of heightened attention to vowel length, recognizing its contrastiveness elsewhere.

Apparent structure-preservation effects in sound change are attributed to Structural Analogy, as stated in (5).

(5)   STRUCTURAL ANALOGY
       In the course of language acquisition, the existence of a
       phonological contrast between A and B will result in more
       instances of sound change involving shifts of ambiguous
       elements to A or B than if no contrast between A and B existed.

Structural Analogy is attributed to the kind of analogical learning which characterizes phonological acquisition (Wedel 2004). Like the FMP in (4), it is not a property of grammars, but a property of the cognitive processes which give rise to grammars.[13] Under Structural Analogy, language-specific priming effects play a role in the course of language acquisition precisely where contrasts are unambiguous. I have already

---

[13] Structural Analogy as a factor in language acquisition is similar in intention to the phonological "priming effect" proposed in Kiparsky (1995: 656) which states that "redundant features are likely to be phonologized if the language's phonological representations have a class node to host them." While Kiparsky's proposal is limited to redundant features and depends on phonological constructs like class nodes, Structural Analogy is not limited to any class of features, and is compatible with any phonological model in which features and segments are represented.

suggested how these effects result in the association between compensatory lengthening sound changes and pre-existing vowel-length contrasts. Other cases where structure-preserving effects are expected are in cases of metathesis, where pre-existing phonotactics can prime reanalysis of ambiguous strings. Again, a tendency in this direction is attested, though it is not absolute (Blevins and Garrett 1998). Structural Analogy has also been invoked in the study of historical syncope rules. Blevins and Blust (2003) demonstrate that syncope of vowels in VC__CV sequences is much more likely in languages which have pre-existing closed syllables than in languages which do not. In general, the effects of Structural Analogy will be more visible in instances of CHANCE and CHOICE than in CHANGE where perceptual biases dominate.

6.5   Phonetic sources of vowel insertion

Many of the world's languages show synchronic rules of vowel insertion. Rules of epenthesis, prothesis, and paragoge are often considered to have an optimising function within the phonology: they serve to syllabify consonants which would otherwise be left stray, or to create unmarked open syllables, or to facilitate the production of certain consonants or consonant clusters. In (2v) one source of paragogic vowels is fortition under consonant release. In this section I suggest two additional sources for sound patterns involving rules of vowel insertion. In one case, a syllabic consonant is reinterpreted as a VC sequence. In another case, vowel epenthesis reflects the inversion of an earlier vowel-syncope rule.

The general view that phonetic variation stems ultimately from the hyper-to-hypo continuum of speech predicts that hyper–hypo patterns will also exist at the phonological level, as grammaticized reflections of this continuum. The existence of both vowel insertion- and vowel-deletion rules in the world's languages can be seen to support this general view. Just as vowel-deletion rules can be seen to have their origins in hypoarticulated speech, so certain vowel-insertion rules appear to stem from aspects of hyperarticulated speech. Consider Crowley's (1998: 14) observation concerning certain word-initial consonant clusters in Erromangan (Sye), a language of Vanuatu: "Word-initial clusters of /n-/ followed by a heterorganic consonant are occasionally pronounced with an intervening unstressed schwa, though only when the word is produced very carefully in isolation. Thus, /nmar/: [nmar ∼ nəmar] 'breadfruit' and /nvaŋ/: [nvaŋ ∼ nəvaŋ] 'food'." This isolated phonetic fact from a little-known language might seem insignificant, but I argue that it is not. On the contrary, in this single fact lies important counterevidence to some of the leading phonological views on the role of epenthesis in synchronic grammars. Let us try to understand why, by reviewing several cases where vowel insertion evolves from instances of listener-based consonant release.

In chapters 4 and 5, the failure to release word-final consonants was suggested as one contributing factor to word-final laryngeal and place neutralizations. However, because release is non-contrastive, there is always the possibility that final consonants will be released. If they are, neutralization is unexpected. In 6.2, some instances of final-vowel insertion, or paragoge, are attributed to the phonologization of audible release. This sound change has occurred independently in the history of many languages including: Kisar (Stresemann 1927: 219–20), Leti (Blevins and Garrett 1993: 542), Dobel (Hughes 1995), Kambera (Klamer 1994) and many of the Central and Western Malayo-Polynesian languages surveyed in Sneddon (1993). Kambera appears to represent the pre-phonologized stage of this development. Roots ending in consonants receive a paragogic [u], but Klamer refers to this vowel as "weak" and notes that it may disappear altogether in rapid speech. The sound change is formalized as an instance of CHOICE + CHANGE: hyperarticulation provides the strongly released final consonants, while misperception allows the release of these consonants to be reinterpreted as reduced vowels.

A similar sound change occurs in word-medial position, where obstruent–sonorant clusters are analyzed with medial vowels. A well-documented case is the evolution of a copy-vowel between $*cl$ clusters in the history of Latin: *facilis* 'easy' $< *faclis$, *pōculum* 'goblet' $< *pōclum$, etc. In this instance, the copy-vowel tells us something about the phonetics of early Latin: apparently there was significant anticipatory articulation of vowel gestures, so that the release of $*c$ was colored by the post-consonantal vowel, giving rise to a copy-vowel percept. A more general instance of a similar sound change is found in the history of West Chadic languages, where, obstruent–sonorant clusters are resolved by an epenthetic vowel colored by the following consonant (Schuh 1978: 254): Ngizim *zapənu*, Bade *sabənu* 'churn' $< *zapnu$; Ngizim *kakəra*, Bade *kakəla* 'load' $< *kakra$, Ngizim *səsuwa*, Bade *təsuwa* 'stalk' $< *səswa$; Ngizim *vaviyu*, Bade *ɓaɓiyu* 'singe' $< *vavyu$.[14] A parallel synchronic rule, known as "Dorsey's Law" is found in Winnebago (Hale and White Eagle 1980; Miner 1989) and has the form $TRV_i \rightarrow TV_iRV_i$: /wakripropro/ [wakiriporoporo] 'spherical bug').[15] In all of these cases, the epenthetic vowel appears to have its source in audible release of the preceding stop.

---

[14] Tone marks on Bade and Ngizim forms have been removed for ease of legibility.

[15] The Winnebago rule and Ngizim-Bade sound change target glides, liquids, and nasals. The inclusion of nasals makes it an unlikely example of perceptual epenthesis of the sort

A subset of common epenthesis rules may be unrelated to consonant release and, as a consequence, do not target oral stops. I will suggest phonetic explanations for two of the most common types here. In the first type, a syllabic sonorant is reinterpreted as a vowel–sonorant or sonorant–vowel sequence. In Mokilese (Harrison 1984: 387), *NC > VNC, where the quality of the initial epenthetic vowel is determined by the quality of the nasal consonant: *nsa > insa, *mwwuj > umwwuj, etc. In the synchronic phonology of Old Armenian, a rule of pre-sonorant epenthesis must be distinguished from other epenthesis rules. And within Germanic, there are both historical pre-sonorant epentheses (e.g. Old Swedish *Cr# > Cer#) and cases of synchronic alternations (e.g. Modern Icelandic Ø → u/ C__r#). Since vowels are typically longer than consonants, and since all languages have syllabic vowels, the perceptual correlates of syllabicity in syllabic sonorants appear to contribute to their reanalysis as vowel–sonorant sequences. The quality of the inserted vowel is predicted to depend on perceptual features of the sonorant, as e.g. in Mokilese.

In the second type of non-release-based epenthesis, long-domain features like those discussed in 6.3 are involved. A VC_F sequence, where F is a long-domain feature, is reinterpreted as a $V_iC_FV_i$ sequence. For example in East Slavic, medial VL > VLV, where V is a non-high vowel and L is a liquid – a change referred to as *Polnoglasie*, while in Negev Bedouin Arab aGC > aGaC, where G is a gutteral. Blevins and Garrett (1998: 522–25) suggest that these epenthesis types have precisely the same perceptual origins as the perceptual metatheses discussed in 6.3.

While many epenthesis rules have their origins in perceptual reanalyses of consonant release, features with elongated cues, or consonant syllabicity, synchronic epenthesis rules may also be inverted instances of earlier syncope rules. Where syncope deletes a medial unstressed vowel, vowel-zero alternations result. In the acquisition of grammar, such rules of vowel deletion may be reinterpreted as rules of vowel insertion. One case of this kind is described for Manam (Lichtenberk 1983: 32–40), and involves vowel insertion at a stem-suffix boundary.

The phonological rule in Manam inserts [i] between a stem-final nasal and a following adnominal suffix, accounting for alternations like *tamim* 'urine, urinate' *tamimigu* 'my urine' *matadaŋ* 'tear' *matadaŋigu* 'my tear,' etc. where epenthetic vowels are in bold. The only consonants which can close syllables in Manam are nasals. For this reason, the epenthesis rule

discussed directly below. However, it could be that both cases are combined instances of reinterpretation of release and perceptual epenthesis. Note that in all cases discussed in this paragraph, an obstruent precedes a sonorant, providing a particularly salient context for obstruent release. See Hall (2002) for a survey of svarabhakti vowels in over 25 languages.

serves no clear syllabic function in the synchronic phonology. Lichtenberk shows that the epenthetic vowels indirectly reflect a historical process of final vowel loss. Word-final high vowels *i, u were lost after nasals in the history of Manam (see 6.6 for an account of similar developments). These high vowels would have been preserved before the adnominal suffixes, and this vowel retention has been reinterpreted as vowel epenthesis by subsequent generations. But this is not the only historically motivated epenthesis rule in the language.

In addition to morphologically restricted epenthesis, Manam appears to have a more general process which inserts [i] between a non-nasal consonant and a following consonant. Since this alternation appears to break up otherwise illicit clusters, it might be assumed to serve a syllabification function in the synchronic grammar. However, as detailed by Lichtenberk, the epenthetic i in this rule reflects Proto-Oceanic *-i, a verbal transitive suffix, which, at some point in the history of Manam, ceased to function as a transitivizer. As Lichtenberk (1983: 36) summarizes: "The original transitive suffix *-i, after being reinterpreted as a new 3sg object suffix, was then lost everywhere except in those cases where there was some motivation for its retention; i.e., in those cases where sequences of two consonants the first one of which was not a nasal would have resulted . . ." In other words, the object suffix *-i underwent the same loss as the word-final vowel mentioned earlier. The result of this vowel loss is the synchronically inverted pattern which appears to insert /i/ to save what would otherwise be an illicit syllable type.[16]

After this somewhat long excursus, we can return to Crowley's (1998: 14) description of careful speech variants in Erromangan: "Word-initial clusters of /n-/ followed by a heterorganic consonant are occasionally pronounced with an intervening unstressed schwa, though only when the word is produced very carefully in isolation. Thus, /nmar/: [nmar ~ nəmar] 'breadfruit' and /nvaŋ/: [nvaŋ ~ nəvaŋ] 'food'." In careful speech, the transition between the first two consonants is delineated by non-overlapping articulations, and a lengthening of the transition between these two articulations, while in casual speech, overlapping gestures are the norm. In the discussion above, small variations like these and their percepts are viewed as the seeds of many sound changes involving the insertion or deletion of vowels. If the explanations suggested above are correct, these Erromangan variants tell us more about expected sound patterns and directions of sound change than might be imagined.

---

[16] In Gilbertese, rule inversion with the same historical origins in final high-vowel loss after nasals takes the form of regular sandhi alternations (Blevins 1997: 237–43).

6.6 Inheritance and convergence: the myth of high-sonority codas

6.6.1 Sonority

It has long been recognized that syllables tend towards sonority profiles which involve a central sonority peak (the syllable nucleus), with an optional rise in sonority towards the peak or nucleus, and an optional fall in sonority after the peak. However, as noted by nearly every person who has looked at this subject carefully, there are two problems with using a sonority algorithm to define syllable structure: first, these sonority profiles are strong tendencies, but they are not without exceptions; second, sonority appears to be relative, and difficult to define outside of the particular context in which a segment appears.

Nevertheless, within the phonology literature, there is general agreement that something like the sonority scale in (6) is useful in defining relationships between segments within the syllable in many of the world's languages.

(6)   Sonority scale (Blevins 1995)

HIGH   LOW
low vowels > mid vowels > high vowels > glides > liquids > nasals > fricatives > oral stops

Sonority scales like the one in (6) have been put to many uses in phonological analyses. In addition to defining overall syllable contours (Hooper 1976; Selkirk 1984), sonority scales have been used to define relations between adjacent syllables (Hooper 1972; Murray and Vennemann 1983), and to define the content of sub-syllabic constituents including nuclei, onsets, codas, and weight units or moras (e.g. Levin 1985; Clements 1990; Blevins 1995a; Zec 1995). Sonority scales have also played a role in syllabification algorithms, where more sonorous segments are given preference as nuclei over less sonorous ones (Levin 1985a; Dell and Elmadloui 1985; Prince and Smolensky 1993).

One generalization that has been claimed to emerge from crosslinguistic studies of syllable structure is that high-sonority codas are preferred over low-sonority codas in the world's languages. Given a syllable $[C_1VC_2]$ where C_1 is the onset, V is the nuclear vowel, and C_2 is the coda, it has been suggested that there is a preference for high-sonority segments in C_2, but no such preference in C_1. There are several ways in which this claimed preference has been incorporated into modern phonological theory. In early work, it takes the form of a syllable-contact condition. The Syllable Contact Law first proposed in Hooper (1972) and later modified by Murray and Vennemann (1983) states that for any heterosyllabic sequence of consonants $C_1.C_2$, there is a preference for C_1 to be more sonorous than C_2. In later formulations, the focus is on syllables in isolation. For example, Clements (1990: 301) defines a Sonority Cycle Principle which states that "the preferred syllable type shows a profile that *rises maximally toward the peak and falls minimally toward the end* ..." Under other approaches, constraints are proposed directly on the coda position (e.g. Itô 1986; Goldsmith 1990), or on possible moras (Zec 1995).

6.6.2   Some facts about codas

Here I suggest that any preference for high-sonority segments over low-sonority segments in the syllable coda, if empirically verifiable, is the result of inheritance and convergence. High sonority codas may arise as a consequence of many different types of sound change. But evidence against a general phonological preference for high-sonority segments can be found in many synchronic sound patterns. First, there is the fact that there are very few languages in the world where codas are restricted to all and only the sonorant consonants of the language. In many languages constraints on codas appear arbitrary, while in others, restrictions on codas can be shown to follow from phonetically motivated vowel-loss processes by which codas evolve. In still other languages, low-sonority codas appear to be preferred. One language of this type is Misantla Totonac. In the Yecuatla dialect of Misantla Totonac described by Mackay (1994, 1999), non-nasal sonorants /w, j, l, h/ are not possible codas, but glottal stop, nasals, fricatives, and oral stops are. Phonological rules delete coda glides, while /l/ and /h/ are neutralized to obstruent [ɬ] in the coda. If glottal stop is treated together with /h/ as a laryngeal glide, then this coda set is discontinuous along the sonority scale. But under any analysis, the preference is clearly for low-sonority [ɬ] over high-sonority codas /l, w, j/.

In the course of investigating the distribution of laryngeal and place features, coda inventories of the languages under investigation were noted. The basic question posed was: are there any languages in which coda elements include all and only high-sonority elements?[17] A partial summary of the results follows. Of the more than 52 languages from at least 22 different families investigated in chapter 4, there were no languages in which codas were limited in this way. Only one language, Mbe (Bamgbose 1967) showed a tendency in this direction. The consonant inventory of Mbe is: /p, b, f, m, t, d, s, ts, dz, n, l, r, ʃ, c, ɟ, j, k, g, h, ŋ, kʷ, kp, gb, w, j̃, w̃/. In

---

[17] Because the glides /w, j/ are often restricted from occurring in post-vocalic position within the syllable even in languages with a wide range of syllable types, the absence of /w, j/ in the class of possible sonorant consonants was not taken to be a significant violation of a tendency for high-sonority codas.

Mbe all consonants except the velar nasal /ŋ/ occur syllable-initially. In the syllable coda, the only consonants found are: /l, r, m, n, ŋ, b/. Codas in Mbe tend to be sonorants, but note that glides are excluded, and /b/ is allowed. Because the survey of laryngeal features was primarily focused on neutralization of laryngeal contrasts in coda position, it was clearly biased towards languages with obstruents in this position. Hence, it is not surprising that no languages were found with only sonorants in the coda. Nevertheless, there are clearly a substantial number of languages which lack any strong preference for sonorant elements in the coda.

Languages investigated in chapter 5 include 47 additional languages from 10 distinct families. From this set, there were two distinct cases of languages where the only codas were sonorants. The first was in certain Chinese languages (e.g. Peking, Lingbao) where codas are restricted to nasal stops. However, in both Peking and Lingbao, /l/, which is more sonorous than the nasals, does not occur as a coda, a property inherited from Middle Chinese. A second set includes some of the Pama-Nyungan languages in the survey: Wajarri, Pintupi/Luritja, and Mbabaram. In these languages, codas are restricted to glides, liquids, and nasals, as they were in Proto-Pama-Nyungan (O'Grady and Fitzgerald 1995 and references therein). While many Pama-Nyungan languages inherited this pattern, fortition in languages like Nhanda (Blevins 2001) and Djinang (Waters 1989) has led to obstruent codas. The preference for sonorant codas then is no more than a feature of inheritance. In Sulawesi languages like Selayar and Bugis where final codas are limited to /ʔ, ŋ/, medial codas include the first halves of geminate obstruents. Also, in these languages word-final *s, r, l have given rise to word-final excrescent vowels, and borrowings with final s, r, l trigger the same vowel-insertion process. If sonorant codas are preferred, why do /r/ and /l/ trigger vowel insertion? One might imagine that the smaller the coda inventory, the stronger the preference for sonorant codas. However, in some languages with very small coda inventories, obstruents are still found. A case is Pawaian, a language of the New Guinea Highlands, with coda consonants /n, l, t/ (Trefry 1969). In sum, in this combined survey of over 100 languages representing dozens of different language families, only three, all Pama-Nyungan, show a clear preference for high-sonority codas. However, as noted, in this case, the sound pattern is an inherited one. In addition, two Chinese languages show only sonorants in the coda, though /l/, a high-sonority element, is excluded.

Since this language sample was arguably biased in many respects, an attempt was made to identify any reported languages where coda consonants included all and only the sonorants of the language in question. The majority of languages restricting coda consonants to sonorants are found in Sub-Saharan Africa and Australia. In Australia, the pattern is one that has generally been inherited without change from Proto-Pama-Nyungan. In Sub-Saharan Africa, the prevalence of tone languages may play an important role in the evolution of codas, since tone-bearing units are limited to sonorants in the majority of the world's languages (Gordon 1999, 2002). Tiv, a non-Bantu tone language of Nigeria, is taken to exemplify the case where the possible set of moraic segments includes all sonorants in the language, including nuclear vowels and codas (Zec 1995). Tiv syllable structure is CV(C), with coda consonants limited to /l, r, m, n, v, ɣ/ and /ŋ/ in ideophones (Abraham 1940; Arnott 1958). Another language where codas are limited to sonorants is Lama (aka Lama), a Gur language of Togo (Ourso 1989; Ourso and Ulrich 1990). Lama consonants include /p t c k kp f s h m n ɲ w l r j/. Of these, only /m n w l r/ occur in the coda, with the palatals excluded. Even in tone languages, however, there are facts which lead one to question the association between codas and high-sonority segments. Consider, for example, the peculiar coda inventories of some Bantoid languages noted by Herbert (1986: 150–51): Elong, codas include /l, N, k, ʔ, p/; common Nyokon codas are /p, N, s, ʔ, r/; and in Djanti, syllables may be closed by /r, k', y, ŋ, n/. In each case, the seeming pattern association of coda position with sonorants is disrupted by the occasional obstruent.

In the majority of the world's languages where closed syllables occur, there does not seem to be a strong preference for sonorants over obstruents. But if a statistical tendency in this direction is observed, what might it be attributed to? In the case of the Pama-Nyungan languages mentioned above, direct inheritance is involved. But are there other factors at work? Are there any recurrent sound changes which result in limited classes of sonorant-only codas? Two recurrent sound changes of this type are detailed below.

6.6.3   Convergent evolution

General rules of unstressed vowel deletion are not predicted to result in any specific restrictions on coda consonants. And many phonologized instances of such rules which take the form of medial syncope are consistent with this view. However, other phonetic factors may play a role in unstressed vowel deletion. Here I look at factors which play a role in the historical loss of final voiceless vowels, and cases where homorganicity plays a role in vowel deletion. In both cases, high-sonority codas result.

In Gilbertese, a Micronesian language, the only possible syllable codas are nasals. The restriction of word-final codas to nasal consonants is due to a sound change involving loss of word-final voiceless high vowels.

In Pre-Gilbertese, word-final voiceless high vowels were lost only after nasal consonants. Following Ohala (1983), Blevins (1997: 243–46) suggests that the critical factor distinguishing post-nasal from other environments is the potential muting property of the preceding nasal consonant. Ohala (1983: 205–6) suggests that nasalization will block (or substantially reduce) the audible flow of air created by turbulence downstream. This reduction in audible airflow makes the (near-silent) voiceless vowels even more difficult to perceive after nasals than elsewhere, and they are lost via CHANGE. A similar sound change was noted for Manam in 6.5. If loss of final voiceless vowels after nasal consonants is a common sound change, then it will result in some languages, like Gilbertese and Manam, where nasals are the only attested synchronic codas.

Another sound change giving rise to high-sonority codas can be attributed to CHANCE. Recall the sound changes schematized in (3) where resolution of a long-domain feature may result in dissimilation, metathesis, or harmony. One subcase of dissimilation may result in vowel loss: this is the case where vowel features are attributed to release features of a preceding consonant. A recurrent sound change with these features is $*mu > m$.

Fijian is often cited as one instance of the small percentage of world languages having only open syllables. This is true for most dialects, but in some, coda consonants are evolving. In Nadrogaa Fijian (Geraghty 1995: 927) which otherwise has only open syllables, unstressed *mu* sequences are commonly reduced to [m]. Variation is indicative of a sound change in progress: *yámu* or *yam* 'mosquito'; *mmá*: < /mu-ma:/ 'your tongue.' A strictly sonority-based view of this variation cannot explain why /m/ and not other sonorants /w, y, r, l, n, ŋ, ŋʷ/ is a preferred coda. I suggest that $m^u > m$ is an extreme case of the dissimilatory changes analyzed in 6.3. The short voiced labial quality of the vowel allows it to be interpreted as a release of the preceding labial consonant. The same $m^u > m$ change has occurred independently in Tawala, an Oceanic language of the Papuan tip cluster (Ezard and Robert 1995: 759), and in some Eastern Bantu languages including Nyanja and Sukuma. In these two languages, the Class 1 and 3 noun prefix /m-/ reflects Proto-Bantu $*mu$- through a recent rule of vowel loss (Herbert 1986: 171). In this case, vowel loss appears to be independent of syllable structure, since it gives rise to word-initial NC clusters, where N is arguably syllabic. Loss of final voiceless vowels after nasals as well as $*mu > m$ dissimilatory changes converge on a higher frequency of nasal codas than would otherwise be expected.

Another potential source of high-sonority codas are common sound changes involving coda-weakening. Bybee (2001: 193), for example, suggests that:

the crosslinguistic patterns of syllable structure are . . . the result of a diachronic tendency by which syllable-final consonants gradually weaken and delete. Such changes can be manifested in various ways: a syllable-final nasal can nasalize the preceding vowel and then delete; [s] can lose its lingual articulation, becoming [h], which then deletes; or a syllable-final obstruent can assimilate to the following obstruent, producing a geminate that degeminates.

However, some of the most common sound changes in the syllable coda (*r*-loss, nasal-loss, *l* > *w*, glide-loss) are those which actually *eliminate* high-sonority codas. Explanations for precisely these patterns are suggested by Kavitskaya (2002), and relate to the perceptual similarity of vowels and following sonorants, as well as relatively long transitions in and out of these sounds. The general pattern is not weakening of low-sonority elements to high-sonority ones, but loss of high-sonority codas.

In cases where high-sonority codas do occur, direct inheritance and convergence appear to be involved. In some language families, like Pama-Nyungan and Bantu, high-sonority codas have been directly inherited by the majority of living daughter languages. In other cases, like Gilbertese and Manam, they reflect voiceless vowel loss after nasals, while in still other cases, like Nadrogaa Fijian, nasal codas are the output of sound changes which appear to be dissimilatory. At the same time, high-sonority codas are often lost in the course of sound change. In sum, there is no single factor which is responsible for high-sonority codas, where they happen to exist, nor is there any clear evidence for phonological constraints which lead to preferences for high-sonority codas over others.

6.7   Some unexplained sound patterns

Despite the great number of common sound patterns which originate in natural sound change, certain recurrent, independent, and well-documented sound changes remain unexplained. Before looking at several cases, it is useful to consider the implications of the preceding discussion for future avenues of investigation. Chapters 4 and 5 demonstrate that the most common sound patterns involving the distribution of laryngeal and place features can be seen to follow from common phonetically motivated sound change, and their patterns of phonologization. And the sections above suggest how a range of other patterns, including common assimilations, lenitions, fortitions, metatheses, and dissimilations may be explained along the same lines. Given the numerous recurrent synchronic sound patterns which *can* be explained in terms of phonetically based sound change, it is not unreasonable to hypothesize that all such recurrent sound patterns have similar origins. In this context, let us look at three examples of recurrent sound change whose origins remain obscure.

The unmarked or most natural syllable type in spoken languages is thought to be CV: a single consonant, the onset of the syllable, followed by a vowel, the nucleus of the syllable (Jakobson 1962: 526). In over fifty Australian Aboriginal languages, however, consonants have been lost from the beginning of words, leaving vowel-initial syllables. As detailed in Blevins (2001b), initial C-loss is not limited to any single genetic or areal group of languages within Australia; it occurs in Western, Central and Eastern Pama-Nyungan languages, and in non-Pama-Nyungan languages as well. Blevins (2001b) explores several factors which may have played a role in this sound change. Segmental lenition and lenition of unstressed pre-tonic syllables has clearly been a factor in some languages. However, in other languages, the most important identifiable conditioning factor for C-loss is utterance-initial position. Utterance- or phrase-initial consonant weakening and loss has been observed as a non-distinctive property of natural speech in Worora, Wajarri, Nhanda, Warlpiri, and Yir-Yoront, while utterance-initial cases of historical C-loss are apparent in Arabana, Baagandji, Maljangaba, Yadliyawara, Nhanda, Nyungar, Warumungu, Yir-Yoront, and Burarra.

A puzzling question is what aspect of utterance-initial consonants leads to their loss. Blevins (2001b) suggests several hypotheses, all open to phonetic investigation. One is that the default setting for the oral tract on initiation of speech is "open" in many Australian languages, leading to more initial lenition than elsewhere. Another possibility is that audible ingressive breathing associated with initiation phrase-initially could reduce perceptual cues for initial consonants. A third possibility is that initial consonants are compensatorily shortened as the vowels following them are lengthened.

A second case of unexplained sound change is the change of y-accretion before /a/ detailed by Blust (1990) for a wide range of Austronesian languages. Blust (1990) presents evidence for this change in the history of Fijian, Motu, Gedaged, the Cristobal-Malaitan languages, the Trukic languages, Buli and Numfor, and several other languages. He argues against the role of universal principles because the addition of y ($= $ [j]) before a appears to be limited to the Austronesian family, and is without clear articulatory or perceptual motivation. While the lack of direct phonetic motivation is not contested, a similar change outside of Austronesian may provide a key to the origins.

A generalized form of y-accretion is found in several Western Desert languages of central Australia. Compare Luritja *anyu*, Pintupi *yanyu* 'same place'; Luritja *ina*, Pintupi *yina* 'friend'; Luritja *umu*, Pintupi *yumu* 'care free,' etc. A potentially significant fact is that in related dialects like Pitjantjatjara there is no contrast between *i*- and *yi*-initial words. One potential origin then of *y*-accretion in Pintupi is based on the non-contrastive nature of phonetic [i], [ji]. From the variant surface forms, Pintupi speakers chose [ji] as "basic," and relate their speech to that of speakers with [i] by a rule of initial-glide insertion, which is extended to other vowel-initial words. Whether or not a similar development is possible for Blust's (1990) Austronesian examples based on word-initial variation between [i] and [ji] remains to be investigated, as do the mechanisms by which such extensions might occur.

Alternatively, Austronesian *y*-accretion may reflect the high frequency of *i#a* sequences in sandhi. Under this account, *y*-accretion is attributed to the natural phonetic reinterpretation of formant transitions as glides (Blevins to appear b).

A third case of unexplained recurrent sound change is the example of low-vowel dissimilation found in a range of Austronesian languages, including Ere, of Manus Island, Papua New Guinea, several Micronesian languages and in many languages of Southern Vanuatu (Blust 1996a, b; Lynch 2003). The sound change in Ere takes *aCa* > *iCa*. There are several interesting constraints on dissimilation in Ere which point to its origins in V-to-V coarticulation. As noted by Blust (1996a: 109), dissimilation does not take place if the two low vowels are separated by a consonant cluster, and it is also blocked by an intervening /h/ or glottal stop. A similar segmental constraint is found in Marshallese (Bender 1969), where low-vowel dissimilation is blocked by an adjacent /h/, /y/, or /w/. Since patterns of low-vowel dissimilation are word internal, exceptionless, and, in some cases, productive, they smack of phonetic naturalness. As of yet, however, no plausible phonetic explanation has been identified.

To say that a particular sound change has no as yet identified phonetic source is not to say that a source will not be found. As Ohala (1993: 261) reminds us:

the ultimate check on any hypothesis about the cause of a particular sound change is to test the hypothesis in the laboratory. If particular sound changes are posited to have a phonetic basis, then one should be able to duplicate the conditions under which they occurred historically and find experimental subjects producing "mini" sound changes that parallel them.

Some hypotheses proposed in this and earlier chapters will be difficult to test in the laboratory because of the widespread influence of English and other world languages. For example, the explanation for the recurrent *t* > *k* changes in Austronesian relates this change to significant burst and VOT properties of these two sounds in contrast to [p]. In theory, the hypothesized perceptual similarity of [t] and [k] could be tested on monolingual speakers of Tahitian, a language whose consonant inventory includes only /p m f v t n r ? h/. However, once a Tahitian speaker is exposed to a language with a *t* versus *k* contrast, perceptual contrasts between these segments will become more salient, with less likelihood that they will be treated as a single category (Ohala 1995b: 91–92). In this case, because most Tahitian speakers will be exposed from birth not only to Tahitian, but also to French or English, a sensitivity to the spectral peak at 3–4 kHz which appears to provide an all-or-nothing perceptual cue to velars (Ohala 1985; Plauché et al. 1996) is expected, and will bias judgments. However, for most of the hypotheses in this and preceding chapters which have not yet been tested in the laboratory, such checks are possible. As work in the laboratory proceeds, we will come closer to understanding the perceptual, articulatory, and general cognitive features which underlie these recurrent sound patterns.

7 The evolution of geminates

> If one attempts to characterize the so-called "inner form" of language . . . one can only do so by tracing the origins of expressions and their basic meanings. And so I cannot conceive how one could with any hope of success think about a language without discovering at least to some extent how it came to be as it is.   Paul (1920: 21–22)

7.1   Why geminates?

In addition to the distinctive features which compose speech, it is generally recognized that a distinction must be made between long and short segments in phonological representations. Long consonants are also called geminates. In this chapter, I investigate the historical origins of long or geminate consonants, and ways in which their synchronic behavior may reflect historical origins. The impetus for this study is two-fold. On the one hand, phonological theory has struggled with various aspects of geminate distribution, representation, and behavior. Geminates have been associated with special properties, including resistance to epenthesis and lenition processes, and have been problematic for theories of syllable weight. On the other hand, the neogrammarian position summarized in Paul's quote above leads us to believe that geminates with different historical origins may give rise to geminates with distinct synchronic properties. Because geminates can arise in many different ways, as I highlight below, and because their phonology has been well studied in many languages, a case study of geminate evolution can provide a basis on which to assess and compare synchronic and historical accounts of geminate phonology.

In chapters 4, 5, and 6, recurrent sound patterns in the world's languages which could not be accounted for by direct inheritance, contact, drift, or chance, were shown to have well-founded historical explanations in the form of recurrent phonetically based sound change. In this chapter, I look at distinct phonetically based sound changes which can converge on the same surface sound patterns – geminate consonants.

Earlier studies of geminate evolution include Goodenough (1963) on Trukese, Blust (1990) on Oceanic, Harrison (1984) on Mokilese, and Blust's (1995) more general study of the phenomenon in Austronesian, with special reference to Berewan. A prediction of Evolutionary Phonology is that distinct historical origins of geminates may give rise to distinct synchronic properties for geminates within and across languages. This prediction is tested wherever possible.

7.2   Phonological and phonetic length

At the phonetic level, length distinctions which correspond to segmental duration are gradient and potentially imperceptible. However, at the phonological level, languages are found to make common distinctions between short and long vowels or consonants, and more rarely, between short, long, and extra-long vowels or consonants. In languages with a phonological contrast between long and short consonants, the most salient acoustic correlate for stop consonant length is closure duration (Lahiri and Hankamer 1988; Hankamer et al. 1989; Cohn et al. 1999; Kraehenmann 2001). On average, long stops have one and a half to three times the acoustic closure duration of short stops in careful speech (Ladefoged and Maddieson 1996: 92).

There is general consensus that the representation of length should be independent of the featural content of the segment. However, phonologists differ as to whether length is represented independent of syllable weight (e.g. the X-slot model of Levin 1985a) or whether length is represented in terms of weight units like moras (e.g. Hyman 1985; Hayes 1989). Some evidence supporting the independence of length and weight is presented below, and a general discussion of this issue can be found in Broselow (1995).

In addition, some languages appear to require a distinction between "true" and "false" geminates. True geminates are single long segments with single-feature bundles. False geminates are sequences of identical short segments. False geminates, or sequences of identical consonants, occur in many languages which do not have true geminates. For example, in English, false geminates occur across word boundaries in compounds like *rat-tail*, *cash-shortage*, *felt-tip-pen*. These are referred to as false geminates because consonant length is not distinctive in English. In English, there are no minimal pairs where consonantal length contrasts are involved.

Though it is sometimes assumed that true geminates involve a single articulatory gesture, while fake geminates involve multiple gestures, there is some evidence that the distinction between false and true geminates does not correspond with any constant articulatory or perceptual correlate. Both true and false geminates may be characterized by a single articulatory gesture, or by two distinct articulatory gestures. Lehiste, Morton, and Tatham (1973) carried out an electromyographic study of the orbicularis oris muscle of the lips, and found that there were two peaks of muscular activity for one speaker pronouncing word-medial geminate /pp/ in Estonian, and for one speaker pronouncing interword /p#p/ in English. On the other hand, an x-ray microbeam study of word-medial geminates in Italian and Japanese does not show double peaks for lip movement in geminate /pp/ (Smith 1992), and a dynamic palatography study by Barry (1985) shows no evidence of two articulatory peaks for English /k#k/ sequences. It is possible then, that the distinction between true and false geminates is, in some languages, a phonological contrast with no clear phonetic correlates.

In phonological treatments it has been argued that morpheme-internal geminates and geminates which arise via assimilation are true geminates, and that in all languages with an underlying consonantal length contrast, true geminates contrast with non-geminate consonants (McCarthy 1981, 1986; Schein and Steriade 1986; Hayes 1986a, b). False geminates are those which arise via morpheme concatenation (without obvious assimilation), and can occur in languages which lack underlying length contrasts. For the purposes of this study, I follow these standard phonological treatments. However, it is worth stressing that nothing in the historical accounts I present hinges on the way in which length is represented. All that is necessary is that phonological contrasts exist between geminates and non-geminates and between true geminates and sequences of identical consonants, and that these contrasts are consistently represented.

7.3   Geminate evolution: general pathways

There are at least seven identifiable pathways by which a single segment or a sequence of non-identical segments can be transformed into a geminate consonant, resulting in the evolution of a consonantal length contrast for a given language. These general pathways are listed in (1).

(1)   General pathways in the evolution of consonantal length
         contrasts
         (a) assimilation in consonant clusters
         (b) assimilation between consonants and adjacent vowel/glides
         (c) vowel syncope

(d) lengthening under stress (including expressive lengthening)
(e) boundary lengthening
(f) reinterpretation of a voicing contrast
(g) reanalysis of identical C+C sequences

In the following paragraphs I will present examples of each type, and then turn to predictions of the evolutionary approach for the synchronic behavior and distribution of geminates. For each case, unless otherwise noted, the documented sound change results in a geminate versus singleton contrast which did not exist prior to the development in question.

7.3.1   Assimilation in CC clusters

Assimilation between adjacent consonants is a common sound change and a common synchronic alternation in the world's languages. Phonetic explanations for different aspects of assimilation were proposed in chapters 4–6, and allow us to understand total assimilation, like that found in the recent history of Nhanda (Blevins 2001). In Nhanda, sonorant–obstruent sequences directly inherited from Proto-Pama-Nyungan have undergone sonorant fortition, giving rise to heterorganic voiceless stop–stop clusters. Subsequent regressive place assimilation gives rise to geminate/singleton contrasts, as illustrated by the minimal pair *nhakka* 'see.PRESENT' ($<$ **nha-t-ka* $<$ **nha-l-ka*) versus *nhaka* 'see.IMPERATIVE.'

While coarticulation may play a role in such changes, it was argued in chapter 5 that perceptual factors are dominant in triggering regressive (as opposed to progressive) major place assimilation. The sound change is schematized in (2). In Proto-Pama-Nyungan and Pre-Nhanda, consonant clusters were limited to word-medial position. As a result, the only place where geminates have evolved via the combination of fortition and assimilation is word-medially.

(2)   Cluster assimilation with resulting geminate
         $C_1 C_2 > C_2 C_2$

In contrast to the Nhanda example, other assimilations resulting in geminates appear to have purely articulatory origins. For example, in Toba Batak **mp > pp, *nt > tt, *ŋk > kk*, and **ns > ts* (Blust 1995: 125). In this sound change, the oral gesture of the post-nasal obstruent is anticipated, and, as a consequence, the nasal stop is produced as an oral stop. A sound change like (2) then may have origins in CHANGE, CHOICE, or both.

7.3.2   Assimilation in VC, GC

Luganda has a contrast between geminate and non-geminate consonants in initial and medial position. Inherited geminates in Luganda are the result of historical assimilation between a consonant and a preceding super-high front vowel (Meeussen, 1967, 1980; Guthrie 1967–71): *-bba-* 'steal' < *-jıb-*, *-dduka-* 'run' < *-jıduk-*, etc. In many Bantu languages the reconstructed super-high noisy vowels have been shown to be associated with the evolution of a noisy consonant or noisy consonant transition (Hyman 1998, 1999). From the range of historical developments documented by Hyman (1999) it seems likely that the phonetic identify of the noisy vowel varied between a more vocalic sound and a syllabic sibilant or fricative vowel.[1] The sound change accounting for Luganda geminates in (3) is similar to (2) except that the segment to which the consonant assimilates was once a vowel, constituting both a potential stress- and tone-bearing unit in the language.

(3)   Assimilation to vowel with resulting geminate
       $V^h C_2 > C_2 C_2$ (Where V^h is a close high noisy vowel)

7.3.3   Vowel syncope between identical consonants

In many Austronesian languages vowel deletion between identical consonants has given rise to geminates (Blust 1990). Vowel deletion in these contexts is a canonical case of CHOICE, where gestural reduction of unstressed vowels results in their eventual loss. Languages showing historical loss of vowels between identical consonants include Mussau of the St. Matthias Archipelago north of New Ireland, Tuvaluan, Kapingamarangi, and other Polynesian outliers (Milner 1958; Biggs 1978), and Trukese and other Micronesian languages (Goodenough 1963). In Dobel (Hughes 1995), there is evidence that the sound change is still in progress: compare k^w *a-k^{w}ása, kk^{w}ása* 'crocodile,' *sa-sár, ssár* 'sandfly,' *tu-tún, ttún* 'mosquito,' etc. In all of these languages, historical CV-reduplication produces prosodic contexts where the loss of pre-tonic unstressed vowels appears limited to the reduplicative context. The general sound change is shown in (4) where the consonant in parentheses is not part of the structural description, but is included for clarity.

(4)   Vowel deletion with resulting geminate
       $\check{V} > \emptyset/(C_i)\_C_i\acute{V}$

---

[1] See Ohala (1975) for aerodynamic factors involved in high-vowel devoicing and frication, and Svantesson (1984) for an acoustic study of fricative vowels in Chinese.

7.3.4 Lengthening under stress

In many languages, a stressed syllable is longer in duration than a segmentally identical unstressed syllable.[2] Stressed syllable lengthening can
take the form of tonic vowel lengthening, post-tonic consonant gemination, syllable-initial consonant lengthening, or any combination of these.
In English, stressed syllables are longer than their unstressed counterparts (Lisker and Abramson 1967). In Rotuman, short stressed vowels
are longer than their unstressed counterparts (Churchward 1940: 73).
In Swedish consonants are long after short vowels in stressed position
and short elsewhere (Engstrand 1999: 141). In Ndjébbana, a non-Pama-
Nyungan language of Australia, there is a geminate/singleton alternation
of stem-initial Cs under prefixation, with geminates preceding stressed
vowels (McKay 1984). And in Hebrew, vowels and consonants are both
longer in stressed syllables (Laufer 1999: 98). The simplest explanation
of lengthening under stress is that length is a direct phonetic manifestation of stress. Perceptual studies support duration as a correlate of
stress in many languages, including English (Fry 1958; Nakatani and
Aston 1978), Czech (Janota 1967), and Italian (Bertinetto 1980). In
many languages duration under stress is non-contrastive, but length
differences in stressed syllables are great enough to give rise to gemi-
nate/singleton contrasts. Post-tonic lengthening under stress is the source
of at least some non-inherited geminates in a range of Austronesian
languages.

In the history of Austronesian, a recurrent change involves the evolution of geminate consonants after schwa (Brandstetter 1916; Blust 1995).
Proto-Austronesian is reconstructed with a four-vowel system: $*a$, $*i$, $*u$,
$*ə$. Based on its reflexes in many languages, $*ə$ is believed to have been
shorter than the other three vowels. The inherited quantity difference
between vowels has resulted in languages where stress on a penultimate
schwa results in lengthening of the following consonant (Blust 1995:
127, 132–33). Post-schwa gemination in /CəCVC/ is found synchronically in Kelabit, Madurese, Sangir, and Buginese (aka Bugis). In related
Isnag and Konjo, a subsequent merger of $*ə$ and $*a$ results in contrastive
gemination after /a/: Proto-Austronesian $*ənəm$ 'six,' Konjo annaŋ but
Proto-Austronesian anak 'child,' Konjo anaʔ.[3]

---

[2] Early studies demonstrating the association between stress and longer duration include
Fry (1955) on English, Rigault (1962) on French, and Jassem et al. (1968) on Polish. See
chapter 4 of Gordon (1999) for a cross-linguistic survey of weight-sensitive stress systems
demonstrating that overall acoustic energy within the syllable rhyme is greater in stressed
syllables than unstressed syllables.

[3] Subsequent assimilations in these languages have given rise to other geminate consonants.

The general sound change involving post-tonic gemination is shown in (5). The phonetic source of this rule is the general association between stress and phonetic duration evidenced in the acoustic and perceptual studies cited above. Syllables are longer under stress, and the phonetic length of consonants is reinterpreted as contrastive.

(5)   Post-tonic gemination
$$\acute{V}C_iV > \acute{V}C_iC_iV$$

In many languages, post-tonic gemination is limited to cases, like the Austronesian example, where intrinsic properties of the stressed vowel are incompatible with lengthening. For example, in Southern Paiute, a Uto-Aztecan language, all obstruents occur as geminates after stressed voiceless vowels (Harms 1966, 1985), while in Norton-Sound Unaliq, an Eskimo language, a consonant following a stressed schwa in an open syllable is geminated (Jacobson 1985). Cases of the sound change in (5) then may be more common after intrinsically "weak" vowels than elsewhere.

Another case of lengthening under stress involves what might be referred to as expressive or emphatic lengthening. Syllable lengthening, including vowel lengthening and consonant gemination, is used for expressive or emphatic purposes in many unrelated languages. See, for example, Churchward (1940: 108–9) on Rotuman vowel protraction and Rasmussen (1979) and Woodbury (1987) on Eskimo expressive lengthening. In West Greenlandic Eskimo, demonstratives showing emphatic gemination include: *'ikka* 'look yonder!' (non-exclamative /ika-/) and *'uvva* 'look here!' (cf. /uva-ne/ 'here where I am pointing'). Similar examples are found in Bengali and Marathi: *ata* 'now' versus *atta* 'now!' (Masica 1989: 122). If emphasis is realized in terms of additional stress, then these examples may be viewed as special cases of stress-induced post-tonic gemination like that shown in (5).

7.3.5   Boundary lengthening

In many languages, a phrase-final syllable is longer in duration than a segmentally identical phrase-medial syllable (Klatt 1975; Wightman et al. 1992). In addition, consonants which are initial within a prosodic domain typically involve greater articulatory amplitude or force, longer duration, and more rigid alignment of articulatory gestures than their non-initial counterparts (Fougeron and Keating 1997; Fougeron 1999). Given these automatic phonetic lengthening processes, it is not surprising to find that articulatory strengthening at the edges of prosodic domains is phonologized in certain languages where segmental lengthening is limited to constituent boundaries.

An interesting case of this sort occurs in Mokilese (Harrison 1976, 1984). In Mokilese, consonant gemination and vowel lengthening are triggered by encliticization. Vowel-initial clitics (e.g. *-o* 'that') trigger gemination of preceding consonants, while consonant-initial clitics (e.g. *-ki* 'with') trigger lengthening of a preceding vowel. Consonant clusters arising through cliticization are unaffected. Harrison (1984: 396) demonstrates that the origin of length in these contexts is not due to segmental or stress effects, and concludes that "Junctural lengthening before enclitics can be viewed as a direct response to their enclitic status."

Examples of Mokilese boundary lengthening with gemination preceding the vowel-initial enclitic *o* 'that' (where = marks a clitic boundary) include: *wɔllo* /wɔl=o/ 'that man,' *wɔlkɔlikko* /wɔl kɔlik=o/ 'that big man,' and *wɔlkɔlik rɔɔmenno* /wɔl kɔlik rɔɔmen=o/ 'those two big men'. The absence of gemination in non-clitic environments is shown by examples like *wɔl ɛmɛn* /wɔl ɛmɛn/ 'one man (emphatic).' Comparative evidence supports reconstruction of Proto-Ponapeaic *-o* 'that.' In this case, then, there is no obvious segmental source for the gemination in the examples above, nor does boundary lengthening appear to have any relationship to stress. Rather, lengthening at the constituent boundary appears to be a phonologized instance of automatic phonetic lengthening at the edge of a prosodic domain. A similar case is reported for the Nobiin variety of Nubian, a Nilo-Saharan language, where cliticization of /-ɔn/ 'and' results in gemination of a stem-final consonant (Bell 1971). A general schema for this sound change is shown in (6), and may be related to phonetic phrase-final lengthening.

(6)   Boundary lengthening
        $VC_iV > VC_iC_i]V$ where] is a phrase-boundary

7.3.6   *Reinterpretation of an obstruent voicing contrast*

In many languages voiceless obstruents are significantly longer than their voiced counterparts (Denes 1955; Lisker 1957; Catford 1977; Westbury 1979; Jaeger 1978, 1983). Given this, we might expect to find laryngeal contrasts subject to phonological reanalysis, with length replacing voicing as the contrastive feature distinguishing the two obstruent series. The sound change is schematized in (7).

(7)   Voicing contrast reinterpreted as length contrast (T a voiceless
        obstruent, D a voiced obstruent)
        $T_i > T_iT_i$
        $D > T$

Voicing of the short consonant is interpreted as an automatic phonetic consequence of lenition, and is "undone," while the intrinsic duration of the voiceless segment is interpreted as underlying.

Though such changes seem possible in principle, I have been unable to find well-documented cases involving inherited vocabulary. There are some synchronic patterns suggestive of such developments, and other cases where the change in (7) has been proposed subject to controversy.

In Didinga (Odden 1983), a Nilo-Saharan Surma language of the southern Sudan, all consonants are automatically lengthened in syllable-final position. As a result, the underlying contrast between short and long consonants in Didinga is neutralized syllable-finally to the geminate category. If Pre-Didinga is reconstructed with the cross-linguistically common rule of syllable-final devoicing, this strange alternation might receive a plausible historical explanation. The voiceless syllable-final consonants of Pre-Didinga were reinterpreted as geminates. A similar sound change might account for the peculiar distribution of obstruent voicing in Meidob Nubian, as described by Thelwall (1983). Intervocalically there is both a voicing and length contrast for oral stops, but word-initially there is no voicing or length contrast.[4] Since word-initial degemination (but not word-initial devoicing) is common cross-linguistically, an earlier reinterpretation of the word-initial voicing contrast as a length contrast, followed by word-initial degemination, would result in the peculiar synchronic distribution of obstruent voicing.

One case where a change of the kind found in (7) has been proposed is in the history of the Dravidian languages. Under the standard view, Proto-Dravidian contained a single laryngeal series of plain voiceless obstruents and voiced sonorants, and had a length contrast for both obstruents and sonorants directly inherited in Malayalam and Tamil (Steever 1998). A different position is taken by Emeneau (1967), where Proto-Dravidian is reconstructed with a voicing contrast. Under Emeneau's account, the ancestral voiced/voiceless contrast is reflected as a geminate/singleton contrast in Malayalam and Tamil, while in most other languages, it is continued unchanged.

One instance of (7) is attested in dialects of Swiss German. In this case a geminate/singleton contrast has been inherited in word-medial and final position, but loanwords provide evidence of the mappings in (7) (Kraehenmann and Lahiri 1999; Kraehenmann 2001). At the time loans entered the language, there was a geminate/singleton contrast in

---

[4] There are very few languages where an obstruent voicing contrast in the environment V_V does not also occur word-initially before a vowel. In Nhanta, where it does not, the voiced/voiceless contrast word-medially can also be analyzed as a singleton/geminate contrast.

medial and final position, but only singletons occurred word-initially. Loanwords with word-initial voicing contrasts from Romance and other languages show a consistent mapping of voiced to singleton and voiceless to geminate in all positions of the word: *poott* 'boat,' *piplə* 'bible,' *snop* 'snob'; *ppaaʀ* 'pair,' *xappə* 'cap,' *kalopp* 'gallop' (Kraehenmann 2001: 140). While loanword phonology can often be viewed in terms of matching to the closest phonetic target, the consistency of correspondences like those just listed shows that speakers perceive the contrast between voiced and voiceless stops in loans, and associate them with their native length contrast. The difficulty of finding well-documented sound changes of this sort suggests that geminate/singleton contrasts are more easily reinterpreted as voicing contrasts than the reverse.

7.3.7   Reanalysis of identical C+C sequences

An obvious source for a geminate/non-geminate contrast is through lexicalization of former heteromorphemic sequences of adjacent identical consonants. In Gooniyandi, a Bunaban language of Australia, there are no morpheme-internal geminates, but across morpheme boundaries, geminate contrasts are found for all consonants, with the exception of the tap (McGregor 1990: 78). Compare *moowa* 'he looks,' *moowwadda* 'we look,' *warangi* 'I stood,' *warangngi* 'I sat,' etc.

McGregor (1990: 78–80) describes the phonetics of the geminate/ singleton contrast as follows:

All geminates are phonetically distinct from the corresponding single consonants, involving longer articulation in the case of nasals, stops and laterals. For geminates of these manners, the articulation is initially weak (giving a lenis syllable final consonant), becoming stronger finally (where the syllable initial articulation is fortis.)

Though, for the most part, geminates in Gooniyandi are limited to transparent heteromorphemic sequences, McGregor (1990: 75) notes that roots which are duplications of meaningless forms, or which are segmentable into historical formatives, show the cluster types found intermorphemically. An example is /gligglig/ 'noise of an eagle' (cf. /gigig/ 'neigh of a horse'). If it has not happened already, it appears to be only a matter of time before the source of geminates in some words becomes opaque, and true morpheme-internal geminates emerge. The development is stated in (8).

(8)   False geminates reinterpreted as true geminates
        $C_i + C_i > C_iC_i$

Nevertheless, it is clear that in some languages without a pre-existing length contrast, sequences of adjacent identical consonants are simplified to singletons both within and across words. This is true for Yurok (Robins 1958: 9), Misantla Totonac (MacKay 1999: 53–54), and Erromangan (Crowley 1998: 28). A comparison of the Yurok, Totonac, and Erromangan cases with Gooniyandi allows us to discredit certain general accounts of degemination. Structure Preservation cannot account for the failure of degemination in Gooniyandi, and the Obligatory Contour Principle is unable to distinguish, without stipulation, the Totonac and Gooniyandi cases, since in both, derived geminates are word-internal.

What is the explanation for the difference between Gooniyandi on the one hand, and Yurok, Totonac, and Erromangan on the other? Given the common phonologization of phonetically conditioned variation, the Yurok, Totonac, and Erromangan sound patterns could have historical roots in patterns of gestural overlap: a sequence of identical adjacent gestures are compressed into a single gesture, resulting in surface degemination. If the phonologization of such processes is what gives rise to automatic degemination, then Gooniyandi is a language where such gestural overlap does not occur. The absence of such a development is not surprising, since in Gooniyandi, the large majority of words end in vowels.[5] General production strategies for overlapping consonantal gestures are expected in languages where consonants come in contact frequently across word boundaries. But in languages where this never occurs (Hawaiian, Cayuvava), or where this occurs rarely (Gooniyandi), speakers may have no general production strategy for the C–C context. Again, this is an articulatory hypothesis which can be tested in the laboratory.

7.4   Geminate inventories and geminate distribution

With the exception of Thurgood (1993), and recent work by Podesva (2000, 2002), geminate inventories and geminate distribution have not, to my knowledge, been the focus of any broad typological cross-linguistic studies. In this section, I will simply point to generalizations over geminate inventories and geminate distribution which are falsified by one or more languages in this survey. The failure to find exceptionless phonological generalizations likely follows from the distinct pathways of geminate evolution just presented. Constraints on geminate inventories may simply

---

[5] All word-final suffixes are vowel final. In the three texts appended to McGregor (1990), aside from English words, and partial words broken by hesitation pauses, there was only a single example of a consonant-final word, the unsuffixed proper name *joolang* (p. 587, Text 3, line 1). In this corpus, then, there was only a single context of potential C–C gestural overlap across a word boundary.

reflect the extent to which certain consonant clusters, but not others, are coarticulated, or subject to perceptually based assimilations. And geminate inventories which result from morpheme concatenation will represent inherited segmental properties of bound versus root morphemes. Finally, geminates which result from emphasis (under stress) or boundary lengthening may be confined to a semantically closed class of words or clitics, with resulting geminate inventory a function of the consonants present in those particular lexical items.

7.4.1   Geminate inventories

Since vowel-length contrasts are more common cross-linguistically than consonant-length contrasts, it is reasonable to speculate as to whether there are any implicational relationships relating to sonority which hold of geminates. The answer appears to be no. Some languages have only geminate sonorants. For example, Gilbertese and Manam have only geminate nasals. At the other extreme, there are languages which have only geminate obstruents. These include Nhanda, Djinang, and Ojibwe. There is little mystery in how most of these systems came to be as they are. The evolution of nasal codas in Gilbertese and Manam was outlined in 6.4. Since the only codas in these languages are nasals, morpheme concatenation may result in geminate nasals when a coda nasal abuts a following onset nasal. In Nhanda, as discussed earlier, geminates are the result of sonorant fortition followed by assimilation. As a consequence, there are no geminate sonorants in the language. In Ojibwa, where geminates are the result of historical assimilation (or buccalization) of earlier laryngeal–obstruent clusters, the length contrast is also limited to obstruents (Bloomfield 1946). A case parallel to Ojibwa, where voiceless geminates are the reflex of earlier hC and $?C$ clusters, is proposed for Anejom̃, a language of Vanuatu (Lynch 2000: 24).

The tendency for geminate oral stops to be voiceless as opposed to voiced is noted by Klingenheben (1927), and has been argued to follow from the aerodynamic properties of stop production (Jaeger 1978; Ohala 1983a). The general argument is that, the longer the stop closure, the more difficult it is to sustain voicing. Supraglottal air pressure build-up will inhibit vocal-fold vibration unless some active step is taken to increase the volume of the supra-glottal cavity.[6] This phonetic explanation accounts straightforwardly not only for the general rarity of voiced

---

[6] The same explanation accounts for sound changes like Sindhi *b: > $ɓ$, since the secondary larynx lowering associated with sustained voicing in *b: may be reinterpreted as a distinctive feature of this sound (Ohala 1983, 1984).

geminate stops, but also for place-based restrictions within the set of voiced stops. For example, in Nubian (Bell 1971), a case of boundary lengthening leads to gemination of all consonants with the exception of /d, dʒ, g/ which devoice in the same context. Under boundary lengthening, however, /b/ is realized as [bː]. Because labial stops create larger supraglottal cavities than other stops produced farther back, voicing can be maintained longer (Ohala 1983a).

However, as with other universal tendencies with well-understood phonetic origins, there is no argument for building the rarity of voiced geminate stops, and the contingent rarity of voiced non-labial stops, into synchronic grammars.[7] Doing so would only duplicate the already existing explanation and complicate the description of other sound patterns. For example, any attempt to build an implicational place contrast into the inventories of voiced geminates would complicate the description of Didinga, which has a geminate contrast for all consonants, including /d/ and /g/, but excluding /j/ and /b/ (Odden 1983). And even a general implicational relationship where voiced geminate obstruents imply voiceless ones, such as that suggested by Thurgood (1993), meets with difficulties in Somali, where there exists a geminate/non-geminate contrast for voiced stops, but no length contrast for voiceless stops (Armstrong 1934; Andrzejewsky 1955; Puglielli 1997).

Similar problems occur with other segment- or feature-specific constraints on geminates. Although there are languages like Hebrew and Tigre where geminate gutturals are prohibited, there are others, like Ge'ez, with contrastive gemination for the same gutturals. And while geminate /h/ is not found in Hindi or Amharic, it does occur in Taba and Marshallese. Geminate glides /y, w/ are the only consonants left out of the geminate contrast in Meidob Nubian and they are also not found geminated in Taba, but geminate glides occur in Marshallese and Dobel, and Dobel also has a contrast between long and short glottal stop. Podesva (2002) proposes a constraint *SS which prohibits geminate voiceless fricatives, based on a claim that geminate fricatives require greater articulatory precision than geminate stops. However, there is no evidence that this constraint plays a general role in restricting geminate inventories. Of the 52 languages listed in Podesva's survey of this feature, only three, Wolof, Chaha, and Gilbertese, lack geminate voiceless fricatives.

Some languages like Totonac, Erromangan, and Yurok do not have a phonological length contrast for consonants, while others like Gooniyandi, Marshallese, and Dobel show length contrasts for all

---

[7] Podesva (2000, 2002) suggests just this, proposing a constraint, *DD, which prohibits voiced geminate obstruents.

non-vocalic segments. Between these two extremes, there is a great range of systems, with no clear instantiation of universal *phonological* constraints on geminate inventories. In many cases, geminate inventories appear to be a direct reflection of specific instances of geminate evolution, or combinations of them, and nothing more. And in cases where cross-linguistic phonological tendencies are evident, e.g. the preference for voiceless over voiced geminate oral stops, they reflect common phonetically based sound change.

7.4.2   Geminate distribution

The geminate/non-geminate contrast in most languages is realized by durational differences in consonants in intervocalic position. For stop consonants, one phonetic realization of length contrasts is extension of the medial closure phase of the stop in its geminate realization. In intervocalic position, the long/short contrast is easily perceived, due to the flanking vowels which delineate the stop closure and release phases. In other positions within the string, it is not as obvious that length contrasts for oral stops (in contrast to sonorants, or fricatives) will be easily perceived.

In Pattani Malay, length contrasts in word-initial position are found for all consonants, including the voiceless unaspirated stops (Abramson 1986: 9). Abramson (1986) observes that the longer geminate closure/constriction durations for sonorants, fricatives, and voiced stops may be cued by intrinsic features of these sounds, however, the same is not true for the voiceless unaspirated stops whose contrast is cued only by a shorter versus longer medial silent gap when these sounds are utterance-medial. Abramson's (1986) perceptual experiments show that speakers do not have difficulty distinguishing these pairs in running speech, and he concludes that long versus short closure duration is a sufficient cue for the geminate/non-geminate contrast. This is not surprising since mean duration of word-initial and word-medial geminate stops (voiced and voiceless) in a carrier phrase was three times longer than their short counterparts (Abramson 1991). In isolation, however, where durational differences are not easily perceived, one cue for initial gemination is amplitude differences in the initial syllable. Other factors which may play a role in initial position are intensity of burst, rate of formant transitions, and fundamental frequency contours.[8]

---

[8] Hatam, a language of Irian Jaya, also has word-initial geminate/singleton contrasts for nasal and oral stops and shows stronger bursts as well as higher F_0 at release for some geminates (Reesink 1999: 13–15).

In Taba (Bowden and Hajek 1999), which also shows word-initial geminate/singleton contrasts, phrase-initial geminates show variation across the hyper-to-hypoarticulation continuum. In careful speech, phrase-initial geminates are realized "with a greater degree of tension and more articulatory force"; while in casual speech "they can be realized with the same reduced tension and articulatory force as singletons" (Bowden and Hajek 1999: 144). This sort of variation in phrase-initial position is expected, since it is precisely in initial position that the closure duration of a voiceless stop is difficult to perceive due to the absence of a cue for the onset of stop closure.

In Swiss German, word-initial geminates are shortened, with neutralization of the length contrast, when a preceding word ends in an obstruent. However, phrase-initally and phrase-finally, the contrast in closure duration between singletons and geminates remains. In phrase-final position, release makes the closure duration audible, and there is no evidence of neutralization. In phrase-initial position, however, perceptual studies show that listeners, who rely on closure duration as the primary cue for this contrast, are unable to distinguish voiceless singleton and geminate stops in this environment (Kraehenmann 2001: 138).

I suggest that the phonetic variation and perceptual neutralization found in these case studies of initial geminates are two distinct sources for divergent pathways of geminate evolution. In careful speech, hyper-articulation of initial geminates can result in shifts from geminate consonants to fortis or aspirated consonants. In normal or casual speech, the geminate closure duration is produced, as in phrase-medial contexts, but insufficient perceptual cues result in a singleton percept, giving rise to the evolution of word-initial degemination. Many instances of each development are found in the historical record. In Tuvaluan, a Polynesian language (Milner 1958), unstressed vowel deletion gave rise to initial geminates which were subsequently reinterpreted as aspirated stops: *ke-kémo > kkémo > kʰémo 'blink'; *pu-púni > ppúni > pʰúni '(be) shut, blocked'; *ta-táki > ttáki > tʰáki 'lead,' etc. in line with hyperarticulation. An instance of the second development is incipient in the Thurgovian dialect of Swiss German, and appears to have occurred in the Lac Simon dialect of Ojibwa, where medial geminates have undergone degemination word-initially (Hock 1991: 163–64).

The other position in which there is evidence for neutralization of geminate contrasts is word/phrase-finally. In this context, non-release gives rise to indistinguishable voiceless oral stop closures for the contrasting geminate and singleton, with resulting historical degemination with source in CHANGE. In dialects of Afar where some final vowels are lost, the geminate contrast has been lost as well. Compare *oob* < *oobb* 'hear' in Eritrea and Wollo with *obbiy* in Shewa and Assab (Bliese 1981: 243). However, in the history of Balto-Finnic, final vowel loss has not resulted in degemination. In Estonian, Proto-Balto-Finnic medial geminates are continued as final geminates: **meekka* > *mɨkk* 'sword,' **hullu* > *hull* 'crazy'; **verkko* > *vɨrrkk* 'net'; **loppu* > *lɨpp* 'end' where voiceless stops have audible release.[9] Other languages with word-final geminate/non-geminate contrasts include Berber dialects (Louali and Puech 1994; Ouakrim 1995; Dell and Elmedlaoui 1985, 1996, 1997) and Saipan Carolinian (Jackson 1984a, b).

Together with the seven pathways of geminate evolution exemplified in 7.3, hyperarticulation of initial geminates, perception-based degemination of initial and final geminates, along with the general aerodynamcis of oral stop voicing, appear to provide historical explanations for the majority of conditions on geminate inventories and distribution. Given these historical explanations, geminate-specific constraints or conditions within the synchronic phonology are unnecessary. There are no clear universals relating to geminate inventory or distribution, and given the distinct pathways by which geminate contrasts can evolve, no absolute universals are expected.

7.5   Geminate inalterability

There is a large literature supporting the generalization that geminates are not subject to certain types of phonological alternations or sound changes (Kenstowicz 1982; Hayes 1986a; Schein and Steriade 1986; Elmedlaoui 1993; Inkelas and Cho 1993; Malone 1993; Kirchner 2000). The bulk of these cases involve what are traditionally referred to as lenition processes: voicing, spirantization, flapping, gliding or complete loss of a consonant. Geminate resistance to such processes is sometimes referred to as geminate inalterability. An often cited case of geminate inalterability is found in Tigrinya (Kenstowicz 1982). In Tigrinya, the singleton velar /k/ spirantizes to [x] in post-vocalic position (cf. *ʕarat-ka* 'bed-2sg.masc,' *kətəma-xa* 'town-2sg.masc'), but this spirantization is blocked in geminates (*k'ətəl-na-kka* 'we have killed you'). Kirchner (2000), summarizing much of the earlier work on this topic, lists nine cases of singleton spirantization, all blocked in geminates, and eight cases of singleton voicing, again all blocked in geminates. The generalization which surfaces is that geminates resist lenition processes which target non-geminates.

---

[9] Estonian data are from Campbell (1998: 53–56) See 8.2.2 and 8.3 for further discussion of the unusual Estonian length contrasts.

The most straightforward explanation of this generalization is the characterization of lenition as a process with origins in gestural reduction, either in terms of magnitude or duration (LaVoie 2001). In 6.2.2, phonetic studies of lenition were shown to be consistent with this characterization, and provided a sound basis for the range of sound changes associated with lenition processes. The historical origins of geminates are irrelevant to this phenomenon. The geminate/singleton contrast involves consonants with longer and shorter closure durations respectively. The longer a stop closure duration is, the less likely it is that gestural reduction will result in a significant change, or a perceived change in manner or voicing features. Because geminates can be on average one and a half to three times longer than their singleton counterparts, an intervocalic process which temporally reduces short [t] closure by half may result in [d] or [ɾ], or the percept of one of these, but the same temporal reduction of geminate [t:] will shorten the segment, perhaps enough for it to be reinterpreted as a short [t], but not enough for any of the other changes typically phonologized as lenition processes. The phenomena of geminate inalterability then is a consequence of the differing signals and percepts which result when short versus long stops undergo gestural reductions. Synchronic grammars do not contain a principle of geminate inalterability. They merely reflect the greater impermeability of long closure durations to phonetic erosion in the form of gestural reduction.[10]

7.6   Geminate integrity

Another generalization concerning the phonology of geminates is that they regularly resist epenthesis rules applying to other structurally parallel consonant clusters (Kenstowicz and Pyle 1973; Guerssel 1977, 1978; Steriade 1982). Given a geminate sequence C_iC_i and a non-geminate sequence C_iC_j, regular epenthesis will split the non-geminate sequence, but is blocked from splitting the geminate. This pattern is referred to as geminate integrity. Languages with reported geminate integrity effects

---

[10] Kirchner (2000) presents a phonological effort-based account of geminate inalterability and lenition. His primary argument against purely phonetic accounts is that they are unable to explain geminate inalterability, but the argument is rather indirect. In order to account for geminate inalterability, phonetic lenition processes must be strict reduction operations. He suggests, however, that there are modifications of the original gestures in lenition which appear to go beyond mere reduction, making the purely phonetic account untenable. None of the examples he provides are convincing, and his argument fails to take into account the important role of perception in sound change. As LaVoie (2001) demonstrates, weakening to true fricatives under lenition does not occur phonetically, and voicing is rare. Stops shorten and/or weaken to approximants, with shortening giving rise to voiced percepts, and approximantization giving rise to phonologization of fricatives.

include Semitic languages (Palestinian Arabic, Tunisian Arabic, Classical Arabic, Moroccan Arabic, Tiberian Hebrew, Amharic), Berber languages, Pero (a Chadic language), and Kolami (Central Dravidian). Early accounts of geminate integrity attribute this property to the phonological representation of full or partial geminate structures. The insertion of an epenthetic vowel is blocked by the linked feature structure of the geminate consonant: if a vowel is inserted, an illicit crossing association line occurs in the phonological representation.[11] One problem with this account is the assumption that epenthetic vowel insertion is a one-step process, since, under many proposals, the epenthetic skeletal slot (or mora) is inserted by one rule, with distinctive features inserted by later redundancy or feature-spreading rules (Levin 1985; Kenstowicz 1994: 415–16). A more serious problem with all standard accounts of geminate integrity is that they do not allow for exceptions, and yet, counterexamples can be found.

In Marshallese, dialects differ in terms of the surface realization of underlying word-initial geminates (Bender 1968, 1999: 51–55). In the Rālik dialect an epenthetic vowel is inserted initially, observing geminate integrity. In the Ratak dialect geminates are split by vowel insertion. Vowel quality is predictable, and the vowel in Ratak only occurs when the form is not preceded by a vowel within the phonological phrase. Recall from the discussion in 7.4.2 that initial geminate contrasts for voiceless oral stops are predictably difficult to perceive in utterance-initial position. Hyperarticulation may occur in this context. If hyperarticulation of initial geminates can lead to a short onset vowel, in the same way that hyperarticulation of final voiceless stops may involve a salient release, the Rālik alternations may be viewed in terms of such developments.

However, what is remarkable in this paradigm from the standpoint of modern phonological theory, is the medial vowel in the Ratak forms. Recall that initial geminates in Marshallese, like several other Oceanic languages investigated earlier, are the result of unstressed vowel deletion in historically reduplicated forms. Once this is recognized, the Ratak forms can be understood as instances of simple rule inversion. In Pre-Marshallese, there was variation between phrase-medial vowelless forms and phrase-initial forms with reduced vowels. In both dialects, phrase-initial forms were generalized, but in the Ratak dialect, the rule of vowel

---

[11] An alternative representational account represents geminates with single root nodes so that there is no formal entity to insert the epenthetic vowel between. However, this alternative is problematic for languages like Kolami (Kenstowicz 1994: 423) where homorganic nasal–stop sequences also show resistance to epenthesis. On the principles of autosegmental phonology, including the constraint against crossing association lines, see Goldsmith (1976).

deletion was interpreted as a rule of vowel insertion, facilitated by the coarticulatory features of the vowel in question. The general prediction of the evolutionary approach is that in any case where a geminate results from a context-sensitive vowel/zero alternation, phonologization of an inverted form of the original sound change may lead to vowel insertion between the two halves of the geminate. Other languages with vowel insertion into geminates include the Lule dialect of Sami (Engstrand 1987) and Modern Hebrew, as analyzed by McCarthy (1986: 238–40).[12]

Structural accounts of geminate integrity also incorrectly rule out insertion of consonants between the two halves of an underlying long vowel. A case of this type is reported by Hayward (1986: 72) for Arbore, an Ethiopian Cushitic language, where: "the second mora of a long vowel and an immediately following laryngeal are transposed when the latter is followed by an obstruent or nasal." Optional alternations include *zeehse* ~ *zehese* 'I caused to melt,' *kee?te* ~ *ke?ete* 'she planted.' This is a classic case of perceptually conditioned metathesis, of the type described in 6.1.2. In this case, the sound change in progress is presumably the result of long-domain features of laryngealization and breathiness which are reinterpreted in a non-historical position.

Representational accounts of geminate integrity are unable to account for cases of rule inversion like that found in the Ratak dialect of Marshallese, nor can they simply describe the interposition of a glide within a long vowel that occurs in Arbore. Any account which prohibits these sound changes or alternation types is too strong. In both Marshallese and Arbore, the sound patterns in question have plausible phonetic explanations which allow us to discover, for each pattern, "at least to some extent how it came to be as it is." If geminate integrity is not an inviolable synchronic constraint, then what it is? What accounts for the common patterns of vowel epenthesis which fail to split geminate structures?

The answer to this question is provided by the studies of place-feature distribution in chapter 5. In many languages, like Japanese, the only surface clusters are homorganic ones. This surface pattern reflects, in part, the common phonologization of regressive place assimilation in consonant clusters. An additional aspect of the Japanese sound pattern is that place features are contrastive only in pre-vocalic position. Now consider the consequences of introducing triconsonantal clusters like *VpptV* into Japanese-type languages. In this sequence, the labial place feature of *pp* violates the surface constraint limiting place to pre-vocalic position. If

---

[12] McCarthy's assumption is that geminate integrity is not violated because at the stage at which the rule applies, vowels and consonants are located on separate autosegmental tiers.

epenthesis is viewed as a means of eliminating the constraint violation, it is not expected to split the geminate, since a surface form like $VpVptV$ will still contain a violation of the same constraint, where p is followed by t, not a vowel. In fact, in both $VpptV$ and $VpttV$, the only single instance of epenthesis which will bring the string in conformity with the constraint limiting place features to pre-vocalic position is the insertion of a vowel *between* the heteroganic singleton and adjacent geminate. Epenthesis rules of exactly this type are attested. In both Pero (Frajzyngier 1980) and Amharic (Hudson 1995: 787–88), epenthesis inserts a vowel between a geminate and an adjacent singleton. However, there are many languages, like the Ait Segrouchen dialect of Berber (Guerssel 1977, 1978), where no epenthesis occurs in triconsonantal clusters including geminates. The obvious, but somehow overlooked, analysis of these cases is that epenthesis does not split geminates because geminates in these positions do not violate any phonotactic constraints in the languages in question.[13]

An additional consideration in sound patterns attributed to geminate integrity are common sources of epenthetic vowels. One attested source of epenthetic vowels described in 6.3 is audible consonant release. In comparing strings like $Vp{:}V$ and $VptV$, the question is whether an audible release might be more common in the second, where stops are heterorganic, than in the first. The answer is clearly yes. Morpheme-internal geminates are characterized by single gestures of long duration. The evolution of segment-internal epenthetic vowels from audible release should be no more common in underlying geminates than in underlying singletons.

Finally, in at least one language, Leti, geminate integrity has been argued to account for different patterns of reduplication (Hume, Muller, and van Engelenhoven 1997). In the synchronic system, the reduplicate prefix immediately follows the stem when a stem is CV initial or geminate initial. If the stem begins with a non-geminate cluster, the reduplicate prefix is infixed between the two members of the cluster. Hume, Muller and van Engelenhoven (1997) attribute this pattern to geminate integrity: infixation does not apply to geminate-initial stems because it would violate geminate integrity.

However, in this case, a diachronic explanation for the observed pattern is possible, and it is the only explanation consistent with another peculiar fact about reduplicated geminate-initial stems: though they begin with CV sequences, they exceptionally pattern with CC-initial forms for the

---

[13] Other patterns are observed. For example, in Afar, where coda and onset clusters are not tolerated, geminates which form part of CCC clusters undergo degemination. The facts described for Swiss German by Kraehenmann (2001) suggest that degemination in these contexts is phonetically natural, and not conditioned by syllable structure.

purposes of nominal prefixal allomorphy (Blevins 1999). Pre-Leti forms like *pepérat and its reduplicant *pe-pepérat undergo regular syncope of the pretonic vowel: *pepérat > ppérat, *pepepérat > *peppérat giving rise to the inherited pattern.

7.7   Moraic and non-moraic geminates

The notion of a "mora" as a unit of weight has been problematic in phonological theory, in particular where geminates are involved (Tranel 1991; Broselow 1995; Davis 2003). The most fundamental problems are descriptive and empirical. There are many languages in which the syllables which count as heavy for the purposes of one phonological pattern must not count as heavy for another. Two examples discussed in Gordon (1999, 2002) are Lhasa Tibetan and Classical Greek.[14] Both languages have weight-sensitive tone and weight-sensitive stress, but the definitions of weight for the two processes must be distinct. In Lhasa Tibetan, stress falls on the first long vowel of the word, and if there is no long vowel, on the first vowel. For the purposes of the stress rule then, syllables with VV rhymes are heavy, and those with V or VC rhymes are light. However, the same definitions of light and heavy will not account for tone distribution. In Lhasa Tibetan, level tones occur on all syllable types, but contour tones are realized only on CVV and CVR syllables, not on CVO or CV syllables (R a sonorant, O an obstruent.) For the purposes of tone assignment then, VV and VR rhymes are heavy, but those with VO or V rhymes are light.

If this was an isolated problem, in Lhasa or Greek, isolated solutions might seem appropriate. However, the bulk of Gordon's (1999, 2002) study demonstrates that the distinct notions of weight involved in tone versus stress are recurrent properties of the world's languages, and that they follow from the differing phonetic content of tone and stress. Gordon's database of 388 languages includes both broad typological comparisons and numerous detailed acoustic studies of unrelated languages. The empirical evidence strongly supports a phonetic basis for divergent weight systems for tone and stress.

Gordon shows that long vowels constitute bimoraic sequences in all tone and stress systems, while post-vocalic sonorant consonants may often count as moras for tone but not for stress. Within stress systems, it is common for all VC sequences to count as heavy, though this is unusual for tone systems. Gordon's most important findings in this area

---

[14] For details of the Classical Greek weight distinctions for stress and tone assignment rules, see Steriade (1991).

concern the phonetic basis of tone and stress. He finds a significant correlation between tone and total sonority in the syllable rhyme; and a significant correlation between stress and overall auditory energy in the syllable rhyme. Implications of Gordon's study for the behavior of geminates are straightforward: post-vocalic geminates should not behave any differently from other post-vocalic consonant clusters in the determination of moraic status for tone or stress. What is at issue is the feature content of the geminate: if it is a high-sonority segment then it is more likely to function as a tone-bearing unit.

Since voiceless unaspirated obstruents have low sonority, and very little acoustic energy, they are not predicted to contribute substantially to syllable weight for the purposes of tone or stress. And yet, there are languages like Luganda where CVV, CVR, and CVO all count as bimoraic for the purposes of tone, while CV does not. Gordon (1999: 97) comments on the surprising nature of this fact, since many of the coda obstruents in Luganda are voiceless and thus cannot carry tone at all. In fact, at the phonetic level, the obstruent is not tone-bearing. As reported by Snoxall (1967), Luganda CVO syllables with falling tone have a "psychological low tone." Phonetically, the CVO syllable realizes only the H of the HL contour, with the L realized as a lowering effect on the tone of the following syllable.

The fact that the phonological analysis of Luganda demands treatment of O in CVO syllables as tone-bearing is unsurprising in the context of geminate evolution. The only inherited obstruents which close Luganda syllables are precisely those which have arisen through assimilation with extra-high vowels, as discussed above. Historically, the vowels conditioning assimilation were tone-bearing units. Under assimilation, the first half of the geminate inherited the tonal association of the earlier vowel, as expected. While Gordon's account of the associations between phonetic properties and phonological weight are convincing, the Luganda facts illustrate the important role of diachronic explanation in the understanding of sound patterns. The assimilation of consonantal features to a preceding super-high noisy vowel, whether perceptual or articulatory in origin, occurred independently of changes in fundamental frequency contours. As a result, Luganda geminate obstruents became tone-bearing units, contrary to the general association between tone and high-sonority segments.

A review of the seven general pathways of geminate evolution in (1) will allow us to make general predictions as to ways in which geminates can acquire weight or moraic status through sound change.

In (1a, b) if the segment to which the consonant assimilates is itself a weight unit for the purposes of stress or tone, as in the case of Luganda just discussed, then the output of assmilation may result in a geminate with phonological weight.

Where vowel syncope gives rise to geminates, as in (1c), moraic geminates are also predicted. Bender's (1999: 55) description of Marshallese geminates may be a case in point:

Even though double consonants are pronounced without an intervening vowel . . . It is as if there were a silent vowel between the two consonants. Since it is thought that a vowel actually did occur there historically, it is as if the speaker observes a moment of silence for the departed vowel, for as long as it would take to utter the vowel and close again for the second consonant, before actually opening for the real vowel of the next syllable.

In cases like (1d) where lengthening under stress is involved, moraic geminates are also expected. An example of this kind is found in Cahuilla, a Uto-Aztecan language. In Cahuilla, stress is assigned to the initial syllable of the stem, and to alternating moras thereafter, where heavy or bimoraic syllables are those with long vowels, diphthongs, and *V?* sequences (Seiler 1965, 1967, 1977; Levin 1988; Hayes 1995: 132–37). A morphological process of intensive gemination, however, gives rise to moraic geminates: *čéxiwèn* 'it is clear' versus *čéxxiwen* 'it is very clear'; *wélnet* 'mean one' versus *wéllnèt* 'very mean one.' Seiler's (1977: 58) description of this process is purely moraic: "As an invariant, we find that the initial syllable receives an extra mora, thus a total value of two mora. As a consequence, the second vowel of the sequence will bear a secondary stress." Hayes (1995: 139) notes that in the Mountain Cahuilla dialect, intensives are formed via vowel, not consonant lengthening: *če:xiwen* and *we:lnet* respectively. In both dialects, lengthening serves the same essential function of giving extra weight to a stressed syllable under emphasis.

In the case of boundary lengthening (1e) and historical reinterpretation of voicing contrasts (1f), moraic geminates are unexpected, unless, prior to the sound change, coda consonants are weight-bearing. It is difficult to test these predictions since so few cases of boundary lengthening are reported in the literature. In the Mokilese case discussed earlier, geminates were pre-existing, and there are no obvious phonological differences between geminates derived by boundary lengthening, and those in other contexts. However, in at least one language, Ngalakgan, a non-Pama-Nyungan language of Australia, where boundary lengthening has also given rise to geminates, there is evidence from stress that geminates are non-moraic (Baker 1999).

The last case to consider is when geminates arise from identical consonant clusters across a morpheme boundary (1g). The prediction is that the input cluster and output geminate will have the same prosodic status in the language, assuming no independent changes in the prosodic system. As far as I am aware, there are no clear counterexamples described in the literature.

7.8   Antigemination

Antigemination refers to sound patterns where phonological syncope rules are sometimes blocked from applying if their output would create a sequence of adjacent identical consonants. This recurrent sound pattern was first characterized and analyzed by McCarthy (1986). McCarthy (1986) argues that antigemination is a consequence of the Obligatory Contour Principle which prohibits adjacent identical elements in phonological representations. Formerly a constraint on lexical representations, the Obligatory Contour Principle (OCP) is extended by McCarthy to exert an active influence on the mapping between underlying and phonological surface forms.

Odden (1988) presents serious theoretical and empirical criticisms of the OCP-based account of antigemination. First, he highlights weaknesses related to phonological representations and notions of adjacency. Within McCarthy's model, antigemination is predicted to apply to tautomorphemic derived $C_i C_i$ sequences, but not to heteromorphemic sequences, since morphemes are claimed to define independent "tiers." Where antigemination is expected but not found morpheme-internally, McCarthy analyzes the segments in question as long-distance geminates. Where antigemination is not expected but attested across morphemes, tier-conflation is claimed to apply prior to syncope. As Odden notes, the freedom to represent $C_i V C_i$ sequences as long-distance geminates when necessary to allow syncope, combined with the freedom to order tier-conflation before syncope to derive intramorphemic antigemination, greatly weakens the predictive power of the model. An important empirical observation is that antigemination is not found in certain languages. Odden concludes that OCP is not a principle of Universal Grammar.

Blevins (to appear b) reviews all cases where antigemination is attributed to the Obligatory Contour Principle. A striking finding is that in nearly every case, the failure of regular syncope to apply between adjacent identical consonants can be attributed to paradigm-internal anti-homophony effects. This is a welcome result, since there is no plausible phonetic explanation for the failure of syncope between identical consonants. McCarthy (1986) reports just such cases in fast speech, and sound changes of precisely this kind were noted in 7.3.3.

8   Some uncommon sound patterns

The range of things that are actually attested in natural languages is determined not only by the possibilities made available by the human cognitive-linguistic ability (which linguistic theory attempts to characterize), but also by contingent facts about the world.

Anderson (1992: 63)

It would be unsafe for speech communities to depend on performance at the very limits of the physical possibilities of a speaker's vocal apparatus. The relationship between absolute anthropophonic possibilities of speech performance on the one hand, and the phonetic selection by a language of some zone within those possibilities on the other, is not one which places phonetic performance at the very outer perimeter of anthropophonic space, as it were.

Laver (1994: 433)

In this chapter, I investigate potential explanations for uncommon sound patterns. For the purposes of this discussion, uncommon sound patterns are those which are limited to a few languages, a few language families, or to a small number of geographic regions.[1]

Certain sound patterns, like many of those summarized in chapters 4–6, are natural and frequent in the world's languages, while others are uncommon or unattested. In contrast to the common pattern of regular word-final obstruent devoicing, regular word-final voicing is unattested, though limited final voicing is found in at least one language, Lezgian, as discussed in 4.7. In chapter 4, the common occurrence of synchronic final devoicing is attributed to common instances of phonetically motivated sound change. Final voicing, on the other hand, is uncommon because there is no documented instance of CHANGE, CHANCE, or CHOICE that will result in a shift of final voiceless obstruents to voiced obstruents. In general, uncommon alternations like final voicing will be the result of analogical change, rule inversion, rule telescoping, or accidental convergence on a particular surface regularity. A study of uncommon sound

---

[1] In this last case, the assumption is that the feature in question may have diffused from one language or language family to another through language contact.

patterns, however, is not limited to uncommon alternation types. Uncommon sound patterns also include rare segment types, infrequent contrasts, and uncommon phonotactics. These uncommon sound patterns are the focus of this chapter. In particular, where alternative accounts may simply designate a particular segment type or contrast as a marked property of a synchronic grammar, Evolutionary Phonology provides explanations for the rarity of certain sound patterns, and suggests that the rarity of other sound patterns may be accidental.

In many cases, limited distribution will follow from "contingent facts about the world," as suggested in Anderson's quote above, including aspects of the human auditory and perceptual system. Final obstruent voicing cannot be understood as a natural phonetic occurrence under CHANGE, CHANCE, or CHOICE, nor is it the result of any common combination of independent changes, or instances of rule inversion. The only remaining pathways of evolution are chance events, including analogical change, resulting in a lexicon where all words ending in obstruents just happen to end in voiced obstruents. However, if this potentially occurring sound pattern is truly unnatural due to contingent facts about the world, then not only should it have low frequency of occurrence, but it is also expected to decay over time. In other words, where natural sound patterns are those which arise via regular sound change with sources in CHANGE, CHANCE, or CHOICE, unnatural sound patterns are those which do not arise via regular sound change, and which may also be eliminated by instances of CHANGE, CHANCE, or CHOICE. Sound pattern frequency, is, in general, not only a function of frequency of genesis but also of frequency of destruction.

In general, sound patterns of the world's languages are not at the "outer perimeter of the anthropophonic space," as emphasized by Laver above. However, there are rare cases where sound patterns appear to push the articulatory or perceptual envelope. In this chapter I take a close look at rare instances of contrast which may actually tax the human perceptual system. In all cases, the contrast in question has arisen as the only inherited phonological feature capable of marking a morphological contrast within an inherited paradigm. Based on this correlation, I suggest that in cases where there is one-to-one association of a phonological feature with a morphological contrast, hyperarticulation by speakers may slow otherwise expected instances of sound change with sources in CHOICE. I also give one example illustrating how sound change may be inhibited by what I call "parasitic perception": in general, a particular percept A may be weak in relation to a competing percept B, but if some sound pattern in the language requires attention to A at the cost of B, then other contrasts relying on A may be parasitically strengthened, inhibiting sound change.

8.1   Uncommon segment types

Surveys of segment inventories (e.g. Maddieson 1984) reveal that certain segment types are cross-linguistically less common than others. For example, front rounded vowels are less common than back rounded vowels, and interdental fricatives are less common than sibilants. Nevertheless, front rounded vowels and interdental fricatives are not uncommon segment types. They are found in many language families throughout the world, and are the common outputs of regular phonetically motivated sound changes of umlaut and lenition respectively. Truly uncommon segment types are those which are limited to a few languages, a few language families, or to a few areal groups.

In (1) general explanations for uncommon segment types are identified.

(1)   EXPLANATIONS FOR UNCOMMON SEGMENTS
    a. b is uncommon because there is no sound change $XaY > XbY$
    b. b is uncommon because there is a sound change $XbY > XaY$
    c. b is uncommon due to random events in cultural evolution and world history

(1a) suggests that a particular sound is uncommon because there is no common sound change which will give rise to it. Uncommon sounds can also have low frequencies because of the high frequency of sound changes which result in their transformation (1b). Finally, the infrequent occurrence of a particular sound could be accidental, unrelated to phonetic sources of sound change: if, prior to 1700, a giant meteor had hit the Earth, resulting in human loss in all continents with the exception of Australia, the subsequent linguistic record would be accidentally skewed. For example, sibilants, which are rare segments in Australian Aboriginal languages, might be unattested. Only by observing language change for centuries after this hypothetical catastrophe would it become clear that the uncommon occurrence of sibilants was not due to (1a) or (1b). The natural evolution of sibilants from stops, affricates, and glides would eventually demonstrate that their earlier absence was accidental.

8.1.1   Clicks

Click sounds are those produced with a velaric ingressive airstream mechanism. As distinctive speech sounds, they are found in the Khoisan languages of southern Africa, in some Southern Bantu languages and Dahalo (a Cushitic language of Kenya) due to borrowing from Khoisan, and in Damin, a secret language used by Lardil speakers of Mornington Island,

Australia (Hale and Nash 1997). In terms of genetic origins, then, clicks appear to have arisen only twice in linguistic history: in Khoisan, where they must be reconstructed for Proto-Khoisan, and in Damin, where they replace common pulmonic egressive sounds in the language of initiates.[2] Since the Damin case does not involve regular sound change, and since there is no evidence bearing on the origins of Proto-Khoisan clicks, the historical record includes no cases where clicks arise from non-clicks through regular phonetically based sound change. This record then is evidence that the uncommon occurrence of clicks in the world's languages relates directly to (1a): there is no common sound change $XaY > XbY$ where a is a non-click, and b is a click.

In the case of clicks, their uncommon occurrence may also be related to (1b): over time, sound change may result in the replacement of clicks by non-clicks. In many Bushman words with clicks, clickless variants coexist, and in some cases, these clickless variants are the only ones heard in the speech of the younger generation (Bleek 1939: 61). In addition, words with the highest token frequencies (pronouns, demonstratives, and verbal particles) have no clicks in the Bushman languages (Bleek 1939), suggesting that association between high frequency and lenition, found in so many languages (Pierrehumbert 2001; Bybee 2001), is instantiated by a shift of velaric ingressive to pulmonic or glottalic egressive airstream mechanism. Additional support for common lenition-based sound changes giving rise to the elimination of clicks is found in some of the Southern Bantu languages which obtained clicks some 500–700 years ago as a result of Bantu–Khoisan intermarriage. Since the time they were introduced, there is evidence of clicks being replaced by non-clicks. In historical times, older Nguni speakers produced dental, palato-alveolar and lateral clicks, while subsequent generations neutralized all series to dental clicks, and new dialects of Nguni appeared where these clicks were replaced by various combinations of non-click consonants (Herbert 1986: 28). A similar situation is reported for North Transvaal Ndebele, where the clicks of previous generations have been replaced by non-clicks (Ziervogel 1959): the palato-alveolar click is reflected as an ejective velar affricate, while nasal clicks are inherited as plain pulmonic egressive velar nasals (Herbert 1986: 29). The same is true in Zulu, where clicks are being replaced by non-clicks in some idiolects and dialects (Louw 1964: 147). The replacement of clicks by non-clicks can be viewed as a general case of articulatory simplification under lenition, with its source in

---

[2] Interestingly, the majority of Bantu words with clicks come from the *hlonipa* vocabulary, a process of taboo word formation where clicks can be replaced by non-clicks and vice versa (Faye 1923–25). Could it be that all instances of click-genesis are the historical result of conscious replacement of non-click sounds by click sounds?

CHOICE. The notion of clicks as complex or difficult articulations is supported by evidence from language acquisition: in Zulu, clicks are the last sounds acquired by children, and are usually replaced by corresponding non-clicks in children's speech (Louw 1964).

Though clicks are uncommon in the world's languages, there is no evidence that they are "at the very limits of the physical possibilities of a speaker's vocal apparatus." On the contrary, the facts noted above all point to clicks as sounds well within the comfort-zone of the anthropo-phonic space referred to by Laver in the introductory quote, both in terms of their articulation, and in terms of their perceptual salience. Ladefoged and Maddieson (1996: 279–80), who have made detailed studies of the phonetics of clicks, come to essentially the same conclusion:

Some clicks are complex articulations; but many are simple sounds, judging from the fact that they are fairly easy to produce. Almost any child can, and probably does, make bilabial, dental and lateral clicks as extralinguistic noises. Nor have we found any real difficulty in teaching students to integrate these sounds into syllables . . . In our experience, most clicks are much easier to teach people to make than ejectives or implosives. Considering also their perceptual salience, it might seem as if they should be highly favoured consonants in the world's languages.

Ladefoged and Maddieson (1996: 280), in fact, are at a loss to explain why clicks are not more common cross-linguistically:[3]

Their desirability is evidenced by the fact that they were readily borrowed from Khoisan into the neighbouring Nguni languages. Their ready acceptance and retention was no doubt facilitated by their phonetic qualities. Indeed, we cannot explain why these easy to make and perceptually optimal consonants are found in so few languages.

However, as we have seen, Ladefoged and Maddieson's remarks are not entirely accurate. As discussed above, late acquisition suggests that clicks are more difficult articulations than others, at least in the context of other speech sounds. In addition, clicks were not "readily borrowed" into the Nguni languages, but were the result of a highly unusual type of bilingualism, with children exposed to Khoisan sound patterns for most of the critical period, with only limited exposure to Bantu. Finally, these sounds were not readily retained, but show clear signs of decay in nearly all the cases in which sound change is documented. In sum, the uncommon status of clicks is not accidental. It can be explained both in terms of the absence in the historical record of sound changes taking

---

[3] The same conclusion is reached by Traill (1997: 115): "If clicks are in a sense 'ideal' segments from an auditory point of view, why are they so limited in their distribution?" He sees no satisfactory answer to this question.

non-clicks to clicks, and by the common reduction of clicks to non-clicks documented above.

8.1.2   Pharyngeals

Another uncommon segment type is the pharyngeal glide or spirant. Though not as genetically limited as clicks, pharyngeals are limited to three geographical zones. In north Africa, they are found in the Semitic and Cushitic families; in south-western Eurasia they are found in the North-West and North-East Caucasian families; and in the north-west of North America, they are found in four separate groups: Haida, Salishan, Wakashan, and Palaihnihan.[4] Unlike clicks, there is good evidence that pharyngeals are stable over time, and that they may be the output of regular sound change. In the context of the typology in (1), their uncommon status must ultimately be attributed to random events in cultural evolution and world history (1c).

To appreciate the difference between pharyngeals and clicks, consider the broad history of pharyngeals within the Semitic family. Proto-Semitic was spoken over 4,000 years ago, and is reconstructed with both voiceless and voiced pharyngeal fricatives or glides. However, despite thousands of years of sound change, pharyngeals have been maintained without change in every major branch of Semitic (Simpson 2002). The general pattern is for pharyngeals to be directly inherited, as they are in North-West and all but two of the South-West Semitic languages. This contrasts with the history of clicks in Southern Bantu discussed above, where, over the past 700 years, clicks have been quickly replaced by non-click sounds.

While pharyngeals show a strong pattern of retention in Semitic, there are many cases of pharyngeal to laryngeal shift, especially in the Cushitic family. Simpson (2002) suggests that mergers of pharyngeals and laryngeals in Cushitic may be due to a specific feature of language contact: where speakers of languages having laryngeals but lacking pharyngeals come in contact with pharyngeals in a second language, there will be a tendency to replace unfamiliar pharyngeals with laryngeals. While this hypothesis must remain speculative, it is the only one which will account for the geographic distribution of pharyngeal loss within Cushitic, and which is consistent with the well-documented Semitic pattern of general pharyngeal inheritance.

Another significant difference between the historical phonology of pharyngeals and that of clicks, is that there are many attested sound changes

[4] See Simpson (2002) for a historical treatment of pharyngeals in each of these language families, with special focus on Semitic and Cushitic. This section is based largely on his findings.

showing pharyngeal genesis. As documented by Simpson (2002), uvular to pharyngeal shifts are well documented in every branch of Semitic: *ʁ > ʕ is most common, occurring in Dathina, Cypriot, Aramaic, Hebrew, Phoenician, Old Akkadian, Soqotri, Ge'ez, and Tigrinya; but *χ > ħ is also attested, occurring in Maltese, Aramaic, Hebrew, Phoenician, Soqotri, Tigrinya, and Harari.

While one might attribute the shift of uvulars to pharyngeals to the pre-existence of a pharyngeal class, uvulars can give rise to pharyngeals in the absence of pre-existing pharyngeal segments. This is true in Haida, Salishan and Wakashan, where there are regular correspondences between pharyngeals and earlier uvulars. For example, in Salishan, pharyngeals are restricted to Southern Interior Salish, and absent in Northern Interior Salish and Coast Salish, where uvulars are found instead (Kinkade 1967). All evidence points to pharyngeals as an innovation in Southern Interior Salish due to a regular uvular to pharyngeal sound change. The same is true for Haida, where pharyngeals are limited to Northern dialects, and in Wakashan, where pharyngeals are restricted to two of the languages of the Nootkan branch.

Since there is a common sound change of uvulars to pharyngeals, and since sound changes eliminating pharyngeals may be the result of contact-induced change, the uncommon occurrence of pharyngeals in the world's languages appears to be accidental (1c). This is consistent with the occurrence of pharyngeals in eight different language families, despite the clustering of these families into three broad geographic regions.

8.2   Uncommon contrasts

Certain phonological contrasts are rare among the world's languages. As with uncommon segment types, uncommon contrasts are defined as those which are limited to a few languages, a few language families, or a few regions in the world. Within Evolutionary Phonology, uncommon contrasts are explained by the same mechanisms of change which account for the common sound patterns documented in chapters 4–6. In general, uncommon contrasts are explained in terms of common mergers or neutralizations as shown in (2).

(2)   EXPLAINING UNCOMMON CONTRASTS
   a. *a versus b* is uncommon because there is a common sound change $XaY > XbY$
   b. *a versus b* is uncommon because there is a common sound change $XbY > XaY$
   c. *a versus b* is uncommon because there is a common sound change $XaY > XcY$ or $XbY > XcY$

8.2.1   *Voiceless vowels*

A phonological contrast between voiced and voiceless vowels has been suggested for only a handful of languages, including: Ik (Nilo-Saharan/Eastern Sudanic; Heine 1975), Dafla (Sino-Tibetan; Ray 1967), Comanche (Armagost 1985, 1986), and Proto-Keresan (Miller and Davis, 1963). This contrast, if it exists, is extremely rare. From a purely phonological perspective, this is surprising, since languages with contrasts between voiced and voiceless sonorants are not uncommon. For example Klamath, Kashaya, Burmese, and Iaai all contrast modal voicing and voicelessness in sonorant consonants.[5]

An evolutionary account of the uncommon contrast between voiced and voiceless vowels makes reference to phonetic sources of voiceless vowels, and to their common subsequent developments. In nearly all languages where voiceless vowels occur, they are predictable allophones of voiced vowels. There are two common types of phonetic vowel devoicing: unstressed vowels may be devoiced independently of consonantal environment, as they are, for example, word-finally in Kwara'ae; or very short vowels may be devoiced when adjacent to voiceless segments, as /i/ and /u/ are in Japanese, when preceded and followed by voiceless obstruents. Both common sources of voiceless vowels may be found in a single language. In Dafla all short /i/s surface as [i̥] (or [j̥]) word-finally, but word-final short [u̥] is found only when preceded by a voiceless consonant. Devoiced allophones of voiced vowels are typically very short. Due to their whispered quality, they are also low-sonority sounds.

If phrase- or word-final devoicing and medial assimilation to neighboring voiceless consonants are two common sources of voiceless vowels, why are there so few cases where voiceless allophones are phonologized? The answer to this question is found if one follows the historical development of voiceless vowels in both contexts. In nearly all cases where word-final unstressed vowel devoicing can be reconstructed, voiceless vowels are ultimately lost. Examples from Gilbertese, Kwara'ae, and Trukic were discussed in section 6.4. Chemehuevi has also lost final unstressed voiceless vowels which are maintained in Southern Paiute, and Dafla has lost all but the tonal reflexes of final [i̥] after sonorants (Ray 1967: 10). In voiceless vowels which originate through assimilation of an adjacent voiceless segment, what inhibits the evolution of contrastive voiceless vowels is the rarity of consonant-voicing rules in the same contexts. Only when an adjacent /h/ or consonant cannot serve as the source of voicelessness is the language learner forced to posit a new category of voiceless vowels.

---

[5] What is rare is for this contrast to be limited to a single sonorant, as discussed in 2.1 for English /w/ versus /ʍ/.

Another factor which may play a role in inhibiting the evolution of phonological voiced versus voiceless vowel contrasts is the fact that many languages have a phoneme /h/ which has similar phonetic properties to voiceless vowels. Consider the case of Comanche (Charney 1993; Armagost 1985, 1986), a Central Numic language of the Uto-Aztecan family, where the phonological status of the voicing contrast in vowels is debated. In Comanche, certain voiceless vowels are allophones of voiced vowels: short unstressed vowels are optionally devoiced phrase-finally and before /s/ or /h/. Medial surface voiceless vowels in Comanche are the result of historical pre-aspiration of geminates: *VCC $>$ VhC $>$ V̥C (4.3.3). In these contexts, there is no strong evidence for phonological voiceless vowels over /Vh/ sequences. If one posits short unstressed voiceless vowels word-medially, they are always in positions where they derive historically from *VhC* clusters, and this analysis can be maintained since /h/ occurs elsewhere in the language. Similar analyses are found for Southern Paiute (Sapir 1930), a related Southern Numic language. In an analysis without voiceless vowels (Chomsky and Halle 1968; Cairns 1978) an abstract /h/ or voiceless obstruent is posited. This abstract segment triggers devoicing of a preceding stressless vowel before deleting; in post-tonic position, it assimilates fully to the following obstruent, resulting in a surface geminate. An analysis with an underlying contrast between voiced and voiceless vowels (Harms 1966, 1985) requires gemination of obstruents following stressed voiceless vowels, and voicing of stressed voiceless vowels in pre-sonorant position. In these two Numic languages, all voiceless vowels are unstressed, and the voiceless segments which once conditioned them in word-medial position no longer surface. There is no question in any of these languages that voiceless vowels contrast with voiced vowels on the surface. However, in languages with an independently occurring /h/ phoneme, there appears to be a tendency to associate occurrences of vowel devoicing with /h/.

However, despite the common loss of final voiceless vowels, and the absence of obstruent voicing rules giving rise to phonemicization of voiceless vowels originating in assimilation to earlier voiceless consonants, there are at least one or two languages which arguably exhibit a voiced versus voiceless vowel contrast. Proto-Keresan is reconstructed by Miller and Davis (1963) with a voiced/voiceless vowel contrast, with this contrast continued in at least one daughter language, Santa Ana. Since both the Keresan languages and Dafla (see above) are tone languages, the role of vowels as tone-bearing units may play a role in slowing down what could be the inevitable – loss of final unstressed word-final voiceless vowels.

Since there are common sound changes which give rise to voiceless allophones of voiced vowels, the uncommon contrast between voiced and voiceless vowels is either accidental, or due to subsequent developments of voiceless vowel allophones. Common loss of voiceless vowels through CHANGE provides part of the explanation for the rarity of this phonological contrast, as do the unlikely dissimilatory changes in contexts of surrounding voiceless obstruents. The common status of /h/ as a phoneme may also play a role, allowing phonetically voiceless vowels to be analyzed as clusters of V + /h/. As with many of the sound patterns detailed in chapters 4–7, the rarity of vocalic voicing contrasts does not follow from any formal principle of phonological theory. In fact, voiceless allophones of voiced vowels are not uncommon, and are often predictable aspects of sound patterns. To understand the rarity of this contrast, it is necessary to investigate why particular instances of phonologization are uncommon. This discussion is meant as a first step in this direction.

8.2.2 Uncommon length contrasts

Many languages have a contrast between short and long tautosyllabic vowels. In Maddieson's (1984) database of 317 languages, 62 or 19.6 percent, have contrastive vowel length. Contrasts between short and long consonants are also common, as suggested by the seven distinct pathways of evolution detailed in chapter 7. Language families with inherited long/short consonant contrasts include Semitic, Cushitic, Dravidian, and Eskimo, and many instances of geminate evolution are documented in chapter 7. However, of the thousands of languages whose sound patterns have been described, only three to five are reported to have a three-way contrast in vowel length (Dinka, Coatlan Mixe, San José Paraíso Mixe, Estonian, Sami, and Yavapai);[6] and only two are claimed to have a three-way contrast in consonant length (Estonian and Sami). To take just one example, in El Paraíso Mixe, we find the lexical contrast: *ʔoj* 'although,' *ʔo:j* 'he went,' *ʔo::j* 'very' (Suárez 1983: 34).

One factor contributing to the rarity of three-way length contrasts cross-linguistically is the rarity of certain preconditions for their evolution. In two varieties of Mixe, Coatlan, and San José Paraíso, extra-long vowels correspond to the long aspirated VVh nuclei of Totontepec Mixe (Suárez 1983: 34). Assuming a sound change V:h > V::, a pre-condition

---

[6] Other languages with a reported three-way vowel-length contrast include KiKamba (Whiteley and Muli 1962), Yurok (Robins 1958), the Applecross dialect of Scots Gaelic (Ternes 1973), and Hopi (Whorf 1946). However, in all of these languages is it clear that duration is not the only feature involved. For example, in Yurok and KiKamba there is evidence that the extra-long vowels constitute *disyllabic* sequences, in contrast to short and long vowels, which are monosyllabic.

for this evolutionary pathway is the existence of a three-way V/V:/V:h contrast. However, such contrasts themselves are uncommon.

A second factor, and perhaps the most significant one, are hypothesized mergers where multiple gradient phonetic contrasts in segment duration are analyzed as binary, not ternary, phonological length contrasts. Many languages show short, long, and extra-long allophones of vowels, but typically, these allophones represent only one or two durational categories.

Though few perceptual studies have been done on the rare ternary durational contrasts noted above, acoustic studies support the view of "crowding" within the perceptual space. In languages with binary length contrasts, the typical ratios of short-to-long segments are very high. Long stop consonants may have one and a half to three times the closure duration of short stops in careful speech while long vowels are typically at least twice as long as short vowels. However, in the three degrees of length measured in Estonian words, average durations for stressed vowels are 118.8 ms for the first degree of length, 204.4 ms for the second degree of length, and 240.4 ms for the third degree of length (Lehiste 1970: 33–34). While the short/long contrast is equivalent to that in many other languages, the 1:1.3 ratio of long to over-long vowels makes these two categories much closer to each other than typical long/short contrasts cross-linguistically. Given the closeness, in this case of the long and extra-long categories, merger of these two as a single "long" category is predicted as a common type of sound change. If this is so, then what really needs to be explained is why such mergers have not occurred in this small set of languages. In 8.3 I suggest that morphological paradigms play a role in the maintenance of these and other perceptually difficult contrasts.

8.2.3   A three-way contrast in nasality

Many languages contrast oral vowels with nasalized vowels. In Maddieson's (1984) database of 317 languages 71, or 22.4 percent, contrast oral and nasalized vowels. Oral vowels typically lack nasal airflow, with the velum raised, while nasalized vowels typically show nasal airflow, with the velum lowered. In many languages, nasalized vowels have originated historically from earlier VN sequences by the common sound change: VN > Ṽ (Hajek 1997). Low-level phonetic nasalization is typically present in vowels which precede nasal segments. If the nasal segment is lost, the nasalization once attributed to it can no longer be, and distinctively nasalized vowels arise (Ohala 1981: 186; 1989; Hajek 1997).

Given the binary physiological contrast on which the nasal/oral contrast is based, the discovery of a language with three degrees of nasalization might seem surprising. However, a three-way contrast between oral, lightly nasalized, and heavily nasalized vowels has been documented for Palantla Chinantec (Merrifield 1963; Ladefoged 1971; Merrifield and Edmonson 1999). In this language, there is a synchronic contrast between oral vowels, lightly nasalized vowels, and heavily nasalized vowels, as in the minimal triplet: ha^{LM} 'so much' (oral); $ha̜^{LM}$ 'he opens it wide' (lightly nasalized); and $hã^{LM}$ 'foam' (heavily nasalized) (Merrifield 1963; Ladefoged 1971; Merrifield and Edmonson 1999).

Merrifield (1963: 5) is quite specific in spelling out both the lexical nature of the contrast, and its phonetic realization:

> certain idiolects of Palantla Chinantec exhibit two degrees of nasalization which occur in identical environments, thus defining lexical contrasts. The actualization of the two degrees differs in quantity and in timing. A heavy nasalization involves full opening of the velic and nasalization of all elements of the syllable. Light nasalization involves late opening of the velic after the vowel has been initiated and not so full an opening as in heavy nasalization.

Merrifield and Edmonson (1999) compare acoustic signals with measurements of nasal airflow and find good support for Merrifield's original observations.

Proto-Chinantec is reconstructed with the oral vowels $*i$, $*e$, $*iu$, $*ia$, $*ɨ$, $*ə$, $*u$, $*a$, all with long and nasalized counterparts (Rensch 1989: 11). Vowel nasalization in Proto-Chinantec could occur after any voiceless stop $*p$, $*t$, $*k$, $*k^w$, or after $*w$, $*r$, or $*y$, and always occurred after nasals $*m$, $*n$, $*ŋ$. In dialects where the three-way contrast is maintained, the heavily nasalized vowels of Palantla Chinantec, which are fully nasalized, reflect Proto-Chinantec nasalized vowels, while the oral vowels reflect Proto-Chinantec oral vowels. Lightly nasalized vowels appear to derive from morphologically complex verbs which consist of a verb root plus the Proto-Chinantec animate marker $*-ŋ$ (Rensch 1989: 23–24). In Palantla Chinantec, the nasal consonant has been lost, with phonetic nasalization once induced by it maintained as a contrastive feature, starting about halfway through the vowel.

That the three-way contrast described for Palantla Chinantec might be difficult in both perceptual and articulatory terms is supported by the fact that it has already been neutralized for many speakers (Merrifield and Edmonson 1999: 306). One interesting feature of this neutralization is its seemingly bi-directional nature. For some speakers, the lightly nasalized form is neutralized to the oral category, while for others, the lightly nasalized forms fall together with the heavily nasalized forms (ibid.) This pattern of bi-directional neutralization for a single feature within a single speech community is quite unusual and suggests a role for both production and perception. If the shift from a nasal consonant to a following oral vowel defines the phonological category of the vowel, then lightly nasalized vowels will be classified together with oral vowels, since both involve velic raising after nasal consonant release. On the other hand, if the percept of nasalization defines phonologically nasalized vowels in contrast to their oral counterparts, then lightly and heavily nasalized categories are expected to merge. The fact that both patterns of neutralization are attested suggests that the contrast between full and partially nasalized vowels may actually sit near the limits of human production and perception. As with rare three-way contrasts in segmental length, I suggest below that morphological paradigms may play a role in the maintenance of these difficult contrasts.

8.3   The role of paradigms in contrast maintenance

In the discussion above, certain uncommon segments and contrasts are argued to be rare due to the uncommon occurrence of sound changes giving rise to them, or the common occurrence of neutralizing sound changes resulting in their elimination, or both. One question which arises is whether there are non-phonological factors which may play a role in inhibiting neutralizing instances of sound change. A related question is, if such factors are discovered, how can factors inhibiting regular sound change be incorporated into the general CCC-model of sound change adopted here?

In Labov's (1994: 328–31) discussion of mergers, he suggests that a complex combination of factors will result in merger as opposed to contrast maintenance. These factors include: the functional load of the opposition involved; the number of minimal pairs that depend on the distinction; the extent to which the distinction depends on minimal pairs; the number of distinctions already made along the particular phonetic dimension; the number of phonetic features on which the opposition depends; the discriminability of the phonetic features on which the opposition depends; and limitations in the range of movements that would avoid merger. This view of merger reflects a general principle of contrast maintenance: if the functional value of a contrast is very low with low token and type frequency of minimal pairs, then merger can occur. However, there is another sense in which we can weigh the functional load of a particular phonological opposition. If the contrast in question directly instantiates a morphological feature within a morphological paradigm, then it bears a heavy functional load; if it is limited to defining non-paradigmatic oppositions, its load is much lighter.

In this subsection rare phonological contrasts are shown to correlate directly with sole markers of paradigmatic oppositions at their point of origin. This correlation suggests that the grammatical role of phonological contrasts can inhibit otherwise common instances of phonetic mergers. Since these common mergers are, in part, a function of phonetic variation, the inhibition of sound change can be localized directly in a speaker's *intention* to maintain a contrast on the basis of its paradigmatic function. Contrast maintenance, as demonstrated by Lindblom (1990a) and Lindblom et al. (1992), can show itself both in terms of more limited variation and through hyperarticulation. A working hypothesis is that it is the morphological role of the uncommon contrasts discussed here that has allowed them to survive. Due to hyperarticulation, sound change with sources in CHOICE has been limited or inhibited, and rare contrasts have been maintained by phonetic enhancement.

In 3.2, the role of teleology in sound change was discussed. In general, sound change is not goal directed, and does not serve the purpose of making speech easier to pronounce, or words easier to discriminate. However, in this one small corner of grammar, where common instances of sound change would result in wholesale obliteration of paradigmatic contrasts, common sound change does appear to be inhibited. Below I briefly review some of the rare contrasts mentioned above where the phonologically contrastive feature is the sole exponent of a morphological feature or category.

Proto-Chinantec is reconstructed with oral and nasalized vowels, and vowel nasalization in Proto-Chinantec could occur after any voiceless stop or oral sonorant, and always occurred after nasals. As noted earlier, in dialects where the three-way contrast is maintained, the heavily nasalized vowels of Palantla Chinantec reflect Proto-Chinantec nasalized vowels, while the oral vowels reflect Proto-Chinantec oral vowels. Lightly nasalized vowels all appear to derive from morphologically complex verbs which consist of a verb root plus the Proto-Chinantec animate marker *-ŋ (Rensch 1989: 23–24). In Palantla Chinantec, the nasal consonant has been lost, with phonetic nasalization once induced by it maintained as a contrastive feature.

The animate/inanimate contrast is a basic one in Chinantec morphosyntax. In Comaltepec Chinantec, the animate gender on verbs occurs when the subject of an intransitive verb is animate, or when the object of a transitive verb is animate (Pace 1990: 31). The Proto-Chinantec animate marker is *-ŋ. I suggest that, in the history of Palantla Chinantec, the partial nasalization induced by this marker was interpreted as a direct exponent of [+animate] in verbs whose inanimate forms had final oral vowels. Since the final nasal suffix was the only marker of [+animate] verbs within certain paradigms, speakers maintained the contrast between half and fully nasalized vowels in order to maintain the animacy distinction in verbs. If, through common coarticulatory processes, nasality had been slightly anticipated in animate verb forms, neutralization of the half-nasalized vowels with the pre-existing class of fully nasalized vowels would have occurred, with loss of the animacy paradigm.

Note that the hypothesized hyperarticulation is intentional, but it is not claimed to be conscious. Speakers hyperarticulate, in this case maintaining the very precise timing of the velum necessary to distinguish fully and partially nasalized vowels; subsequent loss of the final nasal leaves this precise velic timing as the only inherited marker of the previous paradigmatic contrast marked by the animate *-ŋ suffix. However, since this particular contrast may actually push the anthropophonic envelope in terms of both production and perception, it has been lost for many speakers and may, in general, have a half-life of no more than several generations.

Another unique contrast among the world's languages is the three-way length contrast for consonants and vowels in Estonian and other Finnic languages. Compare *sada* 'hundred,' *saada* 'send!' and *saaada* 'to get,' and *lina* 'linen,' *linna* 'city's' and *linnna* 'to the city' (Mürk 1997: 3) for vowels and consonants respectively. As noted by Lehiste (1970: 46), the question of whether Estonian has two or three distinctive lengths for vowels and consonants has been debated for decades. There is no question of a three-way opposition, but researchers disagree as to whether the over-long contrast is ever manifested purely by segmental duration, as opposed to durational contrasts across the syllable rhyme, larger disyllabic unit, or by other features like tone or stress. However, as Lehiste (1970: 46) points out, in a sequence involving a short vowel followed by a long consonant, "the overlength does not extend to the vowel preceding the overlong consonant." Rather, in the third grade, length is created by further lengthening of long consonants in a stressed syllable (Lehiste 1966; Eek 1984). Hence, at least in word-initial stressed syllables with short vowels, the contrast between grades I, II and III in Estonian appears to be realized as a phonetic contrast between a short vowel followed by a short, long, and extra-long consonant respectively.

The origins of the third degree of length are debated as much as their phonological characteristics. In an early paper on the subject, Tauli (1954: 11) points out that many words with over-long initial syllables derive from earlier disyllabic sequences, but also suggests (p. 12) that the over-length in grade III may involve "articulatory overshooting: the more intensive exertion necessary for the pronunciation of the following long vowel has attracted attention to the extent that its more intensive articulation has started with the preceding consonant, therefore it has been articulated longer and more intensely." He points out that the third grade cannot be reconstructed for Balto-Finnic, and assumes that it is an independent development within the history of Estonian proper.

While compensatory lengthening, additional lengthening under stress, and additional lengthening associated with a tonal contour may all be at the root of this contrast, what is particularly notable about extra length is its role in the synchronic system of Estonian nominal paradigms. Due to the loss of the former genitive case marker *-n*, the long versus extra-long grade contrast in Estonian is now the only phonological characteristic distinguishing genitive from partitive for many nouns. Some representative examples are shown in (3).

(3)   Estonian grade contrasts associated with case (Mürk 1997: 6)

nominative (Q3)	genitive (Q2)	partitive (Q3)	gloss
kappp	kappi	kapppi	'cupboard'
kammm	kammi	kammmi	'comb'
küllm	külma	küllma	'cold'

Like the three-way contrast in vowel nasalization which arose in the history of Palantla Chinantec, the consonantal length contrast associated with the third quantity in Estonian is now the only phonological feature distinguishing a particular morphological contrast within the nominal paradigm. For many nouns the contrast between genitive and partitive case is realized solely in terms of consonant length. I suggest that it is this basic paradigmatic function which has allowed this contrast to be maintained in many dialects, inhibiting the otherwise expected neutralization of long and extra-long consonants.

A final case which suggests an association between the maintenance of difficult phonological contrasts and paradigmatic function is the three-way vowel-length contrast noted for Dinka. Andersen (1987, 1990) describes the Agar dialect of Dinka as having 37 monophthongal vowels, including 17 creaky-voiced vowels and 20 breathy-voiced vowels. All monophthongal vowels have three degrees of length, with the exception of creaky and breathy /ɛɛ/ which only shows a long/extra-long contrast.

Andersen (1990) compares the Dinka vowel system with that in Päri, and demonstrates that cognate nouns in the two languages exhibit regular correspondences, where suffixal vowels in Päri have been lost in Dinka, with associated compensatory lengthening. What is striking is that in forms with historical long vowels, compensatory lengthening has given rise to extra-long vowels (see also Kavitskaya 2002). While compensatory lengthening is not an uncommon sound change (see 6.1.3), apart from Dinka, and the possible case of Estonian, no other instances of compensatory lengthening have given rise to a three-way length contrast. As in

Palantla Chinantec and Estonian, the uncommon phonological contrast is the sole exponent of a morphological feature, in this case number.

Historical suffixes, still evident in Päri, are sometimes marked singular and sometimes plural. Instead of the loss of these final unstressed vowels resulting in loss of the plural/singular contrast, phonetic open-syllable length was reinterpreted as phonemic with resulting compensatory lengthening. Given a pre-existing two-way length contrast, long vowels gave rise to extra-long vowels. The paradigmatic contrast between plural and singular, formerly marked by suffixal vowels, was later marked by length contrasts, with length the sole exponent of the feature [±plural] for certain nouns. I suggest that the paradigmatic status of phonetic vowel length as a marker of singular/plural contrasts has contributed to the evolution of a three-way vowel-length contrast in Dinka.[7] At the point at which final vowels were undergoing reduction, speakers intentionally maintained a contrast between plural and singular forms by hyperarticulating the pre-existing phonetic vowel-length differences. It is this grammatically triggered hyperarticulation that inhibited the merger of long and extra-long vowels, and resulted in the rare three-way vowel-length contrast maintained to this day.

A final example of uncommon contrast is a context-sensitive one. While the contrast between long and short voiceless obstruents is common intervocalically, there is good evidence that length contrasts in voiceless stops are typically neutralized utterance- or word-initially (7.4). However, in chapter 7, we saw that initial geminates evolved independently in many Austronesian languages. This instance of multi-genesis suggests either a rethinking of the phonetic explanations for initial length neutralization of voiceless stops, or an alternative force *inhibiting* neutralization in precisely these cases. As in the cases just reviewed, paradigmatic oppositions appear to play an important role.

In the evolution of the word-initial geminate/singleton contrasts described for Dobel, Taba, and Mussau, initial geminates reflect earlier CV-reduplication. Vowel reduction and ultimate loss leaves the initial geminate/singleton contrast as the sole exponent of the paradigmatic opposition once marked by the CV-prefix. In each case, the reduplicated/non-reduplicated paradigm is continued by an initial geminate/non-geminate paradigm. As with the cases described above, the speaker producing vowelless variants hyperarticulates the voiceless geminate stop in order to maintain a paradigmatic contrast. It is these hyperarticulated geminates

---

[7] Verb paradigms also show single morphological features associated with long versus extra-long vowels. For example, the verb 'to roll' is *leer*, with long creaky-voiced /ee/ in its preposed subject form, but *leeer*, with extra-long creaky-voiced /ee/ in the third singular (Andersen 1990).

which are inherited by subsequent generations, resulting in contrast maintenance.

While the role of contrast maintenance is particularly salient where rare phonological contrasts are involved, it can also be found to inhibit sound changes which do not give rise to difficult contrasts. See Blevins (to appear b), where antigemination effects are attributed to paradigmatic contrast maintenance in a range of languages.

In sum, in all cases of rare phonological contrasts where common neutralizing instances of sound change are expected, the maintainance of paradigmatic contrast appears to trigger hyperarticulation, slowing or inhibiting sound change with sources in CHOICE.

8.4   Phonetic priming and contrast maintenance

In 8.3 uncommon phonetic contrasts are maintained due to pre-existing phonology–morphology mappings which endow the phonetic contrast with a high functional load. Another general possibility is that phonetic contrasts may have more strength in some languages than others due to coexisting phonetic contrasts which prime or reinforce the others. A regular sound change may be inhibited due to other sound patterns within a given language which cause listeners to pay particular attention to phonetic features which they might otherwise tend to ignore. These cases are different from instances of Structural Analogy introduced in 6.4. Under Structural Analogy, a pre-existing phonological contrast primes the acquisition of the same contrast. Phonetic priming is the possible case where some distinctive feature of a language results in speakers paying more attention to some phonetic transition or detail than might otherwise be expected, resulting in contrast maintenance. A case of this type is offered from the history of the Pama-Nyungan languages of Australia.

Recall from chapter 5 that common regressive place assimilation in intervocalic NC sequences was accounted for primarily in terms of CHANGE: in VNCV, the place of the nasal is easily misperceived as the place of a following obstruent. This general instance of CHANGE is able to account for both the common regressive nature of place assimilation as sound change, and the finding that the most common consonant clusters cross-linguistically are geminate consonants and homorganic nasal-obstruent clusters. If this account is valid, certain phonotactics like heterorganic NC clusters are expected to be rare cross-linguistically and relatively unstable. Over time, place assimilation in intervocalic heterorganic NC clusters should lead to homorganicity, since there is a tendency for such clusters to be misperceived as homorganic when they are not.

In this light, the Pama-Nyungan languages of Australia represent a typological anomaly.[8] Not only do many of these languages contain non-homorganic nasal–stop clusters, but these heterorganic clusters can be shown to be inherited from a proto-language dating back thousands of years. If the shift from heterorganic to homorganic NC clusters in many languages is an instance of convergent evolution stemming from the perceptual saliency of CV transitions, what phonetic properties have allowed the Proto-Pama-Nyungan non-homorganic NC clusters to survive this long? I suggest that, in this case, the heterorganic NC clusters have been parasitic on primary place features cued by VC transitions: that between retroflex and non-retroflex consonants. Under this account a primary factor in maintenance of inherited nasal place features in VNCV sequences is the additional attention paid to VC transitions in VCV sequences. This attention is required in perception of the phonetic realization of the four-way coronal contrast which existed in Proto-Pama-Nyungan, and which has been inherited in many daughter languages.

Proto-Pama-Nyungan nasals and stops are reconstructed at labial, velar, alveolar, post-alveolar, palatal, and dental points of articulation. Homorganic NC sequences are reconstructed for each place, while heterorganic clusters include: $*np$, $*nk$, $*nc$, $(*n\underline{t})$, $*\eta p$, $*\eta k$, $*\eta p$, $(*\eta k)$. These are exemplified in the the following reconstructions: $*kanpar$ 'spider, poisonous insect'; $*kunka$ 'raw, alive'; $*kunca$ 'pandanus'; $*kun\underline{t}u$ 'strong'; $*\eta a\underline{\eta}ka$ 'beard, facial hair'; $*ku\eta pa$ 'V intr, to whistle'; $*ti\eta ki$ 'narrow, thin; gap in hills'; and $*wan\underline{t}a$-, $wanta$- 'leave, put.' In the following discussion, I focus on the robust contrasts which have been maintained in a majority of daughter languages.

First consider the contrast between [ηp] and other Np clusters, and [ηk] and other Nk clusters, where 'N' represents any nasal. As detailed in Steriade (1998), and summarized in chapter 5, the phonetic cues of retroflex or post-alveolar apical articulations are present primarily in VC transitions (see also Butcher in progress). The lowering of third and higher vowel formants provides a phonetic cue to retroflexion, as opposed to its absence, and the locus of this cue is the vowel preceding C_1 in intervocalic C_1C_2 clusters. Since, in these cases, C_2 is not a coronal consonant, it cannot be reinterpreted as a post-alveolar. The source of retroflexion must be C_1, and, as expected, there is no progressive assimilation.

Now consider the contrast between [ηp] and other Np clusters, and [ηk] and other Nk clusters. Like post-alveolar consonants in post-vocalic pre-consonantal position, the palatal nasals in these positions involve

[8] This section owes much to Alpher (2002), where the development of Proto-Pama-Nyungan NC clusters is detailed.

phonetic cues in the preceding VC transition (Butcher, forthcoming). In this case, pre-palatalization is evident in the raising of F2 of the preceding vowel. As with retroflexion, since C_2 is not a coronal consonant, it cannot be reinterpreted as an alveopalatal. The source of palatalization must be C_1, and, as expected, there is no progressive assimilation.

The question we are left with is why so many Pama-Nyungan languages have maintained *np* versus *mp* and *nk* versus *ɲk* contrasts. Unlike word-final position, where there is the possibility of release, in the intervocalic VC_1C_2V context, C_1 is unreleased, so that the only audible phonetic cues indicating place of articulation are those in the VC transition, and those intrinsic to the nasal itself. However, as far as I am aware, the VC transitions for these contrasting sequences are very much like those in other languages, and so, are unlikely to be the key to understanding the maintenance of place contrasts in this context. Rather, I suggest that the listener's general attention to VC transitions is great enough to offset the common misperception which results in seemingly regressive place assimilation. In this case, a canonical instance of CHANGE, *anpa > ampa*, is inhibited by greater attention to VC transition cues which arises as a natural product of acquiring the retroflex/non-retroflex coronal contrast. Continued work on the phonetics of Australian languages, and general aspects of perception, will allow us to assess the plausibility of this hypothesis, and will further our understanding of some of the unique features of the Pama-Nyungan languages.[9]

8.5   Expected but missing contrasts

In 8.3 and 8.4 accounts are provided of rare contrasts, and unexpectedly stable contrasts. Evolutionary Phonology can also provide an understanding of why certain contrasts are unlikely to be missing in most languages. Consider, for example the contrast between oral and nasal stops. This contrast is extremely common cross-linguistically. In Maddieson's (1984) 316-language sample, there are only four languages which have no phonemic nasal or nasalized segments of any kind. The simplest account of the frequency of nasal/oral contrasts is that the most common types of

---

[9] Other analyses of Australian phonotactics have been proposed, the most extensive being Hamilton's (1995) treatment. Under Hamilton's approach, the phonotactic tendencies which predominate in many Pama-Nyungan languages are the result of ranked synchronic phonological markedness constraints. This contrasts with the account above, where the majority of shared phonotactics of Pama-Nyungan languages are explained through direct inheritance or parallel evolution. In the case of NC place phonotactics, the majority of place contrasts have been passed down from Proto-Pama-Nyungan to daughter languages with little change, resulting in most of the tendencies Hamilton accounts for in synchronic terms.

sound changes involving these segments (voicing, devoicing, contextual assimilation, loss of coda nasals with preceding vowel nasalization) will not lead to neutralization of the oral/nasal contrast in all contexts. For example, if at some starting point, we have a language with stops /p t k/ and /m n ŋ/, and all of these stops occur in word-initial pre-vocalic and intervocalic positions, there is no common phonetically motivated sound change which will neutralize the nasal/oral contrast in these two positions. Nasal weakening, giving rise to the evolution of nasalized vowels, is typical of coda nasals, while assimilation of nasal to oral stops and vice versa is typically limited to consonant clusters. Once established, then, nasal/oral contrasts are expected to be stable over time.

Interestingly, in some of the few languages which do not have a nasal/oral contrast for which historical details are available, the rare phonetics of the nasal consonants themselves appear to have played a role in neutralization of the nasal/oral contrast. Thompson and Thompson (1972) and Kinkade (1985) discuss the shift of nasals to voiced stops in languages of the American north-west coast, including Twana and Lushootseed (Salishan), Quileute (Chimaukan), Makah, and Nitinat (Wakashan). Kinkade's (1985) primary observation is that in this general geographical area, there were at least twelve languages where phonetic records show a rather unusual sound intermediate between nasal and voiced stops. Boas (1911: 565) describes the situation in Lower Chinook as confusing, noting "the occurrence of a labial sound with semi-closure of the nose and weak lip-closure, which is therefore intermediate between *b*, *m* and *w*, with prevalent *m* character. Between vowels the sound approaches *b*." Kinkade (1985:478) demonstrates that "in virtually every littoral language of the Northwest from the 46th to the 50th parallel nasals were sometimes pronounced without full closure of the velum." These semi-nasal semi-oral stops, which I will refer to as "quasi-nasals," were reinterpreted as oral voiced stops in some languages, and as nasals in others.[10] In languages like Twana and others noted above, the reinterpretation of quasi-nasals as oral stops has led to the modern situation where the nasal/oral contrast is absent. The absence of nasal stops in these languages then stems from the prior existence of a rare type of partially nasalized voiced stop. Presumably, the rarity of these partially nasalized stops has the same explanation as the rarity of the three degrees of nasalization described for Palantla Chinantec in 8.2.3. However, unlike the Chinantec case where the half-nasalized vowel was

---

[10] Quasi-nasals should not be confused with pre- or post-nasalized stops where nasal/oral or oral/nasal gestures are sequentially ordered within the confines of a single segment. See Herbert (1986) for a comprehensive study of the phonology of pre-nasalized stops.

the sole marker of a paradigmatic contrast, resisting neutralization, the partially nasalized voiced stops in these North-West-coast languages had no such paradigmatic role. Without the opposing force of hyperarticulation, hypoarticulation combined with misperception would result in their quick reanalysis as either nasal stops or voiced stops in all the languages in which they occurred.[11] Interestingly, as with the Palantla Chinantec half-nasalized vowels, neutralizations in both directions are attested.

In sum, languages without a nasal/oral stop contrast are rare because a nasal/oral stop contrast is typically directly inherited in at least some subset of phonetic contexts. This is due to the fact that there are no phonetically based sound changes which will neutralize the nasal/oral contrast in all contexts. However, if nasal stops shift to highly unstable quasi-nasalized segments, as appears to have occurred at least once in linguistic history, then misperception and sound change due to phonetic variability will inevitably give rise to a shift of these segments to either nasal or oral stops. In the latter case, the oral/nasal contrast is lost.

8.6   Uncommon syllable types

Just as certain contrasts at the segmental level may be uncommon, the same is true in the realm of phonotactics. However, in this domain, uncommon phonotactics appear to be extreme instances of more common ones, with similar evolutionary origins. Consider, for example, the rarity of languages which have tautosyllabic VVVV or CCCCCC sequences. As far as I am aware, only Gilbertese, a Micronesian language is reported to have tautosyllabic VVVV sequences, while only Georgian, a Caucasian language, has tautosyllabic CCCCC sequences. Since there are many languages which allow tautosyllabic VV and even VVV sequences, the rarity of tautosyllabic VVVV appears to be a function of the tendency for long strings of vowels to be syllabified as heterosyllabic sequences. Gilbertese, with monosyllabic sequences like -*kaaei* 'augmentative suffix,' is at one extreme. In Gilbertese, the rhythm of words is mora-based, and syllabification is purely sonority-driven, eliminating ambiguities in vowel count or syllabification which commonly arise in other languages where stress is syllable-based, and syllables may violate general sonority sequencing principles (Blevins and Harrison 1999). And there are many languages with tautosyllabic CC and CCC clusters. In languages with bi- or trisegmental oral stop clusters, stops are typically

---

[11] Kinkade (1985: 480) makes the further observation that spread of the areal feature of quasi-nasals was blocked north of Comox by Northern Wakashan languages which had a pre-existing contrast between oral voiced and nasal stops.

released, allowing identification of contrastive place and/or laryngeal features. In Georgian, we find the same pattern at the phonetic level, but even longer clusters, like *mc'vrtneli* 'trainer' and *gvprckvnis* 'he peels us' (Comrie 1981: 200). Presumably, the audible release of Georgian consonants, and the regular pattern of word-initial stress provide salient cues to segment identification and syllabification.[12] As with the pharyngeals discussed in 8.1.2, there is nothing intrinsically difficult about the production or perception of VVVV in Gilbertese or CCCCCC in Georgian, and there is no evidence that these tautosyllabic sequences are in any way unstable. Rather, the rarity of such systems appears to be the result of the uncommon convergence of significant rules of consonant or vowel loss resulting in long V and C clusters respectively; prosodic systems in which stress-timing, and not syllable-timing, prevails; and unambiguous rules of syllabification.

8.7   Uncommon harmony and blocking patterns

An unusual instance of vowel-height harmony is described by Deith (1932) for Buchan Scots English. The general pattern is that unstressed high vowels become non-high when preceded by stressed non-high vowels. What is particularly unusual about this system is the class of blocking consonants which includes voiced obstruents, as well as certain clusters. Paster (2003) presents a historical phonetic account of this uncommon system: voiced obstruents block harmony due to the laryngeal lowering involved in their production. This lowering may result in lower F1 values in the following vowel, phonologized as non-lowered vowels. The rarity of this pattern is attributed to the combined low frequency of true height harmony and full voicing of medial stops via larynx lowering.

---

[12] I thank Keti Lapiashvili for contributing to my understanding of Georgian phonetics and phonology. Syllabification in Georgian appears to be unambiguous for native speakers with onsets consistently maximized, unless /r/ is involved. It is generally agreed that pre-tonic vowel reduction and loss gave rise to the long word-initial strings of consonants discussed here.

Part III

Implications

Beyond the linguistic universals, everyone's sound patterns, everyone's vocabulary and everyone's grammatical rules, are original. This is because each of us, as a child, worked out the rules afresh . . . This is how we learn to speak. This is how change and originality are built into human language. Dalby (2002: 5)

9 Synchronic phonology

> . . . the universal rules or implicit axioms of grammar aren't really stored
> or located anywhere, and in an important sense, they are not determined
> at all. Instead . . . they have emerged spontaneously and independently
> in each evolving language . . . Deacon (1997: 115)

There are many different ways to study synchronic systems. Structuralist approaches examine formal properties of sounds, words, phrases, and
discourse and extract recurrent patterns. These patterns form the basis of
descriptions that contrast one synchronic system with another, as well as
general statements of linguistic principles whose validity does not depend
on their cognitive status. Within the generative tradition, synchronic
grammars are viewed as reflections of innate linguistic knowledge. Linguistic knowledge is viewed as a type of abstract competence that may or
may not be directly reflected in actual linguistic performance. Contemporary grammatical theory confines itself to the description and explanation
of competence, and delegates aspects of language performance to other
domains of inquiry (e.g. the psychology of human behavior, the physics
of speech, language processing). In this chapter, implications of Evolutionary Phonology are assessed for synchronic phonological models.
While the approach shifts the bulk of explanation from the synchronic to
the diachronic dimension, it also suggests the current relevance of structuralist methods of analysis, and the usefulness of generative divisions
between competence and performance.

9.1   Phonology and language acquisition

Synchronic phonology is a hybrid system of innate and learned structures. A central question in phonological theory is precisely which aspects
of the system are innate and which are learned. Innate properties of
phonological systems are sometimes referred to as phonological universals or aspects of universal grammar. Universals arise in both structuralist
and generative grammars, but have a different status in the two schools.

Within a structuralist account, a linguistic universal can simply reflect an exceptionless cross-linguistic generalization, though its universal status is not represented directly in any of those synchronic systems. In generative analyses, the same universal is claimed to characterize language competence, and is viewed as part of the innate language faculty. This section considers the empirical basis of phonological properties attributed to Universal Grammar within generative accounts.

The attribution of phonological universals to innate properties of the human mind follows one of two common lines of reasoning. One argument is that there is not enough evidence available to the child during the critical learning period to acquire a particular aspect of sound patterns. Since direct learning is not possible due to degenerate input, the phonological characteristic must be innate. As the discussion in 9.1.1 demonstrates, there is little empirical support for this hypothesis in the phonological domain. A second line of reasoning, outlined and supported in 9.1.2 and 9.1.3, bases claims of innateness on studies of human newborns, or children who, for one reason or another, do not have exposure to audible speech. If language learners are not exposed to speech, then any evidence of phonological or phonetic knowledge must be attributed to innate capabilities. In this case the input is not degenerate; it is nonexistent. A review of the literature supports the view adopted throughout this book, that distinctive features and prosodic categories, or perhaps the learning strategies that converge on them, may plausibly be regarded as innate.

The conclusions reached in 9.1.1 and 9.1.2 are based on studies of synchronic phonological systems and infant perception respectively. An independent empirical question is whether any aspects of Universal Grammar are visible in the course of language acquisition. Section 9.1.4 addresses this question. Though the progression from babbling to first words to speech has been interpreted as evidence for phonological markedness constraints, the majority of recurrent sound patterns in child language acquisition appear to derive from production constraints of the maturing articulatory system, and do not reflect language competence.

Since the bulk of evidence examined suggests that most aspects of sound patterns are learned, a question which arises is whether certain domains within phonology present the learner with degenerate, ambiguous, or conflicting structures from which it is difficult to draw valid generalizations. Insufficient, ambiguous, or conflicting evidence could result in places where the grammar is underdetermined, resulting in intraspeaker variability, cross-speaker differences, or both. Section 9.1.5 summarizes research on syllabification relevant to this question.

9.1.1   A wealth of stimulus

Arguments for universality often have a negative or default character in generative accounts. From the claim that a particular property of grammar could not possibly be learned, it is concluded that the property must be part of Universal Grammar. This line of argumentation, known as "the Argument from Poverty of the Stimulus" (APS), remains inexplicit in many generative accounts, though it is very widely assumed. Pullum and Scholz (2002) present a useful dissection and critique of the poverty of stimulus argument, showing that, even in the domain of syntax, where it was first proposed and retains the most plausibility, it is almost entirely unsupported.[1]

To evaluate the claims and implications of the APS, Pullum and Scholz contrast two extreme types of learning, as defined in (1). Data-driven learning (1i) is the case where aspects of linguistic structure are gleaned directly from speech forms that the child is exposed to. This contrasts with "hyperlearning," or "innately primed learning," where learning occurs in the absence of evidence.[2] With these definitions in place, Pullum and Scholz break the APS into the five logical steps in (2), with the key empirical premise in italics.

(1)   TWO KINDS OF LEARNING
    i. <u>Data-driven learning</u>
        Data-driven learning is knowledge of language structure which relies on attention to evidence, specifically, the corpus of utterances to which the child is exposed when they happen to come up in everyday contexts and are uttered in the child's presence. The general conditions on correct reasoning that are germane to learning anything else from evidence are deployed in data-driven language acquisition, but crucially, the learner is assumed *not* to be in prior possession of any information about what languages are like.
    ii. <u>Hyperlearning</u> (aka '<u>Innately primed learning</u>')
        Hyperlearning is knowledge of language structure which is acquired by children without evidence. Innately primed

---

[1] An early critique of the "poverty of stimulus" argument is found in Pullum (1996). For a general survey of potential arguments for innate linguistic knowledge, see Scholz and Pullum (2002).

[2] Though the notion of hyperlearning might seem implausible to the non-linguist, Pullum reminds the reader of its importance within certain grammatical traditions with his opening quote from Hornstein and Lightfoot (1981: 9): "People attain knowledge of the structure of their language for which *no* evidence is available in the data to which they are exposed as children."

learning calls upon inborn domain-specific linguistic
information.

(2)   THE ARGUMENT FROM POVERTY OF THE STIMULUS
   i. Human infants learn their first languages either by
      data-driven learning or by innately primed learning.
   ii. If human infants acquire their first languages via
       data-driven learning, then hyperlearning will never be
       observed in this domain.
   iii. *Hyperlearning does in fact occur in the domain of first-language
        acquisition by infants.*
   iv. Human infants do not learn their first languages by means
       of data-driven learning.
   v. Therefore human infants learn their first languages by
      means of innately primed learning.

Pullum and Scholz (2002) go on to show that, for the four clearest cases
of APS in the literature, the empirical premise in (2iii) is not supported.
In one case, a claimed grammatical property is found to be dubious. In
the three remaining cases, the set of sentences claimed not to be available
to the learner during the acquisition process arguably are. Pullum and
Scholz (2002: 47) conclude that, at least within the syntactic domain,
"the APS still awaits even a single good supporting example."

Now consider how the APS might present itself in phonology. A particular phonological property is observed, but is attributed to Universal
Grammar on the grounds that there is no way a child could learn it
directly from the observable data. Is there any evidence of hyperlearning
in phonology? To answer this question, we can consider three domains
of learning: segment inventories, phonotactics, and alternations. What
would hyperlearning look like in each case? In single-level models containing only phonological surface forms, hyperlearning would take the
form of spontaneous regular "sound change" without phonetic, morphological, or sociolinguistic motivation. Hypothetical examples would
include cases where language learners replace [ð] with [p] in all contexts,
produce all closed syllables as open syllables, or spontaneously voice all
word-final obstruents. No examples of this type are described in the literature on regular sound change.[3] In general then, surface phonetics,

---

[3] The second pattern, of producing all closed syllables as open ones, is documented in the
early stages of languages acquisition. Since in normal language acquisition, a stage with
only open syllables is followed eventually by a stage where syllable codas are produced,
one cannot attribute the open-syllable stage to "hyperlearning" in the strict sense, as the
grammar is not yet mature. In 9.1.4 patterns of this type are attributed to aspects of motor
development.

and associated phonological forms, are usually directly inherited, *modulo* the kinds of articulatory and perceptually motivated sound changes documented in part II.

The situation is somewhat more complicated when multi-level phonological models with underlying and surface forms are considered. Since underlying and surface forms may differ, hyperlearning may arise in cases where an underlying contrast is neutralized in surface forms. If the linguist can find evidence that speakers posit differing underlying forms in the context of absolute neutralization, then, again, hyperlearning is apparent. The historical record is very clear on this point: whereas contextual neutralizations sometimes show evidence of reversals, absolute neutralization rules or mergers are irreversible (Kiparsky 1968). Even so, a limited number of analyses with absolute or near absolute neutralization are found in the literature. One well-known case is the standard generative analysis of the Yowlumne (aka Yawelmani) dialect of Yokuts (Kenstowicz and Kisseberth 1979), based on Newman's (1944) description and Kuroda's (1967) early generative treatment. In this analysis, underlying /u:/ and /o:/ are both posited, though /u:/ undergoes long-vowel lowering to [o:]. The phonological analysis is based primarily on harmony patterns: /u:/ triggers rounding harmony with following high vowels, while /o:/ triggers rounding harmony with following non-high vowels. Since the linguist is able to deduce from this harmony pattern that there are two distinct underlying vowels, /u:/ and /o:/, the question arises as to whether first-language learners can and will do the same. On the basis of surface harmony patterns, will a learner deduce that stem [o:] which only cooccurs with following high round vowels is a distinct *phonological segment* from stem [o:] which cooccurs with following non-high round vowels?

While this question might seem highly language specific, there is a sense in which it encapsulates one of the most fundamental problems in synchronic phonological modeling. When a given phonological alternation can be stated either in terms of morphological generalizations or in terms of phonological conditioning factors, *what generalizations do speakers make based on the available data?*[4] And, *is it necessary to assume that all speakers make the same generalizations?* I return to these important questions in 9.1.5 and 9.3. For the moment, let us conclude the discussion of possible hyperlearning in Yowlumne. Since there is no positive evidence external to the harmony alternations themselves for underlying long high vowels in these contexts, no facts force a phonological analysis.

---

[4] Spencer (1986) addresses this question directly in his discussion of neutral vowels in harmony systems.

Even with a phonological analysis, hyperlearning may not be necessary if speakers can make the same kinds of distributionally based deductions as linguists. And, since morphologically conditioned alternations occur in many of the world's languages, the morphological solution cannot be ruled out *a priori*. Finally, as recognized explicitly by Newman (1944) and Hockett (1967, 1973) sound patterns outside of verb paradigms suggest that long-vowel lowering and vowel harmony are morphologically conditioned alternations (Blevins to appear). We are left to conclude that, as with the syntactic cases discussed by Pullum and Scholz (2002), there is no persuasive evidence of hyperlearning in Yowlumne.

Are there other potential cases of hyperlearning in phonology? One detail of Klamath phonology appears to be learned with little overt evidence (Blevins 2002). Klamath /sʔ/ is, on the surface, ambiguous between a cluster or single glottalized segment. One small corner of Klamath phonology involving prefixation provides evidence for a cluster analysis, but due to the small number of stems with the appropriate structure and their low frequencies, this data may not be available to children in the course of language acquisition. If language learners consistently analyze /sʔ/ as a cluster without evidence from relevant alternations, can this be seen as an instance of hyperlearning? In this case, distributional facts appear to play a primary role. Since /sʔ/ and /ʔ/ occur only before vowels, analyzing /sʔ/ as a cluster means learners need only posit a single generalization regarding the distribution of /ʔ/. Since, in this case, learning is based on distributional evidence directly available in the form of surface-true generalizations, hyperlearning, again, need not be invoked.

Another case where hyperlearning has been invoked is in pidgin and creole grammars (e.g. Lenz 1928; Schuchardt 1979). However, in the few detailed studies of pidgin and creole phonology and phonetics, there are few, if any, properties which cannot be attributed to sound patterns of the substrate language, lexifier language, or to regular sound change. For example, in Singler's (1996) analysis of Vernacular Liberian English, the majority of phonotactic constraints reflect substrate features, while the exceptional possibility of /p/, /b/ as codas in one basilect does not follow from any proposed aspect of Universal Grammar. Similarly, in Tok Pisin, as spoken by the Tolai, substrate influences characterize the earliest years, while later stabilization shows the introduction of /s/ in the pidgin (Mosel 1980). Again, it is difficult to see the introduction of /s/ as a feature determined by Universal Grammar. Strong confirmation of the general principle that pidgins and creoles reflect speakers' learned abilities of pronunciation and perception are found in work on tone languages. As summarized by Mülhäusler (1997: 140), simplification of tone systems is common in pidgins when the majority of users are speakers of a non-tone language, while in contexts where speakers of tone languages adopt a pidgin, tonal contrasts are preserved. A complicating factor in any of these studies is the fact that hyperlearning would have to be applied not only to children, but to adults as well.

Phonological hyperlearning does appear to be necessary in approaches where highly abstract underlying forms are proposed as a consequence of theory-internal considerations. As a hypothetical example, consider a language with surface vowels ã õ ĩ u. If a hypothetical synchronic constraint demands that a language have no more nasalized vowels than oral vowels, then the surface nasalized vowels in this language may be assumed to be underlyingly oral, with an automatic rule of nasalization for all vowels but /u/. However, an obvious question for such an analysis is whether any empirical evidence exists for the posited underlying /a o i/. While this example is hypothetical, certain phonological models demand abstractions of this type. Within Government Phonology (Kaye et al. 1990; Harris 1990, 1997), for example, surface CVC strings are analyzed as vowel-final, where the vowel in question is an "empty-category" with no phonetic substance. In this case, it is not the phonetic data which suggest an abstract vowel, but a theory-internal postulate which demands it. Within Government Phonology, a universal constraint against closed syllables is assumed, and it is this constraint, in conjunction with others, which will inevitably give rise to abstract vowels after coda consonants. Though empty vowels in Government Phonology constitute cases of hyperlearning, their abstract nature, lack of phonetic substance, and theory-internal status, result in no clear means of empirical verification. Hyperlearning in phonology, then, is generally not in evidence.

This should not be surprising. To my knowledge, no one has defined an obvious learnability problem in the acquisition of surface sound patterns *per se*.[5] Phonological systems are finite and relatively small. In contrast to syntactic systems which have been claimed to present the learner with data of "degenerative quality and narrowly limited extent" (Chomsky 1965), phonological systems provide an abundance of stimuli, with productive phonological alternations robustly cued. In one week an infant might hear tens of thousands of sentences. Each of these thousands of sentences will include recurrent examples of the limited stress, tone, syllable, and

---

[5] This is not to say that particular theories do not define unique problems of learnability. For example, in Optimality Theory where constraints are claimed to be innate and universal, constraint ranking must be learned on a language-specific basis. Since the relationship between constraint ranking and surface forms is not direct, problems arise (Hale and Reiss 1998; Hayes 1999; Tesar and Smolensky 2000).

alternation types in the language, and even more examples of tokens of individual segments. By the time an infant reaches the age of eight or nine months, when a first word might appear, the child will have heard hundreds of thousands of tokens of the sound patterns of the native language. The bulk of phonological learning then, for which there is overt evidence, points to data-driven learning. Implicit in this data-driven model is the assumption that infants can perceive all the possible phonetic contrasts which are used to signal meaningful contrasts in sound systems. This is the one area where empirical data support some sort of innate knowledge or capability, as summarized in 9.1.2.

9.1.2   Infant perception

Let us turn now to the general question: what aspects of sound systems follow directly from innate capacities of the human language faculty? Given the small number of absolute universals relating to segment inventories, phonotactics, stress, and tone patterns, our attention must be directed to organizational features of phonological systems as a whole. All phonological systems can be described in terms of strings of segments which contrast in terms of a seemingly closed class of distinctive features. All phonological systems organize segments into prosodic units, with prosodic words fundamental constituents in all languages, and with no upper limit on size. By hypothesis, all of these characteristics may be attributed to the biological endowment of the human species. Evidence for many of these design features as non-learned properties of human language is found by looking at the perceptual capabilities of human infants.

There is now an extensive literature demonstrating that human infants are capable of discriminating nearly all contrastive pairs of sounds and syllables presented to them, with only a few exceptions. In one of the earliest studies of infant perception, Eimas et al. (1971), based on changes in rates of sucking, were able to show infants' abilities to discriminate [pa] versus [ba] and [ta] versus [da], and to show that this discrimination was categorial. When a baby was presented with an exemplar of the /pa/ category followed by an exemplar of the /ba/ category, sucking rate increased, while repetitions of within-category tokens did not give rise to increased sucking rates. Subsequent experiments using both the sucking design and head-turning routines, have been able to demonstrate that in the first days, weeks, and months of life, children are able to distinguish laryngeal, place, and manner contrasts in consonants; vowel quality; differences in syllable duration and composition; distinct pitch and intonation contours; and that they are sensitive to the categories "syllable" and "prosodic word." Infant experiments illustrating these perceptual capabilities include: Aslin et al. 1981; Best et al. 1988; Eimas 1975; Fernald 1985; Fernald and Kuhl 1987; Lasky et al. 1975; Mehler et al. 1988; Streeter 1976; Trehub 1976; Werker et al. 1981; Werker and Tees 1984; and Werker and Lalonde 1988. Useful summaries of experimental evidence can be found in: Aslin 1987; Aslin et al. 1983; Juczyk 1992; Kuhl 1987; and Vihman 1996: 57–65. The fact that infants can discriminate these speech sounds and categories from such a young age is strong evidence that these phonological constructs are innate.

Yet evidence from non-human subjects suggests that humans are not the only living creatures with such perceptual acuity. Chinchillas were the first to show their auditory skills, demonstrating categorical perception for /ta/ versus /da/, /pa/ versus /ba/ and /ka/ versus /ga/ contrasts (Kuhl and Miller 1975, 1978). Not only do chinchillas show similar category boundaries to those used by English speakers, but they also show the same pattern of shifts across place of articulation: the category boundary for /g/ versus /k/ has the longest voicing lag, while that for /b/ versus /p/ has the shortest values. General categorical perception for VOT and place of articulation contrasts has also been observed in macaque monkeys (Kuhl and Padden 1982, 1983), while the Japanese quail has been trained to distinguish /d/ from /b/ and /g/ (Kluender et al. 1987). These studies, combined with the infant perception studies noted above, lend firm support to the view that the perceptual categories which arise again and again in phonological systems are, in part, determined by innate predispositions which characterize the human auditory system. However, predispositions which can also be observed in the behavior of quails, chinchillas, and macaques are by no means obviously unique to the human species.

Furthermore, not all contrasts are easily distinguished by infants. Some experiments show that infants may have difficulties distinguishing between voiceless and voiced fricatives and between labio-dental and dental fricatives (Eilers and Minifie 1975; Eilers 1977). Since adults often confuse these two sound types, it is not surprising that children do the same. Other experiments show that children have more difficulties identifying contrasts in multisyllabic contexts than in simple CV syllables (Trehub 1976; Goodsitt et al. 1984). A question which has yet to be explored is whether certain positions within a word are attended to more carefully than others. One prediction of Evolutionary Phonology is that category neutralization should be more common in the form of neutralizing sound change precisely where difficulties are found in infant perception. Another prediction is that contextual differences in perceptual acuity will be mirrored by differences in the cross-linguistic distribution of contrasts.

9.1.3   Deaf babble

If the perception of newborns provides a window on innate properties of the auditory system, how can we observe the innate articulatory capabilities of infants when they do not talk? In the first few months of life, babies coo, laugh, cry, and may vocalize in very non-specific ways, but there is no clue to the complexities which will soon follow. By the time children start to babble, usually between six and eight months, they have normally been exposed to hundreds of thousands of syllables. Based on this, they begin to extract recurrent patterns from these utterances, and show greater attention to native-language contrasts. With this increased attention to the native language, the one-year-old child is already showing evidence of early language-specific phonological categories (Werker et al. 1981; Werker and Logan 1985; Werker and Lalonde 1988; Werker and Pegg 1992; Werker and Tees 1984). Since language-specific information is already being processed by the child on the verge of babbling, we cannot assume that the articulations which constitute babbling are uninformed by the ambient speech community.[6]

But children who are born deaf are different. A congenitally deaf child will not have exposure to auditory stimuli. Any patterns which emerge from babbling can inform our view of what is, and is not, innate, and inform models of articulatory development and its potential relationship to synchronic phonologies. Locke (1983: 26–38) and Locke and Pearson (1992: 104–6) summarize a range of studies showing that deaf children, though delayed by several months, do babble. This babbling has fewer consonant-like sounds than that of hearing children (Stoel-Gammon and Otomo 1986), but does show some of the same general preferences for segment types as the babbling of hearing children (Locke 1983: 26–38). Stops, nasals, and glides are the most common consonant types; voiceless unaspirated segments are more common than voiceless aspirated ones; and labials and coronals are more common than velars. If, as argued by Locke (1983), these preferences mirror those found in adult phonologies, then it is possible that certain very gross patterns of segmental distribution and frequency reflect the innate articulatory trajectory of early speech.

If one was unconvinced that humans are made to talk, that there are innate predispositions to use speech, even in the absence of auditory input, the prolonged babbling stage of deaf children might give cause to reconsider. Clearly, one does not need to hear speech-like sounds in order to make them. Locke and Pearson (1992), evaluating a range of

---

[6] In fact, cross-linguistic studies of pre-linguistic vocalizations suggest effects of ambient language exposure on production as early as ten months (Boysson-Bardies et al. 1989).

neurological and behavioral data relating to vocal learning, view babbling by both hearing and deaf children as a form of motor practice for speech. Babbling provides children with their own vocalic stimulation, and from this self-produced stimulation, "the child derives production experience and a store of motor-auditory equivalences that enable the expression of internal representations and aural guidance of articulatory movements" (1992: 119). In the following section, evidence is presented that much of what is viewed as "child phonology" is also a consequence of the development of motor skills. These findings are significant, since as performance factors, they may obscure the true nature of a child's language competence.

9.1.4   The illusion of child phonology

The majority of sound patterns observed in child language which deviate significantly from adult patterns, and which are not reflected in sound change, have articulatory origins. The view that children's articulatory behavior during the first years of acquisition reflects developmental processes, and not necessarily grammatical ones, is not new. In Locke's (1983) comprehensive study of language acquisition and its relationship to language change, he observes that:

Just as there is a cross-linguistic tendency for children to express fricatives as stops, so is there a universal tendency for stops to be acquired prior to fricatives. And the same may be said for a number of other patterns, as we have seen. These tendencies are, I believe, the phonetic residue of a biologically driven system of vocal tract movements that become apparent as early as the later periods of premeaningful babbling. (1983: 81)

Less than a decade later, a large amount of data had accumulated, showing that Locke's conclusion was essentially correct, though other factors also played a role. In summarizing this decade of work on the transition from babbling into speech, Vihman (1992: 394) highlights three distinct results in the field:

To begin with, babbling production is clearly rooted in a biological base common to all children . . . However, another line of research has shown conclusively that the child's phonetic production has in some respects begun to be shaped by the particular ambient language to which he or she is exposed even before the first words are attempted . . . Finally, there is equally strong support for the proposition that individual children follow individual paths, drawing their early lexicon largely from the phonetic repertoire which they have established in the course of the babbling period . . .

In later work, Vihman (1996: 217) introduces the study of children's deviant phonological behavior within the larger field of language development with an immediate disclaimer: "These adjustments have been termed (child) phonological rules . . . or processes . . . despite the fact that the relationship to the rules of the *adult* phonology is more apparent than real."[7]

Some recurrent sound patterns in child phonology which appear to reflect articulatory patterns of development and particular motor difficulties during the babbling-to-speech stage are listed in (3) with representative examples.

(3)   CHILD PHONOLOGY ERRORS DUE TO PRODUCTION
       LIMITATIONS
       i. closed syllables produced as open syllables (e.g. *book* as [bʊ])
       ii. context-free cluster reduction (e.g. *stop* as [tap])
       iii. fricatives produced as stops (e.g. *shoe* as [du])
       iv. consonant harmony (e.g. *doggie* as [gaga])
       v. English rhotic produced as non-rhotic (e.g. *red* as [wɛd])

The first thing to notice about these changes is that they can all be viewed in terms of articulatory simplification. In (3i,ii) an entire consonantal gesture is left out; in (3iii), the fine motor control required in creating the narrow channel for fricative noise is omitted; in (3iv), consonant harmony, a target with two distinct points of consonantal articulation, requiring sequential organization of distinct articulators, is simplified to one; and in (3v) the lingual contortions involved in the English rhotic are eliminated, leaving gestures which are nearly identical in form to those of vowels. While all these changes are simplifying, many of the adult phonological processes discussed in earlier chapters are not, including, common processes like velar palatalization ($k \rightarrow t\int$), vowel epenthesis, and post-tonic gemination.

Patterns of individual children support the view that consonant harmony is used to avoid difficult sounds or sound sequences. In the speech of Canta, learning Chinese, consonant harmony appeared in only 5 percent of the data set, but was used almost exclusively to deal with /l/ which she did not yet produce. In Virve's acquisition of Estonian, there were two different early strategies for dealing with liquids and /v/: consonant

---

[7] Empirical evidence as well as learnability considerations lead Hale and Reiss (1998: 658) to essentially the same conclusion: "Deviations from target forms in children's . . . grammars are to be attributed to performance effects, including non-linguistic cognitive and motor processing."

harmony and deletion. And in Sofia's acquisition of Spanish, a majority of words with consonant harmony were three syllables or longer. In each of these cases, there is good evidence that harmony is being used to deal with sound patterns which pose specific production problems for the individual child.[8]

A second property of the changes in (3i–iv) is that they have no parallels in phonetically motivated sound change of the kind documented in part II. This may not be evident on first inspection. The child-language pattern in (3i) looks similar to rules of coda weakening and loss documented for many unrelated languages. However, what is significant is that documented changes involving coda loss are typically gradual, and have specific patterns related to the phonetic content of the feature in question. Recall, for example, the Chinese developments from closed to open syllables discussed in chapter 5. Loss of final stops involved an intermediate stage of neutralization to glottal stop, while loss of final nasals involved an intermediate stage of a final velar nasal or glide. There are few, if any, cases of non-contact-induced change where a language with the same range of codas as Middle Chinese abruptly loses *all* coda consonants.[9] Yet this is the pattern observed again and again in the early stages of child language development.

The same generalization holds for (3ii–iv). Though there are many sound changes involving consonant loss which are contextually determined, there are few, if any, proposed sound changes where cluster reduction is *context free*. Typically, in regular sound change, initial or final clusters are reduced, but intervocalic CC sequences remain; or, heterorganic clusters are (ultimately) reduced, but homorganic clusters are maintained. These patterns differ significantly from those in children's speech where, at a certain stage, all words are composed of V or CV syllables. The stopping of fricatives parallel to (3iii) is also uncommon as a regular sound change. Even in fortition environments, the common realization of a fortis [s] involves longer fricative noise durations, but not a shift to

---

[8] The data summarized here are based on Vihman (1996: appendix B and C). Inkelas and Rose (2002) report an interesting case study of positional neutralization in the acquisition of English which they argue is not the result of articulatory difficulty. In strong positions only, adult /k/ is realized as [t] while /l/ is realized as [y]. Since /k/ and /l/ have distinct allophones in strong and weak positions, this pattern suggests difficulty with the phones in strong position. For /l/, this is supported by evidence of /l/ avoidance prior to the replacement strategy. For /k/, the child, unable to produce a [kʰ] with sufficient aspiration in strong position, may resort to [tʰ] which he finds easier to produce with longer VOT.

[9] Abrupt loss of final consonants does appear to have occurred at least a dozen times in the history of Austronesian languages (Blevins to appear e) and, as an instance of drift, deserves further study.

stop articulation.[10] And the shifts in major place of articulation between /p, t, k, b, d, g/ which occur under child-consonant harmony (3iv) are not known as sound changes, nor are they attested as productive alternations in adult grammars.

While the common child-phonology transform in (3v) is similar to regular instances of sound change, there is good evidence that, in child phonology, it too results from a child's inability to produce a well-formed adult rhotic glide, not from a phonological rule neutralizing the contrast between /w/ and /r/ in English. The first piece of evidence pointing in this direction is what we know about the articulation of rhotics in many English dialects. American English /r/ can be produced in many different ways. At least one common pronunciation of this sound involves simultaneous lip rounding, coronal closure, palatal approximation, and pharyngeal constriction. The coordination of so many gestures during the duration of a single segment is expected to yield a level of difficulty greater than most other English sounds. In this case, the association of (3v) with articulatory difficulty seems well founded, since /r/ is often the last sound to be mastered by English-speaking children, at least to standards of the adult ear. A stronger piece of evidence supporting [w] pronunciation as a child's true attempt to approximate an *r*-like sound is the fact that the child's [w] and the adult [w] are not alike, differing in acoustic intensity, and that children who make these distinctions in their own speech have extremely high success rates distinguishing them (Klein 1969; Menyuk 1971; Hawkins 1973; Kornfeld and Goehl 1974; Faber and Best 1994). In this case, the apparent difference between the child's phonology and that of the adult is an illusion: these children can perceive the adult contrast between [ɻʷ] and [w], and attempt to reproduce it. Though their rhotic reproductions are not recognizable as such to the adult ear, the children themselves can hear the contrast they are making and recognize these two sounds as distinct.

Within Evolutionary Phonology the language learner, as reinventor of the phonological system, is the prime source of regular sound change. This general view has been rejected by many researchers on the grounds that processes like those in (3) do not properly characterize adult phonology.[11]

---

[10] The majority of phonological alternations involving fricative fortition in LaVoie (2001) are inverted instances of historical leniting sound changes. As a consequence, they show fricative to stop in the form of ð → d, but not *s* → *t* or *z* → *d*. Context-free *s* > *t* is attested in Western Tibeto-Burman and Sino-Vietnamese.

[11] For example, Kiparsky (1988), in assessing Andersen's (1973) proposals that sound change originates from abductive learning, in much the way suggested in 2.2, concludes that: "Empirical study of child phonology gives little support for this theory." He also

What these researchers fail to appreciate is that the correspondences in (3) are not properly grammatical: they are transforms of adult speech into the developing vocal apparatus of the young child. In contrast to these transforms, true sound changes resulting from CHANCE will be unobservable when they take place, while those with sources in CHOICE will be barely observable, involving, as they do, minute shifts in vowel formants, VOT, stop duration, etc. which are typically thought to characterize "individual variation." A challenge for future studies of phonological acquisition is to tease apart "individual variation" from minute shifts in systems of oppositions. Only by extensive systematic longitudinal studies of the phonetics of children's speech will we come closer to what could be the strongest evidence for imperfect learning as a primary factor in sound change.

The discussion above highlights the superficial nature of many phonetic or phonological "errors" in children's speech. Though these can be described in terms of phonological rules, the errors have one of two trajectories: either they are simple consequences of immature articulatory development, and disappear with age; or they are real instances of mini-sound change, which may spread through a community, or be diluted by diffusion from other directions. In the first case, the errors are often distinct from alternations seen in adult phonologies; in the second case, errors may be subphonemic and barely noticeable, though similar in content to observed instances of sound change. Combined with the arguments above, there is very little evidence from child-language acquisition for innate phonological constructs apart from distinctive features, and the prosodic units which function as the domains for stress and intonation contours. The actual content of phonological representations appears to be acquired through data-driven learning, with segmental and prosodic categories emerging from the data as a consequence of innate mechanisms for producing and processing speech.

If so much of phonology is learned, and if the data-set that each individual is exposed to is slightly different, it follows that each individual may have a slightly different grammar, as Dalby's (2002) quote at the beginning of part III suggests. Is there evidence in synchronic phonologies for

---

contends that "a general problem with locating sound change in language acquisition is that the class of typical or potential sound changes does not match the class of typical or potential child language processes." Yet research over the past fifteen years suggests that the issues that Kiparsky identifies are non-problems. A child's phonological competence is masked by severe production problems in the early years of speech and can only be assessed accurately by perception experiments during that time, or inspection of the emergent grammar once motoric difficulties are no longer evident. Typical child-language processes in the first three to five years of speech do not match sound changes precisely because, by and large, they reflect performance factors.

the uniqueness of individual grammars? The following section summarizes some of the strongest evidence for phonological knowledge which is learned and non-uniform across a speech community.[12]

9.1.5   Syllabification

Syllables are important constructs in phonological systems, as they serve as the bearers of stress, the domains of harmony, and as templates for prosodic morphology (Blevins 1995). However, it is also clear that syllable structure is usually predictable in a language (Levin 1985). Although in some exceptional cases, non-gliding vowels or non-vocalizing glides must be lexically specified, syllable structure and syllabicity alternations can, for the most part, be derived from the segmental properties of phonological forms. The derived status of syllabification is consistent with the fact that syllabifications within a given language are never contrastive (Blevins 1995; Steriade 1999b). However, since rules of stress assignment and syncope often take syllabified forms as their input, syllabifications cannot be purely surface phenomena either.

The general view in phonological theory, summarized in Blevins (1995), is that word phonotactics reflect conditions on syllable structure, since words are ultimately composed of syllables. However, languages with highly unusual syllabification patterns force a reconsideration of this position. Sommer (1969, 1970) argues that Oykangand, which has only vowel-initial words, syllabifies all medial consonants into the coda. In VCCCV strings, then, the syllabification is VCCC.V. A similar argument has been made by Breen and Pensalfini (1999) for Arrernte, another Pama-Nyungan language. Both of these languages have, independently, undergone the unusual sound change discussed in 6.7 involving initial consonant loss. As a result, all words are vowel-initial. It appears highly significant that these are the only two languages in the world with medial syllabifications giving rise to onset-less syllables, and that they both lack words beginning in consonants. This correlation suggests that it is not the syllable which defines the form of a word, but rather the word which defines the shape of a syllable.

Empirical evidence for syllabifications based on word-edge phonotactics is summarized in Steriade (1999b). She notes two significant aspects

---

[12] For evidence supporting the learned status of detailed phonetic knowledge, including patterns of variation, see Pierrehumbert (1994, 2000, 2001), Bybee (2001), and Warner et al. (2002). Ladefoged and Maddieson (1996) contains many descriptions of articulatory features which differ across speakers. One example is American English /r/, which is produced as an alveolar or post-alveolar approximant for some speakers, but with pharyngeal and palatal constrictions for others without any significant involvement of the tongue blade (1996: 234).

of studies investigating native-speaker judgments of word-internal syllab-ifications. First, in many languages, word-internal syllabification judg-ments vary across speakers. Second, this variation correlates with contexts in which word-internal strings cannot be parsed as a sequence of word-initial and word-final strings. In some languages, like Spanish and many dialects of Arabic, all word-internal strings can be parsed as sequences of word-initial and word-final sequences. As a consequence, syllabification judgments are consistent across speakers. In other languages, like English, even some of the simplest words give rise to uncertainty on the part of speakers. For example, the word *lemon* in American English is problematic since syllabifications *le.mon* and *lem.on* yield syllable types which are not found at word edges. In the first case, [lɛ], with a final non-low lax vowel is parsed, though such lax vowels are otherwise unattested word-finally in English. In the second case, [ən], a truly vowel-initial syllable is posited, though vowel-initial words are typically preceded by glottal stop. In these cases, speakers show variability in where they place the syllable boundary: some place it before [m]; some place it after [m]; and some split the [m] in two, allowing it to close the first syllable and open the second.[13] Steriade (1999b) summarizes psycholinguistic studies from English, Dutch, and Polish which demonstrate uncertainty and speaker variability precisely where word edges cannot be matched to word-internal sequences.

Within the descriptive arena, there are many languages whose word phonotactics cannot be described in terms of sequences of well-formed syllables without special statements. Dixon (1980: 159) makes this point for the phonotactics of many Australian languages. In discussing general properties of disyllabic words of the form $C_1VC_2C_3V(C_4)$ or $C_1VC_5V(C_4)$, he observes that:

It is . . . not possible, for an Australian language, to give a structure $C_1V(C_2)$ for syllables, and then to describe a word as a sequence of these syllables. The possibilities at C_3 may be similar to those at C_1 but they never coincide; similar remarks apply to C_2 and C_4.

Panyjima, a Pama-Nyungan language, reflects a typical case. All words begin with a single consonant and end in a vowel, but there are medial clusters where C_2 is a nasal or liquid. In C_4, then, no consonants are allowed, while in C_2 sonorant consonants occur. The fact that this distri-butional property is not accidental is indicated by a phonological rule of accretion in Panyjima which adds a syllable /-pa/ to any word which would otherwise end in a consonant (Dench 1991). The name of this language

---

[13] For in-depth studies of English syllabification, including words like *lemon*, see Treiman (1983, 1986, 1988) and Treiman and Danis (1988).

and people illustrates the problem raised by word-internal syllabifications: *Pany.ji.ma* [paɲɟima] with initial-syllable final [ɲ] is not consistent with word-level patterns, since all words must end in vowels; *Pa.nyji.ma* fares no better, since the second syllable begins with a consonant cluster, an illicit word-initial pattern; and *Panyj.i.ma* is perhaps the worst of all, since the initial syllable ends in a consonant cluster, unattested word-finally, while the second syllable begins with a vowel, another illicit start for Panyjima words. Unsurprisingly, syllabification judgments for speakers of Nhanda and Wajarri, with similar sound patterns, are highly variable for words with medial clusters, though elsewhere, there is no hesitancy to syllabify CVCV as CV + CV.[14]

Following Steriade (1999b), then, it appears that surface syllabifications evidenced by native-speaker judgments are the result of word-based generalizations like those in (4).

(4)   WORD-BASED SYLLABIFICATION (defaults; may be overridden by other phonotactic constraints)
    a. If C_0 is possible word-initially, then C_0 is possible syllable-initially.
    b. If C_0 is not possible word-initially, then C_0 is not possible syllable-initially.
    c. If C_0 is possible word-finally, then C_0 is possible syllable-finally.
    d. If C_0 is not possible word-finally, then C_0 is not possible syllable-finally
    e. If V_q is possible word-initially, then V_q is possible syllable-initially.
    f. If V_q is not possible word-initially, then V_q is not possible syllable-initially.
    g. If V_q is possible word-finally, then V_q is possible syllable-finally.
    h. If V_q is not possible word-finally, then V_q is not possible syllable-finally

In fact, only these statements are able to handle certain problems of analysis where other approaches fall short. I have already mentioned the highly unusual syllabifications of Oykangand and Arrernte which are supported by productive patterns of reduplication. In this case, reduplication is sensitive to prosodic phonological constituents. If the schema in (4) are invoked, the appropriate syllabifications can serve as input to reduplication. However, if universal syllabification strategies involving obligatory

[14] When CV syllables are produced in isolation, vowels are lengthened, conforming to a bimoraic minimum on phonological words. See Henderson (1998) for similar observations regarding syllabification with speakers of Eastern Arrernte.

onsets and onset-maximization are invoked, the reduplication patterns cannot be accounted for without additional stipulations (Sommer 1969, 1970; Breen and Pensalfini 1999).

Another type of problem which arises in syllable-based phonology is the case where syllabifications necessary for certain phonological processes conflict with those necessary for others, as well as those provided by native speakers. An interesting case of this kind arises in Yurok (Blevins 2003d), where pre-glottalized segments are arguably single segments for the purposes of four distinct phonological processes, but in intervocalic environments, they serve to close preceding syllables for the purposes of stress, and are consistently syllabified by native speakers as sequences of glottal stop + sonorant. In this case, the syllabification schema in (4) also makes the correct predictions. In Yurok pre-glottalized sonorants are neutralized to plain sonorants in word-initial position (see 4.5). In a word like *ke'mow* 'food,' the syllabification *ke.'mow* violates (4b), since glottalized sonorants are not tolerated word-initially in Yurok (see 4.5). However, the alternative, *ke'm.ow*, violates (4f), since words cannot begin with vowels in Yurok either. In this case, segmental fission occurs to satisfy the constraints in (4). While word-based syllabification in Yurok brings up new questions, such as where segmental fission may take place, it is the only analysis in which language-specific *ad hoc* conditions on syllabification are unnecessary.

In sum, there is growing evidence that syllabifications necessary for phonological processes like reduplication and stress assignment, as well as surface syllabifications provided in native speaker judgments, are word-based, as in (4). This contrasts with conventional approaches in which universal constraints like Onset, No-Coda, etc. drive syllabification. While the word-based nature of syllabification may be universal, the word-edge phonotactics on which this syllabification is based are language-specific and learned. An empirical advantage of this approach over others is that it predicts where variability or exceptional processes like fission will occur. Inconsistent or exceptional syllabification is expected precisely where word-medial sequences cannot be parsed into well-formed word-initial + word-final sequences. Where cross-speaker variation results, this can be interpreted as support for the highly individualistic nature of certain aspects of phonological knowledge.

9.1.6   Summary

The evidence from language acquisition and the patterns of word-based syllabification presented in this section argue strongly for data-driven learning in phonology. Within the domain of sounds, there is no poverty of the stimulus. Sounds surround us, and if anything, there is too much information to process, not too little. If synchronic phonologies consist of generalizations in terms of phonological constructs extracted from the speech stream, there are many ways that different language learners can arrive at different generalizations concerning sound patterns. We have already looked at differences in raw input as a source of sound change in CHOICE. Another source of potential cross-speaker differences is cases where surface sound patterns yield word-based syllabification schemas which cannot be applied to word-medial sound sequences. In both cases, differences in individual grammars are attributed to the fact that the majority of phonological knowledge is not innate. This view of phonological knowledge as learned knowledge is at odds with many modern phonological theories which attribute a range of sound patterns to universal constraints which are part of the innate language faculty. The next section suggests that the most widely accepted of these phonological constraints are unnecessary or unmotivated.

9.2   Phonological constraints

The roots of modern generative phonology are often traced to *The Sound Pattern of English* (Chomsky and Halle 1968). The theory proposed in *SPE* involves three separate components: a theory of distinctive features that defines phonological representations; a theory of rules that defines phonological alternations; and a theory of markedness that attempts to impose substantive constraints on the content of the rule component. However, this last component of the theory was only sketched briefly in the final chapter of the book, and had little effect on the development of generative phonology in subsequent years.

Only with new conceptions of phonological representations in the 1980s, including autosegmental features and metrical constituents, did certain typological generalizations regarding the phonetic content of phonological rules become more salient. Some of these generalizations, e.g. the Obligatory Contour Principle, were adopted as universal constraints. Others, such as the naturalness of place assimilation rules, were attributed to properties of phonological representations, in this case, the presence of a place-node within a feature geometry.

However, as more and more relationships between sound patterns and their phonetic content were established, the theoretical inadequacies first noted in chapter 9 of *SPE* could no longer be ignored, leading many phonologists to share Chomsky and Halle's view that, to the extent that formal generative treatments did not relate specific sound patterns to their phonetic content, they had "failed to formulate the principles of linguistic theory, of Universal Grammar, in a satisfactory manner" and had "not made any use of the fact that the features have intrinsic content" (Chomsky and Halle 1968: 400).

In this section, approaches and constraints meant to eliminate this problem are evaluated in light of the arguments for Evolutionary Phonology presented in part II. Section 9.2.1 consolidates arguments against approaches which directly incorporate markedness constraints into synchronic grammars, while sections 9.2.2 and 9.2.3 address two other universal properties which have been attributed to synchronic phonologies, but which do not appear to have solid empirical foundations.

9.2.1   Markedness constraints

In part II, a range of evidence supports diachronic explanations for properties of recurrent sound patterns. With this evidence in mind, we are in a position to evaluate implications of these findings for synchronic phonological models. The central premise of Evolutionary Phonology is repeated in (5) from chapter 1.

(5)   CENTRAL PREMISE OF EVOLUTIONARY PHONOLOGY
        Principled diachronic explanations for sound patterns have
        priority over competing synchronic explanations unless
        independent evidence demonstrates, beyond reasonable doubt,
        that a synchronic account is warranted.

Since the phonologization of phonetically motivated sound change provides principled diachronic explanations for the majority of common and uncommon sound patterns examined in chapters 4–8, markedness constraints which duplicate these explanations should be excised from synchronic grammars. Markedness and naturalness in phonology are emergent properties of synchronic systems. As Deacon (1997: 115) puts it, in the passage that opens this chapter, markedness constraints attributed to Universal Grammar "aren't really stored or located anywhere, and in an important sense, they are not determined at all. Instead . . . they have emerged spontaneously and independently in each evolving language . . ."

Since the classical generative model introduced in *SPE*, minus chapter 9, did not invoke markedness constraints, it is consistent in this respect with the findings of Evolutionary Phonology.[15] However, any model which incorporates substantive universal markedness constraints is not. Let us look briefly at one of the first constraints of this type

---

[15] Of course, in other ways, it is not. Since phonology is learned on the basis of positive evidence, some of the abstract underlying representations in *SPE* could not be motivated within Evolutionary Phonology.

proposed in phonological theory, the Obligatory Contour Principle (Leben 1973; Goldsmith 1976). Is there independent evidence which demonstrates, beyond reasonable doubt, that the OCP is a universal principle of synchronic grammars, and not the emergent consequence of the Feature to Segment Mapping Principle, as suggested in chapter 6?

The Obligatory Contour Principle, in the form stated in (6), has been invoked in a large number of phonological studies to account for everything from underlying tone patterns (Leben 1973) and tonal alternations (Goldsmith 1976; Myers 1991), to root constraints in Semitic (McCarthy 1981) and antigemination, where vowels fail to delete between adjacent identical consonants (McCarthy 1986).

(6)   THE OBLIGATORY CONTOUR PRINCIPLE (OCP)
       Adjacent identical features or feature complexes are prohibited in underlying representations.

In any case where a morpheme-internal feature, or feature complex, is associated with more than one segment, the OCP demands the representation in (7i) and prohibits the representation in (7ii). As stated in (6), the OCP is a perfect candidate for a phonological universal, since, in many languages there is no way that the representation in (7i), demanded by the OCP, can be distinguished from that of (7ii) on the basis of phonetic differences.

(7)   Underlying representations and the Obligatory Contour Principle

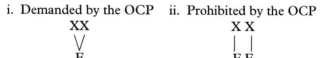

    i. Demanded by the OCP   ii. Prohibited by the OCP

However, the OCP, as stated in (6), is both too strong, and too weak. It is too strong because, though it is invoked to prohibit adjacent H tones, adjacent identical segments, and adjacent specifications of place and laryngeal features, it is rarely invoked to prevent sequence of segments with identical manner features like [nasal], or major class features like [consonantal]. Non-homorganic nasal clusters are found morpheme-internally in Piro Arawakan (Matteson 1965) and in Leti (van Engelenhoven 1995), and in both of these languages there is evidence for two independent [+nasal] specifications. In Piro, short excrescent vowels separate the sequential nasals, as they do in other heterorganic clusters: *him[ᵊ]nanu* 'to be relaxed,' *p[ᵊ]nu* 'beyond.' In Leti, infixation can split morpheme-internal nasal–nasal clusters: *mnina* 'to be calm,' *m-ni-nina* 'calm.' Since, in general, geminate structures are claimed to resist insertion processes, the behavior of these clusters suggests that multiple specifications of nasality are tolerated.[16] We are left to conclude that the Obligatory Contour Principle is not a constraint on all distinctive features, only on some. However, even with this disclaimer, the OCP on place features [coronal], [labial], and [dorsal] is still too strong for languages like Leti. In Leti, initial morpheme-internal coronal clusters like /nt/, /lt/, and /rt/ are also split by reduplicative infixation, as is the initial /mp/ cluster (van Engelenhoven 1995). However, as noted in 7.6, stem-initial geminates in Leti show a different pattern of reduplication, and are not split by the reduplicative infix. If these aspects of sound patterns are attributed to distinct representations like those in (7), then the OCP is too strong, and makes the wrong predictions. A final sense in which the OCP is too strong involves cases of antigemination (see 6.2.3). McCarthy (1986) invokes the OCP to block vowel deletion between adjacent identical consonants, however, Odden (1988) presents serious counterexamples, while Blevins (to appear a) identifies antihomophony effects as primary inhibitors of vowel loss, making the OCP extraneous.

Yet, at the same time, the OCP is also too weak. Recall from 6.4.1 that the tendency for morpheme-internal geminates to show true geminate behavior can be accounted for by the Feature-to-segment Mapping Principle, repeated in (8).

(8)   FEATURE-TO-SEGMENT MAPPING PRINCIPLE (FMP)
        In the learning algorithm which allows listeners to interpret the
        phonetic string as a sequence of segments, a phonetic feature,
        F_p, whose domain overlaps with other segment-defining
        phonetic features, is assumed to have a unique featural source
        [F] in the phonological representation (where [F] may be a
        feature or feature-complex).

As stated, (8) will allow language learners to interpret lexical length contrasts in terms of single associations of feature-bundles to segments, in the absence of evidence to the contrary. But (8) also has other implications for phonological acquisition, as discussed in 6.2. In particular, as stated,

---

[16] While the failure of major class features to take part in the Obligatory Contour Principle might be attributed to fine aspects of segment-internal feature geometry, this will not work for [+nasal]. Many languages show assimilation of nasality between neighboring segments. If [+nasal] is independent for spreading, then it should be independent for the purposes of assessing OCP violations.

(8) not only gives rise to a subset of sound patterns accounted for by the OCP, but also accounts for metathesis sound changes where a feature, or feature complex, inverts its historical position. The OCP, as stated in (7), can only account for dissimilatory instances of alternation or sound change, and says nothing of the seemingly related cases of perceptual metatheses which are handled by the FMP.

One theoretical problem with the OCP, as formulated in McCarthy (1986), is its reliance on notions of tier separation and tier conflation. Representations like that in (7ii) will commonly occur when morphemes are concatenated (see the Gooniyandi data in 7.3.7); if there are no adjustments, the OCP is violated. In order to deal with such violations, McCarthy suggests that morphemes are represented on separate autosegmental tiers, and that tier conflation may apply at different points in the derivation in different languages. The problem is that a language learner has no empirical basis, apart from the OCP facts themselves, on which to motivate tier conflation.

The problems raised briefly with respect to the OCP are not unique to this phonological constraint. Problems with universalist conceptions of geminate integrity and geminate inalterability were also noted in chapter 6. In the case of geminate integrity, the data are consistent with the FMP, with seeming "violations" arising precisely where vowels inserted into geminates are the consequence of rule inversions of earlier patterns of vowel reduction and loss. Marshallese data were discussed in chapter 6, and the facts noted above for Leti and Piro support the same hypothesis. Phonetic sound patterns involving reduced vowels between homorganic consonants are directly inherited, though in synchronic terms these vowels are best viewed as the result of insertion. The non-integrity of geminates will only arise under rule inversion for the simple reason that there is no known instance of CHANGE, CHANCE, or CHOICE which involves the splitting of a single articulation (geminate closure) into two.

Geminate inalterability is not a general property of geminates, but rather, a property of phonological lenition rules. More specifically, within Evolutionary Phonology, geminate inalterability is the phonologization of natural lenition-based sound changes involving gestural reduction. Within the evolutionary approach, the facts are as predicted: phonetic variability for any speaker is characterized by fortition and lenition at opposite ends of the hyper-to-hypoarticulation continuum. Phonologization of lenition as sound change is expected to mirror phonetic aspects of this variation, and it does. Geminates, due to their longer closure durations, are shortened under lenition, but usually not enough to result in a percept of change in voice, manner, etc. As with other sound patterns that reflect natural sound change, there is no need to build geminate inalterability into synchronic grammars.

Additional constraints on sound patterns which appear too strong are those associated with universal tendencies in syllabification. Constraints giving preference to syllables with onsets have been proposed by many researchers (e.g. Clements and Keyser 1983; Itô 1986), but the data reviewed in 9.1.5 show that these proposals are not only too strong, but that they fail precisely in places where words do not begin with consonants. While the algorithms in (4) suggest that universal constraints are not the way to encode syllable phonotactics, an alternative to (4), and to the wholesale abandonment of universal constraints on syllable structure and the OCP, is to construct phonological models in which markedness constraints are violable. This is precisely the step taken by Optimality Theory.

Within Optimality Theory, sound patterns are treated as the consequence of interacting markedness and faithfulness constraints, where all constraints are claimed to be universal and violable (Prince and Smolensky 1993; Kager 1999; McCarthy 2002). Treating constraints as aspects of Universal Grammar means they do not need to be learned; they are innate properties of the language faculty. Treating constraints as violable means that cross-linguistic tendencies can be captured by cross-linguistic differences in constraint ranking. Indeed, a central claim of Optimality Theory is that learning a language involves learning language-specific constraint ranking. Since Optimality Theory directly encodes markedness constraints relating to the content of sound patterns into grammars, it is not compatible with the central premise of Evolutionary Phonology stated in (5).[17]

A clear indication of the problems involved is the increasing number of OT accounts which recognize that specific markedness constraints, like the constraint prohibiting coda voicing, are typically resolved by constraint rankings which result in devoicing or voice assimilation, but not by rankings which involve vowel epenthesis or metathesis, which could also eliminate a constraint violation. Wilson (2001) suggests that the absence of certain rankings should be handled by targeted constraints.

---

[17] This is true, despite the disclaimer of McCarthy (2002: 15) that markedness in OT is "distinct from and a good deal more specific than the more familiar usage of this word in linguistics . . ." McCarthy goes on to admit that OT markedness constraints may "produce results related to this descriptive or typological sense of markedness" but insists that "the formal constraint and the typological observation are two different things."

Targeted constraints within OT not only specify a marked structure, but also express a preference for precisely how that structure is to be avoided. Myers (2002) on the other hand, maintains the OT architecture, but defends the view that the unattested rankings are not problematic since "the patterns they represent are unlikely to arise diachronically through natural sound change on the basis of phonetic patterns." In essence, the approach taken by Wilson (2001) leads OT down the inevitable path of not only encoding the output of common sound patterns, but their phonetic conditioning environments as well. Gaps in the factorial typology are "patched" by incorporating phonological conditioning factors into constraints themselves. On the other hand, Myers' appeal to phonologization as an explanation for unattested constraint rankings leads to the obvious question of why other aspects of sound patterns cannot ultimately be explained in the same terms, with elimination of universal markedness constraints altogether. The logical consequence of this approach is the wholesale abandonment of markedness constraints suggested here.

There are few direct empirical arguments for OT over other approaches. One claim is that within OT, the positions of infixes fall out from the general ranking of phonological constraints over morphological ones (Prince and Smolensky 1993). Under the standard OT account there is no infixation *per se*. Prefixes and suffixes are pushed into the base by highly ranked phonological constraints on prosodic structure. For example, the well-known /-um-/ infix of Malayo-Polynesian languages like Tagalog and Ilokano is treated as a prefix. However, because phonological constraints dominate morphological ones, the alignment of the prefix with the beginning of the word can be overridden by constraints like No-Coda which prohibit closed syllables. The resulting pattern is that the -VC- prefix is infixed when a stem is consonant initial (*k-um-uha-* 'get,' *t-um-awag-* 'call,' etc.), but prefixed when a stem is vowel-initial (*um-asim-* 'turn sour,' *um-akyat-* 'teach,' etc). While this analysis works well for many languages related to Tagalog and Ilokano, it does not work for all languages. In Leti, infixation of the nominalizing prefix can create consonant and vowel clusters, indicative of a Morphology > Phonology mapping (Blevins 1999b), not the reverse. In Pingding Mandarin, infixation gives rise to highly marked consonant clusters which do not occur elsewhere in the language, suggesting problems for the simple view that infixation sites reflect general phonotactic constraints (Lin 2002; Yu 2003). In Atayal, as shown in (9), the different positions of the actor-focus morpheme and the reciprocal/reflexive morpheme provide strong evidence for infixes as morphological primitives (Yu 2002).

(9)   Atayal /m-/ versus /-m-/ (Egerod 1965)

Root	Actor focus	Reciprocal/Reflexive	
kaial	kmaial	mkaial	talk
qul	qmul	mqul	snatch
sbil	smbil	msbil	leave behind
spuŋ	smpuŋ	mspuŋ	measure
hkaŋi?	hmkaŋi?	mhkaŋi?	search

If the position of the Atayal /-m-/ infix is, in fact, language-specific and learned, this raises an obvious and largely unaddressed question: why can the position of infixation not be learned in all languages? Recurrent tendencies in the positioning of -VC- infixes, if they are real, may follow from the evolution of these morphemes as infixes. This is arguably the case in Yurok, where the infix /-eg-/ results from reanalysis of earlier reduplicated *he-ge* < *he-he* as *h-eg-e* (Garrett 2001).

Another area where OT claims greater empirical coverage than alternative approaches is in the treatment reduplication.[18] One generalization which is encoded in Optimality treatments of reduplication is that, all else being equal, reduplication involves total copy of the base form. To capture this, a universal constraint, MAXBR, is proposed which states that there is "no partial reduplication." Under full reduplication, MAXBR is undominated; partial reduplication results when MAXBR is dominated by a templatic constraint, or some combination of other constraints. Another general feature claimed to characterize reduplicative morphology is that phonological structures in reduplicative strings tend to be cross-linguistically unmarked. Optimality Theory attributes this to the fact that reduplicative morphemes are segmentally underspecified. Markedness constraints are normally dominated by faithfulness constraints for lexically specified inputs, and therefore obscured. However, these same markedness constraints are free to emerge in reduplicative morphemes where they are undominated by input faithfulness constraints. Nevertheless, there is now a growing literature on reduplication which contests both of these claims. Inkelas and Zoll (2003) present evidence that reduplication does not involve phonological copying, while data from at least two Solomon Islands languages (Blevins 2003b), as well as Southern Oromo (Cushitic), and Trukese (Micronesian) (Blevins, to appear c), show highly marked syllable types under reduplication, disconfirming OT predictions.

---

[18] Other areas where OT claims greater empirical coverage are in treatments of rule conspiracies and particular types of opacity. In both cases, it is not the universal nature of markedness constraints which is at issue, but the theoretical encoding of these as violable constraints.

It should be stressed that the primary objection to OT is its reliance on universal markedness constraints as a means of capturing typological generalizations across phonological systems. Ranked and violable *language-specific constraints* are compatible with Evolutionary Phonology, provided that the constraints are learnable on the basis of evidence available to the child.[19]

9.2.2   *Structure preservation*

Kiparsky (1982b) observes that phonological alternations that occur internal to phonological words are often limited to alternations between contrastive segments of the language, while no such constraint holds of rules applying across words, which can freely create non-contrastive allophones. For example, in American English where [t] and [ɾ] are non-contrastive, flapping occurs both across and within words: *a[ɾ] a moment's notice*; *wri[ɾ]er*, etc. But there are no rules creating flaps which are limited to word-internal application. This principle, referred to as "Structure Preservation," was incorporated by Kiparsky into the theory of Lexical Phonology, in an attempt to limit the necessity of external rule ordering, and facilitate a child's acquisition of grammar. While Structure Preservation has been abandoned as a universal feature of lexical rules within Lexical Phonology models (Borowsky 1986; Hargus 1988), there is still a strong tendency for phonological alternations within words to respect lexical/phonological contrasts, while those across words need not.

The model of phonologization in 2.2 accounts for the observed generalizations in a straightforward manner. Consider the case of Yurok /s/ palatalization after /i/ noted in 6.2.1. A traditional statement of the rule is shown in (10), with examples illustrating its application. Square brackets in (10a–f) show phonological word boundaries. In (10a, c) the rule is blocked by a phonological word boundary; in (10b, d) it applies across syntactic words, while in (10f) it applies word-internally. In many words like *pi[ʃ]kah* 'salt,' *si[ʃ]on* 'brake fern root,' etc. a non-alternating [ʃ] occurs in the environment of the conditioned alternations in (10).

(10)   Yurok palatalization: a post-lexical rule

$$s \rightarrow [ʃ]/ i \_\_\_$$

a. [yo' ki] [saa'agoc']   'she can speak Yurok'
b. [yo'] [ki ʃaa'agoc']   'she can speak Yurok'

---

[19] For other general critiques of Optimality Theory, see Hale and Reiss (2000) and McMahon (2000). For arguments against markedness constraints like ONSET as triggers of consonant epenthesis, see Blevins (to appear b).

    c. [ti'ni'] [sook]   'what kind is it?'
    d. [ti'ni'ʃook]   'what kind is it'
    e. [wonik-s]   'upward-3subj'
    f. [skeli-ʃ]   'down-3subj'

Yurok /s/ palatalization appears to be at the earliest stages of phonologization, since the [ʃ] allophone is predictable in the post-/i/ environment, both within and across words. This is a typical example of what
Kiparsky (1982b) calls a post-lexical rule. If we go back one step, we
can see how this alternation arose. Presumably, a previous stage of the
language allowed coarticulation in [is] sequences, and this coarticulation
gave rise to progressive mini-sound changes which eventually resulted in
shift from [s] to [ʃ] after [i] on the basis of the high frequency of [ʃ] in this
environment. The question raised is whether, in non-alternating lexemes
like [piʃkah] 'salt,' one should posit /s/ or /ʃ/ in underlying forms. The traditional view taken by *SPE* and much subsequent work, including Lexical
Phonology, is that the lexicon is the repository of unpredictable information, and that only contrastive information is represented in underlying
phonological forms. Since [s] and [ʃ] are in complementary distribution
in Yurok, and their distribution is predictable, an underlying form /piskah/
is posited. It is not until a later stage, when the conditioning /i/ for this
change is lost from certain lexemes, or words are borrowed with [ʃ] in
contexts other than that predicted by the rule in (10), that an underlying
contrast *must be* posited. In other words, phonemic analyses are based on
word-level contrasts. By definition, then, accounts incorporating phonologization limit non-structure-preserving alternations to the post-lexical
component.[20]
    While this is a welcome result, it passes over a fundamental issue.
Though non-predictable distribution allows the linguist to determine the
latest historical point at which [s] and [ʃ] must be considered to represent contrasting segments in developments like those apparent in Yurok,
what evidence is there that Yurok speakers do not come to distinguish
these sounds earlier, despite the failure of [s] and [ʃ] to define lexical
contrasts? One argument raised in support of the traditional approach is
that non-phonemic contrasts are typically indiscernible to native speakers, with predictable allophones treated as instances of "the same sound."

---

[20] Exceptions to this, like the case of English [ŋ] discussed by Borowsky (1986) depend on
abstract phonological forms which are not motivated within EP treatments. If psychological reality is relevant, the fact that English speakers have no problems with *kin*/*king*/*Kim*
triplets suggests that the place contrast for nasals in final position is truly contrastive in
English. Even in word-initial position where English speakers have a hard time *producing*
this contrast without training, they are able to *hear* it.

However, loan phonology involving supposed allophones of a phoneme outside of their predicted range of distribution suggests that the traditional view might be overly conservative. Consider, for example, the fact that English *sheep* is borrowed into Yurok as [ʃip]. Why is the Yurok speaker able to innovate this form, if [ʃ] and [s] are non-contrastive? Similar examples are found in many other languages. To take one well-studied case, in Japanese, the traditional Yamato vocabulary shows complementary distribution of [ɸ]/[h] and [tˢ]/[t], with [ɸ] and [tˢ] occurring only before the high back vowel /ɯ/, and [h] and [t] occurring elsewhere. A phonemic analysis posits underlying /h/ and /t/, with predictable surface allophones before /ɯ/. However, as noted by Itô and Mester (1995: 826–27), this predictability does not limit the extension of [ɸ] and [tˢ] to new environments. On the contrary, these segments define new contrasts in many loanwords (where *f* represents [ɸ]): *faito* 'fight,' *fesutibaru* 'festival,' *eritˢiN* 'Yeltsin,' *kantˢoone* 'canzone,' etc.[21] Clearly Japanese speakers can hear the difference between [ɸ] and [h], and [tˢ] and [t]; if they could not, the pattern of replacements in loans would not display the regularity it does. This evidence strongly suggests, contrary to classical principles of phonemic analysis, that at the time these loans entered the language, each element in the alternating pairs had contrastive potential, despite the fact that it does not function contrastively in the native vocabulary.

In sum, Structure Preservation is, in part, a construct of the methodology by which contrasts are defined in phonological theory. If we translate Structure Preservation into theory-neutral terms, we are left with an association between predictable phonetic alternants outside of the word domain, which may not define lexical contrasts, and predictable phonetic alternants limited to the word domain which must define lexical contrasts. Since these are precisely the associations predicted by phonologization models, they also appear to be emergent properties of grammar.

However, there is another sense in which structure preservation has been associated with sound patterns, and this is in the diachronic dimension. Recall from chapter 6 that many instances of compensatory lengthening and metathesis are structure-preserving in the sense that they do not define new length contrasts or new phonotactics respectively. De Chene and Anderson (1979: 517) suggest that compensatory lengthening is always a structure-preserving change: a length contrast must already exist in a language for compensatory lengthening to evolve. Subsequent studies have shown this to be incorrect. Compensatory lengthening in

---

[21] At the same time, loans with /hɯ/ and /tɯ/ sequences undergo regular alternations supporting a shift of /h/, /t/ to [ɸ], [tˢ] respectively before /ɯ/: *fuupu* 'hoop,' *fuudo* 'hood,' *tsuaa* 'tour,' *tsuna* 'tuna.' See 9.3 for further discussion.

at least eight languages has occurred giving rise to new vowel-length contrasts, including Piro (Matteson 1965), Ngajan (Dixon 1990), Occitan (Morin 1992), and Andalusian Spanish (Hock 1986). However, this set of languages form a minority of the eighty-plus languages with well-documented compensatory lengthening sound changes (Kavitskaya 2001).

In 6.4, the association between compensatory lengthening and pre-existing length contrasts was attributed to Structural Analogy, repeated in (11).

(11)   STRUCTURAL ANALOGY
        In the course of language acquisition, the existence of a
        phonological contrast between A and B will result in more
        instances of sound change involving shifts of ambiguous
        elements to A or B than if no contrast between A and B existed.

Structural Analogy is attributed to the kind of analogical learning which characterizes phonological acquisition (Wedel 2004). It is not a property of grammars, but a property of the cognitive processes which give rise to grammars. Under Structural Analogy, language-specific priming effects play a role in the course of language acquisition precisely where contrasts are unambiguous. In languages with pre-existing unambiguous vowel-length contrasts, a language learner starts to categorize vowels as long or short early on in the acquisition stage. There are two significant consequences of this process. First, ambient "training" in length perception results in increased sensitivity to smaller differences in vowel-length duration, something which speakers exposed to languages without vowel length contrasts will not acquire. Second, the acquisition of two categories on the basis of unambiguous tokens supplies the same two categories for tokens whose short versus long status is intermediate. In languages with no pre-existing length contrasts, these two categories are not present when ambiguous tokens are encountered.

Another place where Structural Analogy may play a role is in the nasal place neutralizations reviewed in chapter 5. Recall that while many languages show a shift of $N > \eta$, N a nasal glide, there are also cases of $N > n$. Rather than invoke underspecification of coronal place (Kiparsky 1995), I suggest that in both cases of sound change, a nasal glide is misperceived as a nasal stop. If a language has other occurrences of [ŋ] in the same context, neutralization to [ŋ] is more likely, since [ŋ] is more perceptually similar to [N] than [n] is. If a language does not have contrastive [ŋ] in the same context, neutralization to [n] may occur. The Middle Chinese developments illustrate the first case, while the shift of final $m > n$ in the history of Finnish may be an example of the second. For further discussion of Structural Analogy in the context of historical "drift," see 10.5.

9.2.3   The Elsewhere Condition

A final constraint to be considered in this section is the Elsewhere Condition (Anderson 1969; Kiparksy 1973), an early formulation of which appears in Pāṇini's Astādhyāyī.[22] The Elsewhere Condition is proposed by Kiparsky (1973) as a condition on rule application. While there are many versions of the Elsewhere Condition in the literature, the general formulation in (12) will suffice for the purposes of the following discussion.

(12)   The Elsewhere Condition (Kiparsky 1982b)
Rules A and B in the same component apply disjunctively to a form F if and only if: (i) the structural description of A (the special rule) properly includes the structural description of B (the general rule), and (ii) the result of applying A to F is distinct from the result of applying B to F. In that case, A is applied first, and if it takes effect, then B is not applied.

A brief review of the phonological examples Kiparsky uses to illustrate the Elsewhere Principle in his 1973 paper suggests its expendability. Two cases, those of stress rules using SPE parentheses notation, and glide/vowel alternations in Rigvedic Sanskrit, are, with the advent of metrical theories of stress and syllabification, no longer instances of disjunctive rule application (Hayes 1980, 1995; Levin 1985). The two remaining cases, are Finnish total assimilation, with deletion elsewhere, and Diola-Fogny place assimilation, with deletion elsewhere. In the Finnish case, the source of apparent "disjunctive" rule order follows from the historical account of geminate inalterability provided in 7.5: geminates, whether full or partial, are subject to less gestural reduction than their singleton counterparts. As a result, where assimilation results in a full or partial geminate, lenition is less likely to apply. The Finnish facts presented by Kiparsky are shown in (13).

(13)   Western Finnish coda *k*-loss and *k*-assimilation (Kiparsky 1973: 95)
Word-final -*k* assimilates to an initial consonant in the following word, and deletes before vowels and pauses. In some dialects, assimilation is optional or inapplicable in certain environments (for example before *h*, *f*, or clusters). The scope of deletion is then correspondingly greater.

[22] See Kiparsky (1973: 94) for the exact passage and its location.

menek#	'go'
menek# pois → menep pois	'go away'
menek#kotiin → menek kotiin	'go home'
menek#alas → mene alas	'go down'

Synchronically, there is no need to refer to rule ordering: since deletion rules can target singleton as opposed to geminate structures, the rule can be appropriately restricted. Notice that this is a case of geminate inalterability, similar to those described in 7.5, but with wholesale deletion as the phonologization of lenition.

The Diola-Fogny facts presented by Kiparsky illustrate a different sound pattern – one which relates to positions of neutralization for major place features documented in chapter 5. In (14) Diola-Fogny forms are shown illustrating the relevant alternations. In (14a), there is place assimilation between a nasal and a following consonant, and no cluster reduction. In (14b–d), there is no place assimilation, and cluster reduction. Note that in (14d) an entire NC cluster deletes. Again, assuming a rule of place assimilation between a nasal and a following oral or nasal stop, as illustrated in (14a), a deletion rule can be proposed which need not be disjunctively ordered with assimilation. The synchronic generalization is that place features are not licensed in pre-consonantal position. Where place features of a consonant or homorganic sequence are not licensed, the segment or segments are deleted.[23] This rule applies wherever its structural description is met; under standard accounts, it will not apply to the output of assimilation due to the singly linked place node.

(14)   Diola-Fogny cluster reduction and place assimilation (Sapir 1965; Kiparsky 1973)

	UR	Surface	
a.	ni-gam-gam	nigaŋgam	'I judge'
	pan-ji-maɲ	paɲjimaɲ	'you (pl) will know'
	ku-bɔɲ-bɔɲ	kubɔmbɔɲ	'they sent'
	na-ti:ŋ -ti:ŋ	nati:nti:ŋ	'he cut (it) through'
	napum kuɲilak	napuŋkuɲilak	'he pushed back the children'
	najum tɔ	najuntɔ	'he stopped there'
	na-mi:n-mi:n	nami:mmi:n	'he cut (with a knife)'
b.	na-laɲ-laɲ	nalalaɲ	'he returned'
	na-yɔkɛn-yɔkɛn	nayɔkɛyɔkɛn	'he tires'
	na-waɲ-a:m-waɲ	nawaɲa:waɲ	'he cultivated for me'

[23] Nasals do not assimilate in place to following palatal nasals: /banɲa/, baɲa 'finish now.'

    c. lɛt-ku-jaw   lekujaw   'they won't go'
       kutɛb sinaŋas   kutɛsinaŋas   'they carried the food'
       ɛkɛt bɔ   ɛkɛbɔ   'death there'
    d. ɛ-rɛnt-rɛnt   ɛrɛrɛnt   'it is light'
       na-maɲj- maɲj   namamaɲj   'he knows'
    e. takun-mbi . . .   takumbi . . .   'he must not . . .'

While the Elsewhere Condition may prove useful in contexts of morphological blocking (Aronoff 1976), there is no evidence for it in the phonological component.[24]

9.2.4   Summary

Section 9.1 presents evidence to support the view that most knowledge of sound patterns, including phonotactics and alternations, are learned aspects of grammar. Section 9.2 evaluates markedness constraints, and other proposed universal constraints, in light of the empirical studies presented in part II. From this discussion, very little universal phonology remains, be it in the form of violable or inviolable constraints. There is simply no case where independent evidence exists for a synchronic account over the plausible and, in many cases, documented, historical alternative.

While methods of analysis have remained constant, Evolutionary Phonology defines a clear shift in the locus of explanation: from synchronic grammars to diachronic developments; from abstract phonological constraints to concrete phonetically based instances of sound change; and from aspects of Universal Grammar to learned, language-specific properties and general learning strategies. The chart in (15), summarizes some of the general reinterpretations and empirical advances which distinguish Evolutionary Phonology from other approaches, where these include *SPE* and its generative derivatives, as well as Optimality Theory.

The next section takes these empirical advances and this shift in perspective as the point of departure for a general redefinition of pure synchronic phonology in terms of formal relationships between surface distributional patterns and notions of contrast. Pure phonology is just one subdiscipline of phonology as a whole. As should be clear from the preceding chapters, a genuine understanding of sound patterns is not possible without detailed phonetic models, historical models, and cognitive models of language acquisition.

---

[24] This is perhaps not surprising in the context of Optimality approaches (Prince and Smolensky 1993; McCarthy 2002) which dispense with ordered rule components.

(15)   EVOLUTIONARY PHONOLOGY IN CONTRAST TO OTHER
        PHONOLOGICAL MODELS
        i. General reinterpretations

General property	Evolutionary Phonology	Other approaches
Recurrent sound patterns	historical phonetic explanations	universal markedness
Uncommon sound patterns	historical phonetic explanations	universal markedness
OCP	FMP (learning strategy)	universal markedness + tier structure
Violations of OCP	not prohibited	no account
Geminate integrity	FMP, string-based phonotactics	no-crossing constraint
Violations of geminate integrity	historical rule inversion	no account

ii. Specific empirical advances within Evolutionary Phonology
     a. New account of final devoicing (chapter 4)
     b. New account of $*t > k$ (chapter 5)
     c. New account of historical structure preservation under
         Structural Analogy, which includes:
         i.   correlation between compensatory lengthening and
              pre-existing vowel length contrast
         ii. correlation between neutralizing $*N > \eta$ versus $N > n$,
              and pre-existing place contrasts
         iii. relationship between syncope and pre-existing closed
              syllables (see 10.5)
     d. New account of variable moraic status of geminates in
         terms of their historical origins

9.3   Pure phonology

With phonology stripped of nearly all universal components, with the
exception of distinctive features and prosodic categories, and with the
majority of recurrent sound patterns explicable in terms of phonetically
motivated sound change, what systematic aspects of synchronic phonology remain to be studied? In table 9.1 eight distinct relationships are
defined between patterns of distribution and sound patterns which may
or may not directly reflect regular phonetically motivated sound change.

Table 9.1 *Pattern distribution and naturalness*

	Productive	Surface-true	Natural
I	+	+	+
II	+	+	−
III	+	−	+
IV	+	−	−
V	−	+	+
VI	−	+	−
VII	−	−	+
VIII	−	−	−

In order to interpret and exemplify each of the pure phonological relationships in table 9.1, specific definitions of "productive," "surface-true," and "natural" are required. In the following discussion, productive sound patterns are those for which there is concrete evidence of a learned generalization on the part of the speaker. This may take the form of a sound pattern which takes part in productive alternations within a given language, or it may take the form of an exceptionless surface sound pattern which is visibly extended to nonce forms, loanword phonology (Silverman 1992; Ulrich 1997), second-language acquisition (Broselow 1979, 1983), poetic devices (Malone 1996), or some other domain. Other evidence for productive sound patterns might be found in aphasiology, where the productive pattern could be lost.

A fine but important contrast is made in table 9.1 between productive patterns and surface-true generalizations. Surface-true generalizations are true statements which can be made about a language for some given point in time. Surface-true generalizations are statements about the data. They may or may not reflect learned generalizations on the part of the speaker. Whether they do is an empirical question, and one of the central questions within pure phonology.

In the last column the sound patterns categorized in the first two columns are distinguished in terms of those which are known to be, or are hypothesized to be, direct reflections of sound change, as modeled in 2.2 and part II, and those which are not.

In table 9.2, sound patterns illustrate the combinations of properties defined in table 9.1. The fact that every combination of features in table 9.1 describes a sound pattern in some language has significant implications for phonological modeling.

First, as stressed in part I, naturalness, as expressed by phonetically motivated sound patterns is not necessarily associated with productivity

Table 9.2 *Sound patterns illustrating distribution-naturalness combinations*

	Language	Sound pattern	Description
I	Yurok	s → [ʃ]/ [i, j] __	sibilant palatalization
II	English	Ø→ [ɹ]/Ṽ__ V	r-insertion
III	Turkish	final stress	final word stress
IV	Lama	Ø→ ə/ɲ __##	final vowel insertion after palatal nasal
V	Japanese	ɸ/__ɯ	limited distribution of [ɸ]
VI	English	*[sC$_i$V̄C$_i$]$_{word}$	homorganicity constraint
VII	Class. Arabic	ʔal=C$_i$→ ʔaC$_i$C$_i$ [cor]	total assimilation
VIII	Paamese	h → v/ $_{Vbstem}$[__	mutation

or surface-true generalizations. Sibilant palatalization in Yurok is productive and natural, but British English *r*-insertion in sandhi, the consequence of inversion of earlier *r*-loss, is not natural.[25] There is no way, in looking at any of the patterns in I–IV of table 9.2, to know *a priori* whether it is natural or not. One must develop a comprehensive theory of phonetically based sound change, and have a historical account of each pattern, before an assessment can be made. Even with sound changes that appear to be productive, surface true, and natural, one cannot be sure that the pattern in question directly reflects a regular sound change until its history is known. For example, if a language shows a regular rule of [j]-insertion before word-initial /i/, this could be a direct phonologization of strengthening in word-initial position, and therefore be classified as natural. But the same change could just as well be the result of rule inversion of an earlier rule of initial [j]-loss before /i/ whose origins lie in misperception of [ji] as [i]. Another question defining pure phonology is when rule inversion can and does take place.

Another aspect of naturalness is that many sound patterns which are highly restricted in their distribution can be just as natural in this sense as others. For example, the Arabic pattern of total assimilation between the /l/ of the definite article /ʔal/ and a following coronal consonant in VII of table 9.2 appears to be a phonologization of extreme coarticulation in a prosodically weak position. A strikingly parallel natural development to that found in Classical Arabic is in progress in many varieties of English.

---

[25] Notice in this case, it is important to adhere to the definition provided above. The rule of *r*-insertion can be *viewed* as natural from the perspective of providing a syllable onset, but as a sound change, segments like [ɹ] do not emerge in this context as the consequence of misperception of the abutting vocalic gestures, or as an articulatory consequence of glide strengthening in the same context. See Blevins (to appear c) for further discussion.

A clear conditioning factor for both of these changes is the weak prosodic status of the article involved. English /ð/ in the article *the* often undergoes total assimilation to a preceding coronal consonant, resulting in surface geminates, e.g. *what's the* as [watssə]. As demonstrated by Shockey (1973, 1977), speakers can use these length differences alone to distinguish *a* from *the*. In phrases like *miss a guy, warn a guy*, Shockey (1977) manipulated the length of [s] in the first case, and [n] in the second. For fricatives with durations of 80–200 ms, speakers heard *the* once the fricative got to about 130 ms. For nasals with durations of 0–120 ms, speakers heard *the* when the nasal got up to 120 ms. That this process is still clearly a function of rate of speech, style, etc., and not a phonological rule, is evidenced by the data on variation presented in Shockey and Bond (1980). In this study of British women's speech, total assimilation was found for *the* preceded by coronal fricatives 56 percent of the time when a woman was talking to her own child, but only 36 percent of the time when talking to another adult. These differences in frequency are precisely the type which are claimed to be significant in the CCC-model of sound change. If children are hearing more instances of total assimilation than other people in the community, they will be more likely to acquire grammars in which total assimilation as sound change takes place. In this case, the predicted sound change is nearly identical to the one found in Classical Arabic.

In III and IV of table 9.2, two sound patterns are listed which are productive but not surface true. Case III involves Turkish word stress. The dominant pattern in Turkish words is for stress to fall on the final syllable. However, there are exceptions to this in placenames, and other small lexical classes, where stress is on the penult or antepenult (Barker 1989). Despite these lexical exceptions, the final stress pattern is productively extended to new loans (Orhan Orgun, personal communication, 2002). An unusual case of productivity, which is not associated with a surface-true sound pattern, is found in Lama (IV). In Lama final /ɲ/ of loanwords is usually realized with a following final schwa (Ulrich 1997).[26] The native Lama vocabulary does not have words ending in final palatal nasals. Furthermore, all obstruents in Lama are followed by a final schwa, while sonorants, /m, n, l, r, w/ cannot be followed by a word-final schwa. Given the distribution of sonorants in the native vocabulary, the word-final [ɲə] pattern in loans cannot be viewed as the extension of a surface-true pattern, nor can it be viewed as "natural" since limited vowel insertion after one particular consonant type is not, as far as I know,

---

[26] In Ulrich's study, of the 19 loans with final [ɲ] in the source language, 15 (79 percent) undergo epenthesis, 1 shows deletion of the nasal, and 3 are unchanged.

an attested sound change. Rather, one must assume in this case that the schwa which appears word-finally is essentially an innovation determined by the failure of [ɲ] and [n] to contrast word-finally in the native vocabulary. If palatalization in Lama is primarily a release feature, the final schwa can be viewed as a consequence of hyperarticulation. Productivity in this instance has a very different quality from the productivity associated with the sound patterns in I and II which directly or indirectly reflect phonetically based sound change. In this case, the absence of a particular sound pattern in the native vocabulary (word-final [ɲ]) gives rise to a phonological innovation which actually violates an independent surface-true generalization regarding the distribution of word-final schwa.[27]

The Japanese pattern in V of table 9.2 has already been discussed in 9.2.2 with respect to structure preservation. Recall that in the traditional Yamato vocabulary, there is complementary distribution of [ɸ] and [h], with [ɸ] occurring only before the high back vowel /ɯ/, and [h] occurring elsewhere. A phonemic analysis posits underlying /h/, with predictable surface allophone [ɸ] before /ɯ/. One surface-true generalization in Pre-Yamato Japanese, then, is that [ɸ] only occurs before /ɯ/. However, this generalization is clearly not extended, since loans freely allow [ɸa], [ɸe], [ɸi], and [ɸo] sequences. Not all surface-true generalizations, even those that result from naturally conditioned sound change, will be extended productively. In this case, the constraint against [h] before /ɯ/ is extended, but its complement constraint, limiting [ɸ] to pre-/ɯ/ contexts is not. This is a case where productivity provides evidence of an active rule (*h→ ɸ/ __ɯ*) or constraint (*ɸɯ*). The question, however, is why the limited occurrence of [ɸ] before /ɯ/ does not lead to similar restrictions in loanwords. Here again, as in Lama, surface phonetic matching between source and target-language phones appears to override surface-true distributional constraints of the (pre-loan) language.

---

[27] This feature of Lama loanwords may be attributed to production rather than competence effects. Note that one of the most common features of loanword phonology and transfer effects in second-language acquisition is the observance of surface-true natural sound patterns, including the distribution of laryngeal features (final devoicing, cluster assimilation, etc.), regular stress patterns, and phonotactics related to consonant release. It could well be that many of these sound patterns do not reflect "productive" phonological processes as much as production strategies which speakers have difficulty altering. Final devoicing of Russian speakers speaking English occurs despite the fact that they may be able to perceive a difference in input forms. They simply cannot reproduce it due to ingrained laryngeal timing strategies. In Hawaiian, with only open syllables, the fact that loanwords undergo vowel epenthesis may not be so much a consequence of syllable-based constraints as production strategies which demand that consonants are released into vowels. See Silverman (1992) and Ussishkin and Wedel (2003) for similar proposals.

The remaining sound patterns listed in VI–VIII have different relations to phonetically motivated sound change. The English pattern in VI represents the fact that no words of the form $[sC_i\breve{V}C_i]_{word}$ are found. As far as I know, this feature of English is wholly accidental. If words like *state* underwent vowel laxing, or *stud* underwent final devoicing, just such a pattern would arise. While the sound pattern, as described, might seem uninteresting, Clements and Keyser (1983) attribute it to a phonological constraint which prohibits just this sequence. However, there is no evidence that speakers disallow such sequences. As noted by Clements and Keyser themselves, shortened words like *stat* (from *statistic*), do not seem anomalous. However, their analysis raises another question at the heart of pure phonological analysis. Is there any fundamental difference between accidental gaps of this sort and non-accidental gaps like the similar dissimilatory constraints found in Arabic, and attributed to the Obligatory Contour Principle (McCarthy 1982)? I return to this question shortly.

The Arabic pattern in VII has already been discussed. It involves total assimilation between article and following coronal-initial noun. Comparison above with similar phonetic facts from English clitic *the* suggests that it has, as its source, gestural reduction under coarticulation. Though it is surface true, there is no evidence of its productivity. In other words, due to the highly unique prosodic domain defined by the article + noun, and the high frequency of this construction, a phonological rule has evolved which is natural, but limited to the article + noun domain, and not extended to other forms with similar consonant sequences. Consider /l/ + coronal sequences in: *?akalna* 'we ate,' *hamalta* 'I carried,' etc. This pattern differs from the other non-productive patterns in VI–VIII in resisting classification as a general lexical rule or constraint.[28]

Sound pattern VIII in table 9.2 shows an $h \to v$ shift verb-initially in Paamese (Crowley 1982). As with many sound patterns which reflect lenition, much rule telescoping can be involved. This alternation on its own is highly unnatural, involving the accretion of true voicing as well as labio-dental place of articulation, but in a context-free version, it is even more unusual. As Crowley (1982: 121) shows, the *h-/v-* alternation is a modern reflex of Proto-Oceanic *$^*p$-/*$^*mp$-, reflecting various layers

---

[28] The fact that such alternations can remain stable and productive in a language for long periods demonstrates the independence of alternation type from lexical versus post-lexical domains in the sense of Kiparsky (1982b). Provided morphosyntactic evidence defines a construction type, construction-specific alternations can be exceptionless and productive (e.g. extended to new instances of the same construction type.) On construction-specific phonology, or co-phonologies see Orgun (1996), Inkelas, Orgun, and Zoll (1997), and Inkelas and Zoll (2003).

of lenition sediments. Given the possibility of phonological alternations which are morphologically governed, and others with purely phonological conditioning factors, what generalizations do speakers make based on the available data? And is it necessary to assume that all speakers make the same generalizations?

For all the patterns in V–VIII, which are classified as non-productive, there is no evidence for extension of the particular sound pattern outside of its domain of occurrence. Obvious cases of non-productive sound patterns involve lexical sound patterns which play no role in synchronic alternations whatsoever. Constraints of this type include the antihomorganicity constraints within Semitic roots (Greenberg 1950; McCarthy 1981, 1988), and the constraints on clusters which hold within stems for Pama-Nyungan languages like Panyjima, but which fail to hold between stems and suffixes. The patterns are characteristic of highly lexicalized sound change, with subsequent layers of grammaticized elements surrounding what was one word. For any of these patterns, a central question which arises is to what extent these fossilized patterns are accessible to the native speaker, and what sorts of generalizations might be made in the course of language acquisition.

A recent study of precisely this question demonstrates that native speakers of Jordanian Arabic have extremely precise knowledge of phonotactic antihomorganicity constraints within the root (Frisch and Zawaydeh 2001), traditionally attributed to the Obligatory Contour Principle. Native speakers were presented with 254 novel verb roots and asked to rate them on a scale of 1–7 on the basis of how much they sounded like Arabic verbs. The stimuli allowed the researchers to determine whether speakers show knowledge of the phonotactic constraints and whether this knowledge reflects the gradient nature of the constraints in question. Their results showed clear evidence for abstract phonotactic constraints, independent of simple lexical statistics. At the same time, the phonotactic knowledge displayed by the subjects revealed gradient patterns which are typically not encoded by standard phonological analyses. Their conclusion is strikingly similar to that reached for other sound patterns in the preceding discussion:

the consonant coocurrence constraints of Arabic are emergent generalizations over the lexicon. In an emergent grammar, phonotactic knowledge is abstract, but not too abstract. The emergent constraints, based on lexical patterns, are language specific and learned . . . The existence of psychologically real emergent phonotactic constraints demonstrates that knowledge of linguistic patterns goes beyond a set of universal principles . . . For phonotactics, at least, the lexicon provides a rich enough source of data for phonological generalizations to be derived directly from lexical patterns. (Frisch and Zawaydeh 2001: 104–5)

This study is not an isolated one. Speakers appear to have very refined scales by which they judge whether or not a word they have never heard before could be a possible word in their language (Ohala and Ohala 1986; Coleman and Pierrehumbert 1997; Bailey and Hahn 2000; Frisch et al. 2000, 2001). The results of these studies suggest that similarity judgments are a complex mix of analogical whole-word comparisons, and assessments based on the relative frequencies of subword units. And in their recent study of Dutch final devoicing, Ernestus and Baayen (2003: 5) show that "speakers predict the characteristics of neutralized segments on the basis of phonologically similar morphemes, stored in the mental lexicon." While these studies might seem quite far from the sound patterns illustrated in table 9.2, it is likely that it is only through continued work of this kind that the true nature of phonological knowledge will be understood.

Pure phonology is the study of the matrix of relationships set out in table 9.1. As suggested above, productivity is a cover-term for a complex body of knowledge which may be gradient, and highly sensitive to properties of the lexicon as a whole, but also reflect innate or emergent categorical knowledge. At the same time, in loan phonology, productivity may reflect surface-to-surface mapping of phones, with no implications for grammatical competence. Surface-true generalizations which can be expressed in terms of phonological primitives are expected to show evidence of productivity. Having extracted notions of naturalness and markedness from synchronic grammars, pure phonology is left to define mappings between phonetic representations and phonological ones which are evident in productive processes. Pure phonology, then, is a modest area within the general domain of phonological description and explanation. It is conceivable that as our knowledge in areas of phonetic science, cognitive development, and neuroscience deepens, this area may become even more circumscribed.

10   Diachronic phonology

> We have a distance to go in restoring the balance between universalist
> and historical explanation, and in giving full weight to the principle that,
> to understand a linguistic system, we must know how it came to be.
>   Labov (1981: 305, citing Jespersen 1924, ch. 2)

Historical linguistics includes the study of language change. For many linguists studying language change, it is taken as given that "to understand
a linguistic system, we must know how it came to be." In this chapter
I will show that the central findings of Evolutionary Phonology are in
concert with this view. The bulk of the arguments presented up to this
point demonstrate that there are good historical phonetic explanations
for most common sound patterns. As suggested in chapter 9, attributing common sound patterns to common phonetically motivated sound
change allows synchronic grammars to be primarily descriptive, liberated
from the burden of explanation and naturalness. This is a welcome result,
since synchronic markedness accounts seem, at best, to duplicate properties of phonetically motivated sound change or raw frequency effects. At
their worst, markedness accounts rule out attested sound patterns, fail
to explain why a particular sound pattern is more or less marked than
some other, and still make reference to historical explanations when a
highly marked pattern arises. Since the bulk of explanation for attested
phonological systems is now pushed into the diachronic dimension, one
must ask whether the proposed model of sound change is consistent with
findings in historical linguistics. This is one question explored in this
chapter.

In this chapter, I highlight the compatibility of a model incorporating CHANGE, CHANCE, and CHOICE with traditional views of sound
change. The precise mechanisms of sound change are not only consistent with the early neogrammarian doctrine that sound change is regular,
but, as argued in 10.1, their formulation as part of a general learning
algorithm results in typical regularity at the level of the individual. At the
same time, the extended typology of phonetic sources of change allows for

abrupt change, as well as transmission of word-based frequency effects on phonetic variation. This combination of properties allows us to take a fresh look, in 10.2, at what Labov refers to as "the neogrammarian controversy": does sound change occur across-the-board, or does it diffuse through the language in a word-by-word fashion? The starting point for our discussion is Labov's (1981, 1994) comprehensive review of the issue and his proposed resolution. Labov's approach predicts that regular sound change and lexical diffusion should display complementary distribution, yet they do not. The only empirically supported conclusion consistent with the CCC-model is that lexical diffusion (without clear phonetic conditioning) *is the diffusion of a completed sound change*. Another issue addressed in this chapter is whether sound change is goal-oriented. In order to eliminate markedness from grammar altogether, it must be demonstrated that markedness is not directly involved in sound change itself. Section 10.3 assembles arguments against the optimizing or goal-oriented nature of sound change. As with synchronic phonological alternations, many sound changes appear to be driven by functional or structural properties of sound systems. However, on closer inspection, these properties turn out to be illusory, accidental, or emergent. The empirical record supports a model in which sound change happens, but it does not happen for any particular reason. Implications of the evolutionary model for studies of natural sound patterns are noted in 10.4, and the role of Structural Analogy in drift is outlined in 10.5.

10.1   The regularity of sound change[1]

One of the central contributions of the nineteenth-century neogrammarians to the study of language was the observation that sound change is typically regular. Shared innovations in the form of regular sound change still constitute the backbone of the comparative method, and there are few posited subgroups which do not share regular sound changes, even if these are taken to be non-probative. The regularity of sound change has been criticized from many different directions, but nearly all historical linguists agree that it holds for some identifiable subset of sound changes. Regularity is characteristic of the phonetically motivated processes discussed in part II, and excludes instances of analogical change and dialect borrowing. The regularity hypothesis is repeated with only minor emendations in nearly every textbook on historical linguistics. Hock (1991: 35), for example, suggests the version in (1).

---

[1] This section is an expansion of an argument first presented in Blevins and Garrett (to appear).

(1)   THE (REVISED) NEOGRAMMARIAN REGULARITY
        HYPOTHESIS (Hock 1991: 35)
        Change in pronunciation which is not conditioned by
        non-phonetic factors is regular and operates without exceptions
        at a particular time and in a particular speech community, with
        possible environmental restrictions.[2]

Two problems that any model of historical phonology must confront are
the precise mechanisms of sound change and the cause of its typical
regularity. In this section the mechanisms of change and the regularity
of change are intimately connected by highlighting implications of sound
change as a special case of phonological acquisition. Since normal phonological acquisition results in the grouping of similar phonetic tokens into
single phonological categories in a regular fashion, sound change should
do the same. In other words, sound change should be regular wherever
general phonological acquisition is regular.

   In chapter 2, the phonetic sources of sound change were broken down
into three basic types: CHANGE, CHANCE, and CHOICE. All regular
sound change is claimed to have its source in one or more of these sources
of phonetic ambiguity, repeated in (2).

(2)   PHONETIC SOURCES OF SOUND CHANGE
        i. CHANGE   S says [anpa]; L hears [ampa]
        ii. CHANCE   S says [ʔa̰ʔ] for /aʔ/; potential analyses of
                      [ʔa̰ʔ] include /ʔa/, /aʔ/, /ʔaʔ/, /a/. L analyzes
                      string as /ʔa/.
        iii. CHOICE   S says [kakata], [kăkata], [kkata] for /kakata/;
                      potential analyses include /kakata/ and /kkata/.
                      L chooses /kkata/.

In each phonetic source, there is inherent ambiguity which can give rise
to reanalysis on the part of the language learner. In CHANGE, a particular
sound pattern has a greater-than-chance likelihood of being misperceived
as some distinct sound pattern. In CHANCE, a particular sound pattern

---

[2] Following the neogrammarian tradition, Hock (1991: 35), adds: "Certain changes
(including dissimilation and metathesis) are exempt from this hypothesis" incorporating
a segregation of major and minor sound change, first proposed by Osthoff and Brugmann
(1878). Major sound changes were regular and could be viewed as the result of gradual
articulatory drift, while minor sound changes (including dissimilation and metathesis)
could not be viewed in this way, and were thought to be more often sporadic. Ohala's
(1993) treatment of dissimilation and Blevins and Garrett's (1998, to appear) work on
metathesis essentially eliminate the need for a distinction between these two types of
sound change.

is ambiguous with respect to the localization of a particular segment or feature. Under CHOICE, the variation inherent in the careful-to-casual speech continuum gives rise to phonetic tokens of the same word with distinct phonological analyses. The indeterminacy in this case is across tokens or sets of tokens, and the listener is faced with the choice of deciding which is the "basic" form.

The CCC-model of sound change covers both subphonemic changes in pronunciation, changes in phonological representations, and shifts from phonetic processes to phonological ones. Let us review some of the general features of this model to see how precise mechanisms of sound change will typically result in regularity. Before doing so, however, it will be useful to revise the regularity hypothesis in (1) in three ways. A first modification involves the recognition of identifiable subclasses of exceptions to the regularity hypothesis. Instead of characterizing sound change as regular, operating without exception, it is more accurate to characterize phonetically based sound change as "typically regular." A second modification replaces "change in pronunciation" with "sound change." This modification is due to the fact that instances of CHANCE and CHOICE may not immediately result in changes in pronunciation, though, over time, such changes are expected. A final modification limits the locus of regularity to the individual, though regularity at the level of the individual will often be reflected by the speech community as a whole. The revised regularity hypothesis is given in (3).

(3)   THE REGULARITY HYPOTHESIS (revised)
        Sound change which is not conditioned by non-phonetic
        factors is typically regular and operates at a particular time for a
        particular speaker, with possible environmental restrictions.

Before examining how the CCC-model gives rise to typical regularity at the level of the individual speaker, I briefly sketch how exceptions to the Regularity Hypothesis are handled within this same model of sound change.

Exceptions to regularity have long been noted and fall into identifiable subsets. These include: cases where analogical change overlays a once regular sound change; sound symbolism; taboo vocabulary; and potential homophony. In the first case, there is nothing interesting to be said. Sound change may appear to be irregular only because a subsequent or competing analogical change is layered on top of it. In cases involving sound symbolism, sounds are imbued with systematic meanings or shades of meaning. Given this, misperception, and reanalysis under CHANGE, CHANCE, and CHOICE are less likely to take place when such a change will destroy the systematicity of the sound–meaning correspondences. In other words, given a high-frequency association between sound S and meaning M in the lexicon, this association will guide listeners to hearing S where S might otherwise be mistaken for some other sound, or analyzed as some other sound. In the case of taboo vocabulary, low token frequency can result in their status as phonological outliers. As demonstrated by Bybee (2001), frequency plays an important role in the speed with which leniting sound changes take place. If taboo words have frequencies below a particular threshold, there may be little evidence of a lenited variant during the acquisition phase, making sound change via CHOICE less likely. Taboo words may also be uttered in contexts where they are typically hyperarticulated; again, this will result in lower probabilities of sound change via CHOICE. Potential homophony also appears to inhibit sound change with sources in CHOICE. The strongest evidence of antihomophony constraints inhibiting sound change involves patterns of antigemination (Blevins, to appear b). Regular syncope occurs except where it would lead to wholesale collapse of paradigmatic oppositions. Since syncope is a classic instance of CHOICE, we can understand exceptions to syncope as cases where hyperarticulation of vowels has higher frequency, due to its paradigmatic role in distinguishing one member of a paradigm from another. Within the CCC-model, this is the only place where "teleology" in the form of "better discriminability" is invoked on the part of the speaker, and it is highly circumscribed. Having some understanding of exceptions to regular phonetically based sound change, we can now proceed to explore why it is typically regular at the level of the individual.

The general model of sound change is shown in (4), repeated from chapter 2. It instantiates the common view that language structure changes as learners reconstruct grammars (Baudouin de Courtenay 1871; Meillet 1925; Bloomfield 1933; Andersen 1973; Dalby 2002). Diagrams in (4) represent phonological forms of the speaker and listener in slash brackets, and surface forms in square brackets. Subscripted Vs indicate a range of phonetic surface variants, with most common exemplars listed first.

(4)   A FORMAL MODEL OF SOUND CHANGE
     i. No sound change

        Speaker   Listener
        /ut/   /ut/
        ↓1   ↑3
        [ut, ʉt, yt . . .]$_{Vi}$ 2 →   [ut, ʉt, yt . . .]$_{Vi}$

ii. CHANGE: sound change via misperception

Speaker	Listener
/θa/	/fa/
↓	↑3
[θa . . .]$_{Vi}$ 2→	[fa . . .]$_{Vj}$

iii. CHANCE: sound change via "mis-application" of phonetic–phonology mapping

Speaker	Listener
/yt/	/ut/
↓1	↑3
[yt . . .]$_{Vi}$ 2→	[yt . . .]$_{Vi}$ ⇒ [ʉt, yt, . . .]$_{Vj}$

iva. CHOICE: sound change from phonetic variation (change in variant frequency)

Speaker	Listener
/ut/	/yt/
↓1	↑3
[yt, ʉt, . . .]$_{Vi}$ 2→	[yt, ʉt . . .]$_{Vi}$
4↑	
[ʉt, yt . . .]$_{Vj}$	

ivb. CHOICE: sound change from phonetic variation (change in variant set)

Speaker	Listener
/ut/	/yʔ/
↓1	↑3
[yʔ . . . yt']$_{Vi}$ 2→	[yʔ . . .]$_{Vj}$
4↑	
[yt', yʔ . . .]$_{Vi}$	

(5)   UNIVERSAL DECOMPOSITION OF SOUND CHANGE

Step 1: Universal and language-specific phonetics give rise to a range of surface forms in natural speech production, abbreviated here by [ ]$_V$ (= [ ] and its phonetic variants), where subscripts indicate identity, or lack thereof, and are listed in order of decreasing frequency.

Step 2: Utterance (set) is perceived 'correctly' (i, iii, iv), or 'incorrectly' (ii).

Step 3: Utterance is associated with a phonological form on the basis of

a. Universal knowledge (features, prosodic categories)

b. General segmentation and pattern matching algorithms

c. Default mapping principle: one-to-one association between features and segments

d. Other ambient sound patterns of the language being acquired

e. Relative frequency of variants

Step 4: Shift in variant frequencies from speaker as child to speaker as adult

Three independent phonetically governed sound changes are illustrated in (4): fronting of the back vowel [u] adjacent to a dental/alveolar consonant under coarticulation, $ut > yt$ (Ohala 1981); $\theta > f$ due to perceptual similarity (6.1.1); and $t' > ?$, the change of a voiceless glottalized (unreleased) stop to a glottal stop, as the simple result of anticipation of glottal closure combined with absence of release which weakens or eliminates place-of-articulation cues for the oral stop (chapter 5).

In (4i), there is no sound change, and both the range of phonetic surface forms and their relative frequencies, and the phonological interpretation of the sequence are directly inherited. In (4iv), two cases of CHOICE are diagrammed, one involving a simple vowel change $ut > yt$ (4iva), and the other a complex change of $ut > y?$ (4ivb). In the latter case, there is an overt change in pronunciation: due to a sound change of $t > t' > ?$ (cf. a similar change in many dialects of English), the t which conditioned vowel fronting is lost. In (4iii), the vowel /u/ is reanalyzed as underlyingly front ([-back]) at the phonological level, but this reanalysis need not express itself directly in the earliest stages of change; the double arrow shows the predicted direction of change discussed further in 10.3. In (4iii) CHANCE is illustrated by the dissimilatory change $yt > ut$. As in (4iv), a change in phonological analysis occurs, with fronting of /u/ viewed as a redundant phonetic feature triggered by the following /t/. This reanalysis is due to predictability of occurrence in surface strings and/or similar phonetic realizations of inherited /ut/ sequences. Again, there may be no perceptible shift of pronunciation in the earliest stages of the change, with predicted direction of change shown by the double arrow. The case of phonologization in (4ii) is an instance of context-free $\theta > f$, an example of CHANGE. Variation plays a direct role in the changes in (4iv), but not elsewhere.

In contrast to earlier models, the model of sound change in (5) admits language-specific variation in phonetic implementation rules, allows for context-free splits and mergers, and directly incorporates the role of variation in change. Though (5) isolates distinct types of sound change, it will often be the case that a single sound change has multiple sources. For example, nasal place assimilation in VNTV is characterized as a canonical instance of CHANGE, though many languages show coarticulation of N and T in non-careful speech, suggesting that CHOICE may also be involved.

The synthesis of different models of sound change can be seen directly in the precise mechanisms of change spelled out in (4) and (5). For example, the neogrammarian hypothesis that variation in production gives rise to seemingly gradual directional deviation from an earlier norm is encapsulated by CHOICE, where variation is the primary source of change. Modern approaches incorporating articulatory phonetic variation as the source of sound change include Articulatory Phonology (Browman and Goldstein 1992) and H&H Theory (Lindblom 1990a). In contrast to the neogrammarian position, however, sound change need not involve cotemporaneous changes in pronunciation. The only two changes in (5) which necessarily involve audible changes in pronunciation are (4ii), a pure case of CHANGE, and (4ivb), a case of CHOICE. In sound changes like (4ivb), the listener's "loss" of one pronunciation is attributed to frequency effects: in CHOICE, frequently used forms will supplant infrequent forms in redefining the central locus of phonetic variation. Ohala's (1971, 1974a, 1981) view of the listener as the source of sound change is instantiated directly, and is most perspicuous in cases where there is no necessary variation in input forms. Bybee's (2001) arguments for frequency effects in sound change are also incorporated: where variation gives rise to sound change, changes in the frequency of a particular variant can redefine the locus of variation for that particular sound pattern. As detailed in 10.2, this speaker-based model of change is also consistent with the trajectories of sound change in speech communities described by Labov (1981, 1994) and others.

However, the most conspicuous feature of the model of sound change in (5) is the extent to which it models general phonological acquisition. The simple case depicted in (4i) is acquisition without change. As an example of the complexities involved in the regular acquisition of phonological categories without change, consider the acquisition of /p/ in English. The acquisition of a category /p/ (in contrast to /b/, /m/, /t/, etc.) is based, in part, on phonetic realizations of words like *pit, pat, pet, pot, put* and *tip, tap, top*, etc. In natural speech the formant values of CV transitions in the first set of words with initial /p/ differ significantly due to properties of the following vowel. At the same time, all initial consonants are aspirated, but voice-onset time for the initial consonant varies within a specific range across tokens of the same word. In the second set of words, with final /p/ formant values of VC transitions differ due to properties of the preceding vowels. At the same time, final consonants are typically unaspirated, unreleased, and glottalized. Nevertheless, these sets of words are learned with initial /p/ or final /p/ respectively because some convergence of phonetic cues with complementary distribution gives rise to a single linguistic category for these contexts. Despite significant and consistent differences in the acoustic/perceptual properties of word-initial and word-final /p/s in English, the identification of these distinct sound patterns as a single phonological category *is regular and operates without exception.*

The acquisition or emergence of phonological categories in speech appears to take place very early. For many categorical distinctions between consonants and vowels whose phonetic cues are local (e.g. vowel quality, consonant place of articulation), there is evidence of language-specific category acquisition as early as ten to twelve months (Werker and Tees 1984; Werker and Lalonde 1988; Werker 1991). And for vowels, perceptual magnet effects have been demonstrated on six-month-old infants (Kuhl 1991, 1995), suggesting proto-categories within the acoustic/ perceptual vowel space. If categories are starting to be acquired this early, before there is evidence for substantial lexical acquisition, then it is easy to see how certain instances of phonological mergers and splits could get started. Categories would start to emerge from the phonetic data without the lexical learning necessary to identify minimal pairs, or to identify sound pairs as alternants of one another. In a very general way, then, child-language phonology, at the earliest stages, is less constrained by lexical pressure than adult grammars (cf. Bernhardt and Stemberger 1998). Furthermore, since the categorial "mislearnings" in (4) do not involve any obligatory change in pronunciation on the part of the listener *qua* speaker, they may slip into the speech community unnoticed.

Despite the growing number of studies of the acquisition of phonological categories, precise mechanisms of acquisition remain unclear. Innate abilities of categorical perception clearly play a role. However, between eight and ten months and ten and twelve months, significant changes in categorial perception of sounds occur, and these changes directly reflect language-specific phonetic boundaries of categories in input forms. Language acquisition gives rise to regular mappings between phonetic tokens and phonological categories; these mappings reflect sensitivity to certain phonetic parameters, and insensitivity to others. In the ccc-model, sound change, at the level of the individual, is just a special case of general phonological acquisition. As such, it is expected to display the same regular mappings between phonetic tokens and phonological categories. The regularity hypothesis, stated in (3), then, falls out as a corollary of the listener-based model of sound change: sound change is typically regular because the general mapping between surface phonetic forms and phonological representations which takes place in normal language acquisition is also regular. Identification of phonetic variation on the basis of lexical identity as well as phonetic cues with complementary distribution gives rise to the regular acquisition of phonological categories. If frequencies of phonetic variants differ from one generation to the next, or if misperception occurs, or if phonetic variation is consistent with two distinct phonological representations, regular sound change may occur. The closer we get to understanding how phonological categories and contrasts are acquired, the closer we will be to understanding the ultimate source of regularity in sound change.

10.2   The neogrammarian controversy

Throughout this book, I have focused on sound change at the level of the individual. All of the instances of phonetically motivated sound change must ultimately have their source in individuals, and the regularity hypothesis follows from general properties of phonological acquisiton at the level of the individual. This is the "raw material" for linguistic change, whether it is generalized across a speech community or not. However, Labov (1963), Weinreich, Labov, and Herzog (1968), Labov (1981, 1994, 2001), and much related work, has shown that speech communities as a whole do not always provide evidence of regular sound change. When looking at speech communities, we find that sound change may be limited to a small number of lexical items; it may be generalized on the basis of analogy; and it may be variable in terms of its domain of application, where variability is determined by social factors. Nevertheless, all of these studies admit that, while the ongoing stages of sound change appear to involve irregularity, the eventual outcome of sound change is regular. While the seeds of sound change may lie in the mechanisms of sound change proposed in (4) and (5), the diffusion of these sound changes within speech communities is determined primarily by social factors and may display word-by-word extension commonly referred to as "lexical diffusion" (Wang 1969, 1977).

Once one identifies the role of the individual in seeding sound change, and the role of social factors in the dissemination of change, the metaphorical parallels between language change and biological evolution break

down.[3] In gross terms, chance genetic mutations are the seeds of biological change, while natural selection is systematic in distributing these
changes across populations. In language, the relationship is inverted. Regular sound change at the level of the individual is the seed of language
change within the wider speech community. However, the dissemination
of sound change is highly irregular and, at times, even whimsical. Within
speech communities, sound change may first be apparent in a small number of words, and only later generalized to other contexts, with generalization dependent primarily on social attitude. If two people speak "the
same language" and have ample exposure to the speech of each other,
then the probability that one will talk like the other may be increased if
one likes, admires, or identifies with the other in some general way, and
will be increased the more the two people talk to each other.

   While the evolutionary metaphor may not be useful at this juncture, the
mechanisms of change laid out in (4) and (5) have properties which make
them compatible with Labovian studies of change-in-progress and lexical
diffusion. The regularity hypothesis stated in (3) has been challenged
by much work in dialectology, where it is generally assumed that "each
word has its own history." The centuries-old debate over whether sound
change occurs across-the-board, or in a word-by-word fashion has been
treated in detail by Labov (1981, 1994, 2001). Labov's (1994) assessment
of the "neogrammarian controversy" provides striking confirmation of
regular sound change at the level of the individual, and lexical diffusion
at the level of speech communities. In this subsection I highlight the
general compatibility of the model of sound change in (4) and (5) with
Labov's conclusions. At the same time, I explore the consequences of the
regularity hypothesis for recalcitrant instances of lexical diffusion. The
most important features of this model of sound change are two-fold. First,
all sound changes, gradual or abrupt, are typically *regular* at the level of the
individual, as laid out in 10.1. Second, different types of sound change are
associated with different types of surface manifestations of change: sound
change can occur *without* noticeable changes in pronunciation (4bii, 4c);
sound change can occur with *gradual* changes in pronunciation (4bi); and
sound change can occur with (relatively) *abrupt* changes in articulation
(4d). Another important feature is the recognition of multiple phonetic
sources for a single sound change.

   After assessing numerous accounts of sound-change-in-progress and
lexical diffusion from a wide range of languages, Labov (1994) provides
a concise summary of his findings, shown in (6).

---

[3] I am grateful to Andrew Garrett for highlighting the breakdown of the evolutionary
metaphor in the context of the diffusion of change within the wider community. See
the related discussion in Labov (2001, ch. 1).

(6)   Characteristics of regular sound change in contrast to lexical
       diffusion (Labov 1994: 542)
       a. **Regular sound change** is the result of a gradual
          transformation of a single phonetic feature[4] of a phoneme in
          a continuous phonetic space. It is characteristic of the initial
          states of a change that develops within a linguistic system,
          without lexical or grammatical conditioning or any degree of
          social awareness ("change from below").
       b. **Lexical diffusion** is the result of abrupt substitution of one
          phoneme for another in words that contain that phoneme.
          The older and newer forms of the word will usually differ by
          several phonetic features. This process is most characteristic
          of the last stages of internal change that has been
          differentiated by lexical and grammatical conditioning, or
          has developed a high degree of social awareness or of
          borrowings from other systems ("change from above").

Labov's characterization of lexical diffusion implies that it is not a true
instance of phonetically based sound change since several phonetic
features may be involved, non-phonetic grammatical features may be
involved, and social factors may be involved as well. His reference to
"the last stages of internal change" suggests that what may be involved is
a *completed sound change* in one dialect or idiolect, which diffuses, via contact, into the speech of others. In fact, this is precisely the characterization
of many cases of diffusion detailed in his book, including the well-known
Philadelphia short **a** split (Trager 1940; Jesperson 1949; Ferguson 1975),
where tense vowels in *man, ham, mad,* etc. have come to contrast with lax
vowels in *mat, hat, sad,* etc.:

The Philadelphia short a split is the continuation of a long-standing pattern of
lengthening of English /a/, which proceeds by changes in lexical rules at a high level
of abstraction. This change is characterized by dialect mixture and by analogical
and other forms of grammatical conditioning, and it typically exhibits lexical
diffusion. (Labov 1994: 538)

Nevertheless, instead of attributing lexical diffusion to the output of regular sound change, or non-phonetic change, Labov continues to view some
instances of lexical diffusion as instances of phonetically based sound

---

[4] It is unclear what Labov means by "a single phonetic feature"; it is unlikely that this refers
to single measurable phonetic parameters like "F_1 value" or "VOT value," since vowel
height is a function of F_1 and F_2, while voicing may involve a set of phonetic features
including VOT, stop duration, V/C duration ratios, F_0 values of adjacent vowels, etc. I
will interpret this more broadly as "a single phonetic feature, or related set of phonetic
features" when referring back to (6a).

change. This is clear in his suggestion that the bifurcation of properties in (6) predicts that different types of sound change will fall into different classes based on their intrinsically defined gradual versus abrupt characteristics. His proposed classification is shown in (7).

(7)   Labov's predictions regarding types of sound change (Labov 1994: 542–43)

Regular sound change (gradual, continuous)	Lexical diffusion (abrupt)
Vowel shifts in place of articulation	Shortening and lengthening of segments
Diphthongization of high vowels	Diphthongization of mid and low vowels
Consonant changes in manner	Consonant changes in place
Vocalization of liquids	Metathesis of liquids and
Deletion of glides and schwa	stops[5]
	Deletion of obstruents

However, the dichotomy in (7) is problematic for several reasons. First, it focuses on the output of sound change, not its phonetic source or the mechanisms which must take place when one sound pattern is interpreted as another. The problems inherent in focusing on sound correspondences were recognized explicitly by Andersen (1973: 790):

Phonetic correspondences have been investigated since the second half of the 19th century, primarily as results of articulatory modifications. But this study has not yielded a theory explaining phonological change; nor can it, for the study of phonetic correspondences divorced from phonemic relations is tantamount to the study of effects isolated from their causes . . . But a typology of diachronic correspondences is not a theory of phonological change. It explains nothing, nor does it suggest what questions the investigator should ask of his data in order to explain them . . .

In this case, reference to sound correspondences ignores multiple potential sources of a single sound change. But multiple sources cannot be ignored, since one and the same sound change is predicted to be gradual if it results from CHOICE or CHANCE, but abrupt if it has CHANGE as its sole source. Under (7), vocalization of liquids is classified as a gradual sound change. While coda weakening of $l > w$, u is commonplace

---

[5] The inclusion of consonant metathesis in (7) is surprising, since, in the entire volume, Labov only mentions one case of consonant metathesis. This is the *TVL > TLV metathesis in the history of South-Central Dravidian, where L is a liquid. and T is a coronal (Krishnamurti 1978; Labov 1994: 539; Blevins and Garrett, to appear: 11, footnote 13).

in the world's languages, and may, in part, relate to articulatory under-shoot, there is also evidence that, due to the similar formant values of F1 and F2 in these sounds, [ɫ] and [w]/[u] are easily confused (Jonasson 1971; Ohala 1974b). The sound change $ɫ > w$, u, then, may have its source in CHANGE, CHOICE, or both, with abrupt changes in surface realization predicted for the first instance, and gradual changes for the second and third. Another change with multiple potential sources is the deletion of obstruents, which Labov assumes to be abrupt. In some cases where obstruent-deletion can be examined over time, evidence points to a complex interaction of CHANGE and CHOICE. One case of this type is the sound change #$kn > n$ which has occurred several times in the history of English. Evidence from modern Scottish dialects and writ-ten seventeenth-century records shows a gradual sound change in Scots English involving loss of consonantal release, subsequent place assimila-tion, and loss: $k^h n > kn > tn > n$ (Catford 1974). The presence versus absence of release of the initial stop, as well as the anticipatory coartic-ulation of the oral stop with the following nasal, are common features of casual speech, and there is no reason to think that they may not all constitute variant pronunciations of the sequence at some point in time. Just such variation has been demonstrated in the production of mod-ern English consonant clusters (e.g. Browman and Goldstein 1990; Byrd 1996). Combined with this variation was the common perception of [tn] and/or [kn] as [n] due to the absence of oral release, a case of CHANGE. As with $ɫ$-vocalization, the loss of initial /k/ may have its source both in coarticulation and misperception, suggesting gradual and abrupt com-ponents, respectively, of a single sound change.

Another problem with the output focus of Labov's classification in (7) surfaces in the treatment of trading relationships. Many sound changes involve simultaneous trading relationships, where one change is gradual, but a simultaneous change is abrupt. Though Labov places "shortening and lengthening" of segments and "metathesis of liquids and stops" in the abrupt category, length is a feature which can arise when a formerly predictable and gradient length contrast splits into two contrast-ing categories. Kavitskaya's (2002) detailed treatment of compensatory lengthening, summarized in 6.1.3, illustrates the difficulty of classifying a sound change like CVCV > CV:C as gradual versus abrupt. Com-pensatory lengthening of this type is the result of historical open-syllable lengthening; this lengthening is phonetically regular, and highly context-dependent, with different degrees of length depending on the manner features of the following consonant. This vowel length is reinterpreted as contrastive when the following vowel is lost.

If it were the case that vowel loss was always abrupt, then we would expect vowel lengthening via compensatory lengthening to be abrupt as well. However, it is well known that vowel loss can show the hallmarks of gradual continuous regular sound change, with durational shortening, neutralization of quality, and devoicing, preceding phonetic loss. In Ponapean historical compensatory lengthening, final vowels are lost, but in closely related languages which show the same "compensatory lengthening," voiceless final vowels are still pronounced (Rehg 1984a, b). In Kwara'ae, where final CV-metathesis is in-progress, the maintenance or loss of a final unstressed voiceless vowel depends on quality of the voiceless vowel, manner of a preceding consonant, and quality of the preceding vowel (Blevins and Garrett 1998: 529–31). In terms of output, the sound change could be written as $V_1CV_2 > V_1V_2C$. Prior to the sound change in-progress, all syllables in Kwara'ae were open. However, after nasals, all voiceless vowels have been lost. If the final vowel sequence consists of a high vowel followed by a non-high vowel, the final vowel is also lost. In addition, citation forms maintain final vowels which are lost in casual speech forms. Compare *iʔa*/*yaʔ* 'fish'; *asila*/*asiəl* 'salty, sweet'; *onolo'n* 'six'; *lif*/*liəh* 'teeth'; *lisa*/*liəs* 'Lisa'; *nuta*/*nuət* 'squid'; *lade*/*lǽɛ'd* 'coral gravel' – where the first of each pair is the citation form, and the second is the common speech form. Vowel loss in Kwara'ae is not complete, but it is clearly gradual, continuous, and regular. In general then, formulas like CVCV > CV:C and $V_1CV_2 > V_1V_2C$ accurately express the phonological reanalyses which have taken place in many languages, but obscure the gradual and continuous nature of change evident in many studies of final vowel loss.

A similar problem arises in the evolution of vowel-length contrasts from earlier obstruent voicing contrasts: Vd > V:t. Here, the gradual decay of obstruent voicing is concomitant with an "abrupt" evolution of a vowel-length contrast, where this abrupt evolution involves no necessary or obvious change in articulation. The sound change, as a whole, is a case of CHOICE, but the particular choice made results in a restructuring of the vowel system with no change in the articulation of vowels. Recall from chapter 4 that devoicing of final obstruents is attributed to the common absence of release in final position and phrase-final lengthening, among other phonetic factors. Though final devoicing is accepted as a completed sound change in many languages including German, Dutch, and Catalan, phonetic studies over the past decade suggest that word-final neutralization of e.g. /t, d/ to [t] is phonetically incomplete (Port and O'Dell 1985; Port and Crawford 1989; and the review in Warner et al. 2002). In all of these languages, there are significant phonetic differences between "neutralized" stops and their non-neutralized counterparts. This finding is not surprising if final devoicing arises from variable and gradient devoicing of obstruents in final position via CHOICE. Interestingly, phonetic studies of many varieties of English show evidence of variable final devoicing. A summary of partial descriptions of phonetic variants of English voiced and voiceless stops in medial and final positions from Kingston and Diehl (1994) is shown in (8).[6] In final position, closure voicing is possible, but it is highly variable. The consistent features associated with voiced segments in this context are longer preceding V duration, shorter stop closure, and a lower F_1 on the preceding vowel.

(8) Partial descriptions of phonetic variants of English stops contrasting for [voice], from Kingston and Diehl (1994: 427, table 1) [emphasis added: JB]

	[+voice]	[−voice]
Intervocalic or post-tonic	**closure voicing**	**no closure voicing**
	shorter closure	longer closure
	longer preceding V	shorter preceding V
	F_1 lower	F_1 higher
	F_0 lower	F_0 higher
Utterance-final and post-vocalic	longer preceding V	shorter preceding V
	closure voicing possible	**no closure voicing**
	shorter closure	longer closure
	F_1 lower	F_1 higher

Given the variable nature of final obstruent voicing, in contrast to other phonetic features, which are invariable, phonologization of length can occur via CHOICE, as illustrated in (9).

(9) Phonologization of final devoicing: gradual surface change under CHOICE

Speaker A	Listener C
/ɛd#/	/ɛːt#/
↓1	↑3
[ɛːt,ɛːd̥. . .]$_{Vi}$ 2→	[ɛːt, ˌɛːd̥. . .]$_{Vi}$ ⇒ [ɛːt, . . .]$_{Vj}$ (No instances of final [d])

The example of sound change in (9) appears to be instantiated in American Appalachian English (Hock 1991: 139). In this dialect, variable devoicing in final position has given rise to final devoicing. In Appalachian

---

[6] The descriptions in (8) do not include post-*s* contexts or flapping contexts. Differences in F_1 and F_0 occur at the edges of adjacent vowels.

English, Standard American English *bed* versus *bet* is phonetically [bɛːt] versus [bɛt] with a phonemic vowel-length contrast, and no final voicing.[7] In sum, the possibility of multiple phonetic sources for a single sound change, and trading relationships involving gradual phonetic shifts but categorial phonological ones, suggest a reconfiguration of the dichotomy in (7), based on the phonetic source of sound change. A revised dichotomy of gradual versus abrupt sound change based on the primary phonetic sources of sound change is proposed in (10).[8]

(10)   Gradual versus abrupt sound change

gradual	*abrupt*
CHANCE(±CHANGE, ±CHOICE)	CHANGE only
CHOICE(±CHANCE, ±CHANGE)	

A second problem with the classification of sound change in (7) is that, even with the suggested modifications in (10), there is evidence of abrupt sound change without lexical diffusion. All reported instances of lexical diffusion involve abrupt change, but not all instances of abrupt change are reflected in patterns of lexical diffusion. One case in point is discussed by Labov himself. This is the word-final shift of labials to velars in Atayal based on Li (1982). Since Atayal word-final *p* > *k* and *m* > *ŋ* involve a "consonant change in place," they are predicted to show the hallmarks of lexical diffusion. However, Labov's careful reconsideration of the Atayal facts using multivariate analysis based on consonantal place of articulation shows a strong dissimilatory tendency: the sound change occurs first if one of the preceding consonants in the word is labial or nasal, and only later when other consonant types precede. Labov summarizes his reanalysis in categorical terms:

To sum up, the application of Neogrammarian techniques to the Atayalic consonant shift data shows that there is no clear evidence to support a mechanism of lexical diffusion, and until such evidence is advanced, we must accept the Atayalic case as an example of Neogrammarian regularity. (Labov 1994: 451)

---

[7] Complete final devoicing would probably be much more common in English dialects, were it not for the influence of orthography on the phonetic realization of this particular contrast once literacy skills are acquired. See Sproat (2000) for several examples where orthography influences phonology, and Warner et al. (2002) for a summary of the mounting literature on phonetic influences of orthographies.

[8] This is similar to the view of Kiparsky (1988, 1995) associating abrupt changes with perception and gradual changes with articulation. However, gradual changes may also have perceptual components, as indicated by the parenthesized material in (10).

While the Atayal example most likely involves dialect mixture, similar changes in relatively small isolated island populations with less dialect variation may yield even "purer" cases of regular abrupt sound change.[9]

One well-described instance of regular abrupt sound change is $q > \textipa{P}$ in Manam (Lichtenberk 1983: 17–21). Manam is an Oceanic language spoken on a small island off the north coast of New Guinea. On Manam Island, there are fourteen villages and Manam is spoken in all of them, with minimal geographic variation (Lichtenberk 1983: 2). The change in progress involves replacement of a uvular voiceless stop with glottal stop: $q > \textipa{P}$. The shift in place of articulation appears to be abrupt in articulatory terms; there is no evidence of glottalization of the uvular. In terms of the phonological system of Manam, this sound change is neither a merger nor split; the consonant inventory of Manam prior to the sound change is /p t q b d g m n ŋ s z l r/; after the sound change, the consonant inventory is /p t ʔ b d g m n ŋ s z l r/. Despite the abrupt nature of this change, Lichtenberk's account gives every indication that it is regular, showing no evidence of lexical diffusion:

> The distribution of the two sounds is determined by two factors: age and geography. In the village of Dangale . . . the age at which the q-$\textipa{P}$ break occurs is roughly 45–50 years; that is, speakers over 45–50 years old use q, while younger speakers use $\textipa{P}$. The critical age is lower in the villages clockwise from Dangale as far as, and including, the village of Dugulaba . . . while it is higher in the neighbouring village counterclockwise . . . and finally only $\textipa{P}$ appears to be used farther in that direction . . . In Dangale, there is remarkably little variation in the use of q and $\textipa{P}$; i.e., a person is either a q-speaker or a $\textipa{P}$-speaker . . . (Lichtenberk 1983: 17–18)

Only one village, Dugulaba, is reported to show variation in the speech of individuals, and this village appears to be the last link in the circular dialect chain. If the chain was not circular, we would expect Dugulaba to have the lowest critical age. However, the neighboring village clockwise has only $\textipa{P}$, and close contact with this village appears to have given rise to variation in speakers who would otherwise show only q. That the pattern, once established, is directly inherited during acquisition is confirmed by a noted exception to the rule. Lichtenberk (1983: 21) reports a 3–4-year-old boy who is a q-speaker, despite the fact that his parents are both

---

[9] Changes reported in Gauchat's (1905) study of Charmey, a Swiss village, come to mind. One feature reported was the use of lj by the oldest generation, and j by the youngest, with variation between lj and j in intervening generations. While the sound change $l^j >$ j appears to be abrupt, the variation noted is most likely the consequence of diffusion of a completed gradual sound change involving articulatory lenition: gradual lenition of the central closure gesture giving rise to lateral airflow, would result in a segment defined only by the remaining palatal approximation, [j]. I know of no evidence suggesting that l^j is commonly misperceived as j.

ʔ-speakers. However, his grandparents were both q-speakers, and the boy appeared to have learned most of his language from them.[10]

A fact that needs to be mentioned is that, with the exception of small children, most Manam speakers are fluent in Tok Pisin (Lichtenberk 1983: 614). Given the abrupt nature of the $q > ʔ$ sound change, the possible external influence of Tok Pisin should be considered. Tok Pisin has two velar consonants /k/ and /g/, no uvulars, and no glottal stop. Hence, the shift of $q > ʔ$ cannot be directly attributed to Tok Pisin sound patterns.[11] In fact, Tok Pisin loans in Manam support the sound change as an independent development in Manam. When Tok Pisin loans are nativized in Manam, ʔ-speakers produce Tok Pisin /k/ as [ʔ], while q-speakers pronounce Tok Pisin /k/ as [q].

The classification in (7) is viewed by Labov as a resolution of the neogrammarian controversy. He concludes:

> This resolution of the Neogrammarian controversy entails a shift of research strategies. It turns aside from the questions, Does every word have its own history?, It is phonemes that change?, Are the Neogrammarians right or wrong?, toward a research program of a different sort. . . . We can then ask, What is the full range of properties that determine the transition from one phonetic state to another? (Labov 1994: 543)

In the discussion above, I have attempted to refine Labov's resolution of the neogrammarian controversy by looking closely at the phonetic source of sound change, and the extent to which this determines the transition from one phonetic state to another. The results are quite striking. First, Labov's dichotomy of gradual versus abrupt sound change in (7) is in need of modification. Only by viewing sound change in terms of phonetic sources can we accurately predict intrinsic properties of change. Adopting the modified dichotomy between gradual and abrupt sound change in (10), there is evidence that both types of sound change are regular.

While hundreds of examples of regular *gradual* sound change in-progress are well documented, there are very few examples of regular abrupt change in-progress of the Manam type reported in the literature.[12] There are at least two plausible reasons for this. First, as discussed above,

---

[10] There is a difference between native q-speakers, like this boy, and ʔ-speakers who attempt to talk like q-speakers. In the second case, [k] is substituted for [q], based, presumably, on Tok Pisin, and allophonic realization of /q/ as [χ] between non-high back vowels is absent.

[11] Tok Pisin influence should result in a shift from $*q > k$. This is exactly what happens when native ʔ-speakers attempt to imitate native q-speakers; they replace [q] with [k].

[12] Other cases of abrupt sound change with no evidence of lexical diffusion at the time of origin include $*θ > f$ in many dialects of British English; $*ʃ > x$ in the history of Spanish; and $*r > ʁ, ʀ$ in southern Scandinavian dialects. I am grateful to Andrew Garrett for bringing these examples to my attention.

many instances of CHANGE (abrupt perceptually based sound change) are "impure," and involve simultaneous coarticulatory effects. A second reason for the rarity of examples of the Manam type is the intrinsic difficulty of catching an abrupt change "in-progress." The sound change must be identified in relatively isolated small populations where the natural age-graded profile of the change can exhibit itself, protected from external influence, and this identification must occur before the completed change takes on social significance, or very close to the time it does. Since abrupt changes are typically perceptually salient, they will often be associated with social variables. Once this association occurs, the distribution of the completed sound change takes on a distinct irregular profile, becoming lexically diffused, with regularity no longer recoverable. This has already occurred in Manam, where the q-pronunciation is associated with prestige (Lichtenberk 1983: 19). An additional complication of the past few decades is the spread of English as a world language, and the "changes-from-above" that may accompany this spread.

In sum, the mechanisms of sound change schematized in (4) and (5) are consistent with the core of neogrammarian and Labovian conceptions of sound change. Phonetically based sound change is typically regular at the level of the individual, and simultaneously affects all lexical items. In some cases, sound change is unobservable (4bii, 4c), while in other cases, just-noticeable differences (4bi), or more salient differences (4bii) are observed. Sound change may be gradual at the surface level (4bi) or abrupt (4d). Direct inheritance of phonetic variation in (4bii) and (4c) gives rise to the variable coexistence of old and new pronunciations in many types of sound change. Regular sound change and lexical diffusion are precisely as Labov characterizes them in (6), with gradual and abrupt characteristics attributable to the phonetic source of change (10). Sound change conditioned by phonetic factors alone is regular. But lexical diffusion is never an instance of sound change conditioned by phonetic factors alone, hence its incipient irregularity (Harris 1985; Garrett 2002: 2). The abrupt substitutions found in lexical diffusion often represent completed regular sound changes; they are abrupt precisely because a sound change has already occurred. Under this analysis, lexical diffusion constitutes one notable subtype of contact-induced change.

10.3   Teleology and sound change

The CCC-model summarized in (4) and (5) is one in which ambiguity inherent in the phonetic signal gives rise to potential change. Each step in (5) is associated with a different type of sound change, and in each step there is unpredictability. In CHOICE, where the source of ambiguity is phonetic variation, though the choice of variant may be based on token frequency, variants result from a combination of universal and language-specific factors, where language-specific phonetics are unpredictable (Kingston and Diehl 1994; Pierrehumbert 2001). In CHANGE, where misperception is involved, we can identify easily confused percepts (Jonasson 1971; Ohala 1974b), and in some cases, common directions of misperception (Ohala 1971; Guion 1998; Plauché 2001), but it does not seem possible to predict instances of misperception in the acquisition of a given individual. In the third step of sound change, where utterances are mapped to phonological forms, there is a closed class of representations available. A laryngealized sequence [ʔa̰ʔ] may be analyzed as /ʔa/, /aʔ/, /ʔaʔ/, /a̰/, /ʔa̰/, /a̰ʔ/, or /ʔa̰ʔ/, assuming there is no other segment which alternates with [ʔ] in the language. While the one-to-one feature-to-segment mapping principle proposed in 6.1.2 will eliminate some of these options in some cases, and pre-existing structural features may give preference to others under Structural Analogy, there appears to be no way, at the moment, of predicting which of the remaining representations will be selected by a given language learner. While the non-deterministic features of this model might appear to be a weakness, I suggest that they properly model the unpredictable nature of language change. As the simplest indicator of the unpredictability, let us reconsider the developments of Sulawesi final consonants discussed in 6.3, and repeated in (11).

(11)   Final consonants in Sulawesi languages (Sneddon 1993)

	Totoli	Talaud	Ratahan	Duri	Makasar	Wolio
*p	p	p:a	p	ʔ	ʔ	ø
*t	t	t:a	ʔ	ʔ	ʔ	ø
*k	k	k:a	k	k	ʔ	ø
*m	m	m:a	m	n	ŋ	ø
*n	n	n:a	n	n	ŋ	ø
*ŋ	ŋ	ŋ:a	ŋ	ŋ	ŋ	ø

There are three general patterns in (11): no change (Totoli); gemination with final vowel insertion (Talaud); and final weakening in the form of place neutralization (Ratahan, Duri, Makasar) and loss (Wolio). There is clearly no built-in directionality of change in the input form, since no change is necessary. Furthermore, one cannot insist that consonants in final position will inevitably weaken, since vowel insertion has occurred in at least one case, giving rise to a strengthened consonant in both perceptual and articulatory terms.[13] Someone looking for predictability in

[13] This is just one counterexample to the view that all phonetically based sound change is due to articulatory reduction, as suggested by Pagliuca and Mowrey (1987) and Mowrey and Pagliuca (1995).

change might start with the results in (11), and reason backwards. Totoli final consonants were not neutralized because they were audibly released, and therefore easily distinguished from one another. It was this audible release which was reinterpreted as a final vowel in Talaud. In the other languages with partial or full place neutralization, final consonants were unreleased giving rise to misperception of place. These are all reasonable suggestions. However, they fail to go back to the ultimate origins of sound change. Why were the reflexes of the proto-segments released in some daughter languages, and non-released in others? Again, a reasonable suggestion would be that in the proto-language, there was variable release. Under CHOICE, one development took the non-released variant as basic, and the other, the released variant as basic. But now we must go back one step further and ask on what basis these instances of CHOICE took place. In line with other documented cases of CHOICE, we might suggest that there were different token frequencies of released versus unreleased stops in different populations. But then, what gave rise to these different frequencies? As far back as we go, we will be forced to posit a difference between populations which does not appear to have a phonetic motivation, but results from stochastic effects of frequency in language use (Bybee 2001). Here we have looked at a case where CHOICE may be the ultimate source of divergence, but we will find the same ultimate unpredictability at the source of any sound change we examine. For CHANGE, we need only look at English dialectology: in some dialects $\theta > f$, in others it is maintained with no change. What factors have given rise to misperception in some dialects, and its absence in others? If we attribute misperception to some distinct acoustic property of θ prior to its misperception, then we push the problem back to the origins of this acoustic divergence. But the facts are staring us in the face: from a single source, sound change may or may not take place.[14]

There are many general arguments against teleology as a force in language change. See, for example, Vincent (1978), Lass (1980), Crowley (1992: 196–202), McMahon (1994), and Lass (1997: 340–52). While these works present compelling arguments against certain types of change as being teleologically motivated, they do not have, as a focus, the elimination of markedness constraints. In the subsections which follow, I argue

---

[14] A sophisticated statistical probabilistic model might be able to demonstrate the non-deterministic nature of change, on the basis of the origins of regular phonetic sound change in the individual. Since each individual, will, by definition, be presented with a distinct set of linguistic exemplars from which to model a grammar, no two individual grammars will be the same. At the level of sound change, it will take some critical mass of similar (phonological) grammars to realize an incipient sound change, and the distribution of these critical masses might be random.

that markedness constraints play no role in determining the direction of sound change. In opposition to Grammont (1933), Martinet (1955), and more recent proposals within Optimality Theory (e.g. Cho 1998; Antilla and Cho 1998), sound changes which appear to be driven by functional or structural properties of sound systems are typically either illusory, accidental, or emergent.

10.3.1 Symmetry and the structure of inventories

Linguists have long remarked on the symmetrical properties of certain consonant and vowel inventories. The consonant system of Klamath (Barker 1964) in (12) shows notable symmetry. For every obstruent, with the exception of /s/ (Blevins 2002), there are three laryngeal series: voiceless unaspirated, voiceless aspirated, and ejective. And for every non-laryngeal sonorant, there are also three laryngeal series: plain voiced, voiceless, and glottalized.

(12)   Klamath consonants

p	t	c	k	q	s	m	n	l	y	w	
pʰ	tʰ	cʰ	kʰ	qʰ		m̥	n̥	l̥	y̥	w̥	h
p'	t'	c'	k'	q'		m'	n'	l'	y'	w'	ʔ

Hundreds of examples of this sort could be cited from genetically unrelated languages. The question is not whether there are emergent tendencies towards symmetry, but what these tendencies reflect, and whether they play a direct role in sound change.

Hock (1991: 153) discusses Celtic developments of Proto-Indo-European $*p$ in this context. The developments are summarized in (13), where a dash indicates a gap in the otherwise symmetrical inventory. The question is whether the gap left by the loss of $*p$ played a role in the change of $*k^w > p$ in British Celtic, or in the borrowing of Latin p into Later Old Irish. If one attempts to motivate $*k^w > p$ by its symmetry-creating function, then one must treat the parallel development of $*g^w > b$ as having independent motivation. In fact, there is every reason to believe that the change of labiovelar stops to plain labials was a single change in British Celtic, with the same phonetic source as other similar changes, e.g. $*k^w > p$ in Proto-Mixe-Zoquean (Longacre 1967), or $k^w > b^w > b$ in Nahuatl (Monzón and Seneff 1984): gestural reduction, as in the Nahuatl case, and perceptual similarity (Ohala and Lorentz 1977; Ohala 1992c). Another weakness of the teleological account is the fact that it is used when convenient; the missing p-slot was not filled in the pre-history of early Early Old Irish.

(13)   Celtic developments of Proto-Indo-European *p
        (Hock 1991: 153)

dialectal Proto-Indo-European	Proto-Celtic	British Celtic
p t k kʷ	- t k kʷ	p t k
b d g gʷ	b d g gʷ	b d g

Early Old Irish	Later Old Irish
-t k kʷ	p t k
b d g -	b d g

An even more striking case of the failure to fill a similar gap occurs in the Otomanguean language family. Proto-Otomanguean is reconstructed with consonants *t *k *kʷ *ʔ *s *h *n *w *j (Suárez 1983: 37). However, Rensch (1983: 308) provides evidence that already in Proto-Otomanguean times, there was a dialect split, with one group having the *p *t *k stop system, and the other corresponding *kʷ *t *k. Of interest is the fact that this ancient dialect split, which goes back thousands of years, has been maintained in daughter languages: many of the Mixtecan, Popolocan, Amuzgo, Chatino, and Chinantecan languages have kʷ reflecting the *kʷ-dialect, with nothing filling the labial gap. Chiapanec-Mangue, Otopamean, Isthmus Zapotec, Tlapanec, and Huave have p reflecting the ancient *p-dialect. Some languages even appear to have grammaticized reflexes of the earlier dialect split: for example, in Jicaltepec Mixtec p replaces kʷ in the "diminutive style" (Bradley 1970). One might argue that symmetry is not relevant, since there is no corresponding voiced or nasal segment in Proto-Otomanguean. However, many of the daughter languages with kʷ have innovated other consonant series, creating new labial segments in different series. For example, in Cuicatec, there are voiced fricatives /β ð/, but the voiceless stop series is still the inherited kʷ t k system, maintaining the labial gap. What this case shows is that the *kʷ *t *k stop system reconstructed for one dialect of Proto-Otomanguean appears to be just as stable as the *p *t *k system of its sister dialect. Despite centuries of change, the kʷ t k system survives in many languages to this day, with no p, and no evidence of goal-oriented change in the service of symmetrical inventories.[15]

---

[15] Of the voiceless stop series /p t k/ and /p' t' k'/, /p/ and /p'/ are more often missing than other points of articulation (Javkin 1977; Pinkerton 1986), though a recent study by Maddieson (2002) suggests that this is a consequence of diffusion in certain parts of the world, and not necessarily the result of regular sound change. This is a welcome result: though labials have weaker stop bursts, all else being equal, this is not likely to result in their loss in pre-vocalic position. Nhanda is one language which appears to have undergone regular p-loss in word-initial position, but /p/ is maintained intervocalically and in post-consonantal pre-vocalic position (Blevins 2001a).

Unless it can be shown that certain sound changes occur with greater than chance frequency where there are more gaps than elsewhere, or that certain sound changes are blocked if they will create asymmetrical systems, there is no clear argument for symmetry-based explanations of sound change. In fact, recurrent *asymmetries* in stop inventories suggest that common phonetic sound change operates blindly when symmetry is at stake. In the case of the voiced-stop series, b d g, g is commonly missing (Chao 1936; Maddieson 1984, 2002). An example is Iaai (Gedney 1965) with consonants /p t k, p^h t^h k^h b d – /. This gap in the stop inventory occurs in unrelated languages around the world, and has a simple aerodynamic explanation: where voicing of oral stops is concerned, the greater the volume of the supralaryngeal air chamber, the longer voicing can be sustained. In other words, all else being equal, voicing can be sustained longest in [b], less long in [d], and for a shorter time still in [g] (Javkin 1977; Ohala and Riordan 1979; Ohala 1983a, 1995a). Of the three voiced stops, [g] is most likely to undergo devoicing to [k], since it is the least compatible with sustained voicing. The frequency of the *g*-gap, and its independent evolution in many different languages, can be taken as evidence that phonetically based sound change is blind to symmetry of phoneme inventory.[16] As a final example of the irrelevance of inventory symmetry to sound change, consider again the q > ʔ shift in Manam. Prior to the change, the stop inventory is /p t q b d g m n ŋ/ and after /p t – b d g m n ŋ ʔ/. If a high value was placed on symmetrical inventories, why would this change occur? Symmetry principles might predict that precisely in cases where one sound could be misperceived as another, movement would be toward gap filling. Under such an account, Manam is predicted to evidence q > k, not the attested q > ʔ.

In sum, there is a great deal of empirical evidence that sound change occurs blindly, without regard for the symmetry of phoneme inventories. Problems inherent to symmetry-related accounts are quite general: sound changes are phonetically natural, and therefore will always be found to occur independently of purported symmetry-related functions in some language; a sound change seen as improving symmetry will occur in one daughter language, or one language family, but not in another; certain asymmetries are recurrent, and have well-understood phonetic explanations; and finally, in cases where a phonetically governed sound

---

[16] A proponent of defeasible constraints might suggest that *g, and other phonetically "grounded" constraints typically outrank symmetry constraints. Under the current account where all regular sound change is argued to be phonetically motivated, sound change, and not symmetry, will be the primary force molding sound inventories. The question for such a model is when and how the proposed symmetry constraints might show themselves, since regular sound change is constant and on-going.

change could give rise to perfect symmetry, changes in the opposite direction are attested. The view that sound change improves inventory symmetry is an illusion. It is offered as a *post hoc* motivation for sound change only in cases where a symmetrical inventory results. In just as many cases, a sound change gives rise to asymmetry, or an asymmetrical system undergoes no change.

Despite the conclusion that sound change is not driven by gap-filling imperatives whose ultimate goal is symmetrical inventories, certain symmetrical tendencies in the structure of segment inventories clearly exist. A great deal of work over the last few decades suggests that these tendencies are emergent properties of sound systems related to gestural efficiency (in the case of consonants) and perceptual distance (in the case of vowels). Phonetic work in this area includes: Liljencrants and Lindblom (1972), Lindblom (1986), Stevens (1989), and Lang and Ohala (1996) on vowel inventories; Lindblom (1984, 1989, 1990a, b), Stevens et al. (1986), Lindblom and Maddieson (1988), Ohala (1992a), Pagliuca (1982), Pagliuca and Mowrey (1987), and LaVoie (2001) on consonant inventories.[17] There are also recurrent symmetrical tendencies which result from sound change. For example, the evolution of ejectives from Tʔ sequences, where T is an oral stop, takes a /p t k/ system to one with /p' t' k'/ as well. Such developments are attested in Yurok (Berman

---

[17] Kiparsky (1995: 653–54) argues against the view of blind sound change on the basis that "a battery of blind sound changes operating on a language should eventually produce systems whose phonemicization by the standard procedures would violate every phonological universal in the book." One example he provides involves phoneme inventories:

why does no sound change ever operate in such a way as to subvert phonological principles, such as implicational universals and constraints on phonological systems? For example, every known language has obstruent stops in its phonological inventory, at least some unmarked ones such as *p, t, k*. If sound change were truly blind, then the operation of context-free spirantization processes such as Grimm's Law to languages with minimal stop inventories should result in phonological systems which lack those stops, but such systems are unattested. (Kiparsky 1995: 641)

There are two problems with this particular example. One is the description of Grimm's Law as context-free spirantization. As demonstrated by Garrett and Hale (1993), and discussed further in 10.4, spirantization is limited to word-initial and post-sonorant environments. Their analysis of Grimm's Law is one of syllable-initial strengthening of voiceless stops to aspirates, with aspiration ultimately giving rise to fricative percepts. A related problem is that there are very few well-documented cases of context-free spirantization in the literature. Where lenition and fortition as phonetically based sound changes are involved, they are limited to weak and strong positions respectively within the word. Since all languages have prosodic domains with weak and strong positions, context-free lenitions and fortitions are rare.

Kiparsky's solution to the problem stated above is a model combining variation and selection similar to the one proposed here, but different in the primary role it ascribes to phonological, not phonetic, primitives, like underspecification, feature-geometry, etc. I am suggesting that these phonological constraints play no role in sound change.

1982), Ineseño Chumash (Ohala, to appear), and many other languages (Fallon 2002). Where symmetrical tendencies exist in segment inventories, then, they appear to have the same emergent status as recurrent patterns of feature and segment distribution.

10.3.2   Gap-filling independent of symmetry: what are chain shifts?

Where symmetry accounts have been proposed to account for certain sound changes involving consonants, within vowel systems, sound change has been argued to fill gaps independent of symmetry. One vowel moves within the acoustic/perceptual vowel space, and an adjacent vowel moves into the space left behind, or is pushed into some other space by the changed vowel. Such developments in vowel systems are commonly referred to as chain shifts. Labov (1994: 118) defines the sequence of events as follows: "A minimal chain shift is a change in the position of two phonemes in which one moves away from an original position that is then occupied by the other." The chain shifts involved in the Swedish changes schematized in (14), are instances of a push chain (Benediktsson 1970): short *a* lengthens, and this triggers a shift of earlier *a:* > *ɔ:* and so on.

(14)   A push-chain in Swedish (Labov 1994: 131)
        a > a:, a:> ɔ:, ɔ: > o:, o: > u:, u: > ü

There is no question that chain shifts exist. A survey of the chain shift literature and a wealth of empirical documentation is provided in chapters 5 and 6 of Labov (1994), including historically complete changes and changes in progress. As with recurrent tendencies towards symmetrical consonant inventories, the question is not if such tendencies exist, but what these tendencies reflect, and whether they play a direct role in sound change.

The most commonly held view is that chain shifts reflect maintenance of contrast. Vowels move together in chain shifts to avoid merger and preserve their contrastive function within the language (Martinet 1955).[18] An obvious problem with this simple account is that vowel mergers occur: witness the merger of /a/ and /ɑ/ in Parisian French where the two phonetic categories gradually approach each other, until they become one (Lennig 1978). Labov (1994: 328–31) suggests that a complex combination of factors will result in merger as opposed to contrast maintenance.

---

[18] Martinet's (1955) formulation also makes reference to the asymmetry of the vowel space, and the phonological insistence on symmetry to explain why, under chain shifts, back vowels have a tendency to front.

These factors include: the functional load of the opposition involved; the number of minimal pairs that depend on the distinction; the extent to which the distinction depends on minimal pairs; the number of distinctions already made along the particular phonetic dimension; the number of phonetic features on which the opposition depends; the discriminibility of the phonetic features on which the opposition depends; and limitations in the range of movements that would avoid merger. This view of merger, then, also reflects a principle of maintenance contrast: if the functional value of a contrast is very low with low token and type frequency of minimal pairs, then merger can occur.

I suggest that chain shifts can naturally emerge from the variability inherent in vocalic articulations as a result of frequency effects in sound change (Pierrehumbert 2001, Bybee 2001), the fact that vocalic categories appear to be structured in terms of prototypes (Grieser and Kuhl 1989; Kuhl 1991), and exemplar models of speech perception (Johnson 1997; Pierrehumbert 2001).[19] The pronunciation of all vowels is variable, and this variability is highly language specific (Bradlow 1995). At the same time, vowels do not show evidence of categorical perception in the same way consonants do. Rather, within a vowel category, some members of the category are judged to be better or more typical exemplars of the category than others. These exemplars, referred to as prototypes, have a special status, and affect perception in a very concrete way. In discrimination tests, it is harder for adult listeners to discriminate between prototypes and surrounding members of the category at some psycho-acoustic distance, than between non-prototypes and other members of the category with the same psycho-acoustic distance. This perceptual warping is referred to as the "perceptual magnet effect," and is summarized succinctly by Kuhl (1991: 99):

Surrounding members of the category are perceptually assimilated to it to a greater degree than would be expected on the basis of real psychophysical distance. Relative to a nonprototype of the category, the distance between the prototype and surrounding members is effectively decreased; in other words, the perceptual space appears to be "warped," effectively shrunk around the prototype. The prototype of the category thus serves as a powerful anchor for the category, and the prototype's functional role as a perceptual magnet for the category serves to strengthen category cohesiveness.

A final ingredient in the account of chain shifts comes from the exemplar theory of speech as formalized by Johnson (1997) and Pierrehumbert

---

[19] The discussion at this point is necessarily cursory. To my knowledge, no one has tested the proposed hypothesis. I refer readers to clear expositions of exemplar theory (Johnson 1997; Pierrehumbert 2001), and perceptual magnet effects (Kuhl 1991, 1995).

(2001). Within exemplar theory, phonological systems emerge from the structured memory of auditory input. By examining consequences of the perception–production loop over time, Pierrehumbert (2001) is able to model important features of sound change, including the role of frequency in the advancement of leniting changes through the lexicon (Bybee 1985a, 2001). Another strength of the model is its ability to account for perceptual-magnet effects of the kind just discussed (Lacerda, to appear). One consequence of the model is that "a new token which is well positioned with respect to a category can actually provide a better example of that category (in being recognized quickly and rated highly) than any actual example of that category that has been previously experienced" (Pierrehumbert 2001: 143). In terms of the mechanisms of change recognized here, this means that a phonetic variant which has newly been heard may instantiate a better example of a particular vowel category than all previously perceived exemplars. Another interesting feature of the model is that the perceptually "best" examples of particular vowel categories may be ones with more extreme formant values than typical productions. This is because the probability for a category label is influenced "both by the activation of exemplars having that label, and by competition from other labels having exemplars in the same area of the cognitive map" (Pierrehumbert 2001: 144; see also Johnson, Flemming and Wright 1993). Since under chain shift the move of one vowel category leaves some of the psycho-acoustic space empty of any prototype, extreme examples of a pre-existing (neighboring) category which fall into the empty space may be judged as better instances of that category, provided they are farther from all exemplars with competing labels than others in their category. There is no reference to maximizing contrast in this model: vowels tend to shift together because of the way vocalic categories are perceived and structured.

I will illustrate the proposed hypothesis with a single chain link. A vowel system begins with /uː/ and /oː/; /uː/ undergoes fronting, and /oː/ raises to /uː/. The link is illustrated in (15), and is attested in many languages, including Swedish, Akha, and North Frisian (Labov 1994, chapter 5).

(15)   A common chain-shift link

      yː, ʉː ←uː

         ↑

        oː

The two linked sound changes are uː > yː, ʉː and oː>uː. Now consider at the micro-phonetic level how the two changes might be related within the current model of sound change. The general case is illustrated in (16), where listed phonetic variants are given in order of token frequency.

(16)   CHOICE as the source of chain shifts

Stage I:	Speaker 1	Listener 1	Speaker 1	Listener 1
	/uː/	/uː/	/oː/	/oː/
	↓	↑	↓	↑
	[uː, ʉː,yː: . . .]ᵥᵢ →	[uː, ʉː,yː: . . .]ᵥᵢ	[oː, ọː, ǫː: . . .]ᵥᵢ→	[oː, ọː, ọː:, . . .]ᵥᵢ
Stage II:	Speaker 1	Listener 1	Speaker 1	Listener 1
	/uː/	/yː/	/oː/	/oː/
	↓	↑	↓	↑
	[ʉː,yː, uː: . . .]ᵥᵢ →	[ʉː,yː: . . .]ᵥᵢ	[oː, ọː, ǫː: . . .]ᵥᵢ →	[oː, ọː,ọː: . . .]ᵥᵢ
Stage III:	Speaker 2	Listener 2	Speaker 2	Listener 2
	(= Listener 1)		(= Listener 1)	
	/yː/	/yː/	/oː/	/uː/
	↓	↑	↓	↑
	[yː, ʉː, . . .]ᵥᵢ →	[yː, ʉː, . . .]ᵥᵢ	[oː, ọː, ǫː: . . .uː]ᵥᵢ →	[oː, ọː,ǫː: . . .uː]ᵥᵢ

Stage I of (16) shows one attested case of language-specific variation: fronted variants of /uː/ occur, though they are not as frequent token-wise as non-fronted variants; and raised and lowered variants of /oː/ occur, but they are not as frequent as non-raised and non-lowered variants. In Stage II, the language learner is exposed to variation where fronted variants of /uː/ have higher frequency than non-fronted variants.[20] The effect of this high frequency is repositioning of the high vowel category: $u\textfollowed> y$ on the part of the listener. When this repositioning occurs, the listener as speaker will continue to produce certain tokens of /oː/ which are close to [uː]. However, it is possible that, all else being equal, these "extreme" examples of the phonological category for /oː/ may be judged by subsequent generations of listeners as better exemplars of the category than the more frequently occuring ones. This is because, as noted above, within exemplar theory, the probability for a category label is influenced both by the activation of exemplars having that label, and by competition from other labels having exemplars in the same area of the cognitive map. In this case, it is the earlier shift of $u\text> y\text$ which allows [uː] to be a potentially better exemplar of /oː/ than [oː] itself. In Stage III, the former listener/learner has become a new speaker; variation for /oː/ shifts in the speaker's own speech due to the extremity effect just noted, but listeners give more weight to extreme formant values due to their lack of competition from exemplars with competing labels, since there is no longer an /uː/ with exemplars occupying this space.

---

[20] Recall from 2.2 that the reasons for these shifts range from high-type frequency of phonetic contexts giving rise to fronting (via coarticulation), to high frequency of particularly common lexemes with strongly fronted vowels, to external influence of a dialect which is one chain-step ahead.

Under this view, chain shifts are not "sound changes" in the usual sense, but gradual remappings of an interconnected system of vocalic prototypes. A general prediction of this hypothesis is that chain shifts will be limited to phonological categories showing prototype effects as opposed to those showing categorical perception. Since consonant perception appears to be categorical, the general prediction is that vowel systems will typically show chain shifting while consonant systems will not. In this context, two potential counterexamples need to be examined.

First, it is sometimes claimed that lenitions and fortitions of the type illustrated in (17) are instances of chain shifting.

(17)   Chained shifts in lenition and fortition
        a. Intervocalic lenition in Gallo-Romance (Bourciez and
           Bourciez, 1967)
           $tt > t/$ V_V, $t > d/$V_V

        b. Post-tonic fortition in Yolgnu languages[21]
           $*b > p/$ V'_V, $*p > pp/$ V'_V

However, it is clear in all reported cases of this type that the changes are instances of the same general phonetically based sound change. In the Gallo-Romance change in (17a), we see evidence of gestural reduction in intervocalic position. This gestural reduction takes the long closure of the geminate to a point where it approaches the duration of short stops in other contexts. For the short t, gestural reduction results in durational shortening as well; voicing in the $t > d$ shift may be due to voice leakage, spontaneous voicing, or a percept of voicing. In the Yolgnu languages, post-tonic lengthening has resulted in a shift of short voiceless stops to geminates, and short voiced stops to short voiceless ones. The fact that the primary feature of fortition is longer closure duration is supported by the behavior of sonorants, which also undergo lengthening in the same context. LaVoie's (2001) study of lenition and fortition and their phonetic sources finds consistent and significant phonetic effects across consonant types in lenition and fortition environments. Though only some of these effects will be phonologized as sound change, as in the Gallo-Romance example, her findings clearly show that lenitions and fortitions affecting multiple series of consonants are expected as regular instances of sound change. No reference to "contrast-maintenance" is needed: the paired changes in (18a) and (18b) have parallel phonetic explanations based on parameters of hypo- versus hyperarticulated speech.

---

[21] This sound change is based on my own interpretation of the Yolgnu facts. See Waters' (1980, 1989) description of Djinang where /p, b/ are contrastive word-initially, but not in post-tonic position, and where post-tonic gemination is still productive for all consonants.

A second quite rare instance of a potential consonantal chain shift involves the $*t > k$ sound changes discussed in 5.4 and 5.5. Recall that $*t > k$ occurs as an independent development within four different groups of Austronesian languages. What is notable about this shift is that it only occurs in languages where an earlier $*k$ has been lost. Blust (1990) notes that the pattern is one of a "drag"-chain: the loss of Proto-Oceanic $*k$ leaves a position within the phoneme inventory which is filled by the $*t > k$ change. Numerous potential teleological accounts of these paired changes can be ruled out. Symmetry of phoneme inventory is unhelpful: the Hawaiian inventory has /n m ŋ/, so the shift of $*t > k$ creates a new t-gap in the system. Unlike some of the vocalic chain shifts discussed by Labov (1994), maintenance of contrast cannot be invoked as a catalyst for change since the shift of $*t > k$ after $*k > ʔ$ does not prevent any potential merger. The principle of least effort also seems unhelpful: there is no clear evidence that [k] requires less effort than [t]. If anything, common velar fronting in child-language acquisition suggests that [k] has a higher level of production difficulty than [t] in the early years (Grunwell 1982). Nor does maximization of perceptual distance seem likely as an impetus for sound change: the acoustic feature [grave] (Jakobson, Fant, and Halle 1952) specifies both [k] and [p], in contrast to [t] which is acute. General appeals to markedness fare no better. The claim that k is simply a better stop than t is not supported by typological studies, and is in conflict with at least some phonological proposals for coronal as the unmarked place of articulation (Paradis and Prunet 1991). The only teleological account which remains is one which has no principled motivation: $*t > k$ takes place to fill the k-gap. Apart from its stipulative nature, this teleological account fails to explain why $*t > k$ takes place in some Polynesian languages (Hawaiian, Samoan, Luangiua), but not others (Tahitian).

In 5.4 I suggested an account of this sound change based on the perceptual simlarities of [t] and [k] in contrast to [p]. The general suggestion was that, in acquiring a language with only [p] and [t] as input oral-stop categories, the language learner makes the association between /t/ and the phonetic features of long VOT and high-amplitude burst, and the association between /p/ and the phonetic features of short VOT and low-amplitude burst. Based on these associations, and the absence of any phonetic exemplars in the neighborhood of [k], [k]s are spontaneously produced as instances of the long VOT and high-amplitude burst category. From this variation, [k] is chosen as the best exemplar of the category "long VOT," and sound change is complete.

These instances of $*t > k$ appear to be the only instances of regular consonant change which show the hallmark of a true chain shift. A gap in the acoustic-perceptual space is opened up, but rather than the gradual movement over time we see in vocalic chains, we find an abrupt categorical shift in consonant place of articulation. I have suggested that this is due to alternative cue-based categorizations of /p t/ stop systems versus /p t k/ stop systems. What the *$t > k$ changes and the vocalic chain shifts discussed above have in common is that a particular exemplar of a category which is distant from the original prototype may actually be interpreted as a better exemplar of the category in question.

In sum, I have suggested that vocalic chain shifts are the combined result of intrinsic variation with the prototype structure of vocalic categories. Chain shifts can arise naturally when a formerly occupied area of the psycho-acoustic space is opened up, with variation giving rise to better prototypes of a pre-existing category in the newly opened space. This hypothesis cannot be directly extended to consonant shifts, since consonant perception appears to be categorical and not structured with prototypes. The independent *$t > k$ changes in Austronesian constitute potential counterexamples to this hypothesis. However, the phonetically based classification of stops by phonetic features of VOT and burst amplitude is potentially gradient, allowing for the same general treatment as the more common vocalic chain shifts.

10.3.3   Lenition and the minimization of articulatory effort

Many sound changes have been attributed to minimization of articulatory effort. These include: consonant shortening, lenition, and loss; vowel shortening, centralization, reduction and loss; final devoicing; and assimilation under coarticulation. A non-teleological model of lenition was presented in chapter 6. Lenition processes are common because across the hyper-to-hypoarticulated speech continuum (Lindblom 1990a), lenited forms will always exist. If these forms, due to their high frequency, become the basis of phonological categorization in the course of language acquisition, then lenition, as sound change, will have occurred. Extensive phonetic support for this model is found in LaVoie (2001). Here, I highlight the non-teleological nature of the proposed account.

A good example of the range of variation possible in surface forms is found in Florentine Italian (Giannelli and Savoia 1979).

(18)   The hyper-to-hypoarticulation continuum in Florentine Italian

	slow/ careful	moderate/ natural	fast/ careless	extremely fast/ careless	
a.	/la tavola/	la θavola	la θ̬avola	la (ð̬)aoḷa	la aoḷa 'the table'
b.	/e dɔrme/	e dɔrme	e ð̬ɔrme	e ð̬ɔrm̩e	e ɔrm̩e 's/he sleeps'
c.	/brutto/	brutto	brutto	brutto	bruθθo 'ugly'
d.	/freddo/	freddo	freddo	freddo	freððo 'cold'

The forms in (18a, b) show that intervocalic short voiced stops can be produced as stops in slow or careful speech, while short voiceless stops are typically spirantized. At moderate and faster rates of speech, all short stops are spirantized, and at the fastest rate of speech, stops can be lost altogether. For the geminates in (18c, d), the situation is slightly different; geminates, having longer closure durations, may undergo gestural reduction, but this reduction only results in lenition at the fastest rate of speech. The fact that many sound changes can be viewed in terms of effort minimization results from the fact that these sound changes reflect phonologizations of the temporal compressions and gestural reductions, like those shown in (18), which commonly occur in casual speech. There is no need to invoke "effort minimization" as an independent principle driving sound change: real-time gestural reduction and compression give rise to precisely the variation from which common and recurrent instances of leniting sound change can and do evolve.

In this context, it is worth considering the strong claim that all regular phonetically motivated sound change involves minimization of articulatory effort (Pagliuca and Mowrey 1987; Mowrey and Pagliuca 1995; Bybee 2001: 77–81).[22] First, consider sound changes whose sources lie in misperception, like $\theta > f$. I know of no studies suggesting that labiodental fricatives involve less articulatory effort than dental fricatives; in fact, since dental fricatives are frequently the lenited counterparts of dental stops, while bilabial fricatives result from lenition of bilabial stops, there is the suggestion in sound-change typology that labio-dental fricatives involve more articulatory effort than dental fricatives. Another perceptually based change is the neutralization of place of articulation in certain positions, like the word-final $p > k$ and $m > \eta$ changes in Atayal discussed in 10.2. Here again, there is little evidence bearing on the articulatory effort involved in labial as opposed to velar stops: both points of articulation are made use of in at least one consonant in all of the world's languages, and both appear early in the course of language acquisition.

The strongest argument against the view of effort minimization as the guiding force in sound change is the existence of sound changes which involve segmental lengthening, strengthening, and vowel insertion. LaVoie (2001, chapter 2) provides a cross-linguistic summary of strengthening processes, including occlusivization, frication of glides, and gemination, and several examples have already been mentioned in this chapter. Recall from (11) the Totoli reflexes of Sulawesi final consonants which show final vowel insertion and gemination. Even under the

---

[22] Bybee's (2001: 78) position on whether all sound change stems from assimilation (retiming) or reduction is that the proposal is "of considerable theoretical interest and should definitely be attempted." However, after examining several counterexamples she concludes that "strengthening does take place under certain conditions" (p. 81).

most liberal definition of lenition as gestural reduction or overlap, it is difficult to view this as a weakening process. Another example of historical strengthening is the post-tonic lengthening of Yolgnu languages. Other examples of post-tonic fortition in Australian languages include $l > t$ in Nhanda (Blevins 1999a, 2001a) and pre-stopping of laterals in Arrernte (Koch 1997). In general, lengthening and fortition under stress are common cross-linguistically, and instantiate the commonly noted phonetic association between stressed syllables and articulatory force.

In sum, there is little evidence that effort minimization plays a direct role in sound change. The intrinsic properties of slow versus fast speech and careful versus casual speech provide phonetic transforms of the speech stream which occur in all well-documented languages. Phonetic strengthenings and weakenings are measurable at the opposite ends of the speech continuum, and it is the phonologization of variable leniting events at the non-careful end of the continuum which ultimately give rise to regular instances of leniting sound change.

10.3.4   Polarization and the maximization of perceptual contrast

Whereas maintenance of contrast is proposed as a goal of chain shifts, maximization of perceptual contrast has also been suggested as a driving force in sound change. The view that sound change improves contrast was proposed as early as Passy (1890: 227) and plays a major role in Martinet's (1955) conception of sound change. In more recent times, the principle of maximal contrast has been most closely associated with phonetic work on vowel systems, starting with Liljencrants and Lindblom (1972) and continuing in work on hypoarticulation (e.g. Lindblom et al. 1992; Johnson et al. 1993). In this section, I argue that the principle of maximal perceptual contrast suffers the same general weakness as that of articulatory ease: it is too strong, since complete mergers and contextual neutralizations are quite common; and it is also too weak, since it does not account for the fact that sound change results in maximizing perception only where it has a clear source in CHANGE, CHANCE, or CHOICE.

Outside of the chain shifts already discussed, reference to contrast maximization in sound change is not common. Hock (1991: 75 passim) uses the term "polarization" to refer to cases where there is a tendency to mark "phonological distinctiveness by an increase in phonetic distinctiveness." For example, in his discussion of palatalization in Indo-European, Hock attributes the change of palatalized velars to pure palatals to maximization of phonological contrast. "For velars . . . polarization is accomplished most easily by the shifting of the palatalized segments toward the palatal area of articulation" (1991: 76). However, Guion (1998) makes a strong case that velar palatalization is perceptually conditioned, and that velar palatalization arises from a perceptually conditioned reanalysis of faster speech. Given that coarticulation between velars and high vowels is common in fast speech, her findings that velars are highly confusable with palato-alveolar affricates allow for an account of velar palatalization which makes no direct reference to perceptual contrast. Palatalized velars often shift to palato-alveolars because they sound like palato-alveolars.

As another potential case of contrast maximization, we can again examine the reflexes of final $*p$, $*t$, $*k$ shown in (11). In order to maximize contrast, the stops in Totoli are audibly released, and the language is spared from the final place neutralization attested in Duri, Makasar, and Wolio. But if sound change serves to maximize contrast, why has only Totoli been able to make use of this principle? In the spirit of optimality accounts, one might propose that contrast maximization and articulatory ease are competing constraints, with distinct rankings in the different daughter languages. Then we must ask why the different daughter languages have different constraint rankings? If this results from hypotheses based on auditory input, then *why not refer directly to that input as the ultimate source of the distinct pathways of change*? As suggested above, in this case, the hyper-to-hypoarticulated continuum of the proposed proto-language will contain both audibly released and non-released final consonants. The high frequency of audible release in one dialect may give rise to the Totoli pattern, while higher frequency of non-released stops may result in the attested patterns of final neutralization. No reference to contrast maximization is necessary.

The one exception, already mentioned, is in cases where a sound change would give rise to homophony, especially where whole paradigms are involved. If the analysis of antigemination in Blevins (to appear b) is correct, general syncope can be blocked where it would lead to homophony for contrasting forms within a paradigm. Within this account, hyperarticulation yields antigemination and arises precisely where speakers are attempting to maximize a perceptual contrast.

In sum, there is little evidence that maximization of perceptual contrast, independent of paradigm-internal homophony, plays a direct role in sound change. The intrinsic properties of hyper- versus hypoarticulated speech provide phonetic transforms of the speech stream which occur in all documented languages. Coarticulation may give rise to instances of misperception, which may or may not be viewed as maximizing perceptual distance. And sound changes involving strengthening will appear to maximize contrast, though their ultimate source will always be statable without reference to contrast maximization.

10.4   Naturalness and reconstruction

The evolutionary approach to sound change is consistent with the major findings in historical linguistics. Phonetically based sound change is regular, but may be gradient, involving slight changes in articulatory or perceptual targets, or abrupt, involving articulatory leaps. Sound change may have its source in surface phonetic variation, the ambiguity of long-domain features, misperception, or any combination of these. But the implications of the evolutionary approach go far beyond simple confirmation of historical principles. One of the central claims of this model is that recurrent sound patterns in synchronic phonological systems reflect recurrent sound change. A direct consequence of this approach is that regular sound change is the locus of naturalness in phonology.[23]

From a methodological perspective, there are two ways natural phonological processes can be studied directly: by looking closely at cases of regular sound change, and sound change in progress, and by the techniques of experimental phonetics and phonology. The study of synchronic phonological systems alone will never yield a precise understanding of natural sound patterns, since, as detailed in chapter 3, regular sound patterns may be the output of morphological analogy, the end result of rule telescoping or rule inversion, or the end result of accidental convergences on an exceptionless surface sound pattern. In any of these cases, a regular synchronic sound pattern will not directly reflect regular sound change. There is some irony in this state of affairs. For many decades, phonologists have struggled with ways of incorporating naturalness into synchronic accounts. Now, it appears that naturalness plays no role in synchronic systems, and that the only domain in which pure natural phonology will be reflected is in the study of regular sound change.

While detailed studies of regular sound change and speech perception and production will continue to inform our view of what sound patterns are natural, cross-linguistic studies of phonetic variation in speech may illuminate our understanding of sound change. By assuming that the patterns of phonetic variation for a proto-language have the same properties as attested continuums of hyper-to-hypoarticulated speech, and that phonetically natural sound change may have its source in this variation, phonetic reconstruction can be the key to understanding certain

---

[23] Recall from chapters 2 and 3 that Evolutionary Phonology distinguishes itself from Natural Phonology (Stampe 1973; Donegan and Stampe 1979) by providing a formal model of sound change, including subphonemic change and phonologization, and by providing historical explanations for both natural and unnatural sound patterns. The historical explanations for the rarity of certain segment and contrast types in chapter 8 also go well beyond the limited domain of explanation of Natural Phonology.

recalcitrant cases of sound change. An example from the well-studied history of Indo-European is instructive.

As is well known, the first step in Grimm's Law by which voiceless stops become fricatives has one systematic exception: voiceless stops do not become fricatives if they are preceded by obstruents. The general pattern is illustrated in (19), with exceptions for series 1 shown in (20).

(19)   Grimm's Law (Garrett and Hale 1993: 1)

	Stops before Grimm's Law	Output of Grimm's Law
series 1	$*p *t *k *k^w$	$*f *\theta *x *x^w$
series 2	$*b *d *g *g^w$	$*p *t *k *k^w$
series 3	$*b^h *d^h *g^h *g^{wh}$	$*b *d *g *g^w$

(20)   One exception to Grimm's Law (Garrett and Hale 1993: 2)

$*p *t *k *k^w$ unchanged after obstruents

	Stops before Grimm's Law		Output of Grimm's Law	
a.	$*g^h ástis$	>	$*g^h ástis$	> Gothic *gasts* 'guest'
b.	$*stéig^h eti$	>	$*stéig^h e\theta i$	> Gothic *steigi θ* 's/he climbs'
c.	$*nák^w tū$	>	$*náx^w tū$	> Gothic *naht* 'night (acc. sg.)'
d.	$*kaptás$	>	$*xaftás$	> Old High German *haft* 'taken'

Garrett and Hale (1993) suggest that the Grimm's Law shift of voiceless unaspirated stops to voiceless fricatives involved an intermediate stage where voiceless stops were aspirated. They further suggest that as with many modern languages (e.g. English), this allophonic aspiration was limited to syllable-initial position, and was therefore absent after $*s$, and after other obstruents (20c, d).[24] Under this analysis, there were originally two allophones for each consonant in series 1 of (19): $*p *t *k *k^w$ after obstruents, and $*p^h *t^h *k^h *k^{wh}$ elsewhere. Aspiration under Grimm's Law gave rise to a common instance of CHANGE: a perceptual reinterpretation of phonetic aspiration as fricative noise. As such, this sound change did not affect the unaspirated allophones of the voiceless stops. By recognizing phonetically based allophony in Proto-Germanic, one can account naturally for the seeming exceptions to Grimm's Law.

To illustrate how a similar methodology may suggest solutions where there are many more historical uncertainties, consider Proto-Algonquian $*\theta$ as reconstructed by Bloomfield (1946: 87). There is some debate as to whether this segment was phonetically a voiceless dental fricative [θ], or a voiceless lateral fricative [ɬ]. Reflexes of the segment include θ (Arapaho), t (Cree, Atsina, Cheyenne), and l (Miami, Delaware, Abenaki). The changes $*\theta > ɬ$ and $*ɬ > \theta$ are both assumed to be equally "natural"

---

[24] Since the first stop in the voiceless stop clusters in (20c, d) does undergo Grimm's Law, the facts suggest that in all clusters of this type, the whole cluster is specified as [spread glottis], with phonetic realization of this feature on only the first consonant.

due to the perceptual similarity of the two sounds. However, $*\theta > l$ does not look phonetically natural, as noted by Picard (1984). Lenition of [θ] typically involves voicing, shortening, and ultimate loss, as in (18), not the addition of a lateral gesture. In addition, there are Proto-Algonquian etyma in which either $*l$ or $*\theta$ is possible (Goddard 1982: 21, footnote 18). One possibility is that Proto-Algonquian $*ł$ had voiced and voiceless phonetic realizations. Devoicing of /l/ is common cross-linguistically: it occurs in English (after word-initial /s/), in Misantla Totonac where /l/ is realized as [ł] in syllable codas, and has arguably occurred in the history of Yurok, where /l/ and /ł/ are in near complementary distribution, with /l/ in pre-vocalic position, and /ł/ elsewhere (Blevins and Garrett 2001). By recognizing a proto-phoneme $*ł$ in Algic, with voiced and voiceless phonetic variants, sound changes posited for daughter languages can be better understood as phonetically natural processes.

10.5   Towards a theory of drift

Recurrent, or parallel changes in related languages which cannot be attributed to chance, universals or diffusion, have been categorized as instances of *drift* (Sapir 1921). Under drift, languages which are no longer in contact are believed to move in similar directions due to the continued, independent operation of inherited structural pressures which are arguably language specific. One goal of historical linguistics is to define relationships between inherited structural pressures and changes which have been identified as instances of drift. Work in this area is not voluminous but includes Lakoff (1972), Vennemann (1975, 1988), Campbell and Ringen (1980), and Andersen (1987).

For any source of ambiguity in the CCC-model of sound change, we can view "drift" as the case where two potential phonological analyses, A and B, compete, and one of them has already been unambiguously identified elsewhere, while the other has not. In the case of compensatory lengthening discussed in 6.4 and 9.2.2, the emergence of a long and short vowel contrast from unambiguous tokens can give rise to shifts where vowels of ambiguous, intermediate lengths, are analyzed by learners as long. This priming effect is attributed to Structural Analogy, repeated in (21).

(21)   STRUCTURAL ANALOGY
        In the course of language acquisition, the existence of a
        phonological contrast between A and B will result in more
        instances of sound change involving shifts of ambiguous
        elements to A or B than if no contrast between A and B existed.

Recall that Structural Analogy is attributed to analogical learning which is thought to characterize phonological acquisition (Wedel 2004). Structural Analogy as a factor in language acquisition is similar in intention to the phonological "priming effect" proposed in Kiparsky (1995: 656) which states that "redundant features are likely to be phonologized if the language's phonological representations have a class node to host them." However, it differs in at least three significant ways from Kiparsky's proposal. First, it is not limited to "redundant" features; since the phonological system is being acquired, and since markedness constraints play no role, there is no sense in which any feature is more or less redundant than any other in the course of phonological acquisition. Second, it is independent of particular theory-internal details (e.g. class nodes); whatever model is used to represent, say, vowel length, Structural Analogy predicts that compensatory lengthening as instances of CHANCE will be more common in languages having pre-existing contrasts than in languages which do not. Finally, Structural Analogy is not limited to segmental contrasts, but also has implications for stress patterns, syllable structure, and other potentially non-local sound patterns.

Extension of Structural Analogy to drift involving vowel syncope is detailed in Blevins and Blust (2003). Based on instances of apparent drift within the Austronesian language family, it is suggested that the pre-existence of unambiguous word-final closed syllables plays a role in sound change. Stated as a universal tendency, the claim is that languages with closed syllables show a tendency to syncopate short unstressed vowels in VC^VCV strings, while languages without closed syllables do not exhibit parallel syncopating sound changes. This universal tendency is attributed to Structural Analogy: an ambiguous . . . C^VC . . . sequence which could be analyzed as . . . CVC . . . or as . . . C.C . . . is resolved in favor of categories or strings which can be unambiguously identified. In languages with word-final closed syllables, syncope is much more common than in languages which lack word-final closed syllables.

This general account of drift makes sense not only of individual sound changes, but also of sound changes which, cumulatively, appear to converge on certain syllabic templates. Consider, for example, the evolution of open syllables in the history of Slavic, sometimes referred to as the Slavic "open-syllable conspiracy" (Hock 1991: 161–62). The earliest sound change in the sequence of documented changes appears to be the loss of certain word-final consonants. Subsequent changes involving metathesis, epenthesis, resyllabification, and loss of word-medial coda consonants, which occur over the next several hundred years (Nowak 2002), may be viewed as a consequence of Structural Analogy. Once final consonants are lost, there are fewer "unambiguous" tokens of

C-final syllables. As a result, sound patterns which are ambiguous between closed and open syllables, are less likely to be analyzed as closed syllables.

Structural Analogy may also be responsible for learned aspects of syllabification like those discussed in 9.1.5. Consider the case of Cheke Holo (aka Maringe, Hograno, and A'ara), a language of Santa Isabel in the Solomon Islands. In Cheke Holo, all words end in vowels, but can begin with V, C or CC. Medial consonant clusters are syllabified as complex CC onsets (White et al., 1988; White 1995; Blevins 2003b). Since there are no unambiguous instances of closed syllables in the language, medial VCCV is analyzed as V.CCV, not as VC.CV. Although the Cheke Holo facts may not smack of "drift" in the traditional sense, they are parallel, under this analysis, to attested cases of Slavic resyllabification where certain *VC.CV sequences are reflected as V.CCV.

11　Beyond phonology

> Our ignorance of the laws of variation is profound.　Darwin (1859)

The previous chapters present a sustained argument that many common sound patterns are the result of parallel evolution. Certain sound changes are frequent due to intrinsic properties of speech: some sounds or sound sequences are more likely to be misperceived than others (CHANGE); certain features with long temporal domains are harder to localize than others (CHANCE); and inherent variation along the careful/casual or hyper-to-hypoarticulated speech continuum gives rise to variants with multiple categorical interpretations (CHOICE). A plausible working hypothesis is that all regular spontaneous sound changes fall into one or more of these categories. Moreover, from this perspective, once historical explanations are found for common sound patterns, the same phonetic explanations need not, and indeed *should not*, be encoded in synchronic grammars. Synchronic grammars show no bifurcation of "natural" versus "unnatural" phonological alternations. Regular alternations are learned quickly and easily. Exceptionless alternations are typically productive. However, as summarized in chapter 9, there is only a tendency for surface-true generalizations to directly reflect natural sound change. There is no evidence that phonetic explanations play any role in synchronic phonological systems, and certain "marked" segment types and sound patterns appear to be no more unstable, historically, than unmarked ones.

If the language faculty is an integrated (cognitive) system, with multiple subcomponents, as suggested by decades of accumulated data on language deficits (Kean 1985; Caplan 1987; Bates and Wulfeck 1989; Grodzinsky 1990; Clahsen 1999) and lexical priming (Katz et al. 1987; Marslen-Wilson et al. 1993, 1994), and if an evolutionary view is on the right track, then one might expect to find historical explanations for distributional patterns of other linguistically significant units. This chapter outlines a number of cases of this sort. The first section suggests how manual/visual patterns in signed language support the idea that recurrent sound patterns are emergent properties of grammar. This is followed by several brief case studies of morphological and syntactic patterns which violate suggested universals, but have well-understood historical sources. The conclusion outlines the application of an evolutionary approach to grammatical description and explanation, emphasizing the goal of capturing surface-true generalizations and productive rules of grammar.

11.1 Beyond spoken language: the visual patterns of sign language

Not all natural human languages are spoken languages. In Deaf communities in many parts of the world, independent signed languages have evolved. For example, British Sign Language is distinct from French and American Sign Language, and these languages do not appear to be related to Chinese Sign Language, Nicaraguan Sign Language, or Hausa Sign Language. Sign languages of the Deaf are "fully developed human languages independent of the languages spoken in the linguistic communities in the same region" (Wilcox 1990: 141). There are nearly as many different signed languages as there are Deaf communities, leading at least one researcher to suggest that "there is no single country in the world where deaf people have no sign language" (Andersson 1990: 157).

Where spoken languages are articulated using the larynx, vocal folds, and mouth, and perceived with the ears, signed languages are articulated primarily with the hands and face, and perceived with the eyes. Despite these significant modal differences, there is good evidence that signed language uses the same general neural structures as spoken languages, and that signed languages and spoken languages have similar patterns of acquisition (Bellugi and Klima 1990; Newport and Meier 1987; Kyle and Woll 1991). Signed languages also show evidence of the same distinct levels of representation as spoken languages: visual "phonetics," visual "phonology," morphology, syntax, and semantics. Given the numerous parallels between signed and spoken language, an obvious question is *why* such parallels exist.

In the realm of phonology, one answer which has been proposed is that the parallels reflect aspects of Universal Grammar (Liddell and Johnson 1989; Sandler 1989; Wilbur 1990; Brentari 1995). On this view, segments, features and syllables, are taken to be organizational phonological primitives. Within each domain, modality-specific content is manipulated or categorized. So while spoken languages have features like [voiced], [nasal], etc. which refer to articulatory, acoustic, and perceptual properties of sounds, sign languages have features like [spread], [hooked], [closed], etc., to refer to specific handshapes. While these approaches have illuminated many aspects of sign language structure, Uyechi (1996) presents the first theoretical framework in which the visual phonology of sign language is based not on theories of spoken language phonology, but on primary data from sign language.

In her study of visual patterns in American Sign Language (ASL), Uyechi (1996) demonstrates that there are difficulties in applying spoken language constructs to sign language data. Her focus on the modality differences between speech and sign highlights expected and attested differences between the two modalities. Most generally, where auditory perception must take place over a temporal interval, visual perception can occur at a discrete point in time, or over time intervals. This asymmetry between the two modalities results in strikingly different phonological atoms: in spoken language, the atoms of speech are segments, which require time intervals to be produced and perceived; in sign language, the proposed atoms of speech are what Uyechi refers to as "transition units." The range of properties associated with segments in spoken languages and transition units in sign are summarized in (1), adapted from Uyechi (1996: 225).

(1)   A comparison of phonological atoms in spoken and signed language

Spoken language segments	Signed language transition units
a. A segment associates a time unit with a feature complex.	A transition unit associates a time unit with a spatial unit.
b. A segment represents a time interval.	A transition unit represents a time interval, specified by distinct endpoints.
c. All segments are temporally ordered.	Transition units may be temporally ordered, or simultaneous (unordered).
d. A segment represents all the properties of an articulatory gesture.	A transition unit represents part of the properties of an articulatory gesture.

Uyechi (1996: 225) summarizes the comparison as follows:

The segment and transition unit are similar because they relate gestural information to time, and because they mediate between that combination of information and the next level of organization – for spoken language phonology, the syllable, and for visual phonology, the cell. But after that initial set of similarities, the properties of the constructs diverge. Specifically, they differ in their interpretation of time and their organization of information.

She observes further that:

> Whereas the constructs in spoken language phonology are distinctive features that classify segments, the constructs in visual phonology such as location and orientation are dyadic relations that specify relations between constructs. From this perspective the differences are unlikely to be resolved by adjusting the organization of the spoken language phonology to accommodate the properties of the visual phonology, or tweaking the constructs of visual phonology to more closely resemble spoken language constructs. (Uyechi 1996: 227)

In other words, although there are gross structural similarities in the organization of lower-level units, which are not individually meaningful, onto larger units that are, visual phonology has properties which follow directly from the fact that multiple image parameters can be represented at a single point in time (e.g. handshape, location, orientation, facial expression). The fact that all sign languages share these features follows from the modality: over time, patterns of movement, location, handshape, etc., will converge on systems where transition units, with the properties specified in (1), emerge, since such systems represent smooth motoric patterns and salient visual images. As shown by the work of Bellugi and Fischer (1972) and Klima and Bellugi (1979), although the average duration of a single sign is longer than a single word in spoken languages, sentence production rate is similar in both modalities, due to simultaneous expression in sign.

Of course, modality differences are expected, if grammar is malleable and not entirely mode-specific. From an evolutionary perspective, in which the majority of sound patterns constitute language-specific learned information, the facts of sign language phonology are not problematic. The Deaf language learner may come to the task of language acquisition with neural circuitry capable of distinguishing voiced from voiceless sounds, nasal from oral sounds, etc. However, without auditory input, these categories are not defined, and are ultimately replaced with visual phonological features if the learner is raised in a signing environment. Under this approach, the set of primitives in need of replacement is quite small: phonological features, syllables, and possibly higher-level prosodic constituents. Under other conceptions of grammar, for example, Optimality Theory, the mode-specific nature of sign language is more problematic. With an Optimality approach, an extensive collection of constraints for spoken languages must cooccur with signed language constraints, with every human being endowed with grammatical notions of markedness for both spoken and signed utterances. While such a scenario is not inconceivable, there is at present no reason to believe that humans are in fact endowed with parallel inventories of highly mode-specific constraints.

11.2   Evolutionary morphology: words and paradigms

Morphology is traditionally defined as the study of word structure. In many morphological studies, markedness and universality have been invoked to account for recurrent tendencies in word and paradigm structure. In this section I discuss two morphological constraints proposed in the literature, one related to morphological constituency, and the other to morphological feature structure. In both cases, I suggest that the proposed universals, like many of the sound patterns discussed in part II, are emergent properties of grammar. The particular counterexamples discussed suggest that these morphological constraints have no formal status in the synchronic morphological systems of individual languages. Word structure thus appears to be another area of grammar where "our ignorance of the laws of variation is profound." I suggest, however, that as our understanding of potential pathways of evolution within morphological systems deepens, so will the likelihood of finding explanations for recurrent aspects of word and paradigm structure.

11.2.1   Constraints on affix order

The claim that word-internal affixes are sequenced according to grammatical principles goes back at least to Jakobson ([1957] 1971b: 146). In this work, Jakobson suggests that affixes are sequenced according to their category affinity. This same idea has been suggested in more recent work on morpheme order and scope based on broader typological studies. The basic idea is that a morpheme Y, with scope over a morpheme X, occurs outside of X within the word (Bybee 1985a, b; Baker 1985, 1988; Alsina 1999; Rice 2000). Schematically, in a language with stems and suffixes, the structure of the word will be [[stem] . . . X . . . Y . . .] where Y has scope over X. The inverse ordering *[[stem] . . . Y . . . X . . .] is ungrammatical, unless X can be interpreted as having scope over Y. In the works just cited, the term "scope" refers to semantic compositionality, in some cases expressed via intermediate syntactic operations or representations. I will refer to these approaches generally as those making use of "scope constraints" on affix order. Two general questions arise. First, do scope constraints on morpheme order adequately describe the patterns of affix order which exist in the world's languages? Second, if there is a tendency for morpheme order to reflect syntactic or semantic compositionality, does this tendency reflect synchronic scope constraints, or can it be viewed as an emergent property of grammar?

In answer to the first question, there is ample evidence that scope constraints do not adequately describe the patterns of affix order which exist in the world's languages. See, for example, Hewitt (1979), Ackerman (2002), and Hyman (2002) for examples from Georgian, Hungarian and Bantu respectively. In answer to the second question, two recent studies of suffix ordering within the Bantu verb highlight the role of inheritance and grammaticization independent of semantic scope in accounting for morpheme order (Good 2001; Hyman 2002). Bybee et al. (1991: 19) take a more general position with respect to morpheme order: "grammatical material develops whatever position it happens to be in when grammaticization occurs." Together, these studies suggest that constraints on morpheme order are language-specific, learned, properties of languages, and that scope constraints may play no role in synchronic grammars.

11.2.2 *Paradigm leveling and markedness*

In many languages, inflected word forms are organized into inflectional paradigms. Within paradigms, certain morphological features have traditionally been taken to constitute the unmarked members of oppositions. Notably, Jakobson (1932) proposes an asymmetrical analysis of agreement features in Russian, where unmarked features include singular and third person. The unmarked status of third person in contrast to second and first persons is echoed in the work of Kuryłowicz (1964), Watkins (1962), Greenberg (1966b), Bybee (1985a), J. P. Blevins (2001) and many others. Originally, the unmarked status of third-person-singular forms was proposed to account for their wider syntactic distribution. For example, third person singular forms are used in impersonal constructions where they may indicate the absence of person marking (Jakobson 1932; J. P. Blevins 2001). The unmarked status of third-person forms has also been claimed to have morphotactic implications: third-person-singular forms can be minimally distinct from stem forms, because they encode no additional marked features (Kuryłowicz 1964). It is this same unmarked status which allows third-person forms to serve as the basis for paradigm leveling, since third-person-singular forms can be reinterpreted as basic stems (Watkins 1962).[1]

However, an example of paradigm leveling in the history of Yurok casts doubt on the role of universal markedness in paradigm leveling.

---

[1] This tendency for paradigm leveling to take third-person-singular forms as pivots is sometimes referred to as "Watkins' Law," referring to Watkins' (1962) observation of this tendency in the evolution of Indo-European verbal inflection.

As detailed in Blevins (to appear c), leveling in pronominal prefix verbs is to first-person-singular indicative forms, despite the fact that third-singular verb forms are morphotactically and morphosyntactically the least marked verb forms in the language.[2] In this particular case leveling is clearly not the result of phonological change, nor is there any other analogical source for the leveling in question. The primary significance of this example is to illustrate that while there might be an observed tendency for paradigms to level to phonologically or morphologically "unmarked" forms, this tendency cannot be elevated to the status of a universal constraint on paradigm leveling.

11.3   Evolutionary syntax: understanding grammar

Syntax is traditionally concerned with the study of phrase and clause structure. Many syntactic studies appeal to putatively universal constraints that incorporate some notion of markedness to account for recurrent word-order patterns, or nearly exceptionless associations between features and syntactic categories. An instructive example is Greenberg's Universal No. 3: "Languages with dominant VSO order are always prepositional" (Greenberg 1966a: 78). While this generalization holds for the majority of languages with fixed VSO constituent order, there are notable exceptions: e.g. Persian combines VSO word order with post-positions. Nevertheless, there is a clear tendency for verb-initial languages to have prepositions and for verb-final languages to have post-positions. This correlation is often referred to as cross-category harmony. The explanations for cross-category harmony range from accounts based on semantic analogy and grammatical simplicity (e.g. Hawkins 1979, 1983) or processing ease (Hawkins 1991), to those in which the tendency is formulated as an inviolable constraint (e.g. the "head parameter" of X-bar theory as proposed by Jackendoff 1977 and developed by Chomsky 1981, 1982). Given the extent to which emergent sound patterns reflect historical sound changes, it does not seem unreasonable to ask whether tendencies like cross-category harmony may likewise reflect the historical origin of adpositions, specifically the fact that many derive from verbs (or nouns).

11.3.1   The emergence of cross-categorial harmony

As it turns out, the historical literature contains a great many well-documented cases of verbs or auxiliaries shifting to adpositions in a range

---

[2] See J. P. Blevins (2001) where these two types of markedness are distinguished.

of unrelated languages. Consider Norman's (1988: 161) general statement on the history of prepositions in Chinese languages:

From a historical perspective it is clear that Chinese prepositions all derive from earlier verbs; some grammarians still consider them a type of verb . . . Even from a purely synchronic perspective, the verbal nature of prepositions is evident, since in many cases the same words that function as prepositions still function as full verbs as well.

An example is the locative verb *zài* in Mandarin, which can serve as a main locative verb, or as a locative preposition, and which derives historically from a locative main verb. Given the fixed word order V-O within the Chinese verb phrase, the category shift of verbs to adpositions has given rise to prepositional phrases P-NP. In other words, the simple category shift of verbs to adpositions accounts directly for the cross-category harmony of verb phrases and prepositional phrases found in the majority of Chinese languages.

The Chinese case has a mirror image in the Senufo languages discussed by Carlson (1991). In these Gur languages, constituent order is basically SOV. Direct objects precede the verb, but obliques follow, while an auxiliary element separates S and O. In line with the tendency for cross-category harmony, the language has post-positions. Carlson (1991: 205) summarizes his hypothesis:

the simple postpositions of Senufo languages descend from verbs. These verbs were used transitively in a case marking function, that is, they added locative, dative and benefactive arguments to the clause, one per verb, in a manner common to many serializing languages. It should be pointed out that such a use of serial verbs is already highly grammaticalized. The etymologies proposed . . . show that most of these verbs were already highly abstract long before the proto-Senufo stage. The development of a category of postpositions thus represents one part of the over-all trajectory of these morphemes from less to more grammaticalized.

An example of a post-position derived from an earlier verb is *na/la* 'at, on, to,' found in all the Senufo languages. This locative post-position derives from an earlier main verb **na* 'be at.'

Lichtenberk (1991) presents a detailed study of the evolution of verbs into prepositions in To'aba'ita, an Oceanic language. The basic word order of To'aba'ita is SVO, so the categorical shift of verbs to adpositions again results in cross-category harmony: verb phrases and prepositional phrases are both head-initial for the simple reason that verbs have become prepositions, with no independent changes in word order. Compare To'aba'ita *fasi/fa'isi*, the ablative preposition with verbal cognates in related Cristobal-Malaitan languages: Kwara'ae *fa'asi* 'leave, forsake, depart from'; Lau *fasi* 'lose.'

I follow many others in viewing the most significant factor in cross-categorial harmony between verb phrases and adpositional phrases as the common grammaticization of verbs into adpositions. The change in category of verbs to adpositions is one facet of general grammaticization patterns: lexical items evolve phonologically and semantically into grammatical elements, and eventually into bound forms (see Givón 1971; 1979; Lehmann 1982; Heine and Reh 1984; Traugott and Heine 1991; Mithun 2001). The position of grammatical elements and bound forms is expected to reflect the original position of the lexical material it evolved from, all else being equal. Within this approach, the frequency of certain types of grammaticization, e.g. the category shift of locative verbs to locative adpositions, gives rise to the observed tendency for cross-categorial harmony in word order between verb/complement and adposition/complement. This tendency is an emergent property of grammar. There is no universal which demands cross-categorial harmony, nor is there any markedness constraint which prohibits it. Understanding this syntactic tendency in terms of grammaticizition will allow us to better understand counterexamples to it, and various other properties of newly grammaticized adpositions which reflect their former status as verbs.

11.3.2 Rare combinations of syntactic features

Certain syntactic patterns are extremely rare in the world's languages. As an example, consider the fact that tense, aspect, and mood features are realized on verbs, auxiliaries, whole clauses, or as adverbial modifiers in most of the world's languages. Tense, aspect, and mood (TAM) are categories which specify features of the basic predication or event (Chung and Timberlake 1985). The most general proposal put forth to account for common realization of TAM as morphosyntactic features of verbs or verbal projections is that of structural isomorphism (Behaghel 1923–32; Vennemann 1973; Haiman 1985; Bybee 1985a, b). Under such accounts, linguistic structure reflects conceptual structure, and the proximity or cooccurence of elements within a clause is essentially iconic.

In many syntactic frameworks, the inherent specification of predicates for TAM features is directly encoded, so that any deviation from the morphosyntactic realization of these features on predicates is difficult to describe. Within Lexical Functional Grammar (Bresnan 2000) and Head-driven Phrase Structure Grammar (Pollard and Sag 1994), TAM features are typically passed from heads to mother nodes. Other frameworks pose similar restrictions. Within Role and Reference Grammar (Van Valin 1993) aspect is a nuclear operator which only modifies the predicate, while tense is an operator with clausal scope. And within the

Government and Binding framework (Chomsky 1981, 1986), the syntactic category INFL (inflection, a realization of tense and agreement features) is defined as the head of a clause, which selects a VP complement. All of these frameworks take the high frequency of TAM marking on verbs or clauses as an indicator of naturalness. Tense marking of nominals is unexpected and, in some frameworks, difficult to describe.

The rarity of true tense marking on nouns is well supported by cross-linguistic studies (Sadler and Nordlinger 2002). In fact, the morphological realization of tense on nominals is so rare that descriptions of such systems have given rise to initial reactions of incredulity on the part of researchers. Consider, for example, Dixon's (1976: 263) reaction to Mathews (1904) and Wurm (1972), who both describe Gurnu, an Australian language, as having a tense contrast realized directly on pronouns:

W[urm] uncritically repeats grammatical misstatements that originated in the "amateur literature"; in no case has any attempt been made to check original sources and re-examine a controversial problem. Thus W[urm] (83, 133) follows Capell 1956 in believing that "in some of the dialects of the Darling Group, the initial consonant of the personal pronouns undergoes change for tense; e.g. in Gurnu the first person singular pronoun forms for present, past and future are "ŋaḍu, waḍu, and gaḍu." This originated with Mathews 1904. Mathews was a surveyor and amateur linguist who gathered material on a considerable number of Australian languages between 1897 and 1912; he frequently doctored his fieldnotes for publication and . . . all his work must be treated with caution. An examination of Mathews' notebooks . . . reveals that what Mathews described as inflection of pronouns for tense was in fact the operation of a phonological sandhi-type rule. The canonical forms for tense morphemes appear to have been PRES-*ŋuna-*, PAST -*ŋaw-*, FUT -*rag-*; pronominal subject normally followed the verb, and its initial consonant would be dropped after a tense-final consonant. We thus have *bulga-ŋuna-ŋaḍu* 'I am hitting,' *bulga-ŋgaw-aḍu* 'I hit (past),' and *bulga-rag-aḍu* 'I will hit.' There is no alternation in the initial segment of any pronoun when it follows a vowel-final word, or occurs sentence-initially.

However, in this case, Wurm's descriptions were based not only on a careful reading of earlier sources, but also on work with some of the last speakers of the Baagandji dialects. Wurm and Hercus (1976) are able to show that, however one judges Mathews' skills as a linguist, in this instance, he seems to have had some of the facts right. The pronominal paradigms for Gurnu presented in Wurm and Hercus (1976: 40) show distinct present, past, and future forms for all pronouns: compare first singular absolutive present *ŋaba* with its past form *waba* and future form *gaba*. Wurm and Hercus (1976) demonstrate that the form of the tense-marked pronouns is independent of its linear position within the phrase and that the distinct phonological forms of pronouns cannot be attributed to a post-verbal (or general post-vocalic) sandhi rule.

The evolution of tense marking in Gurnu pronouns is not altogether mysterious. As suggested in Dixon's quote above, and by Wurm and Hercus (1976), the ŋ/w/g alternation of the tense-marked pronouns may originate from sandhi effects of an immediately preceding verb. Closely related dialects show relatively fixed verb-pronoun order, with pronouns grammaticized as verbal affixes or enclitics, and phonological sandhi at the verb-pronoun boundary (Wurm and Hercus 1976; Hercus 1982). Comparative evidence shows that the present-tense forms with initial ŋ reflect the original form of the independent (non-tense-marked) pronouns. Under the sandhi account, present-tense forms in Gurnu reflect the sequence verb stem + pronoun without change. I suggest that Gurnu past-tense forms with initial /w/ reflect resegmentation of bound pronouns like those in Baagandji (Hercus 1982: 109–10, 128), while those with initial /g/ can be analyzed as the consequence of phonological rule inversion applied to formerly V-initial bound pronouns.

Though tense marking of pronouns is extremely rare in the world's languages, synchronic accounts must be flexible enough to describe systems like that found in Gurnu. At the same time, we might question whether the rarity of such systems is something that should be encoded in synchronic grammars, or whether it is better viewed as another emergent property of grammar. In this Gurnu example, at least five independent factors seem to have played a role in the grammaticization of tense as a pronominal feature: (i) earlier inflected verbs with regular phonological effects on following pronouns including initial C-loss under sandhi (attested in all other dialects of Baagandji); (ii) limitation of the general C-loss sandhi rule to this particular context (attested in all other dialects of Baagandji); (iii) failure of post-verbal pronouns to undergo complete grammaticization as bound morphemes (similarly for pronouns in possessive constructions in Gurnu); (iv) reinterpretation of word boundary at the verb-pronoun boundary (cf. English *a newt* < *an ewt*, *a nickname* < *an eke-name*, etc.); (v) independent C-loss in pronouns giving rise to C-insertion for remaining V-initial bound pronouns (cf. other cases of phonological rule inversion). None of these factors is rare in isolation. However, the low probability of these factors cooccurring in a single language can be viewed as one factor contributing to the rarity of tense-aspect-mood marking of this type on pronouns.

11.4   The evolutionary approach: summary and implications

This chapter extends an evolutionary approach to other linguistic domains, suggesting how particular aspects of sign language structure, word structure, and phrase structure can be seen as emergent properties of grammar. Where historical explanations are available, there is no need to encode these tendencies within synchronic grammars, either as markedness constraints or structural primitives. The majority of the world's recurrent sound patterns can be attributed to common, phonetically motivated, sound changes. It could well be that recurrent tendencies in other areas of grammar are also susceptible to an analysis in terms of recurrent historical pathways of grammaticization. An evolutionary perspective would thereby greatly reduce the scope of synchronic grammatical descriptions, eliminating all properties that can be explained independently. In particular, innate predispositions would not simply be assumed for recurrent properties of synchronic grammars, but would be reserved for those common features that can be shown, without question, not to reflect parallel evolution among languages, or direct inheritance.

Given the important role of pathways of grammaticization in sections 11.2 and 11.3, it is worth stressing that not *all* aspects of morphological structure are claimed to reflect earlier syntax, nor are *all* universal morphological and syntactic tendencies attributed to pathways of grammaticization. As should be clear from the Yurok and Gurnu examples discussed above, sound patterns, paradigm structure, morphosyntactic realization rules, and syntactic categories may all play a role in change. The evolutionary position developed above thus differs little from that of Anderson (1992: 350) when he suggests that:

we cannot accept morphological structure uncritically as a reflection of (earlier) syntactic structure. This does not at all mean we should abandon the search for syntactic bases for morphological form, however: in fact, exactly the opposite is true. There is every reason to believe that much morphology does represent the reanalysis of earlier syntactic complexity; but since the relation between the two sorts of structure is not simple and direct, it is important to explore the principles involved in the process of morphologization.

As stressed in chapters 9 and 10, an evolutionary approach places phonological naturalness and explanation primarily within the domain of sound change as it occurs naturally in the course of language acquisition. Experimental phonology and phonetics will continue to discover easily confused percepts, just-noticeable differences along various continua, and the precise articulatory mechanisms of hyper- versus hypoarticulated speech. These studies will allow us to better understand more instances of regular sound change in terms of the microcosms of CHANGE, CHANCE, and CHOICE. And this new form of understanding may further free synchronic grammars from the burden of explanation and naturalness. By examining a range of unusual cases, it is hoped that we will come to understand the types of variables which can play a role in morphologization, and the ways that combinations of common properties may converge on uncommon grammatical systems. Synchronic morphological and syntactic accounts may then – like phonology – be liberated from the weight of comprehensive explanation.

The data in part II suggest that the majority of recurrent sound patterns in the world's languages reflect common instances of sound change, and leave few identifiable universal features of phonological systems. Some potential universals involve combinatorial categories, such as distinctive features, segments, and prosodic categories. If most other aspects of sound patterns are learned and language-specific, then it would not be surprising if other components of grammar had similarly low ratios of innate-to-learned properties. The role of learning has been uncontested in the area of lexical acquisition and storage. When a word is learned, a direct association between sound and meaning is established. During the early years of language acquisition, children learn thousands of sound-to-meaning correspondences, and at particular stages, dozens of new words can be acquired in a single day. Another area where language-specific learning has been uncontested is in the realm of phonetics. Phoneticians have long known that two categories, e.g. voiced versus voiceless sounds, will have different category boundaries in different languages. There is mounting evidence that phonetic instantiation of phonological categories is learned, language-specific, and based directly on auditory experience. One general implication of the evolutionary approach is that *most* of the content of traditional descriptive grammar constitutes learned aspects of human behavior. Phonological, morphological, and syntactic descriptions rarely posit more than several dozen rules or constraints. As long as these constraints are learnable from linguistic surface forms, classifying them as learned properties of the linguistic system is entirely unproblematic.

The focus on surface forms is deliberate. As demonstrated in part II, a significant number of recurrent sound patterns constitute inviolable surface constraints. In chapter 9 the majority of surface-true patterns show evidence of productivity. If we view productive sound patterns as those which are generalized to new environments, then productive patterns are those which can be directly inferred from surface phonetic strings. The association between generalizations which can be derived directly from surface forms and productive phonological rules or constraints is, surely, highly significant. This is reflected in the way that phonological theory has moved steadily closer to modeling surface forms. Nonetheless, certain morphological and syntactic models remain highly abstract, in that they posit linguistic structures which have no direct surface instantiations, and are motivated primarily by theory-internal considerations. In contrast, the present study supports the idea that language acquisition, and not just lexical acquisition, is primarily "data-driven," in the sense of Pullum and Scholz (2002).

Combining an evolutionary perspective on recurrent patterns with a data-driven view of acquisition offers a highly empirical, and minimally abstract, conception of grammar. Among other consequences, this type of approach shifts the burden of proof, so that underlying structures which do not surface in the corpus of utterances available to the language learner must be explicitly justified by some type of explicit evidence or argumentation, and cannot simply be assumed. In the same way, no grammatical analysis which fails to distinguish productive from non-productive patterns can be regarded as descriptively adequate.

Chapter 9 demonstrates how Evolutionary Phonology combines structural methods of analysis with the important generative separation of performance and competence. An important difference between Evolutionary Phonology and many alternative models, emphasized in preceding chapters, is that markedness is excised from synchronic grammars. In models where markedness is associated with token frequency, direct reference is made to frequency effects themselves. In models where featural markedness is claimed to predict the direction of phonological neutralization, phonetically based sound change is a better predictor than intrinsic feature values due to the context-dependent nature of so many common sound changes.

The elimination of markedness is part of a more general program of constraining the scope of the synchronic grammar. This program is, to a great extent, theory-neutral. The evolutionary approach to phonology, morphology, and syntax is not a theory of what synchronic grammars *must* encode, but rather what they *need not* encode as properties of Universal Grammar. Any cross-linguistic tendency which has a straightforward historical explanation should be excised from statements of Universal Grammar, unless it can be independently motivated. Within synchronic systems, an adequate grammatical description needs to distinguish productive from non-productive processes, and to be able to express the categorial knowledge available to speakers. The standard assumption in generative grammar is that grammars are uniform across speakers. However, the current approach allows, and indeed predicts, more flexibility, since so much of grammar is learned. In the same way that words will have slightly different meanings for individual speakers based on differing experiences in their usage, so grammars may be slightly different for individuals where surface forms do not lead uniquely to one grammatical analysis.

Previous chapters suggest that recurrent sound patterns in the world's languages are the result of direct inheritance, coupled with errors in transmission which are retained or eliminated by the natural selective forces of the human perceptual and articulatory system. Sound patterns evolve over time, and parallel evolutionary developments can be understood in terms of the natural selectional role of the listener as language learner. An intrinsic property of human speech is its phonetic variability: all phonological categories have variable realizations along specific phonetic parameters. This phonetic variability often serves as the source of sound change, and can be likened to "random" genetic mutations. Though phonetic variability itself may be viewed in terms of minimizing effort (natural speech) and maximizing contrast (careful speech), the sound change which occurs during language transmission when one of these variants is adopted at the expense of the other appears to be based on frequency in language use. Under this view, effort minimization and contrast maintenance do not play a direct role in sound change. From the perspective of the language learner, then, the variability inherent in grammar can be considered "random," with change modeled on probabilistic terms. In other grammatical domains, distinguishing the source of variation from forces which give rise to change under variation may allow for more illuminating treatments of recurrent grammatical change.

Natural selection in the world of sounds has proved a useful and instructive metaphor. Phonetic features which are easily perceived in a particular context are maintained, while those which are easily misperceived are often lost. The stability of a particular sound or sound sequence over time suggests that it is highly adaptive, even if it is not widely distributed in the world's languages. To my knowledge, no one has studied grammar from precisely this perspective. Those interested in aspects of Universal Grammar have consistently focused on directions of language change. In contrast, there have been few, if any, major cross-linguistic studies of grammatical features and constructions which are *most resistant to change*. Studies of grammatical stability may enable us to identify new areas of linguistic convergence and reflect on their origins. Finally, the evolutionary model defines innate interpretive biases, ambiguity, and variation as the three primary sources of change in the natural history of sound systems. The same primary sources of change are suggested for morphology and syntax, with parallel evolution giving rise to recurrent morphological and syntactic structures in the world's languages.

References

Abraham, R. C. 1940. *A dictionary of the Tiv language*. Hertford: Stephen Austin and Sons.

Abramson, Arthur S. 1986. The perception of word-intitial consonant length: Pattani Malay. *Journal of the International Phonetic Association* 16: 8–16.

1991. Amplitude as a cue to word-initial consonant length: Pattani Malay. In M. Rossi et al. (eds.), *Proceedings of the 12th International Congress of Phonetic Sciences*, 98–101. Université de Provence, Aix-en-Provence.

Ackerman, Farrell. 2002. Morphosemantic mismatches and realization-based lexicalism. In Elaine J. Francis and Laura A. Michaelis (eds.), *Mismatch: form-function incongruity and the architecture of grammar*, 83–116. Stanford: CSLI Publications.

Aitchison, Jean. 1996. *The seeds of speech: language origin and evolution*. Cambridge: Cambridge University Press.

Albright, Adam. 2002. Base selection in analogical change: a German/Yiddish comparison. Paper presented at the Berkeley Linguistic Society, February 2002.

Alpher, Barry. 2002. Reconstructing the common ancestor of the Pama-Nyungan languages, a phylogenetic group. Paper presented at the Workshop on Subgrouping in Australian Languages, at the Fifteenth International Conference on Historical Linguistics. To appear in Claire Bowern and Harold Koch (eds.), *Subgrouping in Australian languages*. Amsterdam: John Benjamins.

Alsina, Alex. 1999. Where's the mirror principle? *The Linguistic Review* 16:1–42.

Andersen, Henning. 1973. Abductive and deductive change. *Language* 49: 765–93.

Andersen, Torben. 1987. The phonemic system of Agar Dinka. *Journal of African Languages and Linguistics* 9: 1–27.

1990. Vowel length in Western Nilotic languages. *Acta Linguistica Hafniensia* 22: 5–26.

Anderson, Stephen R. 1969. West Scandinavian vowel systems and the ordering of phonological rules. Doctoral dissertation, MIT.

1981. Why phonology isn't "natural." *Linguistic Inquiry* 12: 493–539.

1985. *Phonology in the twentieth century*. Chicago: University of Chicago Press.

1992. *A-morphous morphology*. Cambridge: Cambridge University Press.

Anderson, Victoria B. 1997. Perception of coronal consonants in some Australian languages. Ms., UCLA.

Andersson, Yerker. 1990. The deaf world as a linguistic minority. In S. Prillwitz and T. Vollhaber (eds.), *Sign language research and application: proceedings of the International Congress on Sign Language Research and Application*, Hamburg, 1990, 155–61. Hamburg: Signum.

Andrzejewsky, B. W. 1955. The problem of vowel representation in the Isaaq dialect of Somali. *Bulletin of the School of Oriental and African Studies* 17: 567–80.

Antilla, Arto and Young-mee Yu Cho. 1998. Variation and change in Optimality Theory. *Lingua* 104: 31–56.

Archangeli, Diana. 1984. Underspecification in Yawelmani phonology and morphology. Doctoral dissertation. Cambridge, MA: Massachusetts Institute of Technology. [Published by Garland Press, New York, 1988.]

Archangeli, Diana and Douglas Pulleyblank. 1994. *Grounded phonology*. Cambridge, MA: MIT Press.

Armagost, James L. 1985. On predicting voiceless vowels in Comanche. *Papers in Linguistics* 10.2: 1–15.

  1986. Three exceptions to vowel devoicing in Comanche. *Anthropological Linguistics* 28: 255–65.

Armstrong, L. E. 1934. The phonetic structure of Somali. *Mitteilungen des Seminars für Orientalische Sprachen* (Berlin) 37.3: 116–61.

Arnold, E. N. 1994. Investigating the origins of performance advantage: adaptation, exaptation, and lineage effects. In P. Eggleton and R. Vane-Wright (eds.), *Phylogenetics and ecology*, 123–68. London: Academic Press.

Arnott, D. W. 1958. The classification of verbs in Tiv. *Bulletin of the School of Oriental and African Studies* 21: 111–33.

Aronoff, Mark. 1976. *Word formation in generative grammar*. Cambridge, MA: MIT Press.

Aslin, R. N. 1987. Visual and auditory development in infancy. In J. D. Osofsky (ed.), *Handbook of infancy*, 2nd edition, 5–97. New York: Wiley.

Aslin, R. N., D. B. Pisoni, B. L. Hennessy, and A. J. Perey. 1981. Discrimination of voice onset time by human infants: new findings and implications for the effects of early experience. *Child Development* 52: 1135–45.

Aslin, R. N., D. B. Pisoni, and P. W. Jusczyk. 1983. Auditory development and speech perception in infancy. In M. Haith and J. Campos (eds.), *Handbook of child psychology*, vol. 2: *Infancy and developmental psychobiology*, 573–687. New York: Wiley.

Austerlitz, Robert. 1966. *Finnish reader and glossary*. Bloomington: Indiana University Press.

Bach, Emmon, and Robert Harms. 1972. How do languages get crazy rules? In R. Stockwell and R. Macaulay (eds.), *Linguistic change and Generative Theory*, 1–21. Bloomington: Indiana University Press.

Bagemihl, Bruce. 1995. Language games and related areas. In J. Goldsmith (ed.), *The handbook of phonological theory*, 697–712. Oxford: Basil Blackwell.

Bailey, Todd M. and Ulrike Hahn. 2000. Determinants of wordlikeness: phonotactics or lexical neighborhoods? Ms., Oxford University.

Baker, Brett. 1999. Word structure in Ngalakgan. Doctoral dissertation. University of Sydney.

Baker, Mark. 1985. The mirror principle and morphosyntactic explanation. *Linguistic Inquiry* 16: 373–415.

    1988. Incorporation: a theory of grammatical function changing. Chicago: University of Chicago Press.

Bamgbose, Ayo. 1967. Notes on the phonology of Mbe. *Journal of West African Languages* 4: 5–11.

Barker, Chris. 1989. Extrametricality, the cycle, and Turkish word stress. In Junko Ito and Jeff Runner (eds.), *Phonology at Santa Cruz*, vol. 1: 1–34. Syntax Research Center, University of California, Santa Cruz.

Barker, M. A. R. 1963. *Klamath Dictionary*. University of California Publications in Linguistics 31. Berkeley: University of California Press.

    Klamath grammar. University of California Publications in Linguistics 32. Berkeley and Los Angeles: University of California Press.

Barnes, Jonathan. 2002. Positional neutralization: a phonologization approach to typological patterns. PhD dissertation, University of California, Berkeley.

Barry, Martin. 1985. A palatographic study of connected speech processes. *Cambridge Papers in Phonetics and Experimental Linguistics* 4: 1–16.

Bates, Elizabeth and Beverley Wulfeck. 1989. Crosslinguistic studies of aphasia. In Brian MacWhinney and Elizabeth Bates (eds.), *The Crosslinguistic study of sentence processing*, 328–71. Cambridge: Cambridge University Press.

Baudouin de Courtenay, Jan. 1871/1972. Some general remarks on linguistics and language. In Stankiewicz (ed.) 1972: 49–80.

    1895/1972. An attempt at a theory of phonetic alternations. In Stankiewicz (ed.) 1972: 144–212.

    1897/1972. Statement of linguistic principles. In Stankiewicz (ed.) 1972: 213–15.

    1972. *A Baudouin de Courtenay anthology: the beginnings of structural linguistics*, ed. E. Stankiewicz. Bloomington: Indiana University Press.

Baum, D. A. and A. Larson. 1991. Adaptation reviewed: a phylogenetic methodology for studying character macroevolution. *Systematic Zoology* 40: 1–18.

Beckman, Mary E. 1986. *Stress and non-stress accent*. Dordrecht: Foris.

    1999. Implications for phonological theory. In William J. Hardcastle and Nigel Hewlett (eds.), *Coarticulation: theory, data and techniques*, 199–225. Cambridge: Cambridge University Press.

Beddor, P. S. and Evans-Romaine, D. In press. Acoustic-perceptual factors in phonological assimilations: a study of syllable-final nasals. *Rivista di Linguistica* 7. [Special issue on *The phonetic basis of sound change*, ed. Carol A. Fowler.]

Behaghel, Otto. 1923–32. *Deutsche Syntax*, vols. I-IV. Heidelberg: Carl Winter.

Bell, H. 1971. The phonology of Nobiin Nubian. *African Language Review* 9: 115–59.

Bellugi, U. and S. D. Fischer. 1972. A comparison of sign language and spoken language: rate and grammatical mechanisms. *Cognition* 1.3:173–200.

Bellugi, U. and E. S. Klima. 1990. Properties of visual spatial languages. In S. Prillwitz and T. Vollhaber (eds.), *Sign language research and application: proceedings of the International Congress on Sign Language Research and Application*, Hamburg, 1990, 115–43. Hamburg: Signum.

Bender, Byron W. 1968. Marshallese phonology. *Oceanic Linguistics* 7: 16–35.
  1969. *Spoken Marshallese.* Honolulu: University of Hawai'i Press.
  (ed.) 1984. *Studies in Micronesian Linguistics,* Pacific Linguistics C-80.
  Canberra: Australian National University.
  1999. Marshallese grammar (chapters 1, 2). Ms., University of Hawai'i.
Benediktsson, Hreinn (ed.) 1970. *The Nordic languages and modern linguistics.*
  Reykjavik: Societas Scientarium Islandica.
van Bergem, D. R. 1995. Perceptual and acoustic aspects of lexical vowel reduction, a sound change in progress. *Speech Communication* 16: 329–58.
Berkovits, Rochele. 1993. Utterance-final lengthening and the duration of final-
  stop closures. *Journal of Phonetics* 21: 479–89.
Berman, Howard. 1982. Two phonological innovations in Ritwan. *International
  Journal of American Linguistics* 48: 412–20.
Bernhardt, Barbara Handford and Joseph P. Stemberger. 1998. *Handbook of
  phonological development: from the perspective of constraint-based nonlinear
  phonology.* San Diego: Academic Press.
Bertinetto, P. M. 1980. The perception of stress by Italian speakers. *Journal of
  Phonetics* 8: 385–95.
Best, C. T., G. W. McRoberts, and N. M. Sithole. 1988. Examination of the
  perceptual re-organization for speech contrasts: Zulu click discrimination
  by English-speaking adults and infants. *Journal of Experimental Psychology:
  Human Perception and Performance* 14: 245–360.
Bever, Thomas and D. Terence Langendoen. 1972. The interaction of speech
  perception and grammatical structure in the evolution of language. In
  R. Stockwell and R. Macaulay (eds.) *Linguistic change and generative theory,*
  32–95. Bloomington: Indiana University Press.
Biggs, Bruce. 1978. The history of Polynesian phonology. In S. A. Wurm and Lois
  Carrington (eds.), *Proceedings of the Second International Conference on Aus-
  tronesian Linguistics.* Pacific Linguistics C-61. Canberra: Australian National
  University. Fasc. 2: 691–716.
Blake, B. 1979. *A Kalkatungu grammar.* Pacific Linguistics 3–57. Canberra:
  Australian National University.
Bleek, D. F. 1939. A short survey of Bushman languages. *Zeitschrift für Eingebore-
  nensprachen* 30: 52–72.
Blevins, James P. 1995. Syncretism and paradigmatic opposition. *Linguistics and
  Philosophy* 18: 113–52.
  2000. Markedness and agreement. *Transactions of the Philological Society* 98:
  233–62.
Blevins, Juliette. 1992. Review of *An essay on stress* by M. Halle and J.-R. Vergnaud,
  Language 68: 159–65.
  1993a. Klamath laryngeal phonology. *International Journal of American Linguistics* 59: 237–79.
  1993b. A tonal analysis of Lithuanian nominal accent. *Language* 69:
  237–73.
  1993c. Gilyak lenition as a phonological rule. *Journal of Australian Linguistics*
  13: 1–21.
  1994a. A place for lateral in the feature geometry. *Journal of Linguistics* 30:
  301–48.

1994b. The bimoraic foot in Rotuman phonology and morphology. *Oceanic Linguistics* 33: 491–516.

1994c. A phonological and morphological reanalysis of the Maori passive. *Te Reo* 37: 29–53.

1995a. The syllable in phonological theory. In J. Goldsmith (ed.), *The handbook of phonological theory*, 206–44. Oxford: Basil Blackwell.

1995b. Review of J. A. Edmondson and K. J. Gregerson (eds.), *Tonality in Austronesian Languages*. *Oceanic Linguistics* 34: 238–43.

1996. Mokilese reduplication. *Linguistic Inquiry* 27.3: 523–30.

1997. Rules in optimality theory: two case studies. In I. Roca (ed.), *Derivations and constraints in phonology*, 227-60. Oxford: Clarendon Press.

1999a. Nhanda and its position within Pama-Nyungan. *Oceanic Linguistics* 38: 297–320.

1999b. Untangling Leti infixation. *Oceanic Linguistics* 38: 383–403.

2001a. *Nhanda: an Aboriginal language of Western Australia*. Oceanic Linguistics Special Publications in Linguistics, Number 30. Honolulu: University of Hawai'i Press.

2001b. Where have all the onsets gone? Initial consonant loss in Australian Aboriginal languages. In J. Simpson, D. Nash, M. Laughren, P. Austin, and B. Alpher (eds.), *Forty years on: Ken Hale and Australian languages*, 481–92. Pacific Linguistics 512. Canberra: Research School of Pacific and Asian Studies.

2002a. The independent nature of phonotactic constraints: an alternative to syllable-based approaches. In Caroline Féry and Ruben van de Vijver (eds.), *The syllable in optimality theory*, 375–403. Cambridge: Cambridge University Press.

2002b. Klamath /s?/ clusters. *International Journal of American Linguistics* 67: 467–74.

2002c. Notes on sources of Yurok glottalized consonants. In L. Hinton and L. Buszard-Welcher (eds.), *Proceedings of the meeting of the Hokan-Penutian Workshop*, 1–18. Survey of California and other Indian Languages, Report 11.

2003a. The phonology of Yurok glottalized sonorants. *International Journal of American Linguistics* 69: 371–96.

2003b. Yurok syllable weight. *International Journal of American Linguistics*. 69: 4–24.

2003c. A note on reduplication in Bugotu and Cheke Holo. *Oceanic Linguistics* 42: 499–505.

To appear a. Antigemination: natural or unnatural history? In P. Nowak and C. Yoquelet (eds.), *Proceedings of BLS 21*.

To appear b. Consonant epenthesis: natural and unnatural histories. In Jeff Good (ed.), *Proceedings of the Workshop on Explaining Linguistic Universals*. Oxford University Press.

To appear c. Periphrastic agreement in Yurok. In F. Ackerman and J. P. Blevins (eds.), *Proceedings of the Workshop on Periphrasis*. Stanford, CA: CSLI Publications.

To appear d. A reconsideration of Yokuts vowels. *International Journal of American Linguistics* 70.

To appear e. The mystery of Austronesian final consonant loss. *Oceanic Linguistics* 43: 179–84.

Blevins, Juliette and Robert Blust. 2003. Towards a theory of drift: patterns of Austronesian syncope. Ms., University of California, Berkeley.

Blevins, Juliette and Andrew Garrett. 1992. Ponapean nasal substitution: new evidence for rhinoglottophilia. In L. A. Buszard-Welcher, L. Wee, and W. Weigel (eds.), *Berkeley Linguistics Society* 18: 2–21.

1993. The evolution of Ponapeic nasal substitution. *Oceanic Linguistics* 32: 199–236.

1998. The origins of consonant-vowel metathesis. *Language* 74: 508–56.

2001. Two problems in Yurok (and Wiyot) historical phonology and morphology. Paper presented at the 33rd annual Algonquian Conference, University of California, Berkeley.

To appear. The evolution of metathesis. In Bruce Hayes, Robert Kirchner, and Donca Steriade (eds.), *Phonetically driven phonology*. Cambridge University Press.

Blevins, Juliette and Sheldon P. Harrison. 1999. Trimoraic feet in Gilbertese. *Oceanic Linguistics* 38: 203–30.

Blevins, Juliette and Doug Marmion. 1994. Nhanta historical phonology. *Australian Journal of Linguistics* 14: 193–216.

1995. Nhanda glottal stop. *Oceanic Linguistics* 34: 139–60.

Bliese, Loren F. 1981. *A generative grammar of afar*. Summer Institute of Linguistics, University of Texas at Arlington.

Bloomfield, Leonard. 1933. *Language*. New York: Holt.

1946. Algonquian. In H. Hoijer (ed.), *Linguistic structures of native America*, 85–129. New York: Viking Fund.

Blust, Robert. 1979. Coronal-noncoronal consonant clusters: new evidence for markedness. *Lingua* 47: 101–17.

1984. A Mussau vocabulary, with phonological notes. *Papers in New Guinea Linguistics* 23: 159–208. Pacific Linguistics A-69. Canberra: Australian National University.

1990. Three recurrent changes in Oceanic languages. In J. H. C. S. Davidson (ed.), *Pacific island languages: essays in honour of G. B. Milner*, 7–28. London: University of London, School of Oriental and African Studies.

1995. Notes on Berawan consonant gemination. *Oceanic Linguistics* 34: 123–38.

1996a. Low vowel dissimilation in Ere. *Oceanic Linguistics* 35: 96–112.

1996b. Low vowel dissimilation in Oceanic languages: an addendum. *Oceanic Linguistics* 35: 305–9.

2003. Must sound change be phonetically motivated? Ms., University of Hawai'i. To appear in *Diachronica*.

Boas, Franz. 1911. Chinook. In F. Boas (ed.), *Handbook of American Indian languages*, 559–677. Bureau of American Ethnology Bulletin no. 40, pt. I. Washington, DC: Government Printing Office.

Borgstrøm, C. H. 1937. The dialect of Barra in the Outer Hebrides. *Norsk Tidsskrift for Sprogvidenskap* 8: 71–242.

Borowsky, Toni. 1986. *Topics in the lexical phonology of English*. PhD dissertation, University of Massachusetts, Amherst.

Bourciez, Edouard and Jean Bourciez. 1967. *Phonétique française: étude historique*. Paris: Editions Klincksieck.

Bowden, John and John Hajek. 1999. Taba. In *Handbook of the International Phonetic Association: a guide to the use of the International Phonetic Alphabet*, 143–46. Cambridge: Cambridge University Press.

Boysson-Bardies, B. de, P. Hallé, L. Sagart, and C. Durand. 1989. A cross-linguistic investigation of vowel formants in babbling. *Journal of Child Language* 14: 211–27.

Bradley, C. H. 1970. *A linguistic sketch of Jicaltepec Mixtec*. Summer Institute of Linguistics Publications 25. Norman, OK: Summer Institute of Linguistics and University of Oklahoma.

Bradlow, A. 1995. A comparative acoustic study of English and Spanish vowels. *Journal of the Acoustical Society of America* 97.3: 1916–24.

Brandstetter, Renward. 1916. *An introduction to Indonesian linguistics*. Translated by C. O. Blagden. London: The Royal Asiatic Society.

Breen, Gavan and Rob Pensalfini.1999. Arrernte: a language with no syllable onsets. *Linguistic Inquiry* 30: 1–25.

Brentari, Dianne. 1995. Sign language phonology: ASL. In J. Goldsmith (ed.), *The handbook of phonological theory*, 615–39. Oxford: Basil Blackwell.

Bresnan, Joan. 2000. *Lexical-functional grammar*. Oxford: Basil Blackwell.

Bright, William. 1957. *The Karok language*. University of California Publications in Linguistics 13. Berkeley: University of California Press.

 1978. Sibilants and naturalness in Aboriginal California. *Journal of California Anthropology, Papers in Linguistics* 1978. 39–63.

Briscoe, E. J. 2000. Grammatical acquisition: inductive bias and coevolution of language and the language acquisition device. *Language* 76: 245–96.

 (ed.) In press. *Linguistic evolution through language acquisition: formal and computational models*. Cambridge: Cambridge University Press.

Broselow, Ellen. 1979. Cairene Arabic syllable structure. *Linguistic Analysis* 5: 345–82.

 1983. Non-obvious transfer: on predicting epenthesis errors. In S. Gass and L. Selinker (eds.), *Language transfer in language learning*. Rowley, MA: Newbury House.

 1995. Skeletal positions and moras. In J. Goldsmith (ed.), *The handbook of phonological theory*, 175–205. Oxford: Basil Blackwell.

Browman, C. P. and L. Goldstein. 1990. Tiers in articulatory phonology, with some implications for casual speech. In J. Kingston and M. Beckman (eds.), *Papers in laboratory phonology*, vol. I: *Between the grammar and physics of speech*, 341–76. Cambridge: Cambridge University Press.

 1992. Articulatory phonology: an overview. *Phonetica* 49: 155–80.

Brown, G. 1977. *Listening to Spoken English*. London: Longman.

Brown, Herbert A. 1968. *A dictionary of Toaripi*. Oceania Linguistic Monographs 11.

 1973. *The Eleman language family*. Pacific Linguistics C-26: 279–375. Canberra: Australian National University.

 1986. *A comparative dictionary of Orokolo, Gulf of Papua*. Pacific Linguistics C-84. Canberra: Australian National University.

Brugmann, Karl. 1878. Das verbale Suffix *â* im indogermanischen, die griechische Passivaoriste und die Sogen, aeolische Flexion der Verba contracta. *Morphologische Untersuchungen* 1: 1–91.

Buckley, Eugene 1994 *Theoretical aspects of Kashaya phonology and morphology.* Stanford, CA: CSLI Publications.

Butcher, Andy. In progress. The phonetics of Australian languages. Ms., Flinders University.

Bybee, Joan L. 1985a. *Morphology: a study of the relation between meaning and form.* Amsterdam: John Benjamins Publishing Company.

1985b. Diagrammatic iconicity in stem-inflection relations. In John Haiman (ed.), *Iconicity in syntax,* 11–48. Amsterdam: John Benjamins.

2001. *Phonology and language use.* Cambridge: Cambridge University Press.

Bybee, Joan L. and Paul Hopper (eds.). 2001. *Frequency and the emergence of linguistic structure.* Typological Studies in Language 45. Amsterdam and Philadelphia: John Benjamins.

Bybee Joan L., William Pagliuca, and Revere D. Perkins. 1991. On the asymmetries in the affixation of grammatical material. In W. Croft, K. Denning and S. Kemmer (eds.), *Studies in typology and diachrony,* 1–39. Typological Studies in Language 20. Amsterdam and Philadelphia: John Benjamins.

Byrd, Dani. 1996. Influences of articulatory timing in consonant sequences. *Journal of Phonetics* 24: 209–44.

Cairns, Charles E. 1978. Universal rules and vocalic devoicing in Southern Paiute. *Linguistic and literary studies in honor of Archibald A. Hill,* vol. 2. M. A. Jazayery, E. C. Polome, and W. Winter (eds.), *Descriptive Linguistics,* 213–26. The Hague: Mouton.

Campbell, Lyle. 1998. *Historical linguistics: an introduction.* Edinburgh: Edinburgh University Press.

Campbell, Lyle and Jon Ringen. 1980. Teleology and the explanation of sound change. In Wolfgang Dressler (ed.), *Phonologica 1980,* 57–68.

Caplan, David. 1987. *Neurolinguistics and linguistic aphasiology.* Cambridge: Cambridge University Press.

Carlson, Robert. 1991. Grammaticization of postpositions and word order in Senufo languages. In E. Traugott and B. Heine (eds.), *Approaches to grammaticalization,* vol. II: 201–23. Typological Studies in Language 19. Amsterdam and Philadelphia: John Benjamins.

Carstairs-McCarthy, Andrew. 1999. *The origins of complex language: an inquiry into the evolutionary beginnings of sentences, syllables, and truth.* Oxford: Oxford University Press.

Catford, J. C. 1974. "Natural" sound changes: some questions of directionality in diachronic phonetics. *Papers from the Parasession on Natural Phonology,* 21–29. Chicago: Chicago Linguistic Society.

1977. *Fundamental problems in phonetics.* Edinburgh: Edinburgh University Press.

Chao, Y.-R. 1936. Types of plosives in Chinese. *Proceedings of the 2nd International Congress of Phonetic Sciences,* 106–10. Cambridge: Cambridge University Press.

Charles-Luce, J. 1985. Word-final devoicing in German: effects of phonetic and sentential contexts. *Journal of Phonetics* 13: 309–24.

Charney, Jean. 1993. *A grammatical sketch of the Comanche language.* Lincoln: University of Nebraska.

Chene, Brent E. de and Stephen R. Anderson. 1979. Compensatory lengthening. *Language* 55: 505–35.

Cho, Young-mee Yu. 1998. Language change as reranking of constraints. In Richard M. Hogg and Linda van Bergen (eds.), *Historical Linguistics 1995*, vol. 2: 45–62. Amsterdam and Philadelphia: John Benjamins.

Choi, John D. 1992. Phonetic underspecification and target interpolation: an acoustic study of Marshallese vowel allophony. PhD dissertation, University of California, Los Angeles. [UCLA Working Papers in Phonetics 82.]

Chomsky, Noam. 1965. *Aspects of the theory of syntax*. Cambridge, MA: MIT Press.

1981. *Lectures on government and binding*. Dordrecht: Foris.

1982. *Some concepts and consequences of the theory of government and binding*. Cambridge, MA: MIT Press.

1986. *Barriers*. Cambridge, MA: MIT Press.

Chomsky, Noam and Morris Halle. 1968. *The sound pattern of English*. New York: Harper & Row.

Chung, Sandra and Alan Timberlake. 1985. Tense, aspect, and mood. In T. Shopen (ed.), 202–58. *Language typology and syntactic description*, vol. III: Cambridge: Cambridge University Press.

Churchward, C. Maxwell. 1940. *Rotuman grammar and dictionary*. Sydney: Methodist Church of Australasia, Department of Overseas Missions.

Clahsen, Harald. 1999. Linguistic perspectives on specific language impairment. In William C. Ritchie and Tej K. Bhatia (eds.), *Handbook of child language acquisition*, 675–704. London: Academic Press.

Clements, G. N. 1990. The role of the sonority cycle in core syllabification. In J. Kingston and M. Beckman (eds.), *Papers in laboratory phonology*, vol. 1: *Between the grammar and the physics of speech* 283–333. Cambridge: Cambridge University Press.

Clements, G. N. and S. Jay Keyser. 1983. *CV Phonology: a generative theory of the syllable*. Cambridge, MA: MIT Press.

Cohn, Abigail C., William H. Ham and Robert J. Podesva. 1999. The phonetic realization of singleton-geminate contrasts in three languages of Indonesia. In John J. Ohala, Yoko Hasegawa, Manjari Ohala, Daniel Granville, and Ashlee C. Bailey (eds.), *Proceedings of the 14th International Congress of Phonetic Sciences*, vol. 1: 587–90. Berkeley: Department of Linguistics, University of California, Berkeley.

Colarusso, John. 1985. Pharyngeals and pharyngealization in Salishan and Wakashan. *International Journal of American Linguistics* 51: 366–68.

1988. *The Northwest Caucasian languages: a phonological survey*. New York: Garland.

Coleman, John and Janet Pierrehumbert. 1997. Stochastic phonological grammars and acceptability. *Proceedings of the third meeting of the Association for Computational Linguistics special interest group in computational phonology*, 49–56. Somerset, NJ: Association for Computational Linguistics.

Crowley, Terry. 1982. *The Paamese language of Vanuatu*. Pacific Linguistics B-87. Canberra: Australian National University.

1992. *An introduction to historical linguistics.* 2nd edition. Oxford: Oxford University Press.

1998. *An Erromangan (Sye) grammar.* Oceanic Linguistics Special Publication no. 27. Honolulu: University of Hawai'i Press.

Dalby, Andrew. 2002. *Language in danger.* London and New York: Penguin Press.

Darwin, Charles. 1859. *On the origin of species by means of natural selection, or, the preservation of favored races in the struggle for life.* London: John Murray.

1871. *The descent of man.* New York: D. Appleton.

Dave, Radhekant 1977. Retroflex and dental consonants in Gujarati: a palatographic and acoustic study. *Annual Report of the Institute of Phonetics, University of Copenhagen (ARIPUC)* vol. 11: 27–155.

Davies, J. 1851. *A Tahitian and English Dictionary with introductory remarks on the Polynesian language and a short grammar of the Tahitian dialect with an appendix.* Tahiti: London Missionary Society's Press. [Reprinted by Editions Haere Po no Tahiti.]

Davis, Stuart. 2003. The controversy over geminates and syllable weight. In Caroline Féry and Ruben van de Vijver (eds.), *The syllable in optimality theory,* 77–98. Cambridge: Cambridge University Press.

De Boer, Bart. 2000. Emergence of sound systems through self-organization. In C. Knight et al. (eds.), *The evolutionary emergence of language: social function and the origins of linguistic form,* 177–98. Cambridge: Cambridge University Press.

2001. *The origins of vowel systems.* Oxford: Oxford University Press.

Deacon, Terrence. 1997. *The symbolic species.* New York: Penguin Books.

Dell, François, and Mohamed Elmedlaoui. 1985. Syllabic consonants and syllabification in Imdlawn Tashlhiyt Berber. *Journal of African Languages and Linguistics* 7: 105–30.

1996. On consonant releases in Imdlawn Tashlhiyt Berber. *Linguistics* 34: 357–95.

1997. Les geminées en berbère. *Linguistique Africaine* 19: 5–55.

Demolin, Didier. 2000. The search for primitives in phonology and the explanation of sound patterns: the contribution of fieldwork studies. Paper presented at the Seventh Conference on Laboratory Phonology, Nijmegen, Netherlands. June 2000.

Dench, Alan. 1991. Panyjima. In R. M. W. Dixon and Barry Blake (eds.), *Handbook of Australian languages,* vol. 4: 124–243. Oxford: Oxford University Press.

Denes, P. 1955. Effect of duration on the perception of voicing. *Journal of the Acoustical Society of America* 27: 761–64.

Denning, K. 1990. The diachronic development of phonological voice quality, with special reference to Dinka and other Nilotic languages. Doctoral dissertation, Stanford University, Stanford, CA.

Dieth, Eugen. 1932. *A grammar of the Buchan dialect (Aberdeenshire): descriptive and historical.* Cambridge: W. Heffer & Sons Ltd.

Dinnsen, D. and Charles-Luce, J. 1984. Phonological neutralization, phonetic implementation and individual differences. *Journal of Phonetics* 12: 49–60.

Dixon, R. M. W. 1976. Review of *Languages of Australia and Tasmania* by S. A. Wurm. *Language* 52: 260–66.

1980. *The languages of Australia*. Cambridge: Cambridge University Press.

1990. Compensatory phonological changes: an example from the northern dialects of Dyirbal. *Lingua* 8: 1–34.

1991. Mbabaram. In R. M. W. Dixon and B. Blake (eds.), *Handbook of Australian languages* vol. 4: 348–402. Oxford: Oxford University Press.

1997. *The rise and fall of languages*. Cambridge: Cambridge University Press.

Doak, Ivy. 1992. Another look at Coeur d'Alene harmony. *International Journal of American Linguistics* 58: 1–35.

Dobzhansky, T. 1951. *Genetics and the origin of species*. 3rd edition, revised. New York: Columbia University Press.

Donegan, Patricia and David Stampe. 1979. The study of natural phonology. In Daniel A. Dinnsen (ed.), *Current approaches to phonological theory*, 126–73. Bloomington: Indiana University Press.

Eek, A. 1984. Problems of quantity in Estonian word prosody. *Estonian Papers in Phonetics* 1984–1985. 13–66.

Egerod, S. 1965. Verb inflexion in Atayal. *Lingua* 15: 251–82.

Eilers, R. E. 1977. Context-sensitive perception of naturally produced stop and fricative consonants by infants. *Journal of the Acoustical Society of America* 61: 1321–36.

Eilers, R. E. and F. D. Minifie. 1975. Fricative discrimination in early infancy. *Journal of Speech and Hearing Research* 18: 158–67.

Eimas, P. D. 1975. Auditory and phonetic coding of the cues for speech: discrimination of the [r-l] distinction by young infants. *Perception and Psychophysics* 18: 341–47.

Eimas, P. D., E. R. Siqueland, P. W. Jusczyk, and J. Vigorito. 1971. Speech perception in infants. *Science* 171: 303–6.

Elmedlaoui, Mohammed. 1993. Gemination and spirantization in Hebrew, Berber, and Tigrinya: a fortis-lenis module analysis. *Linguistica Communicatio* 5: 121–76.

Emeneau, Murray B. 1967. The South Dravidian languages. *Journal of African and Oriental Studies* 87: 365–413. [Reprinted in M. B. Emeneau, *Dravidian studies: selected Papers*. Delhi: Motilal Barsidass, 1994: 71–161.]

Engstrand, Olle. 1987. Preaspiration and the voicing contrast in Lule Sami. *Phonetica* 44: 103–16.

1999. Swedish. In *Handbook of the International Phonetic Association: a guide to the use of the International Phonetic Alphabet*, 140–42. Cambridge: Cambridge University Press.

Ernestus, Mirjam and Harald Baayen. 2003. Predicting the unpredictable: interpreting neutralized segments in Dutch. *Language*: 5–38.

Evans, Nick. 1995. Current issues in the phonology of Australian languages. In John A. Goldsmith (ed.), *The handbook of phonological theory*, 723–61. Cambridge, MA: Blackwell.

Everett, Daniel. 1986. Piraha. In D. C. Derbyshire and G. K. Pullum (eds.), *Handbook of Amazonian languages*, vol. 1: 200–325. Berlin: Mouton de Gruyter.

Ezard, Bryan and Yailo Robert. 1995. Tawala. In Darell T. Tryon (ed.), *Comparative Austronesian dictionary*, Part 1: Fascicle 2: 757–66.

Faber, Alice and Catherine T. Best. 1994. The perceptual infrastructure of early phonological development. In Susan D. Lima, Roberta L. Corrigan and Gregory K. Iverson (eds.), *The reality of linguistic rules*, 261–80. Amsterdam: John Benjamins.

Fallon, Paul D. 2002. *The synchronic and diachronic phonology of ejectives*. New York and London: Routledge.

Faye, C. U. 1923–25. The influence of the "Hlonipa" on the Zulu clicks. *Bulletin of the School of Oriental and African Studies* 3: 757–82.

Ferguson, Charles A. 1966. Assumptions about nasals; a sample study in phonological universals. In J. H. Greenberg (ed.), *Universals of language*, 53–60. Cambridge, MA: MIT Press.

  1975. "Short a" in Philadelphia English. In E. Smith (ed.), *Studies in linguistics in honor of George L. Trager*, 259–74. The Hague: Mouton.

  1990. From esses to aitches: identifying pathways of diachronic change. In W. Croft, K. Denning, and S. Kemmer (eds.), *Studies in typology and diachrony*, 59–78. Typological Studies in Language 20. Amsterdam and Philadelphia: John Benjamins.

Ferguson, Charles A., Lise Menn, and Carol Stoel-Gammon. 1992. *Phonological development: models, research, implications*. Timonium, MD: York Press.

Fernald, A. 1985. Four-month-old infants prefer to listen to motherese. *Infant Behavior and Development* 8: 181–95.

Fernald, A. and P. K. Kuhl. 1987. Acoustic determinants of infant preference for motherese speech. *Infant Behavior and Development* 10: 279–93.

Firchow, Irwin and Jacqueline Firchow. 1969. An abbreviated phoneme inventory. *Anthropological Linguistics* 11: 271–76.

Firth, J. R. 1948. Sounds and prosodies. *Transactions of the Philological Society*: 127–52.

Fitch, W. Tecumsah. 2000. The evolution of speech: a comparative review. *Trends in Cognitive Sciences* 4: 258–67.

Fischer-Jørgensen, Eli. 1975. *Trends in phonological theory*. Copenhagen: Academisk Forlag.

Flemming, Edward. 1995. Auditory representations in phonology. PhD dissertation, University of California, Los Angeles.

  2001. Scalar and categorical phenomena in a unified model of phonetics and phonology. *Phonology* 18: 7–44.

Fougeron, Cécile. 1999. Aspects phonétiques de la position forte: renforcement articulatoire et coordination temporelle. Paper presented at the Roundtable on Lenition and Fortition, Nice, France, June 1999. Ms., Laboratoire de Psycholinguistique, Université de Genève.

Fougeron, C. and P. A. Keating. 1997. Articulatory strengthening at edges of prosodic domains. *Journal of the Acoustical Society of America* 101.6: 3728–40.

Foulkes, Paul. 1997. Historical laboratory phonology – Investigating /p/ > /f/ > /h/ changes. *Language and Speech* 40: 248–76.

Frajzyngier, Zygmunt. 1980. The vowel system of Pero. *Studies in African Linguistics* 11: 39–74.

Frisch, Stefan A., N. R. Large, and D. B. Pisoni. 2000. Perception of wordlikeness: effects of segment probability and length on processing nonword sound patterns. *Journal of Memory and Language* 42: 481–96.

Frisch, Stefan A. and Bushra Zawaydeh. 2001. The psychological reality of OCP-place in Arabic. *Language* 77: 91–106.

Frisch, Stefan, B. A. Zawaydeh, and D. B. Pisoni. 2001. Emergent phonotactic generalizations in English and Arabic. In J. Bybee and P. Hopper (eds.), *Frequency and the emergence of linguistic structure*, 159–79. Amsterdam: John Benjamins.

Fry, Dennis B. 1955. Duration and intensity as physical correlates of linguistic stress. *Journal of the Acoustical Society of America* 27: 765–68.

1958. Experiments in the perception of stress. *Language and Speech* 1: 126–52.

Fujimura, O., M. Macchi, and L. A. Streeter. 1978. Perceptions of stop consonants with conflicting transitional cues: a cross-linguistic study. *Language and Speech* 21: 337–46.

Garrett, Andrew. 2001. Reduplication and infixation in Yurok: morphology, semantics, and diachrony. *International Journal of American Linguistics* 67: 264–312.

2002. Sound change and lexical transfer: evidence from *Wuthering Heights*. Ms., University of California, Berkeley.

Garrett, Andrew and Juliette Blevins. To appear. Morphophonological analogy. In Sharon Inkelas and Kristin Hanson (eds.), *The nature of the word: essays in Honor of Paul Kiparsky*. Cambridge, MA: MIT Press.

Garrett, Andrew and Mark Hale. 1993. The phonetics and phonology of Grimm's and Verner's Laws. Paper presented at the Linguistic Society of America Annual Meeting. Ms., University of California, Berkeley.

Gauchat, Louis. 1905. L'unité phonétique dans le patois d'une commune. In *Aus Romanischen Sprachen und Literaturen: Festschrift Heinrich Morf*, 175–232. Halle: Diemeyer.

Gedney, W. J. 1965. Yay, a Northern Tai language in North Vietnam. *Lingua* 14: 180–93.

Geraghty, Paul. 1995. Western Fijian (Nadroga). In Darell T. Tryon (ed.), *Comparative Austronesian dictionary*, Part 1: Fascicle 2: 925–30.

Ghazeli, Salem. 1977. Back consonants and backing coarticulation in Arabic. PhD dissertation, University of Texas at Austin.

Gianelli, Luciano and Leonardo Savoia. 1979. Indebolimento consonantico in Toscoana. *Revista Italiana di Diallettologia* 2: 23–58.

Gimson, A. C. 1962. *An introduction to the pronunciation of English*. London: Edward Arnold.

Givón, Talmy. 1971. Historical syntax and synchronic morphology: an archaeologist's field trip. In *Papers from the Chicago Linguistic Society* 7: 394–415.

1979. *On understanding grammar*. New York: Academic Press.

Goddard, Ives. 1982. The historical phonology of Munsee. *International Journal of American Linguistics* 48: 16–48.

Goldsmith, John. 1976. Autosegmental phonology. PhD dissertation, MIT, Cambridge, MA. Distributed by the Indiana University Linguistics Club, Bloomington. [Published by Garland Press, New York, 1979.]

1990. *Autosegmental and metrical phonology.* Oxford: Blackwell.

Good, Jeff. 2001. Causativization and applicativization in Bantu: evidence for an evolutionary approach to morpheme ordering restrictions. Ms., University of California, Berkeley.

Goodenough, Ward H. 1963. The long or double consonants of Trukese. *The Proceedings of the Ninth Pacific Science Congress,* 1957, vol. 3: 77–86.

Goodsit, J. V., P. A. Morse, J. N. Ver Hoeve, and N. Cowan. 1984. Infant speech recognition in multisyllabic contexts. *Child Development* 55: 903–10.

Gordon, Matthew. 1999. Syllable weight: phonetics, phonology and typology. PhD dissertation. Los Angeles: UCLA.

Gordon, Matthew. 2002. A phonetically-driven account of syllable weight. *Language* 78: 51–80.

Gordon, Matthew and Peter Ladefoged. 2001. Phonation types: a cross-linguistic overview. *Journal of Phonetics* 29: 383–406.

Gould, S. J. 1983. The hardening of the modern synthesis. In M. Grene (ed.), *Dimensions of Darwinism.* Cambridge: Cambridge University Press.

1990. *An urchin in the storm.* London: Penguin.

Gould, S. J. and R. C. Lewontin. 1979. The spandrels of San Marco and the Panglossian paradigm: a critique of the adaptationist programme. *Proceedings of the Royal Society of London,* B, 205: 581–98.

Grammont, Maurice. 1933. *Traité de phonétique.* Paris: Delagrave.

Greenberg, Joseph. 1950. The patterning of root morphemes in Semitic. *Word* 6: 162–81.

1966a. Synchronic and diachronic universals in phonology. *Language* 42: 508–17.

1966b. Some universals of grammar with particular reference to the order of meaningful elements. In Joseph H. Greenberg (ed.), *Universals of grammar,* 2nd edition, 73–113. Cambridge, MA: MIT Press.

1978. Diachrony, synchrony, and language universals. In J. H. Greenberg, C. A. Ferguson, and E. A. Moravcsik (eds.), Universals of human language, vol. 3: 47–82. Stanford, CA: Stanford University Press.

Grieser, D. and P. K. Kuhl. 1989. Categorization of speech by infants: Support for speech-sound prototypes. *Developmental Psychology* 25: 577–88.

Grodzinsky, Yosef. 1990. *Theoretical perspectives on language deficits.* Cambridge, MA: MIT Press.

Grunwell, P. 1982. *Clinical phonology.* London: Croom Helm.

Guerssel, Mohamed. 1977. Constraints on phonological rules. *Linguistic Analysis* 3: 267–305.

1978. A condition on assimilation rules. *Linguistic Analysis* 4: 225–54.

Guion, Susan G. 1996. Velar palatalization: coarticulation, perception, and sound change. PhD dissertation, University of Texas at Austin.

1998. The role of perception in the sound change of velar palatalization. *Phonetica* 55: 18–52.

Guthrie, Malcom. 1967–71. *Comparative Bantu*, vols. I–IV. Farnborough: Gregg International Publishers.

Hagège, Claude. 1993. *The language builder: an essay on the human signature of linguistic morphogenesis.* Amsterdam: John Benjamins.

Hagège, Claude and André Haudricourt. 1978. *La phonologie panchronique.* Paris: Presses Universitaires de France.

Haiman, John. 1985. *Natural syntax.* Cambridge: Cambridge University Press.

Hajek, John. 1997. *Universals of sound change in nasalization.* Publications of the Philological Society 31. Oxford: Blackwell.

Hale, Kenneth. 1964. Classification of Northern Paman languages, Cape York Peninsula, Australia: a research report. *Oceanic Linguistics* 3: 248–65.

  1976a. Phonological developments in particular Northern Paman languages. In P. Sutton (ed.), *Languages of Cape York*, 7–40. Canberra: Australian Institute for Aboriginal Studies (AIAS).

  1976b. Phonological developments in a Northern Paman language: Uradhi. In P. Sutton (ed.), *Languages of Cape York*, 41–49. Canberra: Australian Institute for Aboriginal Studies (AIAS).

Hale, Kenneth and David Nash. 1997. Lardil and Damin phonotactics. In Darrell Tryon and Michael Walsh (eds.), *Boundary Rider: Essays in honour of Geoffrey O'Grady*, 247–59. Pacific Linguistics C-136. Canberra: Australian National University.

Hale, Kenneth and Josie White Eagle. 1980. A preliminary metrical account of Winnebago accent. *International Journal of American Linguistics* 46: 117–32.

Hale, Mark and Charles Reiss. 1998. Formal and empirical arguments concerning phonological acquisition. *Linguistic Inquiry* 29: 656–83.

  2000. "Substance abuse" and "dysfunctionalism": current trends in phonology. *Linguistic Inquiry* 31: 157–69.

Halle, Morris. 1962. Phonology in generative grammar. *Word* 18: 54–72.

Halle, Morris and G. N. Clements. 1983. *Phonology workbook.* Cambridge, MA: MIT Press.

Hall, Nancy. 2002. Svarabhakti as unordered segments. Paper presented at the LSA Annual Meeting, San Francisco, January 2002.

Hamilton, Philip. 1995. Constraints and markedness in the phonotactics of Australian Aboriginal languages. Doctoral dissertation, University of Toronto.

Hankamer, Jorge, Aditi Lahiri, and Jacques Koreman. 1989. Perception of consonant length: voiceless stops in Turkish and Bengali. *Journal of Phonetics* 17: 283–98.

Hardcastle, William J. and Nigel Hewlett (eds.). 1999. *Coarticulation: theory, data, and techniques.* Cambridge: Cambridge University Press.

Hargus, Sharon. 1988. *The lexical phonology of Sekani.* New York: Garland.

Harms, Robert T. 1966. Stress, voice and length in Southern Paiute. *International Journal of American Linguistics* 32: 228–35.

  1985. The locus of hampered voice in Southern Paiute. *International Journal of American Linguistics* 51: 438–41.

Harris, John. 1985. *Phonological variation and change. Studies in Hiberno-English.* Cambridge: Cambridge University Press.

1990. Segmental complexity and phonological government. *Phonology* 7: 255–300.

1997. Licensing inheritance: an integrated theory of neutralization. *Phonology* 14: 315–70.

Harris, Roy (ed.). 1996. *The origin of language.* Bristol: Thoemmes Press.

Harris, Zellig. 1951. *Methods in structural linguistics.* Chicago: University of Chicago Press.

Harrison, Sheldon P. 1976. *Mokilese reference grammar.* Honolulu: University of Hawai'i Press.

1984. Segmental quantity in Mokilese: a synchronic and diachronic study. In Byron W. Bender (ed.), *Studies in Micronesian Linguistics,* 375–401. Pacific Linguistics C-80. Canberra: Australian National University.

Haudricourt, A.-G. 1968. La langue de Gomen et la langue de Touho en Nouvelle-Calédonie. *Bulletin de la Societé de linguistique* 63: 218–35.

Hawkins, J. A. 1979. Implicational universals as predictors of word order change. *Language* 55: 618–48.

1983. *Word order universals.* New York: Academic Press.

1991. Seeking motives for change in typological variation. In W. Croft, K. Denning, and S. Kemmer (eds.), *Studies in typology and diachrony,* 95–128. Typological Studies in Language 20. Amsterdam, Philadelphia: John Benjamins.

Hawkins, S. 1973. Temporal coordination of consonants in the speech of children: preliminary data. *Journal of Phonetics* 1: 181–217.

Hawkins, S. and A. Slater. 1994. Spread of CV- and V-to-V coarticulation in British English: implications for the intelligibility of synthetic speech. *Proceedings of ICSLP 84* (1): 57–60.

Hayes, Bruce. 1980. A metrical theory of stress rules. Doctoral dissertation, MIT. [New York: Garland, 1985.]

1986a. Inalterability in CV phonology. *Language* 62: 321–51.

1986b. Assimilation as spreading in Toba Batak. *Linguistic Inquiry* 17: 467–99.

1989. Compensatory lengthening in moraic phonology. *Linguistic Inquiry* 20: 253–306.

1995. *Metrical stress theory.* Chicago: University of Chicago Press.

1999. Phonetically driven phonology: the role of Optimality Theory and inductive grounding. In M. Darnell, F. J. Newmeyer, M. Noonan, E. Moravcsik, and K. Wheatley (eds.), *Functionalism and formalism in linguistics,* vol. I, *General Papers,* 243–85. Amsterdam: John Benjamins.

Hayes, Bruce, Robert Kirchner, and Donca Steriade (eds.). To appear. *Phonetically driven phonology.* Cambridge: Cambridge University Press.

Hayward, R. J. 1986. *The Arbore language.* Kuschitische Sprachstudien 2. Hamburg: Buske.

Heine, Bernd. 1975. Ik – eine ostafrikanische Restsprache. *Afrika und Übersee* 59: 31–56.

Heine, Bernd and Mechthild Reh. 1984. *Grammatical categories in African languages.* Hamburg: Helmut Buske.

Henderson, Eugenie. 1949. Prosodies in Siamese. *Asia Minor* 1: 189–215.

Henderson, J. B and Bruno Repp. 1982. Is a voiced consonant released when followed by another stop consonant? *Phonetica* 39: 71–82.

Herbert, Robert K. 1986. *Language universals, markedness theory, and natural phonetic processes*. Trends in Linguistics, Studies and Monographs 25. Berlin, New York, and Amsterdam: Mouton de Gruyter.

Hercus, L. A. 1982. *The Bāgandji language*. Pacific Linguistics B-67. Canberra: Australian National University.

Hewitt, B. G. 1979. (in collaboration with Z. K. Khiba) *Abkhaz*. Lingua Descriptive Series. Amsterdam and New York: North Holland Publishers.

Hjelmslev, Louis. 1953. *Prolegomena to a theory of language*. Trans. Francis Whitfield. Madison: University of Wisconsin Press.

Hock, H. H. 1986. Compensatory lengthening: in defense of the concept "mora." *Folia Linguistica* 20: 431–60.

1991. *Principles of historical linguistics*. The Hague: Mouton de Gruyter.

Hockett, Charles F. 1955. *A manual of phonology*. *International Journal of American Linguistics* Memoir 11.

1967. The Yawelmani basic verb. *Language* 43: 208–222.

1973. Yokuts as testing ground for linguistic methods. *International Journal of American Linguistics* 39.63–79.

Hoijer, Harry. 1933. Tonkawa: an Indian language of Texas. *Handbook of American Indian Languages* 3: 1–148.

Hombert, Jean-Marie, John J. Ohala and William G. Ewan. 1979. Phonetic explanations for the development of tones. *Language* 55: 37–58.

Hooper, J. B. 1972. The syllable in phonological theory. *Language* 48: 525–40.

1976. *Introduction to natural generative phonology*. New York: Academic Press.

Hornstein, Norbert and David Lightfoot. 1981. Introduction. *Explanation in linguistics: the logical problem of language acquisition*, 9–31. London: Longman.

Houlihan, K. and G. K. Iverson. 1979. Functionally-constrained phonology. In D. A. Dinnsen (ed.), *Current approaches to phonological theory*, 50–73. Bloomington: Indiana University Press.

Householder, F. W. 1956. Unreleased /ptk/ in American English. In M. Halle (ed.), 235–44. *For Roman Jakobson*. The Hague: Mouton.

Hudson, Grover. 1995. Phonology of Ethiopian languages. In J. Goldsmith (ed.), *The handbook of phonological theory*, 782–97. Oxford: Basil Blackwell.

Hughes, Jock. 1995. Dobel (Aru). In Darell T. Tryon (ed.), *Comparative Austronesian dictionary*, Part 1: Fascicle 1: 637–50.

Hume, Elizabeth V. and Keith Johnson. 2001. *The role of speech perception in phonology*. San Diego: Academic Press.

Hume, Elizabeth, Jennifer Muller, and Aone van Engelenhoven. 1997. Nonmoraic geminates in Leti. *Phonology* 14: 371–402.

Hurford, James R. 1990. Nativist and functional explanations in language acquisition. In I. M. Roca (ed.), *Logical issues in language acquisition*, 85–136. Dordrecht: Foris.

Hurford, James R., Michael Studdert-Kennedy and Chris Knight (eds.). 1998. *Approaches to the evolution of language*. Cambridge: Cambridge University Press.

Hussein, Lufti. 1990. VCV coarticulation in Arabic. *Ohio State Working Papers in Linguistics.* 88–104.

Hyman, Larry M. 1972. Nasals and nasalization in Kwa. *Studies in African Linguistics* 3: 167–205.

1973. The role of consonant types in natural tonal assimilations. In L. M. Hyman (ed.), *Consonant types and tone,* 151–79. University of Southern California.

1975. *Phonology: theory and analysis.* New York: Holt, Rinehart, and Winston.

1977. Phonologization. In A. Juilland (ed.), *Linguistic Studies offered to Joseph Greenberg,* 407–18. Saratoga, CA: Alma Libri.

1985. *A theory of phonological weight.* Publications in Linguistic Sciences 19. Dordrecht: Foris.

1998. La morphologie et la "fricativation" diachronique en Bantou. *Mémoires de la Société de Linguistique de Paris.* Grammaticalisation et Reconstruction.

1999. Lenition and fortition in Bantu. Paper presented at the Round Table on Lenition and Fortition, Nice.

2002. Suffix ordering in Bantu: a morphocentric approach. Ms., University of California, Berkeley.

Inkelas, Sharon, Cemil Orhan Orgun, and Cheryl Zoll. 1997. Implications of lexical exceptions for the nature of grammar. In I. Roca (ed.), *Constraints and derivations in phonology,* 393–418. Oxford: Clarendon Press.

Inkelas, Sharon and Young Mee Cho. 1993. Inalterability as prespecification. *Language* 69: 529–74.

Inkelas, Sharon and Yvan Rose. 2002. Positional neutralization in first language acquisition. Paper presented at TREND, University of California, Berkeley.

Inkelas, Sharon and Cheryl Zoll. 2003. A morphological theory of reduplication. Ms., University of California, Berkeley and MIT.

International Phonetic Association, The. 1999. *Handbook of the International Phonetic Association: a guide to the use of the International Phonetic Alphabet.* Cambridge: Cambridge University Press.

Irschick, D. J., C. C. Austin, K. Petren, R. N. Fisher, J. B. Losos, and O. Ellers. 1996. A comparative analysis of clinging ability among pad-bearing lizards. *Biological Journal of the Linnean Society* 59.1: 21–35.

Itô, Junko. 1986. Syllable theory in prosodic phonology. Doctoral dissertation, University of Massachusetts, Amherst. GLSA.

Itô, Junko and Armin Mester. 1995. Japanese phonology. In John Goldsmith (ed.), *The handbook of phonological theory,* 817–38. Cambridge, MA: Blackwell.

Jackendoff, Ray. 1977. *X-bar syntax.* Cambridge, MA: MIT Press.

2002. *Foundations of language: brain, meaning, grammar, evolution.* Oxford and New York: Oxford University Press.

Jackson, Frederick H. 1984a. Reflexes of Proto-Oceanic in the Trukic languages of Micronesia. In B. W. Bender (ed.), *Studies in Micronesian Linguistics,* 259–80. Pacific Linguistics C-80. Canberra: Australian National University.

1984b. Selecting an orthography for Saipan Carolinian. In B. W. Bender (ed.), *Studies in Micronesian Linguistics,* 237–58. Pacific Linguistics C-80. Canberra: Australian National University.

Jacobson, Steven A. 1985. Siberian Yupik and Central Yupik prosody. In Krauss (ed.), *Yupik Eskimo prosodic systems: descriptive and comparative studies* 25–45. Fairbanks: Alaska Native Language Center.

Jaeger, Jeri J. 1978. Speech aerodynamics and phonological universals. *Proceedings of the Annual Meeting of the Berkeley Linguistics Society* 4: 311–29.

1983. The fortis/lenis question: evidence from Zapotec and Jawoñ. *Journal of Phonetics* 11: 177–89.

Jakobson, Roman. 1929. Remarques sur l'évolution phonologique du russe comparée à celle des autres langues slaves. *Travaux du Cercle linguistique de Prague* 2. Reprinted in *Selected writings*, vol. 1: *Phonological studies*. The Hague: Mouton.

Jakobson, Roman. [1932] 1984. Zur Struktur des russischen Verbums. *Charisteria Guilelmo Mathesio Quinquagenario* 74–83. Reprinted 1984 as "Structure of the Russian verb" in *Russian and Slavic grammar*, ed. Linda R. Waugh and Morris Halle, 1–12. Janna Linguarum 106. Berlin: Mouton.

1937. On ancient Greek prosody. *Studies presented to Kazimierz Woyzcickiz zagadnien poetyki VI*, Wilno.

1962. *Selected writings* vol. 1: *Phonological studies*. The Hague: Mouton.

1971a. *Selected writings*, vol. I: *Phonological studies*. Second edition. Berlin, Amsterdam, and New York: Mouton.

1971b. *Selected Writings*, vol. II: *Word and language*. Berlin, Amsterdam, and New York: Mouton.

(ed.) 1975. *N. S. Trubetzkoy's letters and notes*. The Hague: Mouton.

Jakobson, Roman, Gunnar Fant, and Morris Halle. 1952. *Preliminaries to speech analysis*. Technical Report 13, MIT Acoustics Laboratory. Cambridge, MA: MIT Press.

Jakobson, Roman and Morris Halle. 1956. *Fundamentals of language*. The Hague: Mouton.

Janota, P. 1967. Perception of stress by Czech listeners. In *Proceedings of the Sixth International Congress of Phonetic Sciences*. 457–61.

Janson, Tore. 1983. Sound change in perception and production. *Language* 59: 18–34.

Jassem, W., J. Morton, and M. Steffen-Batóg. 1968. The perception of stress in synthetic speech-like stimuli by Polish listeners. *Speech Analysis and Synthesis* 1: 289–308.

Javkin, H. 1977. Towards a phonetic explanation for universal preferences in implosives and ejectives. *Proceedings of the Annual Meeting of the Berkeley Linguistics Society* 3: 559–65.

Jesperson, Otto. [1886]1933. Zur Lautgesetzfrage. In *Linguistica: selected papers in English, French and German*. Copenhagen and London. (Originally published in 1886. Reprinted in Wilbur 1977).

1924. *The philosophy of grammar*. London: Allen and Unwin.

1949. *A modern English grammar on historical principles. Part I: Sounds and spellings*. London: George Allen & Unwin.

Johnson, Keith. 1997. Speech perception without speaker normalization. In K. Johnson and John W. Mullennix (eds.), 145–65. *Talker variability in speech processing*. San Diego: Academic Press.

Johnson, Keith, E. Flemming, and R. Wright. 1993. The hyperspace effect: phonetic targets are hyperarticulated. *Language* 69: 505–28.

Jonasson, J. 1971. Perceptual similarity and articulatory re-interpretation as a source of phonological innovation. *Quarterly Progress and Status Report*, Speech Transmission Laboratory, Stockholm, 1/1971: 30–41.

Jun, Jongho. 1995a. Place assimilation as the result of conflicting perceptual and articulatory constraints. *West Coast Conference on Formal Linguistics* 14: 221–37.

1995b. Perceptual and articulatory factors in place assimilation: an Optimality-theoretic approach. PhD dissertation, University of California, Los Angeles.

Jusczyk, Peter W. 1992. Developing phonological categories from the speech signal. In Charles A. Ferguson, Lise Menn and Carol Stoel-Gammon (eds.), *Phonological development: models, research, implications*, 17–64. Timonium, MD: York Press.

Kager, R. 1999. *Optimality Theory*. Cambridge: Cambridge University Press.

Kähler, Hans. 1946/1949. Ethnographische und linguistische Studien von dem Orang laut auf der Insel Rangsang an der Ostküste von Sumatra. *Anthropos* 51/54: 1–31, 757–85.

1960. Ethnographische und linguistische Studien über die Orang darat, Orang akit, Orang laut und Orang utan im Riau-Archipel und auf den Inseln an der Ostküste von Sumatra. *Veröffentlichungen des Seminars für Indonesische und Südseesprachen der Universität Hamburg*, vol. 2. Berlin: Dietrich Reimer.

Katz, Leonard, Suzanne E. Boyce, Louis M. Goldstein, and Georgije Lukatela. 1987. Grammatical information effects in auditory word recognition. *Cognition* 25: 235–63.

Kavitskaya, Darya. 2002. *Compensatory lengthening: phonetics, phonology, diachrony*. New York: Garland.

Kawasaki, H. 1986. Phonetic explanations for phonological universals: the case of distinctive vowel nasalization. In John J. Ohala and Jeri Jaeger (eds.), *Experimental phonology*, 81–103. New York: Academic Press.

Kaye, J., J. Lowenstamm, and J.-R. Vergnaud. 1990. Constituent structure and government in phonology. *Phonology* 7: 193–231.

Kean, M.-L. 1975. *The theory of markedness in generative grammar*. PhD dissertation, MIT, Cambridge, MA. [Distributed by the Indiana University Liguistics Club, Bloomington, 1980.]

(ed.) 1985. *Agrammatism*. New York: Academic Press.

Keating, Patricia. 1985. Universal phonetics and the organization of grammars. In Victoria A. Fromkin (ed.), *Phonetic linguistics: essays in honour of Peter Ladefoged*. 115–32. Orlando: Academic Press.

1988. Underspecification in phonetics. *Phonology* 5: 275–92.

Kenstowicz, Michael. 1982. Gemination and spirantization in Tigrinya. *Studies in the Linguistic Sciences* 12: 103–22.

1994. *Phonology in generative grammar*. Oxford: Blackwell.

Kenstowicz, Michael and Charles Kisseberth. 1979. *Generative phonology*. New York: Academic Press.

Kenstowicz, Michael and Charles Pyle. 1973. On the phonological integrity of geminate clusters. In M. Kenstowicz and C. Kisseberth (eds.), *Issues in phonological theory*, 27–43. The Hague: Mouton.

Key, Mary Ritchie. 1968. *Comparative Tacanan phonology, with Cavineña phonology and notes on Pano Tacanan relationship*. The Hague: Mouton.

Kingston, John. 1985. The phonetics and phonology of the timing of oral and glottal events. Doctoral dissertation, University of California, Berkeley.

1990. Articulatory binding. In J. Kingston and M. Beckman (eds.), *Papers in laboratory phonology*, vol. 1: *Between the grammar and the physics of speech*, 406–34. Cambridge: Cambridge University Press.

Kingston, John and Randy L. Diehl. 1994. Phonetic knowledge. *Language* 70: 419–54.

Kinkade, M. Dale. 1967. Uvular-pharyngeal resonants in Interior Salish. *International Journal of American Linguistics* 33: 224–31.

1985. More on nasal loss on the Northwest coast. *International Journal of American Linguistics* 51: 478–80.

Kiparsky, Paul. 1965. Phonological change. Doctoral dissertation. Cambridge, MA: Massachusetts Institute of Technology.

1968. Linguistic universals and linguistic change. In E. Bach and R. Harms (eds.), *Universals in linguistic theory*, 170–202. New York: Holt.

1973. "Elsewhere" in phonology. In S. Anderson and P. Kiparksy (eds.), *A festschrift for Morris Halle*, 93–106. New York: Holt, Rinehart and Winston.

1982a. *Explanation in phonology*. Dordrecht: Foris.

1982b. Lexical phonology and morphology. In I.-S. Yang (ed.), 3–91. *Linguistics in the morning calm*. Seoul: Hanshin.

1988. Phonological change. In Frederick J. Newmeyer (ed.), *Linguistics: the Cambridge survey*, vol. 1: *Theoretical foundations*, 363–415. Cambridge: Cambridge University Press.

1995. The phonological basis of sound change. In John Goldsmith (ed.), *The handbook of phonological theory*, 640–70. Cambridge, MA: Blackwell.

2002. Sound change and the organization of phonology. LSA keynote address. Linguistic Society of America Annual Meeting, January 4, 2002, San Francisco.

Kirchner, Robert. 2000. Geminate inalterability and lenition. *Language* 76: 509–45.

Klamer, M. 1994. *Kambera: a language of Eastern Indonesia*. HIL Dissertations, 11. The Hague: Holland Academic Graphics.

Klatt, Dennis. 1975. Vowel lengthening is syntactically determined in a connected discourse. *Journal of Phonetics* 3: 129–40.

Klatt, Dennis H. and Laura C. Klatt. 1990. Analysis, synthesis, and perception of voice quality variations among female and male talkers. *Journal of the Acoustical Society of America* 87: 820–57.

Klein, R. 1969. Acoustic analysis of the acquisition of acceptable [r] in American English. Paper presented at the 1969 SRCD Convention, Santa Monica, CA.

Klima, Edward S. 1964. Negation in English. In J. Fodor and J. Katz (eds.), *The structure of language*, 246–323. Englewood Cliffs, NJ: Prentice Hall.

Klima, E. S. and U. Bellugi. 1979. *The signs of language*. Cambridge, MA: Harvard University Press.

Klingenheben, A. 1927. Stimmtonverlust bei Geminaten. In *Festschrift Meinhof*. Hamburg: Kommissionsverlag von L. Friederichsen & Co. 134–45.

Kluender, K. R., R. L. Diehl, and P. R. Killeen. 1987. Japanese quail can learn phonetic categories. *Science* 237: 1195–97.

Knight, Chris, Michael Studdert-Kennedy, and James R. Hurford (eds). 2000. *The evolutionary emergence of language: social function and the origins of linguistic form.* Cambridge: Cambridge University Press.

Koch, Harold. 1997. Pama-Nyungan reflexes in Arandic languages. In Darrell T. Tryon and Michael Walsh (eds.), *Boundary rider: essays in honour of Geoffrey O'Grady*, 271–302. Pacific Linguistics C-136. Canberra: Australian National University.

Kohler, K. J. 1979. Dimensions in the perception of fortis and lenis plosives. *Phonetica* 36: 332–43.

Kohler, Klaus J. 1998. The development of sound systems in human language. In James R. Hurford et al. (eds.), *Approaches to the evolution of language*, 265–78. Cambridge: Cambridge University Press.

Kornfeld, J. R. and H. Goehl. 1974. A new twist to an old observation: kids know more than they say. In A. Bruck, R. A. Fox, and M. W. LaGaly (eds.), *Papers from the Parasession on Natural Phonology*, 210–19. Chicago: Chicago Linguistic Society.

Kraehenmann, Astrid. 2001. Swiss German stops: geminates all over the word. *Phonology* 18: 109–45.

Kraehenmann, Astrid and Aditi Lahiri. 1999. Phonological quantity contrast in Swiss German stops: history and acoustics. Ms., University of Konstanz.

Krauss, Michael E. 1982. Proto-Athapaskan *kin Chipewyan, 1742–1800: philological evidence. *International Journal of American Linguistics* 48: 73–82.

Krishnamurti, Bh. 1978. Areal and lexical diffusion of sound change. *Language* 54: 1–20.

Kruszewski, Miko ai. 1881. *Über die Lautabwechslung.* Kazan'.

1883. *Očerk nauki o jazyke.* Kazan'.

Kuehn, D. P. and K. Moll. 1976. A cineradiographic study of VC and CV articulatory velocities. *Journal of Phonetics* 4: 303–20.

Kuhl, P. K. 1980. Perceptual constancy for speech sound categories in early infancy. In G. H. Yeni-Komshian, J. F. Kavanagh, and C. A. Ferguson (eds.), *Child phonology*, vol. 2: 199–261. New York: Academic Press.

1987. Perception of speech and sound in early infancy. In P. Salapatek and L. Cohen (eds.), *Handbook of infant perception*, vol. 2. New York: Academic Press.

1991. Human adults and human infants show a "perceptual magnet effect" for the prototypes of speech categories, monkeys do not. *Perception and Psychophysics* 50: 93–197.

1995. Mechanisms of developmental change in speech and language. *Proceedings of the International Congress of Phonetic Sciences, Stockholm*, vol.2: 132–39.

Kuhl, P. K. and J. D. Miller. 1975. Speech perception by the chinchilla: voiced-voiceless distinction in alveolar plosive consonants. *Science* 190: 69–72.

1978. Speech perception by the chinchilla: identification functions for synthetic VOT stimuli. *Journal of the Acoustical Society of America* 63: 905–17.

Kuhl, P. K. and D. M. Padden. 1982. Enhanced discriminability at the phonetic boundaries for the voicing feature in macaques. *Perception and Psychophysics* 32: 542–50.

1983. Enhanced discriminability at the phonetic boundaries for the place feature in macaques. *Journal of the Acoustical Society of America* 73: 1003–10.

Kühnert, Barbara and Francis Nolan. 1999. The origin of coarticulation. In William J. Hardcastle and Nigel Hewlett (eds.), *Coarticulation: theory, data and techniques*, 7–30. Cambridge: Cambridge University Press.

Kuroda, S.-Y. 1967. *Yawelmani phonology*. Cambridge, MA: MIT Press.

Kurylowicz, J. 1964. *The inflectional categories of Indo-European*. Heidelberg: Winter.

Kyle, J. G. and B. Woll. 1991. *Sign language: the study of deaf people and their language*. Cambridge: Cambridge University Press.

Labov, William. 1963. The social motivation of sound change. *Word* 19: 273–309.

1972. *Sociolinguistic patterns*. Philadelphia: University of Pennsylvania Press.

1981. Resolving the neogrammarian controversy. *Language* 57: 267–308.

1994. *Principles of linguistic change*, vol. 1: *Internal factors*. Oxford and Cambridge, MA: Blackwell.

2001. *Principles of linguistic change*, vol. 2: *Social factors*. Oxford and Cambridge, MA: Blackwell.

Lacerda, F. To appear. Distributed memory representations generate the perceptual-magnet effect. *Journal of the Acoustical Society of America*.

Ladefoged, Peter. 1971. *Preliminaries to linguistic phonetics*. Chicago: University of Chicago Press.

Ladefoged, Peter and Ian Maddieson. 1996. *The sounds of the world's languages*. Oxford: Blackwell.

Ladefoged, Peter, Kay Williamson, Ben Elugbe, and Ann Angela Uwalaka. 1976. The stops of Owerri Igbo. *Studies in African Linguistics*, Supplement 6: 147–63.

Lahiri, Aditi and Jorge Hankamer. 1988. The timing of geminate consonants. *Journal of Phonetics* 16: 327–38.

Lahiri, Aditi and Allard Jongman. 1990. Intermediate level of analysis: features or segments. *Journal of Phonetics* 18: 435–43.

Lakoff, Robin. 1972. Another look at drift. In Robert P. Stockwell and R. K. S. Macaulay (eds.), *Linguistic change and generative theory*, 172–98. Bloomington: Indiana University Press.

Lang, C. E. and Ohala, J. J. 1996. Temporal cues for vowels and universals of vowel inventories. *Proceedings of ICSLP 96, October 3–6, 1996*. [4th International Conference on Spoken Language Processing, Philadelphia]. Wilmington: University of Delaware. Vol. 1: 430–33.

Larson, Allan and Jonathan B. Losos. 1996. Phylogenetic systematics of adaptation. In M. R. Rose and G. V. Lauder (eds.), *Adaptation*. 187–220. San Diego: Academic Press.

Lasky, R. E., A. Syrdal-Lasky, and R. E. Klein. 1975. VOT discrimination by four to six and a half month old infants from Spanish environments. *Journal of Experimental Child Psychology* 20: 215–25.

Lass, Roger. 1980. *On explaining language change*. Cambridge: Cambridge University Press.

1984. *Phonology*. Cambridge: Cambridge University Press.

1997. *Historical linguistics and language change*. Cambridge: Cambridge University Press.

Laufer, Asher. 1999. Hebrew. In *Handbook of the International Phonetic Association: a guide to the use of the International Phonetic Alphabet*, 96–99. Cambridge: Cambridge University Press.

Laver, John. 1994. *Principles of phonetics*. Cambridge: Cambridge University Press.

LaVoie, Lisa M. 1996. Consonant strength: results of a data base development project. *Working Papers of the Cornell Phonetics Laboratory* 11: 269–316.

2001. *Consonant strength: phonological patterns and phonetic manifestations*. New York and London: Garland.

Leben, William. 1973. Suprasegmental phonology. PhD dissertation, MIT, Cambridge, MA.

Lehiste, Ilse. 1966. *Consonant quantity and phonological units in Estonian*. Indiana University Publications, Uralic and Altaic Series, vol. 65. Bloomington, IN: Indiana University.

1970. *Suprasegmentals*. Cambridge, MA: MIT Press.

Lehiste, Ilse, Katherine Morton, and M. A. A. Tatham. 1973. An instrumental study of consonant gemination. *Journal of Phonetics* 1: 131–48.

Lehmann, Christian. 1982. *Thoughts on grammaticalization: a programmatic sketch*. Cologne: Institut für Sprachwissenschaft, Universität zu Köln.

Lehmann, Winfred P. 1992. *Historical linguistics: an introduction*. 2nd edition. Holt, Rinehart and Winston: New York.

Lennig, Matthew. 1978. Acoustic measurement of linguistic change: the modern Paris vowel system. Doctoral dissertation, University of Pennsylvania.

Lenz, Rodolfo. 1928. *El Papiamento, la lengua criolla de Curaçao*. Santiago de Chile: Balcells.

Levin, Juliette. 1983. Reduplication and prosodic structure. Ms., MIT, Cambridge, MA.

1985a. *A metrical theory of syllabicity*. Doctoral dissertation, MIT, Cambridge, MA.

1985b. Reduplication with reference to syllable structure: Umpila. *MIT Working Papers in Linguistics*, vol. 6, ed. D. Archangeli, A. Barss, and R. Sproat, 133–59. Cambridge, MA: MIT Press.

1987a. Constraints on syllabification in French: eliminating truncation rules. In D. Birdsong and J.-P. Montreuil (eds.), *Advances in Romance linguistics*, 253–73. Publications in Language Sciences, no. 29. Dordrecht: Foris.

1987b. Underspecification Theory and Korean vowels. In S. Kuno, J. Whitman, I.-H. Lee, S.-Y. Bak, and Y.-S. Kang (eds.), *Harvard Studies in Korean Linguistics II*, 404–20. Hanshin Publishing Co., Seoul.

1987c. Between epenthesis and excrescence: what happens after redundancy rules. In M. Crowhurst (ed.), *Proceedings of the West Coast Conference on Formal Linguistics*, vol. 6: 187–201. Stanford: The Stanford Linguistic Association.

1988a. Generating ternary feet. In D. Fruchter, J. Levin, and J. Liu (eds.), *Texas Linguistic Forum* 29: 97–113. The University of Texas at Austin.

1988b. Bidirectional foot construction as a window on level ordering. In M. Hammond and M. Noonan (eds.), *Theoretical morphology*, 339–52. Orlando: Academic Press.

Li, Paul Jen-Kuei. 1982. Linguistic variations of different age groups in the Atayalic dialects. *The Tsing Hua Journal of Chinese Studies*, new series, 14: 167–91.

Lichtenberk, Frantisek. 1983. *A grammar of Manam*. Oceanic Linguistics Special Publication 18. Honolulu: University of Hawai'i Press.

1991. On the gradualness of grammaticalization. In E. Traugott and B. Heine (eds.), *Approaches to grammaticalization*, vol. I: 37–80. Typological Studies in Language 19. Amsterdam and Philadelphia: John Benjamins.

Liddell, Scott K. and Robert Johnson. 1989. American Sign Language: the phonological base. *Sign Language Studies* 64: 195–278.

Lieberman, Philip. 1984. *The biology and evolution of language*. Cambridge, MA: Harvard University Press.

Lightfoot, David. 1999. *The development of language: acquisition, change and evolution*. Oxford: Blackwell.

Liljencrants, J. and B. Lindblom. 1972. Numeric simulation of vowel quality systems: the role of perceptual contrast. *Language* 48: 839–62.

Lin, Yen-Hwei. 2002. Faithfulness, alignment, and markedness in Pingding Er Infixation. Ms., Michigan State University.

Lindblom, B. 1984. Can the models of evolutionary biology be applied to phonetic problems? In M. P. R. van den Broecke and A. Cohen (eds.), *Proceedings of the 10th International Congress of Phonetic Sciences*, 67–81. Dordrecht: Foris.

1986. Phonetic universals in vowel systems. In J. J. Ohala and J. J. Jaeger (eds.), *Experimental phonology*, 13–44. Orlando, FL: Academic Press.

1989. Phonetic invariance and the adaptive nature of speech. In B. A. G. Elsendoorn and H. Bouma (eds.), *Working models of human perception*, 139–52. London: Academic Press.

1990a. Explaining phonetic variation: a sketch of the H&H theory. In William Hardcastle and Alain Marchal (eds.), *Speech production and speech modelling*, 403–39. Dordrecht: Kluwer.

1990b. On the notion of "possible speech sound." *Journal of Phonetics* 18: 135–52.

1998. Systemic constraints and adaptive change in the formation of sound structure. In James R. Hurford et al. (eds.), *Approaches to the evolution of language*, 242–64. Cambridge: Cambridge University Press.

Lindblom, B., S. Brownlee, B. Davis, and S.-J. Moon. 1992. Speech transforms. *Speech Communication* 11: 357–68.

Lindblom, B., S. Guion, S.-J. Moon, and R. Willerman. 1995. Is sound change adaptive? *Rivista di Linguistica* 7.1: 5–37.

Lindblom, Björn, Peter MacNeilage, and Michael Studdert-Kennedy. 1984. Self-organizing processes and the explanation of phonological universals. In Brian Butterworth, Bernard Comrie, and Östen Dahl (eds.), *Explanations for language universals*, 181–203. New York: Mouton.

Lindblom, B. and Maddieson, I. 1988. Phonetic universals in consonant inventories. In L. M. Hyman & C. N. Li (eds.), *Language, speech, and mind: Studies in honor of Victoria A. Fromkin*, 62–80. London: Routledge.

Lisker, L. 1957. Closure duration and the intervocalic voiced-voiceless distinction in English. *Language* 33: 42–49.

Lisker, Leigh and Arthur S. Abramson. 1967. Some effects of context on voice onset time in English stops. *Language and Speech* 10: 1–28.

Locke, John L. 1983. *Phonological acquisition and change.* New York: Academic Press.

Locke, John L. and Dawn M. Pearson. 1992. Vocal learning and the emergence of phonological capacity: a neurobiological approach. In Charles A. Ferguson, Lise Menn and Carol Stoel-Gammon (eds.), *Phonological development: models, research, implications,* 91–129. Timonium, MD: York Press.

Lombardi, Linda. 1991. Laryngeal features and laryngeal neutralization. Doctoral dissertation, University of Massachusetts, Amherst.

Longacre, R. 1967. Systematic comparison and reconstruction. *Handbook of Middle American Indians* 5: 117–59.

Louali, Maïma and Gilbert Puech. 1994. Les consonnes "tendues" du berbère: indice perceptuels et corrélats phonétiques. *Etudes et Documents berbères* 11: 217–23.

Louw, J. A. 1964. The consonantal phonemes of the lexical root in Zulu. *Afrika und Übersee* 48: 127–52.

Lynch, John. 2000. *A grammar of Anejom̃.* Pacific Linguistics 507. Canberra: Australian National University.

2003. Low vowel dissimilation in Vanuatu languages. *Oceanic Linguistics* 42: 359–406.

MacEachern, Margaret R. 1997. Laryngeal co-occurrence restrictions. Doctoral dissertation, UCLA.

MacKay, Carolyn J. 1994. A sketch of Misantla Totonac phonology. *International Journal of American Linguistics* 60: 369–419.

1995. *A Veneto lexicon: the dialect of Segusino and Chipilo.* Venice: Unione dei Triveneti nel mondo.

1999. *A grammar of Misantla Totonac.* Salt Lake City: University of Utah Press.

Maddieson, Ian. 1984. *Patterns of sounds.* Cambridge: Cambridge University Press.

1998. Why make life hard? Resolutions to problems of rare and difficult sound types. In B. K. Bergen, Madeleine C. Plauche, and Ashlee C. Bailey (eds.), *Proceedings of the 24th Annual Meeting of the Berkeley Linguistics Society,* 367–80. Berkeley: Berkeley Linguistics Society.

2002. Typological patterns – geographical distribution and phonetic explanation. Talk presented at the Linguistic Society of America Annual Meeting, San Francisco. January 2002.

2003. Vowel spacing in four-vowel systems (Abstract). *Journal of the Acoustical Society of America,* vol. 113.

Maddieson, Ian, Caroline Smith, and Nicola Bessell. 2001. Aspects of the phonetics of Tlingit. *Anthropological Linguistics* 43: 135–76.

Majors, Tivoli Jane. 1998. Stress dependent harmony: phonetic origins and phonological analysis. PhD dissertation, University of Texas at Austin.

Malécot, A. 1956. Acoustic cues for nasal consonants: an experimental study involving tape-splicing technique. *Language* 32: 274–84.

1958. The role of releases in the identification of released final stops. *Language* 34: 370–80.

Malone, Joseph. 1993. *Tiberian Hebrew phonology*. Winona Lake, IN: Eisenbrauns.

1996. Orthometric patterns and pre-phonetic interfacing: a reply to Manaster Ramer. *Phonology* 13: 119–25.

Manuel, Sharon. 1999. Cross-language studies: relating language-particular coarticulation patterns to other language-particular patterns. In William J. Hardcastle and Nigel Hewlett (eds.), *Coarticulation: theory, data and techniques*, 179–98. Cambridge: Cambridge University Press.

Marslen-Wilson, William, Mary Hare, and Lianne Older. 1993. Inflectional morphology and phonological regularity in the English mental lexicon. *Proceedings of the 15th Annual Conference of the Cognitive Science Society*. Hillsdale, NJ: Erlbaum.

Marlsen-Wilson, William, Lorraine K. Tyler, Rachelle Waksler, and Lianne Older. 1994. Morphology and meaning in the English mental lexicon. *Psychological Review* 101: 3–33.

Martinet André. 1955. *Economie des changements phonétiques*. Berne: Francke.

1961. *Eléments de linguistique générale*. Paris: P. Colin.

Masica, C. P. 1989. *The Indo-Aryan languages*. Cambridge: Cambridge University Press.

Mathews, R. H. 1904. Langage des Kurnu, tribu d'indigènes de la Nouvelle Galles du Sud. *Bulletins et Mémoires de la Société d'Anthropologie de Paris*, ser. 5, V: 133–39.

Matteson, E. 1965. *The Piro (Arawakan) language*. Berkeley: University of California Press.

Matisoff, James A. 1975. Rhinoglottophilia: the mysterious connection between nasality and glottality. In C. A. Ferguson, L. M. Hyman, and J. J. Ohala (eds.), *Nasálfest: papers from a symposium on nasals and nasalization*, 265–87. Stanford: Language Universals Project, Dept. of Linguistics, Stanford University.

McCarthy, John J. 1979. Formal problems in Semitic phonology and morphology. Ph.D. dissertation, MIT, Cambridge, MA.

1981. A prosodic theory of nonconcatenative morphology. *Linguistic Inquiry* 12: 373–418.

1982. Prosodic templates, morphemic templates, and morphemic tiers. In H. van der Hulst and N. Smith (eds.), *The structure of phonological representations*, vol. 1: 191–223. Dordrecht: Foris.

1986. OCP effects: gemination and antigemination. *Linguistic Inquiry* 17: 207–63.

1988. Feature geometry and dependency: a review. *Phonetica* 43: 84–108.

1991. Synchronic rule inversion. In L. A. Sutton, C. Johnson, and R. Shields (eds.), *Proceedings of the 17th Annual Meeting of the Berkeley Linguistics Society*, 192–207. Berkeley, CA: Berkeley Linguistic Society.

2002. *A thematic guide to optimality theory*. Cambridge: Cambridge University Press.

McCarthy, J. J. and A. Taub. 1992. Review of C. Paradis and J.-F. Prunet (eds.), *The special status of coronals: internal and external evidence*. *Phonology* 9: 363–70.

McGregor, William. 1990. *A functional grammar of Gooniyandi*. Amsterdam: John Benjamins.

McKay, Graham. 1984. Stop alternations in Ndjébbana (Kunibidji). *Papers in Australian Linguistics* 16: 107–17.

McMahon, April M. S. 1994. *Understanding language change*. Cambridge: Cambridge University Press.

2000. *Change, chance and Optimality*. Oxford: Oxford University Press.

Meeussen, A. E. 1967. Bantu grammatical reconstructions, *Africana Linguistica* 3: 79–121.

1980. *Bantu lexical reconstructions*. Revised edition. Tervuren: Musée Royal de l'Afrique Centrale. Archives d'anthropologie nº 27. [Original 1969.]

Mehler, J., P. W. Jusczyk, G. Lambertz, N. Halstead, J. Bertonici, and C. Amiel-Tison. 1988. A precursor of language acquisition in young infants. *Cognition* 29: 143–78.

Meillet, Antoine. 1925. *La méthode comparative en linguistique historique*. Oslo.

Menyuk, P. 1971. Clusters as single underlying consonants: evidence from children's productions. Paper presented at the International Congress of Phonetic Sciences, Montreal, Canada, August 22–28, 1971.

Merrifield, William R. 1963. Palantla Chinantec syllable types. *Anthropological Linguistics* 5.5: 1–16.

Merrifield, William R. and Jerold A. Edmonson. 1999. *International Journal of American Linguistics* 65: 303–23.

Miller, G. A. and F. E. Niceley. 1955. An analysis of perceptual confusions among some English consonants. *Journal of the Acoustical Society of America* 27: 338–52.

Miller, W. R. and I. Davis. 1963. Proto-Keresan phonology. *International Journal of American Linguistics* 29: 310–30.

Mills, Roger F. 1975a. Proto South Sulawesi and Proto Austronesian phonology. Doctoral dissertation, University of Michigan.

1975b. The reconstruction of Proto South Sulawesi. *Archipel* 10: 205–24.

Milner, G. B. 1958. Aspiration in two Polynesian languages. *Bulletin of the School of Oriental and African Studies* 21: 368–75.

Miner, Kenneth. 1989. Winnebago accent: the rest of the data. *Anthropological Linguistics* 31: 148–72.

Mithun, Marianne. 2001. Actualization patterns in grammaticalization: from clause to locative morphology in Northern Iroquoian. In H. Andersen (ed.), *Actualization: linguistic change in progress*, 143–68. Amsterdam and Philadelphia: John Benjamins.

Mohanan, K. P. 1991. On the bases of radical underspecification. *Natural Language and Linguistic Theory* 9: 285–325.

Monzón, Cristina and Andrew Roth Seneff. 1984. Notes on Nahuatl phonological change $k^w \rightarrow b$. *International Journal of American Linguistics* 50: 456–61.

Moon, S.-J. and B. Lindblom. 1994. Interaction between duration, context and speaking style in English stressed vowels. *Journal of the Acoustical Society of America* 96.1: 40–55.

Morin, Yves-Charles. 1992. Phonological interpretations of historical lengthening. Paper presented at the Seventh International Phonology Meeting, Krems.

Morpurgo-Davies, Anna. 1998. *History of linguistics,* vol. 4: *Nineteenth century linguistics.* London: Longman.

Mosel, Ulrike. 1980. *Tolai and Tok Pisin.* Pacific Linguistics B-73. Canberra: Australian National University.

Mowrey, Richard and William Pagliuca. 1995. The reductive character of articulatory evolution. *Rivista di Linguistica* 7: 37–124.

Mülhäusler, Peter. 1997. *Pidgin and Creole linguistics.* Expanded and revised edition. Westminster Creolistics Series 3. Westminster: University of Westminster Press.

Mürk, Harri William. 1997. *A handbook of Estonian: nouns, adjectives, and verbs.* Indiana University Uralic and Altaic Series vol. 163. Bloomington, IN: Indiana University Press.

Murray, Robert and Theo Vennemann. 1983. Sound change and syllable structure in Germanic phonology. *Language* 59. 514–28.

Myers, Scott. 1991. Persistent rules. *Linguistic Inquiry* 22: 315–44.

2002. Gaps in factorial typology: the case of voicing in consonant clusters. Ms., University of Texas at Austin.

Nakatani, Lloyd H. and Carletta H. Aston. 1978. Acoustic and linguistic factors in stress perception. Ms., Bell Laboratories. [As summarized in Beckman 1986: 60–62, 174–75.]

Nater, H. F. 1984. *The Bella Coola language.* Canadian Ethnology Service Paper 92. Ottawa: National Museum of Man.

Newman, Stanley. 1944. *Yokuts language of California.* Viking Fund Publications in Anthropology vol. 2, New York.

Newport, E. L. and R. Meier. 1987. The acquisition of American Sign Language. In D. I. Slobin (ed.), *The cross-linguistic study of language acquisition,* vol. 1: *The data,* 881–938. Hillsdale, NJ: Lawrence Erlbaum.

Nord, Lennart. 1976. Perceptual experiments with nasals. *Quarterly Progress and Status Report, Speech Transmission Laboratory* (KTH, Stockholm) 1976: 5–8.

Nowak, Pawel M. 2002. A new look at the Slavic open syllable conspiracy. Paper presented at TREND, University of California, Berkeley.

Norman, Jerry. 1988. *Chinese.* Cambridge: Cambridge University Press.

Nyman, M. 1978. Lexicalization out of casual speech: the Greek-Latin synizesis. In *Four linguistic studies in classical languages.* Helsinki: Department of General Linguistics, University of Helsinki.

Odden, David. 1983. Aspects of Didinga phonology and morphology. In M. Lionel Bender (ed.) *Nilo-Saharan Language Studies,* 148–76. Monograph no. 13, Committee on Northeast African Studies. Michigan State University, African Studies Center.

1988. Anti antigemination and the OCP. *Linguistic Inquiry* 19: 451–75.

Ohala, J. J. 1971. The role of physiological and acoustic models in explaining the direction of sound change. *Project on Linguistic Analysis Reports* (Berkeley) 15: 25–40.

1972a. Physical models in phonology. In A. Rigault and R. Charbonneau (eds.), *Proceedings of the 7th International Congress of Phonetic Sciences, Montreal, 22–28 August 1971.* The Hague: Mouton. 1166–171.

1972b. How to represent natural sound patterns. *Project on Linguistic Analysis* (Berkeley) 16: 40–57.

1974a. Experimental historical phonology. In J. M. Anderson and C. Jones (eds.), *Historical linguistics II. Theory and description in phonology*, 353–89. [Proceedings of the 1st International Conference on Historical Linguistics. Edinburgh, 2–7 Sept. 1973.] Amsterdam: North Holland.

1974b. Phonetic explanation in phonology. In A. Bruck, R. A. Fox, and M. W. LaGaly (eds.), *Papers from the Parasession on Natural Phonology*, 251–74. Chicago: Chicago Linguistic Society.

1975. Phonetic explanations for nasal sound patterns. In C. A. Ferguson, L. M. Hyman, and J. J. Ohala (eds.), *Nasálfest: papers from a symposium on nasals and nasalization*, 289–316. Stanford: Language Universals Project.

1976. A model of speech aerodynamics. *Report of the Phonology Laboratory* (Berkeley) 1: 93–107.

1978a. Southern Bantu vs. the world: the case of palatalization of labials. *Proceedings of the Berkeley Linguistic Society, Annual Meeting* 4: 370–86. [Reprinted in: *Report of the Phonology Laboratory* (Berkeley) 2: 47–62 (1978).]

1978b. The production of tone. In V. A. Fromkin (ed.), *Tone: a linguistic survey*, 5–39. New York: Academic Press. [Reprinted in *Report of the Phonology Laboratory* (Berkeley) 2: 63–117 (1978).]

1978c. Phonological notations as models. In W. U. Dressler and W. Meid (eds.), *Proceedings of the 12th International Congress of Linguists, Vienna, Aug. 28–Sept. 2, 1977*, 811–16. Innsbruck: Innsbrucker Beiträge zur Sprachwissenschaft. [Reprinted in *Report of the Phonology Laboratory* (Berkeley) 2: 38–46 (1978).]

1979a. The contribution of acoustic phonetics to phonology. In B. Lindblom and S. Öhman (eds.), *Frontiers of speech communication research*. 355–63. London: Academic Press.

1979b. Universals of labial velars and de Saussure's chess analogy. *Proceedings of the 9th International Congress of Phonetic Sciences* 2: 41–47.

1980. The application of phonological universals in speech pathology. In N. J. Lass (ed.), *Speech and language: advances in basic research and practice*, vol. 3: 75–97. New York: Academic Press.

1981. The listener as a source of sound change. In Carrie S. Masek, Robert A. Hendrick and Mary Frances Miller (eds.), *Papers from the parasession on language and behavior*, 178–203. Chicago: Chicago Linguistic Society.

1983a. The origin of sound patterns in vocal tract constraints. In P. F. MacNeilage (ed.), *The production of speech*, 189–216. New York: Springer.

1983b. The phonological end justifies any means. In S. Hattori and K. Inoue (eds.), *Proceedings of the XIIIth International Congress of Linguists, Tokyo, 29 Aug. – 4 Sept. 1982*, 232–43. Tokyo. [Distributed by Sanseido Shoten.]

1983c. The direction of sound change. In A. Cohen and M. P. R. v. d. Broecke (eds.), *Abstracts of the Tenth International Congress of Phonetic Sciences*, 253–58. Dordrecht: Foris.

1985. Around *flat*. In Victoria A. Fromkin (ed.), *Phonetic linguistics: essays in honor of Peter Ladefoged*, 223–41. Orlando, FL: Academic Press.

1986. Phonological evidence for top-down processing in speech perception. In J. S. Perkell and D. H. Klatt (eds.), *Invariance and Variability in speech processes*, 386–97. Hillsdale, NJ: Lawrence Erlbaum.

1987. Explanations in phonology: opinions and examples. In Wolfgang U. Dressler, Hans C. Luschützky, Oskar E. Pfeiffer, and John R. Rennison (eds.), *Phonologica 1984: Proceedings of the Fifth International Phonology Meeting, Eisenstadt, 25–28 June 1984*, 215–25. London: Cambridge University Press.

1989. Sound change is drawn from a pool of synchronic variation. In L. E. Breivik and E. H. Jahr (eds.), *Language change: contributions to the study of its causes*, 173–98. Series: Trends in Linguistics, Studies and Monographs no. 43. Berlin: Mouton de Gruyter.

1990a. There is no interface between phonetics and phonology. A personal view. *Journal of Phonetics* 18: 153–71.

1990b. The phonetics and phonology of aspects of assimilation. In J. Kingston and M. Beckman (eds.), *Papers in laboratory phonology*, vol. 1: *Between the grammar and the physics of speech*, 258–75. Cambridge: Cambridge University Press.

1992a. The segment: primitive or derived? In Gerard J. Docherty and D. Robert Ladd (eds.), *Papers in laboratory phonology*, vol. 2: *Gesture, segment, prosody*, 166–83. Cambridge: Cambridge University Press.

1992b. Alternatives to the sonority hierarchy for explaining the shape of morphemes. *Papers from the Parasession on the Syllable*, 319–38. Chicago: Chicago Linguistic Society.

1992c. What's cognitive, what's not, in sound change. In Günter Kellermann and Michael D. Morrissey (eds.), *Diachrony within synchrony: language history and cognition*, 309–55. Duisburger Arbeiten zur Sprach- und Kulturwissenschaft 14. Frankfurt am Main: Peter Lang Verlag.

1993. The phonetics of sound change. In Charles Jones (ed.), *Historical linguistics: problems and perspectives*, 237–78. London: Longman.

1994a. Towards a universal, phonetically-based, theory of vowel harmony. *Proceedings, ICSLP 94*, Yokohama, Sept. 18–22, 1994. 491–94.

1994b. Hierarchies of environments for sound variation; plus implications for "neutral" vowels in vowel harmony. *Acta Linguistica Hafniensia* 27: 371–82.

1995a. Phonetic explanations for sound patterns: implications for grammars of competence. K. Elenius and P. Branderud (eds.), *Proceedings of the 13th International Congress of Phonetic Sciences, Stockholm, 13–19 August 1995*. vol. 2: 52–59.

1995b. The perceptual basis of some sound patterns. B. Connell and A. Arvaniti (eds.), *Papers in laboratory phonology*, vol. 4: 87–92. Cambridge: Cambridge University Press.

1995c. Speech perception is hearing sounds, not tongues. *Journal of the Acoustical Society of America* 99: 1718–25.

1996a. The relation between phonetics and phonology. In W. Hardcastle and J. Laver (eds.), *Handbook of phonetics*, 674–94. Oxford: Blackwell's.

1996b. The relation between sound change and connected speech processes. In A. P. Simpson and M. Pätzold (eds.), *Sound patterns of connected speech: Description, models and explanation*, 201–6. Arbeitsberichte Nr. 31, Institut für Phonetik und digitale Sprachverarbeitung, Kiel.

To appear. Emergent obstruents. To appear in D. Demolin and M. Dominicy (eds.), *Studies in sound change*. Amsterdam: Benjamins.

Ohala, J. J. and M. Amador. 1981. Spontaneous nasalization. *Journal of the Acoustical Society of America* 68: S54–S55. [Abstract]

Ohala, J. J. and M. G. Busà. 1995. Nasal loss before voiceless fricatives: a perceptually-based sound change. [Special issue on *The phonetic basis of sound change*, ed. Carol A. Fowler] *Rivista di Linguistica* 7: 125–44.

Ohala, J. J. and Lorentz, J. 1977. The story of [w]: an exercise in the phonetic explanation for sound patterns. *Proceedings of the Annual Meeting of the Berkeley Linguistic Society* 3: 577–99. [Reprinted in *Report of the Phonology Laboratory* (Berkeley) 2: 133–55 (1978).]

Ohala, J. J. and M. Ohala. 1986. Testing hypotheses regarding the psychological manifestation of morpheme structure constraints. In J. J. Ohala and J. J. Jaeger (eds.), *Experimental phonology*, 239–52. San Diego: Academic Press.

Ohala, J. J. and C. J. Riordan 1979. Passive vocal tract enlargement during voiced stops. In J. J. Wolf and D. H. Klatt (eds.), *Speech communication papers*, 89–92. New York: Acoustical Society of America.

Öhman, S. E. G. 1966. Coarticulation in VCV utterances: spectrographic measurement. *Journal of the Acoustical Society of America* 39: 151–68.

Orgun, Cemil Orhan. 1996. Sign-based morphology and phonology: with special attention to Optimality Theory. PhD thesis, University of California, Berkeley.

Osthoff, H. and K. Brugmann. 1878. Vorwort. *Morphologische Untersuchungen* 1.iii–xx.

Ouakrim, Omar. 1995. *Fonética y Fonología del Bereber*. Cerdanyola des Vallès: Universitat Autónoma de Barcelona, Servei de Publicacions.

Ourso, Meterwa. 1989. Lama phonology and morphology. Doctoral dissertation, University of Illinois, Urbana.

Ourso, M. and C. Ulrich. 1990. Sonorant-strengthening in Lama. *Studies in the Linguistic Sciences* 20: 135–47.

O'Grady, Geoff and Susan Fitzgerald. 1995. Triconsonantal sequences in Proto-Pama-Nyungan. *Oceanic Linguistics* 34: 454–71.

Pace, Wanda Jane. 1990. Comaltepec Chinantec verb inflection. In W. R. Merrifield and C. R. Rensch (eds.), *Syllable, tone and verb paradigms*, 21–62. Studies in Chinantec languages 4. Summer Institute of Linguistics Publications in Linguistics 95. Arlington, TX: SIL and the University of Texas at Arlington.

Pagliuca, William. 1982. Prolegomena to a theory of articulatory evolution. Doctoral dissertation, SUNY, Buffalo, Buffalo, NY.

Pagliuca, William and Richard Mowrey. 1987. Articulatory evolution. In A. G. Ramat, O. Carruba, and G. Bernini (eds.), *Papers from the 7th International Conference on Historical Linguistics*, 459–72. Amsterdam: Benjamins.

Paradis, C. and J-F. Prunet (eds.). 1991. *The special status of coronals: internal and external evidence*. Phonetics and Phonology 2. San Diego: Academic Press.

Passy, P. 1890. *Etude sur les changements phonétiques*. Paris: Librairie Firmin-Didot.

Paster, Mary. 2003. Vowel height harmony and blocking in Buchan Scots English. Ms., University of California, Berkeley.

Paul, Hermann. 1886. *Prinzipien der Sprachgeschichte*. Halle.

1920. *Prinzipien der Sprachgeschichte*. 5th edition. Halle: Niemeyer. [English translation of 2nd edition: *Principles of language history*, 1889. New York: Macmillan.]

Phillips, Betty S. 2001. Lexical diffusion, lexical frequency, and lexical analysis. In Joan Bybee and Paul Hopper (eds.), *Frequency and the emergence of linguistic structure*, 123–36. Amsterdam: Benjamins.

Picard, Marc. 1984. On the naturalness of Algonquian ł. *International Journal of American Linguistics* 50: 424–37.

Pierrehumbert, Janet. 1994. Knowledge of variation. *Papers from the parasession on variation, 30th meeting of the Chicago Linguistic Society*, 232–56. Chicago: Chicago Linguistic Society.

1999. What people know about sounds of language. *Studies in the Linguistic Sciences* 29: 111–20.

2001a. Exemplar dynamics: word frequency, lenition, and contrast. In Joan Bybee and Paul Hopper (eds.), *Frequency and the emergence of linguistic structure*, 137–58. Amsterdam: Benjamins.

2001b. Stochastic phonology. *Glot International* 5: 195–207.

Pinkerton, S. 1986. Quichean (Mayan) glottalized and nonglottalized stops: a phonetic study with implications for phonological universals. In J. J. Ohala and J. J. Jaeger (eds.), *Experimental phonology*, 125–39. Orlando, FL: Academic Press.

Plauché, Madelaine. 2001. Acoustic cues in the directionaly of stop consonant confusions. Doctoral dissertation, University of California, Berkeley.

Plauché, Madelaine, Cristina Delogu, and J. J. Ohala. 1996. Asymmetries of consonant confusions. *Journal of the Acoustical Society of America* 100: 2693.

Podesva, Robert J. 2000. Constraints on geminates in Buginese and Selayarese. *West Coast Conference on Formal Linguistics* 19: 343–56.

Podesva, Robert J. 2002. Segmental constraints on geminates and their implications for typology. Talk presented at LSA Annual Meeting, San Francisco, January.

Pollard, Carl and Ivan Sag. 1994. *Head-driven phrase structure grammar*. Chicago: University of Chicago Press.

Port, R. and R. Crawford. 1989. Incomplete neutralization and pragmatics in German. *Journal of Phonetics* 17.4: 257–82.

Port, R. F. and M. O'Dell 1985. Neutralization of obstruent voicing is incomplete. *Journal of the Acoustical Society of America* 70: S10.

Prince, Alan and Paul Smolensky. 1993. Optimality theory: constraint interaction in generative grammar. Ms., Rutgers University, New Brunswick and University of Colorado, Boulder. [RuCCS TR-2. New Brunswick, NJ: Rutgers Center for Cognitive Science.]

Puglielli, Annarita. 1997. Somali phonology. In Alan Kaye (ed.), *Phonologies of Asia and Africa*, 521–35. Winona Lake, IN: Eisenbrauns.

Pulleyblank, Doug. 1986. *Tone in lexical phonology*. Dordrecht: Reidel.

Pullum, Geoffrey K. 1996. Learnability, hyperlearning, and the poverty of the stimulus. *Proceedings of the 22nd Annual Meeting of the Berkeley Linguistic Society*. 498–513.

Pullum, Geoffrey K. and Barbara C. Scholz. 2002. Empirical assessment of stimulus poverty arguments. *The Linguistic Review* 19 (special issue, nos. 1–2: A review of the "Poverty of Stimulus Argument", ed. Nancy Ritter): 9–50.

Raphael, Lawrence. 1981. Durations and contexts as cues to word-final cognate opposition in English. *Phonetica* 38: 126–47.

Rasmussen, Jens Elmegård. 1979. *Anaptyxis, gemination and syncope in Eskimo: a diachronic study.* Travaux du Cercle Linguistique de Copenhague, vol. 18. Copenhagen: C. A. Reitzels Boghandel.

Ray, Punya Sloka. 1967. Dafla phonology and morphology. *Anthropological Linguistics* 9: 9–14.

Recasens, Daniel. 1987. An acoustic analysis of V-to-C and V-to-V coarticulatory effects in Catalan and Spanish VCV sequences. *Journal of Phonetics* 15: 299–312.

Reesink, Ger P. 1999. *A grammar of Hatam, Bird's Head Peninsula, Irian Jaya.* Pacific Linguistics C-146. Canberra: Research School of Pacific and Asian Studies, Australian National University.

Rehg, Kenneth L. and Damien Sohl. 1981. *Ponapean reference grammar.* Honolulu: University Press of Hawai'i.

Rehg, Kenneth L. 1984a. The origins of "compensatory lengthening" rules in Micronesian languages. In Byron W. Bender (ed.), *Studies in Micronesian Linguistics*, 53–39. Pacific Linguistics C-80. Canberra: Australian National University.

1984b. On the history of Ponapean phonology. In Byron W. Bender (ed.), *Studies in Micronesian Linguistics*, 281–316. Pacific Linguistics C-80. Canberra: Australian National University.

Reichard, Gladys. 1925. *Wiyot grammar and texts. University of California Publications in American Archeaology and Ethnology* 22: 1–215.

Rensch, Calvin R. 1983. Otomanguean isoglosses. In T. A. Sebeok (ed.), *Current Trends in Linguistics*, vol. 11: *Diachronic, Areal and Typological Linguistics*, 295–316. The Hague: Mouton.

1989. *An etymological dictionary of the Chinantec Languages.* Studies in Chinantec languages 1. Summer Institute of Linguistics Publications in Linguistics 87. Arlington, TX: SIL and the University of Texas at Arlington.

Repp, B. H. 1977. Perceptual integration and selective attention in speech perception: further experiments on intervocalic stop consonants. *Status Report on Speech Research* (Haskins Laboratories) 49: 37–69.

1978. Perceptual integration and differentiation of spectral cues for intervocalic stop consonants. *Perception and Psychophysics* 24: 471–85.

Repp, B. and H.-B Lin. 1989. Acoustic properties and perception of stop consonant release transients. *Journal of the Acoustical Society of America* 85: 379–95.

Repp, Bruno H. and Katyanee Svastikula. 1987. Perception of the [m]-[n] distinction in VC syllables. *Haskins Laboratories Status Report on Speech Research* 91: 157–75.

Rice, Keren. 2000. *Morpheme order and semantic scope: word formation in the Athapaskan verb.* Cambridge Studies in Linguistics 90. Cambridge: Cambridge University Press.

Rigault, André. 1962. Rôle de la fréquence, de l'intensité et de la durée vocaliques dans la perception de l'accent en français. *Proceedings of the 4th International Congress of Phonetic Sciences*, 735–48.

Ringe, Donald. 1999. How hard is it to match CVC-roots? *Transactions of the Philological Society* 97.2: 213–44.

Ritchie, James A. 1999. R myth-athesis: a perception based approach at understanding some r-related sound changes. In Irmengard Rauch and Gerald F. Carr (eds.), *New insights in Germanic linguistics I*, 211–22. New York: Peter Lang.

2000. Causation in sound change: perception-based monophthongization in Old High German. PhD dissertation, University of California, Berkeley.

Robins, R. H. 1958. *The Yurok language: grammar, texts, lexicon.* University of California Publications in Linguistics vol. 15. Berkeley and Los Angeles: University of California Press.

1997. *A short history of linguistics.* London: Longman.

Rose, Michael R. and George V. Lauder. 1996. *Adaptation.* San Diego: Academic Press.

Ross, Malcolm. 1998. Proto Oceanic phonology and morphology. In Malcolm Ross, Andrew Pawley and Meredith Osmond (eds.), *The lexicon of Proto Oceanic*, vol. 1: *Material culture*, 15–35. Pacific Linguistics C-152. Canberra: Australian National University.

Ryan, M. J., J. H. Fox, W. Wilczynski, and A. S. Rand. 1990. Sexual selection for sensory exploitation in the frog *Physalemus pustulosus. Nature London* 343: 66–67.

Ryan, M. J. and A. S. Rand. 1993. Sexual selection and signal evolution – the ghost of biases past. *Philological Transactions of the Royal Society of London* B340: 187–95.

Sadler, Louisa and Rachel Nordlinger. 2002. Nominal tense, aspect and mood marking. Talk presented at the San Diego Morphology Workshop.

Sampson, Geoffrey. 1970. On the need for a phonological base. *Language* 46: 586–626.

Sandler, Wendy. 1989. *Phonological representation of the sign: linearity and nonlinearity in American Sign Language.* Dordrecht: Foris.

Sapir, David. 1965. *A grammar of Diola Fogny.* West African Monographs 3. London: Cambridge University Press.

Sapir, Edward. 1921. *Language.* New York: Harcourt-Brace.

1925. Sound patterns in language. *Language* 1: 37–51.

1930. The Southern Paiute language: Southern Paiute, a Shoshonean language. *Proceedings of the American Academy of Arts and Sciences* 65, 1: 1–296.

1938. Glottalized continuants in Navaho, Nootka, and Kwakiutl, with a note on Indo-European. *Language* 14: 248–74.

Saussure, Ferdinand de. 1949. *Cours de linguistique générale.* 4th edition. Paris: Payot.

Scheibman, Joanne. 2001. Local patterns of subjectivity in person and verb type in American English conversation. In Joan Bybee and Paul Hopper (eds.), *Frequency and the emergence of linguistic structure*, 61–89. Typological Studies in Language 45. Amsterdam and Philadelphia: John Benjamins.

Schein, Barry and Donca Steriade. 1986. On geminates. *Linguistic Inquiry* 17: 691–744.

Schmidt, J. 1885. Die Entstehung der griechischen aspirierten perfecta. *Zeitschrift für vergleichende Sprachforschung* 27: 309–14.

Scholz, Barbara C. and Geoffrey K. Pullum. 2002. Searching for arguments to support linguistic nativism. *The Linguistic Review* 19 (special issue, nos. 1–2: A Review of "The Poverty of Stimulus Argument," ed. Nancy Ritter): 185–224.

Schuchardt, Hugo. 1979. *The ethnography of variation: selected writings on pidgins and creoles.* Trans. T. L. Markey. Ann Arbor: Karoma.

Schuh, Russell. 1978. Bade/Ngizim vowels and syllable structure. *Studies in African Linguistics* 9: 247–83.

Seiler, Hansjakob. 1965. Accent and morphophonemics in Cahuilla and Uto-Aztecan. *International Journal of American Linguistics* 31: 50–59.

  1967. Structure and reconstruction in some Uto-Aztecan languages. *International Journal of American Linguistics* 33: 135–47.

  1977. *Cahuilla grammar.* Banning, CA: Malki Museum Press.

Selkirk, L. 1984. On the major class features and syllable theory. In M. Aronoff and R. T. Oehrle (eds.), *Language sound structure,* 107–33. Cambridge, MA: MIT Press.

Shibatani, Masayoshi. 1990. *The Languages of Japan.* Cambridge: Cambridge University Press.

Shockey, L. 1973. Phonetic and phonological properties of connected speech. Doctoral dissertation, Ohio State University.

  1977. Perceptual test of a phonological rule. *Haskins Laboratories Status Report on Speech Research,* SR-50: 147–50.

Shockey, L. and Z. S. Bond. 1980. Phonological processes in speech addressed to children. *Phonetica* 37: 267–74.

Sievers, E. 1881. *Grundzüge der Phonetik.* Leipzig: Breitkopf and Hartel.

Silverman, Daniel. 1992. Multiple scansions in loanword phonology: evidence from Cantonese. *Phonology* 9: 289–328.

Simpson, Andrew. 2002. Gutterals in diachronic perspective: the case of pharyngeal merger and loss in Semitic and beyond. Ms., University of California, Berkeley.

Singler, John Victor. 1996. An OT account of Pidgin phonology: coda consonants in Vernacular Liberian English. *Proceedings of the 22nd Annual Meeting of the Berkeley Linguistic Society.* 375–86.

Skousen, Royal. 1972. On capturing regularities. *Chicago Linguistic Society* 8: 567–77.

  1989. *Analogical modeling of language.* Dordrecht, Boston, and London: Kluwer.

  1992. *Analogy and structure.* Dordrecht, Boston, and London: Kluwer.

Slis, Iman 1986. Assimilation of voice in Dutch as a function of stress, word boundaries and sex of speaker and listener. *Journal of Phonetics* 14: 311–26.

Smith, Caroline. 1992. The timing of vowel and consonant gestures. PhD dissertation. Yale University, New Haven.

  1997. The devoicing of /z/ in American English: effects of Local and Prosodic context. *Journal of Phonetics* 25: 471–500.

Sneddon, J. N. 1993. The drift towards final open syllables in Sulawesi languages. *Oceanic Linguistics* 32: 1–44.

Snoxall, R. A. 1967. *Luganda–English dictionary*. London: Oxford University Press.

Sommer, Bruce. 1969. *Kunjen phonology: synchronic and diachronic*. Pacific Linguistics B-11. Canberra: Australian National University.

1970. An Australian language without CV syllables. *International Journal of American Linguistics* 36: 57–58.

Spencer, Andrew. 1986. Vowel harmony, neutral vowels and autosegmental theory. *Lingua* 69: 3–21.

Sproat, Richard William. 2000. *A computational theory of writing systems: studies in natural language processing*. Cambridge: Cambridge University Press.

Stampe, David L. 1969. The acquisition of phonetic representation. *Papers from the 5th Regional Meeting of the Chicago Linguistic Society*. Chicago: Chicago Linguistic Society.

1973. A dissertation on natural phonology. Doctoral dissertation: University of Chicago. [Published by Garland Press, New York, 1979.]

Stankiewicz, E. 1972. (ed.) *A Baudouin de Courtenay anthology: the beginnings of structural linguistics*. Bloomington: Indiana University Press.

Steels, Luc. 1998. Synthesizing the origins of language and meaning using coevolution, self-organization and level formation. In James R. Hurford, et al. (eds.), 384–404. *Approaches to the evolution of language*. Cambridge: Cambridge University Press.

Steever, Sanford B. (ed.) 1998. *The Dravidian languages*. London: Routledge.

Stemberger, J. P. and C. Stoel-Gammon. 1991. The underspecification of coronals: evidence from language acquisition and performance errors. In C. Paradis and J.-F. Prunet (eds.), 181–99. *The special status of coronals: internal and external evidence*. San Diego: Academic Press.

Steriade, Donca. 1982. Greek prosodies and the nature of syllabification. PhD dissertation, MIT.

1991. Moras and other slots. *Formal Linguistic Society of Midamerica* 1: 254–80.

1993. Closure, release, and nasal contours. In M. Huffman and R. A. Krakow (eds.), *Nasals, nasalization, and the velum. Phonetics and Phonology 5*. San Diego: Academic Press. 401–70.

1995. Underspecification and markedness. In J. Goldsmith (ed.), *The handbook of phonological theory*, 114–74. Oxford: Blackwell.

1998. Licensing retroflexion. Ms., UCLA.

1999a. Phonetics in phonology: the case of laryngeal neutralization. In Matthew Gordon (ed.), *Papers in phonology*, vol. 3: 25–145. UCLA Working Papers in Linguistics 2. Los Angeles: Department of Linguistics, University of California.

1999b. Alternatives to syllable-based accounts of consonantal phonotactics. In Osamu Fujimura, Brian Joseph, and B. Palek (eds.), *Proceedings of the 1998 Linguistics and Phonetics Conference*, 205–42. Prague: Karolinum Press.

2001. Directional asymmetries in place assimilation: a perceptual account. In Elizabeth Hume and Keith Johnson (eds.), *Perception in phonology*, 219–50. New York: Academic Press.

Stevens, Kenneth N. 1972. The quantal nature of speech: Evidence from articulatory-acoustic data. In P. B. Denes and E. E. David Jr. (eds.), *Human communication: a unified view*, 51–66. New York: McGraw Hill:
  1989. On the quantal nature of speech. *Journal of Phonetics* 17: 3–45.
Stevens, K. N., S. J. Keyser, and H. Kawasaki 1986. Toward a phonetic and phonological theory of redundant features. In J. S. Perkell and D. H. Klatt (eds.), *Invariance and variability in speech processes*, 426–49. Hillsdale, NJ: Lawrence Erlbaum.
Stewart, Ian. 1998. *Life's other secret*. New York: Wiley.
Stoel-Gammon, C. and K. Otomo. 1986. Babbling development of hearing impaired and normally hearing subjects. *Journal of Speech and Hearing Disorders* 51: 33–41.
Story, G. L. and C. M. Naish. 1973. *Tlingit verb dictionary*. Fairbanks: Alaska Native Language Center.
Streeter, L. A. 1976. Language perception of 2-month-old infants shows effects of both innate mechanisms and experience. *Nature* 259: 39–41.
Stresemann, Erwin. 1927. *Die Lauterscheinungen in den ambonischen Sprachen*. Supplement 10 of *Zeitschrift für eingeborenen-Sprachen*. Berlin: Dietrich Reimer.
Studdert-Kennedy, Michael. 1998. Introduction: the emergence of phonology. In James R. Hurford et al. (eds.), *Approaches to the evolution of language*, 169–76. Cambridge: Cambridge University Press.
Suárez, Jorge A. 1983. *The Mesoamerican Indian languages*. Cambridge: Cambridge University Press.
Svantesson, J. 1984. Vowels and diphthongs in Standard Chinese. *University of Lund Department of Linguistics Working Papers* 27: 209–35.
Tauli, Valter. 1954. The origin of the quantitative system in Estonian. *Journal de la société finno-ougrienne* 57: 1–19.
Ternes, Elmar. 1970. *Grammaire struturale du Breton de l'île de Groix*. Heidelberg: Carl Winter Universitaetsverlag.
  1973. *The phonemic analysis of Scottish Gaelic. Based on the dialect of Applecross, Ross-shire*. Forum Phoneticum 1. Hamburg: Helmut Buske Verlag.
Tesar, Bruce and Paul Smolensky. 2000. *Learnability in Optimality Theory*. Cambridge, MA: MIT Press.
Thelwall, Robin. 1983. Meidob Nubian: phonology, grammatical notes, and basic vocabulary. In M. Lionel Bender (ed.) *Nilo-Saharan Language Studies*, 97–113. Monograph no. 13, Committee on Northeast African Studies. Michigan State University, African Studies Center.
Thomason, Sarah G. 1986. On changes from palatalized labials to apical affricates. *International Journal of American Linguistics* 52: 182–85.
Thomason, Sarah Grey and Terrence Kaufman. 1988. *Language contact, creolization, and genetic linguistics*. Berkeley and Los Angeles: University of California Press.
Thompson, Laurence C. and M. Terry Thompson. 1972. Language universals, nasals, and the Northwest coast. In M. Estellie Smith (ed.), *Studies in linguistics in honor of George L. Trager*, 441–56. The Hague: Mouton.
Thráinsson, H. 1978. On the phonology of Icelandic aspiration. *Nordic Journal of Linguistics* 1: 3–54.

Thurgood, Graham. 1993. Geminates: a cross-linguistic examination. In Joel Ashmore Nevis, Gerald McMenamin, and Graham Thurgood (eds.), *Papers in honor of Frederick H. Brengelman on the occasion of the twenty-fifth anniversary of the Department of Linguistics, CSU Fresno*, 129–39. Fresno, CA: Department of Linguistics, California State Univerisity, Fresno.

1999. *From Ancient Cham to modern dialects: two thousand years of language contact and change.* Oceanic Linguistics Special Publications in Linguistics 28. Honolulu: University of Hawai'i Press.

Thurston, William. 1987. *Processes of change in the languages of North-Western New Britain.* Pacific Linguistics Series B-99. Canberra: Australian National University.

Tiersma, Pieter Meijes. 1985. *Frisian reference grammar.* Foris: Dordrecht.

Tieszen, Bozena Jozefa. 1997. Final stop devoicing in Polish: an acoustic and historical account for incomplete neutralization. PhD dissertation, Univeristy of Wisconsin, Madison.

Traill, A. 1997. Linguistic phonetic features for clicks. In Robert K. Herber (ed.), *African linguistics at the crossroads. Papers from Kwaluseni 1st World Congress of African Linguistics, Swaziland, 18–22. VII. 1994*, 99–117. Cologne: Rüdiger Köppe Verlag.

Tranel, Bernard. 1991. CVC light syllables, geminates and moraic theory. *Phonology* 8: 291–302.

Trager, George L. 1940. One phonemic entity becomes two: the case of "short a." *American Speech* 17: 30–41.

Traugott, Elizabeth Closs and Bernd Heine (eds.). 1991. *Approaches to grammaticalization*, vols. I and II. Typological Studies in Language 19. Amsterdam and Philadelphia: John Benjamins.

Trefry, D. 1969. *A comparative study of Kuman and Pawaian – Non-Austronesian languages of New Guinea.* Pacific Linguistics B-13. Canberra: Australian National University.

Trehub, S. E. 1976. The discrimination of foreign speech contrasts by infants and adults. *Child Development* 47: 466–72.

Treiman, Rebecca. 1983. The structure of spoken syllables: evidence from novel word games. *Cognition* 15: 49–74.

1986. The division between onsets and rimes in English syllables. *Journal of Memory and Language* 25: 476–91.

1988. Distributional constraints and syllable structure in English. *Journal of Phonetics* 16: 221–29.

Treiman, Rebecca and C. Danis. 1988. Syllabification of intervocalic consonants. *Journal of Memory and Language* 27: 87–104.

Troike, Rudolph C. 1996. Sketch of Coahuilteco. In Ives Goddard (ed.), *Handbook of North American Indians*, vol. 17: 644–65. Washington, DC: Smithsonian Institution.

Trubetzkoy, Nikolai S. 1929. Zur allgemeinen Theorie des phonologischen Vokalsystems. *Travaux du Cercle Linguistique de Prague*, no. 1: 39–67.

1935. *Anleitung zu phonologischen Beschreibungen.* Association international pour les études phonologiques. Brno: Circle Linguistique de Prague.

1939. Grundzüge der Phonologie. *Travaux du Cercle Linguistique de Prague*, no. 7.

Ulrich, Charles H. 1997. Loanword adaptation in Lama: testing the TCRS model. *Canadian Journal of Linguistics* 42: 415–63.

Urbanczyk, Susanne 1995. Patterns of reduplication in Lushootseed. Doctoral dissertation, University of Massachusetts, Amherst.

  1996. Aspiration and Lushootseed Syllable Structure. Paper read at the LSA Annual Meeting, San Diego.

Ussishkin, Adam and Andrew Wedel. 2003. Gestural motor programs account for asymmetries in loanword adaptation patterns. Talk presented at the LSA Annual Meeting, January, Atlanta, Georgia.

Uyechi, Linda. 1996. *The geometry of visual phonology.* Stanford, CA: CSLI Publications.

Van Bergem, Dick. 1994. A model of coarticulatory effects on the schwa. *Speech Communication* 14: 143–62.

van Engelenhoven, Aone. 1995. A description of the Leti Language (as spoken in Tutukei). Doctoral dissertation, University of Leiden, Leiden.

Van Valin, Robert Jr. 1993. (ed.) *Advances in role and reference grammar.* Amsterdam and Philadelphia: John Benjamins.

Vennemann, T. 1972a. On the theory of syllabic phonology. *Linguistische Berichte* 18: 1–18.

  1972b. Rule inversion. *Lingua* 29: 209–42.

  1973. Explanation in syntax. In John Kimball (ed.), *Syntax and semantics,* vol. II. New York: Academic Press.

  1975. An explanation of drift. In Charles N. Li (ed.), *Word order and word order change,* 269–305. Austin: University of Texas Press.

  1988. *Preference laws for syllable structure and the explanation for sound change.* Berlin: Mouton de Gruyter.

Vihman, Marylyn May. 1992. Early syllables and the construction of phonology. In Charles A. Ferguson, Lise Menn and Carol Stoel-Gammon (eds.), *Phonological development: models, research, implications.* 393–422. Timonium, MD: York Press.

Vihman, Marylyn May. 1996. *Phonological development: the origins of language in the child.* Cambridge, MA and Oxford: Blackwell.

Vincent, Nigel. 1978. Is sound change teleological? In Jacek Fisiak (ed.), *Recent developments in historical linguistics.* 409–30. The Hague: Mouton.

Wang, W. S.-Y. 1959. Transition and release as perceptual cues for final plosives. *Journal of Speech and Hearing Research* 2: 66–73.

  1969. Competing sound change as a cause of residue. *Language* 45: 9–25.

  1977. *The lexicon and phonological change.* The Hague: Mouton.

Wang, M. and R. Bilger. 1973. Consonant confusions in noise: a study of perceptual features. *Journal of the Acoustical Society of America* 54: 1248–66.

Warner, Natasha, Jongman, Allard, Sereno, Joan, and Kemps, Rachel. 2002. Sub-phonemic durational differences in production and perception. Ms., Max Planck Institute and University of Arizona.

Waters, Bruce. 1980. Djinang phonology. *Papers in Australian Linguistics* no. 14: 1–71. Pacific Linguistics A-60. Canberra: Australian National University.

  1989. *Djinang and Djinba – a grammatical and historical perspective.* Pacific Linguistics C-114. Canberra: Australian National University.

Watkins, Calvert. 1962. *Indo-European origins of the Celtic verb*, vol. I: *The sigmatic aorist*. Dublin: Dublin University Press.

Watkins, Laurel. 1984. *A grammar of Kiowa*. Lincoln: University of Nebraska Press.

Watson, Ian. 1999. Phonetics, phonologization, and French nasal vowels. *Oxford University Working Papers in Linguistics, Philology & Phonetics* 4: 157–73.

Wedel, Andrew. 2004. Self-organization and the development of higher-order phonological patterns. PhD Thesis, University of California, Santa Cruz.

Weinreich, Uriel, William Labov, and Marvin Herzog. 1968. Empirical foundations for a theory of language change. In W. Lehmann and Y. Malkiel (eds.), *Directions for historical linguistics*, 96–188. Austin: University of Texas Press.

Werker, J. F. 1991. The ontogeny of speech perception. In I. G. Mattingly and M. Studdert-Kennedy (eds.), *Modularity and the motor theory of speech perception: proceedings of a conference to honor Alvin M. Liberman*. Hillsdale, NJ: Lawrence Erlbaum.

Werker, J. F., J. H. V. Gilbert, K. Humphrey, and R. C. Tees. 1981. Developmental aspects of cross-language speech perception. *Child Development* 52: 349–55.

Werker, J. F. and C. E. Lalonde. 1988. Cross-language speech perception: initial capabilities and developmental change. *Developmental Psychology* 24: 672–83.

Werker, J. F. and J. S. Logan. 1985. Cross-language evidence for three factors in speech perception. *Perception and Psychophysics* 37: 35–44.

Werker, Janet F. and Judith E. Pegg. 1992. Infant speech perception and phonological acquisition. In Charles A. Ferguson, Lise Menn and Carol Stoel-Gammon (eds.), *Phonological development: models, research, implications*, 285–311. Timonium, MD: York Press.

Werker, J. F. and R. C. Tees. 1984. Cross-language speech perception: Evidence for perceptual reorganization during the first year of life. *Infant Behavior and Development* 7: 49–63.

Westbury, J. R. 1979. Aspects of the temporal control of voicing in consonant clusters in English. PhD dissertation, University of Texas at Austin.

White, Geoffrey M., Francis Kokhonigita and Hugo Pulomana. 1988. *Cheke Holo (Maringe/Hograno) dictionary*. Pacific Linguistics C-97. Canberra: Australian National University.

White, Geoffrey M. 1995. Maringe (Cheke Holo). In Darell T. Tryon (ed.), *Comparative Austronesian dictionary*, Part 1: Fascicle 2: 787–91. Berlin: Mouton de Gruyter.

Whiteley, W. H. and M. G. Muli. 1962. *Practical Introduction to Kamba*. London: Oxford University Press.

Whorf, B. L. 1946. The Hopi language. In C. Osgood (ed.), *Linguistic structures of native America*, 159–83. Viking Fund Publications in Anthropology no. 6. New York: Viking Fund.

Widdison, K. 1991. The phonetic basis for s-aspiration in Spanish. PhD dissertation, University of California, Berkeley.

Wightman, Colin W., Stefanie Shattuck-Hufnagel, Mari Ostendorf, and Patti J. Price. 1992. Segmental durations in the vicinity of prosodic phrase boundaries. *Journal of the Acoustical Society of America* 91.3: 1707–17.

Wilbur, Ronnie B. 1990. Why syllables? What the notion means for ASL research. In *Theoretical Issues in Sign Language Research*, vol. I: *Linguistics*, Susan D. Fischer and Patricia Siple (eds.), 81–108. Chicago: University of Chicago Press.

Wilcox, Sherman. 1990. The structure of signed and spoken languages. *Sign Language Studies* 67: 141–51.

Willerman, Raquel. 1994. Phonetics of pronouns: the articulatory bases of markedness. PhD dissertation. University of Texas at Austin.

Williamson, Kay. 1973. More on nasals and nasalization in Kwa. *Studies in African Linguistics* 4: 115–38.

Wilson, Colin. 2001. Consonant cluster neutralization and targeted constraints. *Phonology* 18: 147–97.

Woodbury, Anthony. 1987. Meaningful phonological processes: a study of Central Alaskan Yupik Eskimo prosody. *Language* 63: 685–740.

Wurm, S. A. 1972. *Languages of Australia and Tasmania*. Janua linguarum, series critica, 1. The Hague: Mouton.

Wurm, S. A. and L. Hercus. 1976. Tense-marking in Gurnu pronouns. *Papers in Australian Linguistics* 10: 33–49.

Yip, Moira. 1995. Tone in East Asian languages. In J. Goldsmith (ed.), *The handbook of phonological theory*, 476–94. Oxford: Basil Blackwell.

Yu, Alan C. L. 2003. The phonology and morphology of infixation. Doctoral dissertation, University of California, Berkeley.

2001. Explaining final obstruent voicing in Lezgian: phonetics and history. Ms., University of California, Berkeley. To appear in *Language*.

Zec, Draga. 1995. Sonority constraints on syllable structure. *Phonology* 12: 85–129.

Ziervogel, D.1959. *A grammar of Northern Transvaal Ndebele*. Pretoria: J. L. van Schaik Ltd.

Zipf, George K. 1935. *The psycho-biology of language: an introduction to dynamic philology*. Boston: Houghton Mifflin.

Language index

Subject index